CULTURE
& FOREIGN POLICY

Culture
& Foreign Policy

edited by
Valerie M. Hudson

LYNNE
RIENNER
PUBLISHERS

BOULDER
LONDON

Published in the United States of America in 1997 by
Lynne Rienner Publishers, Inc.
1800 30th Street, Boulder, Colorado 80301

and in the United Kingdom by
Lynne Rienner Publishers, Inc.
3 Henrietta Street, Covent Garden, London WC2E 8LU

Library of Congress Cataloging-in-Publication Data
Culture and foreign policy / edited by Valerie M. Hudson.
    p.   cm.
  Includes bibliographical references and index.
  ISBN 1-55587-640-4 (alk. paper)
    1. International relations and culture.   2. United States—Foreign
relations.   I. Hudson, Valerie M., 1958–
JX1255.C828   1997
327.1—dc20   96-32051
                                                                              CIP

British Cataloguing in Publication Data
A Cataloguing in Publication record for this book
is available from the British Library.

Typeset by Letra Libre, 1705 14th Street, Suite 391, Boulder, Colorado 80302

Printed and bound in the United States of America

The paper used in this publication meets the requirements
of the American National Standard for Permanence of
Paper for Printed Library Materials Z39.48-1984.

5· 4   3   2   1

To Dave, Ben, Ariel, Joe, and John

Forever Now

Contents

Part 4
Afterword

Acknowledgments

I gratefully acknowledge the assistance of those who helped make this book a reality. First and foremost, the David M. Kennedy Center for International and Area Studies of Brigham Young University provided valuable tangible resources. Louis Floyd, my research assistant, spent many hours putting the manuscript in final form—and went the extra mile in doing so. Lynne Rienner's encouragement and vision sustained me throughout the project, as did the comments of the anonymous reviewers. Finally, the unflagging support of my husband and children was a constant source of joy and strength to me.

1

Culture and Foreign Policy: Developing a Research Agenda

Valerie M. Hudson

During the Cold War, it was possible for scholars to overlook the effects of culture on foreign policy: One could argue that the constraints of the bipolar rivalry dwarfed, in large part, the domestic idiosyncrasies of nations. However, in the post–Cold War era, that luxury no longer exists. Nations—even the great powers—now obviously define national interest as much in terms of particularistic domestic motivations and imperatives as in terms of international balance of power considerations. The fault lines between civilizations are theorized to be the engine of interstate conflict in the post–Cold War world (see Huntington, 1992); literature on nationalism and the formation of national identity is expanding tremendously (see, for example, Gurr and Harff, 1994; Gottlieb, 1993; Golan, 1994; Appleby, 1994). A sure sign of growth, a new section of the International Studies Association entitled "Ethnicity, Nationalism, and Migration" was formed in 1995.

The research agenda of the field of foreign policy analysis (FPA) is well suited to offer explanation of foreign policy and foreign policy making in this new and uncertain post–Cold War age. Foreign policy analysis strives for actor-specific theory, which combines the strengths of general theory with those of country expertise. Using this approach, foreign policy analysis scholars have examined the psychology of world leaders, small group dynamics in foreign policy making bodies, foreign policy bureaucratic politics, the relationship between domestic political exigency and resulting foreign policy behavior, and so forth. The least developed angle of analysis in the subfield is the study of how societal culture affects foreign policy choice.

This is not surprising, for several reasons. First, the study of how cultural differences affect behavior has been, for the most part, the domain of social sciences other than international relations.[1] Most scholarly work on culture is to be found in the journals of anthropology, sociology,

1

social psychology, organizational behavior, and other related disciplines. In part, the paucity of such literature in international relations stems from the now discredited work on national character from earlier this century. Though a few substantial works have been written since that time in international relations and comparative politics, the trouble is, according to Lucian Pye, author of several such works, that culture quickly becomes "the explanation of last resort" (Pye, 1991:504). Everything that cannot be explained by existing theories in foreign policy analysis is ascribed to "cultural differences." However, explanations of last resort (e.g., "The Chinese act that way because that is the Chinese way") are virtually never explanations at all (Pye, 1988:6).

The time has come to move forward in the study of how culture affects foreign policy. This collection of essays hopefully constitutes a useful step in that direction. The purposes of this opening chapter are several: to overview the evolution of thinking about culture and foreign policy, to assess the current state of research, to clarify the most useful theoretical concepts and frameworks, and to investigate appropriate and innovative methodologies for empirical study in this field—in other words, to begin to outline a coherent research agenda for those interested in the topic.

First, however, we must clarify our central concepts.

CONCEPTUALIZING CULTURE, CONCEPTUALIZING FOREIGN POLICY

Culture is both one of the most elusive and most easily understood concepts in social science. It is easily understood because we have all had the experience of interacting with someone whose background led them to do and say things that seemed surprising or unpredictable. When was the last time your mother-in-law visited you and decided to clean house? Culture's consequences are very real, even to lay observers.

The elusiveness of culture becomes apparent when one attempts to define it in a theoretical sense. The difficulty is not so much centered on what to *include* in such a definition, but rather what to *exclude*. The vagueness of culture's boundaries are echoed in the all-encompassing but pithy definitions of culture found in the social science literature: for example, culture is the "human-made part of the environment" (Herskovits, 1955), culture is "the software of the mind" (Hofstede, 1991), culture is "a set of schedules of reinforcement" (Skinner, 1981), culture is "any interpersonally shared system of meanings, perceptions, and values" (*Millennium*, 1993).

Things do not become any clearer as one moves to more detailed definitions of culture. The following five have been chosen not for their uniqueness as definitions, but for their typicality in the theoretical literature on culture:

1. "I use the term culture to mean an organized body of rules concerning the ways in which individuals in a population should communicate with another, think about themselves and their environments, and behave toward one another and towards objects in their environments" (Levine, 1973).

2. "Culture consists in patterned ways of thinking, feeling and reaction, acquired and transmitted mainly by symbols, constituting the distinctive achievements of human groups, including their embodiments in artifacts; the essential core of culture consists of traditional (i.e., historically derived and selected) ideas and especially their attached values" (Kluckhohn, 1951).

3. "Culture is a set of human-made objective and subjective elements that in the past have increased the probability of survival and resulted in satisfaction for the participants in an ecological niche, and thus became shared among those who could communicate with each other because they had a common language and they lived in the same time and place" (Triandis, 1994).

4. "Culture [consists] of learned systems of meaning, communicated by means of natural language and other symbol systems, having representational, directive, and affective functions, and capable of creating cultural entities and particular senses of reality. Through these systems of meaning, groups of people adapt to their environment and structure interpersonal activities" (D'Andrade, 1984).

5. "[Culture is] an historically transmitted pattern of meanings embodied in symbols, a system of inherited conceptions expressed in symbolic form by means of which men communicate, perpetuate, and develop their knowledge about and attitudes towards life" (Geertz, 1973).

With definitions like these,[2] it is not hard to see why culture became "the explanation of last resort" for a field such as international relations, which was heavily influenced by behavioralism. What "crucial experiment" could be constructed capable of falsifying the hypothesis that culture affects what nations do in the international arena? Indeed, all human activity—including foreign policy—becomes both a product of and a component of culture. The seamlessness of culture rendered problematic early behavioralist attempts to separate and then relink in causal fashion the independent variable of culture and the dependent variable of national policy; we call these early attempts of the 1940s and 1950s the "national character studies." If the German national character could be described as "methodical," their policy would evince the same characteristic; ditto for the "stoic" Russians and "xenophobic" Japanese. National character studies were vulnerable to criticism on several grounds: methodological, theoretical, and moral. For example, the methodologies used predisposed one toward potentially tautological inferences: If a sample group perceived Germans as methodical, this proved significant psychological inducement to perceive whatever Germans did as methodical. Likewise, on theoretical grounds, the fact that individual variation within national groups always exceeded variation between national groups on any given characteristic was very troubling. Last, national character studies seemed a natural bedfellow of the "racial psychology" studies, whose worst excesses contributed a "scholarly" rationale for the evil policies of national socialism.[3]

What hampered these early efforts to find an interface between studies of culture and studies of national policy may not necessarily prevent the emergence of a culture/foreign policy research agenda now. The confluence of several factors provides some optimism on this score:

1. The post–Cold War world demands that international relations take nationalism and the politics of national identity very seriously. Furthermore, the theory and study of national foreign policy making, otherwise known as FPA, has made tremendous strides in the direction of actor-specific theory over the last twenty years. Actor-specific theory is arguably the most conducive approach to incorporating cultural factors into the study of national policy.

2. The theory and study of culture and its effects have matured greatly since the 1950s in such fields as sociology, social psychology, anthropology, and organizational behavior.

3. As a result of these two developments, there is now a small interface between "culture research" and "foreign policy research." In addition, the search for new methodologies to improve upon or replace standard behavioralist techniques of inquiry in international relations has resulted in a greater ability to both ask and answer questions regarding the effect of culture on foreign policy.

Let us take each point in turn.

Actor-Specific Theory in International Relations

The discipline of international relations is at a point of serious introspection caused by the catalytic shock of the end of the Cold War. Others (Gaddis, 1992; Haftendorn and Tuschoff, 1993) have written of the failure of international relations (IR) theory to predict that profound change. I do not intend to reiterate that argument here. Rather, I wish to argue that the real failure of IR theory lies not with the theories, which could never have been capable of predicting, for example, the end of the

Cold War, but with us, who failed to recognize that incapacity. Our failure was in elevating actor-general theory (where human actors appear invisible) to a status where it came to be seen as the pinnacle, if not the entirety, of IR theory. That it is neither does not detract from the usefulness of such theory to the study of IR; it merely puts that usefulness into perspective. The end of the Cold War provides an occasion to regain such perspective, by providing us with a stark display of how unhelpful actor-general theory can be in certain important circumstances.

The source of all international politics and all change in international politics is human beings, singly and collectively. Yes, certain balances of power in the international system (e.g., the Cold War bipolar system) may constrain the repertoire of action of these human actors, but ultimately, with every system transformation, we rediscover that the power of the human will and imagination involved was greater than that of the straitjacket of the system's rules. During periods of stable system constraints, prediction of general patterns of international behavior without reference to the actual human actors concerned may be within reach. Nevertheless, even during such periods, actor-general theories will be limited to posing and exploring ahistorical, contentless, "big" questions, such as the Security Dilemma.

If actor-general theory cannot and should not be the entirety of IR theory, could not its complement be theories that investigate the *source of change* in actor-general theory's scope conditions and the *source of diversity* within a given international system—humans singly and in groups? They are the content that actor-general theories assume but do not investigate. Alexander George calls this complement "actor-specific" theory (George, 1994). This work, the research core of the IR subfield of foreign policy analysis, is data intensive; it also requires country expertise and is time consuming. Despite this, the number of scholars engaged in actor-specific theorizing and research is growing, not shrinking, in part because the questions being asked in the FPA subfield are the questions to which we need answers in the post–Cold War era. There is now no stable and predictable system in the international arena; now more than ever objective indices will not suffice as inputs to expected utility equations. What foreign policy effects will we see if Boris Yeltsin dies suddenly? What if Kurdistan becomes a more coherent entity? To questions such as these being asked in 1997, abstract, actor-general theory will not give the type of answers we would find most useful.

The actor-specific theory of FPA "unpacks" the black box of decisionmaking in international affairs. FPA has several recognized research areas that contribute to its overall thrust: (1) personal characteristics, cognitive process, and reasoning of national authorities, (2) governmental politics (including small/advisory group processes, organizational/bureaucratic forces, and legislative bargaining), (3) domestic political imperatives and opposition, (4) regime and societal differences (this is where the study of the effects of culture on foreign policy would find its niche, theoretically speaking), and (5) integrative studies (studies that attempt to integrate findings from all the other levels of analysis).

Furthermore, foreign policy analysis is a bridging field. It can be envisioned as the theoretical hub of a wheel whose spokes reach out to abstract international relations theory, the foreign policy making community, and the comparative politics subfield of political science. All three end points would "meet" together, as it were, through the hub of foreign policy analysis. Mainstream IR theory, as we have seen, is largely abstract, actor-general theory. Comparative politics offers a wealth of actor-specific information but remains a weak field in terms of theory building. The interface between international relations, the study of internation relations, and comparative politics—the study of national policy and politics—is the study of *foreign policy*. Foreign policy analysis, which is the actor-specific theory of foreign policy, has the ability to ground IR theory and simultaneously theorize comparative politics at this substantive meeting place of the two subdisciplines (foreign policy study). Furthermore, both abstract IR theory and atheoretical comparative politics information can contribute more effectively to the foreign policy making community through the medium of foreign policy analysis. Foreign policy makers need the complexity and detail of actor specifics *together with* explanatory and predictive power and the potential to identify manipulable variables, which are the hallmarks of good theory (Hudson with Vore, 1995).

Although an integral part of actor-specific theory of foreign policy must be the exploration of culture's consequences, this is arguably the least developed research area in FPA. As we will see, a small interface does exist, but it must be enlarged for FPA to realize its potential as a bridging field. Before we explore the existing interface between culture research and foreign policy research, it would be wise to examine the current status of research in the study of culture.

The Study of Culture

The study of culture has had a fascinating genesis, worthy of many book-length treatments in its own right. The journey from the thought of Emile Durkheim, Max Weber, Talcott Parsons, Margaret Mead, and others, through the hiatus of such thought in the 1960s, to the renaissance of the study of culture in the 1980s is an intellectual journey well worth taking. This essay, however, will concentrate on the noteworthy themes of the renaissance period for their possible applicability to the development of a culture/foreign policy research agenda.

Although definitions of culture continue to be very inclusive of the human experience, one can detect a subtle trifurcation in the conceptualization of culture in recent works. Some scholars emphasize culture as *the organization of meaning;* others view culture as primarily *value preferences;* and a third group of scholars conceptualize culture as *templates of human strategy.* Of course, a natural reaction is to assert that culture includes all three elements, and indeed it is futile to impose a hard and fast distinction between the different conceptions. Furthermore, it may be perilous to unweave what appears to be an intricately woven social garment. We may "destroy" what we mean by culture by picking at its facets. The call to advance new methodologies that will allow for a more holistic, yet still quasi-causal, explanation of culture's effects on behavior has gone out (Yee, 1996), but we are still far from achieving that laudable goal. In the meantime, such analytical schemes as proposed in this chapter may have to serve as a springboard for more sophisticated thinking along these lines. Why begin with an analytical framework? Because, as we have seen, the more inclusive view of culture is the least useful in a research sense—at least at this point of theoretical development. The particular emphasis of the three groups of scholars has allowed each to ask (and answer) more concrete questions about the consequences of culture than was possible in earlier periods. Indeed, a close look at the five longer definitions presented earlier will reveal the following emphases.

Culture as the organization of meaning.   If culture is a system of shared meaning, how is it constructed, perpetuated, and modified? Also, how does one system of shared meaning compare to another system, and what are the ramifications of interaction between two very different ontologies? Because meanings are shared through interpersonal expression, the study of such expression, whether it be art, writing, film, or conversation, is often the focus of such analysis. The classic work in this category would be Clifford Geertz's (1973) *Interpretation of Cultures.* Geertz insisted that a structural-functional explanation of, say, a Balinese cockfight, would miss the more holistic *meaning* the cockfight held for the community. In what way can an outsider become privy to meaning within a society? Alluding to the Whorfian hypothesis (Whorf, 1956) that language itself colors thinking, many researchers look to language use as a key. One approach, for example, is to analyze public discourse on issues of high controversy. Luker (1984), for example, in tracing the contorted evolution of public moral discourse on abortion, discovers that the meaning of *abortion* has seesawed back and forth over the centuries and has depended in large part on those authorities who were accepted as having highest legitimacy in the society at the time. Others have asked how it is that scientists come to regard a finding as "important" or even "scientific" in the first place (see, for example, Root-Bernstein, 1989; Pickering, 1984). Comparisons of the meanings of certain phenomena from one culture to another have uncovered some startling and unsuspected differences (see Triandis, 1994:97–99; Bleiker, 1993). Nor need we be confined to analyzing verbal communication—nonverbal messages as well can construct and share meaning. Differences in nonverbal communication can derail otherwise normal interactions: one oft-cited example is the propensity of the Japanese to smile when being reprimanded (see Argyle, 1975).

Culture as value preferences. This view of culture follows the lead of Weber, Parsons, and others in suggesting that culture tells us what to want, to prefer, to desire, and thus to *value.* Such motivations prompt certain predictable behaviors—"syndromes"—in cultures. To the extent that culture has been studied in modern political science and international relations, this is the primary approach taken (Almond and Verba's [1963] *Civic Culture: Political Attitudes and Democracy in Five Nations* would be the classic example[4]). Hofstede's seminal study (1980) dimensionalizes cultures according to their affinity for four factors: individualism, masculinity, uncertainty avoidance, and power distance. Hofstede was able to show a nonrandom geographic pattern of cultures with respect to such values. The immense literature on organizational behavior in different cultures starts primarily from a Hofstede-type theoretical basis (see McDaniels and Gregory, 1991; Tse et al., 1988). Other conceptual schemes exist—for example, Triandis (1994:156–179) discerns three cultural dimensions, which may interrelate to form unique cultural proclivities: cultural complexity, cultural "tightness," and individualism.

Closer to home, the work of Douglas and Wildavsky (1982) can be placed in this category as well. Wildavsky, for instance (building on the work of Douglas), classifies cultures into four types: fatalist, hierarchist, egalitarian, and individualist. He is able to predict the responses of each type of culture to resource scarcity, nature, change, alliances, and other broad issues (see Wildavsky, 1987; Thompson, Ellis, and Wildavsky, 1990). Other political scientists have used this approach to focus on a particular culture (see Pye, 1968; Solomon, 1971). There is also a growing research effort in the comparative study of ethical systems. Continuing the approach of Max Weber's pioneering work on the ethics of Protestantism, Hinduism, and Confucianism (Weber, 1930, 1951a, 1951b, 1963), a new generation of scholars compares traditions of moral reasoning in dealing with common ethical problems (see Green, 1978; Little and Twiss, 1978; Chidester, 1987; Carman and Juergensmeyer, 1990). Such differences in moral reasoning based on culture may skew traditional assumptions of rational-choice theory (see, for example, Sen, 1982, 1987). They may also lead to distinctive patterns of economic development, with some cultures possessing a distinct advantage because of their cultural values (see Kahn, 1993).

Culture as templates for human strategy. One group of scholars argues that the values espoused by members of a culture are not sufficient to explain actual behavior by those members. Often there is great slippage between professed ends and the actual use of means. These scholars assert that the more important explanatory variable is the capability advantages bestowed by one's culture. Individuals will play the game their culture has conditioned them to play *well.* Indeed, Swidler goes so far as to say: "Action is not determined by one's values. Rather, action *and* values are organized to take advantage of cultural competences. . . . What endures is the way action is organized, not its ends. . . . People will come to value ends for which their cultural equipment is well suited" (Swidler, 1986:275, 276, 277). What culture provides its members is a repertoire or palette of adaptive responses from which members build off-the-shelf strategies of action. What matters is not the whole of culture, but rather "chunks" of "prefabricated" cultural response. We may not be able to predict choice and construction of a particular response by a particular member of the culture, but we can know *what is on the shelf* ready and available to be used or not. As Linton argues, "Individuals tend to imitate the culture patterns of their society when confronted by a new situation, then to take thought as the situation is repeated and try to adjust these patterns to their individual needs" (Linton, 1945:104). A related approach is taken by the "dramaturgical school," in which culture provides scripts and personae that are reenacted and subtly modified over time within a society (see Wuthnow, 1987; Kurtz, 1986).

It is in this area of cultural research that we also find efforts linking cultural background with information-processing proclivities. Studies from many fields have pointed out that rationality itself may mean different things in different cultures (see, e.g., Motokawa, 1989). For instance, Douglas and Wildavsky (1982) discovered that fatalistic cultures do not engage in probabilistic thinking and thus perceive risk taking (a subfield of rational-choice study) in a very different fashion from nonfatalistic cultures. Ehrenhaus (1983) argues that culture may predispose a person to certain types of explanations and certain types of attribution and inferencing. This, in turn, makes particular errors in reasoning (Type I or Type II errors) more prevalent in some cultures than in others.

The Interface

As noted previously, there does exist a small interface between the study of culture and the study of foreign policy. To illuminate this interface literature, I have tried to make a distinction between (1) foreign policy studies with little or no attention paid to cultural factors, (2) cultural studies of particular nations ("country studies," "area studies") with no specific implications for foreign policy, and (3) cultural studies of particular nations or regions with identifiable implications for foreign policy research. Only the last category of research is included. However, the other two categories of research are potential sources of theoretical and empirical insight that should not be overlooked as a research agenda linking culture and foreign policy is developed.

Shared systems of meaning in foreign policy and foreign policy making. Rather than accepting preferences and beliefs in international relations at face value, a new generation of scholars asks how they were formed. Deconstructing statements of international reality, these scholars untangle the threads that culminated in the articulation of such statements. Many of the threads would fall under the first category of culture definitions: shared, evolving meanings conditioned by historical precedent and contemporary experience. We see and believe and desire what our horizons of the moment permit us to see and believe and desire—but these horizons are constantly shifting.

One lesson for the culture/foreign policy research agenda to be derived from postmodernist criticism is that it may be fruitless to search for an exclusively *political* culture. The notion that political science studies some subset of culture called political culture is long-standing (see Almond and Verba, 1963; Inglehart, 1988). Yet, at least from a cursory reading of recent U.S. politics, it is almost impossible not to see the political horizons shift their shape according to trends in broader societal culture, and vice versa. (Why does the Speaker of the House of Representatives defend a policy position with reference to a Spencer Tracy movie? How would Bill Clinton's horizons be different if Doonesbury had chosen a box of Wheaties instead of a floating waffle as his symbol?)

Definitions of political culture are virtually indistinguishable from definitions of general culture. Here is one: Political culture is all of the discourses, values, and implicit rules that express and shape political action and intentions, determine the claims groups may and may not make upon one another, and ultimately provide a logic of political action. Cross out every *political:* "Culture is all of the discourses, values, and implicit rules that express and shape actions and intentions. . . ." Sounds like our earlier definitions, does it not? The postmodern critique suggests that things "political" can be deconstructed and shown to have their roots in broad systems of shared meaning. To snip the overtly political elements of culture from their roots is to cut the researcher off from the wellsprings and source of change and permutation of political horizons. After all, another definition of culture is "common ways of dealing with social problems" (Triandis, 1994:17). Dealing with social problems (or, dressed up in political science jargon, "value allocation processes in situations of conflict over scarce resources") *is* the study of politics. Nor should we forget the important feminist contribution on this score: The personal is the political.

However, it is in politics that cultural conversations become most explicit: What ends should the nation pursue? Using what means? Foreign policy is arguably at the very high end on a continuum of conversational explicitness (though it may not seem so from the receiving end!) Foreign policy is first a formal affair because, second, foreign policy concerns relations with outgroups. Outgroups serve simultaneously as a source of national identity (we are not like them) *and* as a threat to national identity (we must resist becoming like them). Thus, we are led to theorize that the relationship between a culture and the acts it performs in the international arena must be fairly strong. Vertzberger sums up the conundrum this way:

> It is extremely difficult to positively prove the causal links, direct and indirect, between societal-cultural variables and foreign-policy-related information processing. The difficulty in directly observing societal-cultural effects, however, does not prove the opposite, that is, that societal-cultural influences are minor or negligible. I believe that the influences are important, even though they are not always tangible and easily observable. (Vertzberger, 1990: 261)

If one were to search for systems of shared meaning in foreign policy and foreign policy making, how would one go about it, methodologically speaking? Let us examine three research efforts: Sylvan, Majeski, and Milliken (1991); Boynton (1991); and Tunander (1989). All three projects seek to uncover the meaning, the basis, and the rules of political discourse in concrete circumstances (see also Chan, 1993; and Alker et al., 1991). The first two works cited are within-nation studies, and Tunander's is a between-nation study.

Sylvan, Majeski, and Milliken examine the mountains of material generated by the U.S. national security establishment with reference to the conduct of the Vietnam War. They question the origins of war policy recommendations in this material: When did a statement become a "bona fide" recommendation? How did it fit into the flow of recommendations and counterrecommendations? How did persuasion occur? On what doxa was the entire discourse based? Sylvan et al. schematically map the river of recommendations in order to answer such questions. They see their work as a *cultural* investigation: "Our emphasis is cultural: how, within a particular foreign policy community, certain statements are fitted together into a comprehensible recommendation. . . . [Our model] must of necessity take into account the construal within a particular culture of certain statements as arguments, evidence, conclusions, and so forth. . . . Our concern is with how, for a given bureaucratic and political culture, various statements are taxonomically related to each other so as jointly to compose a bona fide policy recommendation" (1991:327–328).

Boynton uses the official record of hearings of congressional committees to investigate how committee members make sense of current events and policies. By viewing the questions and responses in the hearings as an unfolding narrative, Boynton is able to chart how "meaning" crystallizes for each committee member, and how they attempt to share that meaning with other members and with those who are testifying. Boynton posits the concept of "interpretive triple" as a way to understand how connections between facts are made through plausible interpretations. He is then able to illuminate how plausibility is granted to an interpretation—in effect, ascertaining which interpretations are plausible within the cultural context created by the hearings.

Tunander offers an innovative semiotic explanation of U.S.-Soviet naval moves in the North Atlantic as "signs" in a complex conversation taking place between the two nations (Tunander, 1989:169–180). Taking off from Derrida's "the missile is a missive," Tunander sees these naval maneuvers as part of the body language of states. In Tunander's view, the navy is the principal character in a hyperreal drama: The navy "speaks about his mad brother" (cruise missiles) and "plays with the key to the lion's cage" (strategic bombers and ICBMs) (1989:174). Episteme (science) and doxa (opinion) merge in a strange game of shifting perceptions. This game becomes a culture unto itself, with participants able to communicate shared meaning that may be opaque to others within their own societies.

Differences in values and preferences in foreign policy and foreign policy making. Much of the work concerning cultural effects on international negotiation examines the effects on such negotiations of cultural differences in value preferences (see Cohen, 1991).[5] For example, because the government of the People's Republic of China (PRC) must base its legitimacy on its superior virtue and morality (in line with Confucian culture), it must explicitly pass moral judgment on the conduct of other nations. To assert moral claim to advantage in negotiation, the PRC will pass negative moral judgment on the other party before entering into serious negotiation with it. From the Western point of view, this is the last thing a nation would do on the eve of serious negotiations. It would be permissible to talk about the unfairness of the status quo before negotiation, but a negative moral judgment of another nation's actions would more likely presage a Western nation's disengagement from serious negotiation (see Shih, 1993). The Western approach, too, derives from its unique Judeo-

Christian values. Similar to the study of values in international negotiation is the study of values with reference to strategy. In the 1980s, a body of literature on "comparative strategic culture" developed to explain persistent differences between the United States and the USSR on military strategy (see Booth, 1979; Gray, 1986). Why did the United States eschew strategic and civil defense in favor of mutual assured destruction (MAD), while the Soviet Union embraced defense to the point of adopting a war-fighting strategy contradictory to MAD? Scholars of strategic culture pointed to cultural and historical differences predisposing each nation to the choice it actually made, simultaneously noting the inevitable anxiety these choices would cause in the other nation.

Studies in international relations paralleling the "cultural syndrome" studies in other disciplines also exist. In its broadest sense, "national role conception" (Holsti, 1970) describes a national syndrome with respect to the nation's external relations (in its more specific application, national role conception studies resemble more the dramaturgical-style studies discussed in the next section). A nation's leaders rise in part because they articulate a vision of the nation's role in world affairs that corresponds to deep, cultural beliefs about the nation. In the rhetoric and action of these leaders, one may discern the nature of this role. Holsti's labels for such roles include "bridge," "isolate," "mediator," "bastion of the revolution," "defender of the faith," "regional leader," and so forth. Holsti and others (see Wish, 1980; Walker, 1987; Seeger, 1992; Breuning, 1992; and Chapters 5 and 7 in this book) could then investigate the degree of concordance between expected role behavior/rhetoric and actual behavior/rhetoric. Breuning, for instance (see Chapter 5), is able to trace differences in the assistance-giving behavior of Belgium and the Netherlands to differences in the two nations' national role conceptions, despite the nations' ostensible similarities in most other respects.

The next step in this line of inquiry is to trace in more detail how certain cultures come to conceive of their nation's roles in particular ways. Sampson (1987) and Sampson and Walker (1987) are two such attempts. Specifically, Sampson and Walker, in contrasting Japan and France, assert that cultural norms of dealing with subordinates and superordinates in organizational settings within the nation will be applied by those nations when dealing with subordinates and superordinates in the international arena. Sampson and Walker compare Japan and France on their reaction to and emphasis on group harmony, indebtedness, concern/dependency on others, a superior's empathy for an inferior, collaboration and consultation, and sense of responsibility owed within an organization. They find that Japan's and France's profound differences on these values result in equally profound, but now predictable and understandable, differences in national role conceptions.

Prefabricated templates of action in foreign policy and foreign policy making. In international relations, the work of Leites (1951), George (1969), Walker (1977), and others on the operational code comes closest to this conceptualization of culture. Defining an operational code involves identifying core beliefs of a leader or group, as well as preferred means and style of pursuing goals. It is this last half of the operational code definition that helps us determine what templates of action may exist within a nation with respect to foreign policy. For example, in elucidating the "Bolshevik" operational code, one finds some explicit maxims on political action, such as maximize one's gains rather than satisfice, but avoid adventuristic actions where the outcomes are either maximum payoff or maximum loss; and push to the limit and pursue one's opponent even if he lets up, but be prepared to engage in strategic retreat rather than suffer large losses in strength (George, 1969). George is then able to demonstrate how these maxims for action were followed by the Soviet Union in its relationship with the United States.

Such action maxims can affect broader aspects of cognitive processing as well. Ball asserts that Asian culture predisposes one to take a longer-term perspective than other cultures: He quotes Sukarno as saying, "We, the Indonesian people, have learned not to think in centimeters or meters, not in hours or days. We have learned to think in continents and decades" (Ball, 1992:5). Hermann (1979) has found evidence that certain cultures are more likely to exhibit particular aspects of decision-making and interpersonal styles than others; for example, she found that Middle Eastern leaders were much more distrustful of others than leaders from other cultures and therefore more likely to discount discrepant information. Furthermore, certain types of leaders are predisposed toward specific styles of foreign policy making (structure of decision groups, method of resolving disagreement, etc.), and the prevalence of certain types of leaders varies according to region and culture (see Hermann, 1987). Gaenslen (1989) persuasively shows that cultures that rely on consensual decisionmaking may not be as open to dissonant information—even from reliable sources—as cultures in which majority vote is sufficient for decisionmaking. Vertzberger (1990) asserts that certain cultures may predispose one to abstractive versus associative reasoning, and to universalistic versus case particularistic reasoning.

As noted earlier, the more specific approach to "national role conception" provides an interesting parallel to the dramaturgical approach to culture. In international relations, the work of Shih (1993), Etheredge (1992), and others falls into this category (see also Esherick and Wasserstrom, 1990), as does the work of Katzenstein presented in this book (see Chapter 3). Shih and Katzenstein both feel that Chinese foreign policy behavior corresponds to relatively specific scripts of action inherited from exemplary episodes in that nation's history. The reenactment of such scripts allows Chinese foreign policy to be meaningful to the Chinese themselves. According to Shih, "The Chinese style of organizing world politics is more dramatic than realist. . . . Every drama can and will be repeated till the demise of the moral regime" (Shih, 1993:201, 197). Shih then analyzes several Chinese scripts, the knowledge of which allows for the reconciliation of otherwise contradictory Chinese foreign policies.

Katzenstein argues that a Chinese script virtually unknown to Westerners, but forefront in the minds of Chinese on both sides of the strait, was seen as the template for eventual resolution of Taiwan's anomalous status. Etheredge, in his study of U.S. national security policy, persuasively argues that such policy is incomprehensible without an understanding of important U.S. dramatic requirements: "All power relationships are a dramatic art, and one creates and manages power as an exercise in applied psychology, shaping a dramatic presence that, in the minds of others, becomes their experience of reality" (Etheredge, 1992:62). The logic of being impressive imposes theatrical requirements far different from those of strict rationality. To try to understand U.S. nuclear strategy without a knowledge of the impression the United States was trying to make with its strategy would be to conclude that the United States was acting irrationally. It was not acting irrationally, but it was *acting*—a very specific role for both internal and external audience consumption.

DEVELOPING A RESEARCH AGENDA

If, as elucidated above, the building blocks for a research agenda investigating the link between culture and foreign policy already exist, where would we go from here? Let us address that question by seeking to define the parameters of that research agenda. Although it is too early to say a research agenda exists, addressing the following questions is a first step in that direction. To begin forging some general agreements among the scholars who will be active in this subfield, I proffer some broad (but certainly not definitive) opinions on each point.

1. What conceptual definitions of culture are most applicable to the study of foreign policy? Are there differences in usefulness depending upon whether one conceives of culture as a system of shared meaning, as a set of value preferences, as a toolkit of skills, or as an expectation for certain script enactments?

There is no one "right" definition of culture. However, a particular definition may be better suited to the type of study one wishes to conduct. If one is primarily interested in knowing what a nation will do next in a certain international situation, a dramaturgical definition may be more useful. If one is interested in how internal forces in society are persuaded to support a foreign policy, the politics of shared meaning would be a good place to start.

2. Are there meaningful conceptual differences between social culture, political culture, religious culture, elite culture, popular culture, ethnic culture, and the like? If so, which are most relevant to the study of foreign policy?

As previously mentioned, in my opinion, such distinctions are not very meaningful, or even helpful, to the researcher. The only exception would be in the case of elite culture, which can be vastly different from mass culture. For example, Indian elites traditionally have life experiences very different from those of nonelites. One major component of this difference is lengthy schooling in Britain. Indian elites thus may be thought of as a unique subculture within the society. The idiosyncrasies of this subculture would putatively be crucial to understanding Indian foreign policy.

3. What is the appropriate level of analysis for the study of culture's effects on foreign policy? Whose culture should students of foreign policy examine: that of the elites, the general populace, or the leader? Can one specify microcultures: Yale graduates who served in the military, for instance? How theoretically or practically useful would the concept of microcultures be?

Microcultures exist and can be important in understanding action. At Brigham Young University, I live in a powerful microculture. However, the importance of such microcultures depends on the homogeneity of the group being analyzed. If the entire top echelon of the U.S. national security establishment were all educated at, say, Princeton, it would be prudent to inquire into the intricacies of Princeton microculture. There may be cultures (such as the Indian example above) where the study of microcultures would be useful. However, as a general rule, it is probably unnecessary to study microcultures to determine the broad effects of culture on foreign policy.

4. Are there different "cultures" for different foreign policy issues? Can one identify, say, a "strategic culture" that is fairly insulated from the culture governing more general matters of foreign policy?

The strategic culture concept is persuasive. However, strategic culture may be more the product of a microculture at work than any meaningful compartmentalization of cultural thinking on foreign policy issues. Nevertheless, Dellios (in Chapter 8 of this book) provides a case study in which she is able to link Chinese strategic culture to broad cultural understandings within Chinese society. The end of the Cold War should allow more artificial strategic cultures to give way to more culturally rooted ones.

5. How can one determine the extent to which cultural factors are affecting any given foreign policy? How can one distinguish between, say, idiosyncratic personality factors and their effect, and culture and its effect? To what extent is culture in a mutually constructive relationship with other FPA variables, such as style of small group interactions, and so forth? What is the relationship between culture and notions of rational choice in foreign policy?

If culture has the potential to affect all aspects of rational-choice modeling, from the very conception of utility to notions of cost, risk, and even probability itself, then the study of differences in rational choice from culture to culture will become a growth field in the near future. In the meantime, conceptualizing culture as an indirect variable affecting foreign policy through other variables may be a useful starting point of inquiry in the culture and foreign policy research agenda. After all, theories linking advisory group size and composition to foreign policy behavior (for example) and foreign policymaking process are already in place. Why not just walk the cat back in a theoretical sense and ask why certain structures and compositions are found in a given nation? (See Chapter 6 in this book for such an attempt.) Why not ask if types of groups are nonrandomly distributed among cultures?

These are fairly easy ways in which we can build upon existing theories in foreign policy analysis. On a related point, however, distinguishing cultural effects from other effects may not be the optimum way to think about our theoretical task. Culture presumably pervades all aspects of human existence. Rather, we can determine (a) whether a phenomenon was concordant with cultural expectations (if it was not, how could culture be part of the explanation?) and (b) what latitude was "allowed" by culture in a particular circumstance (e.g., if a group could use either unanimity or a working majority to reach a decision, then to the extent that the choice of resolution method affected the ultimate decision, such effect could not be ascribed to culture). It is imperative that conceptual work on this issue progress for the research agenda to begin in earnest. Breuning, in Chapter 5 of this book, addresses this issue head-on in a most constructive fashion.

6. Assuming questions about the most useful conceptualization of culture and its facets can be resolved, how does one operationally describe culture? What indicators would be theoretically justifiable? What primary evidence would constitute a defensible basis for asserting that any given culture possessed any given character?

Given the infancy of the "interface" between culture studies and foreign policy studies, it is premature to talk about specific schemes by which to operationally describe culture. However, we can talk about desiderata for schematic candidates: (a) they would be cross-nationally applicable, (b) they would be cross-nationally grounded, (c) they would be capable of capturing the dynamics of cultural change over time, and (d) they would be susceptible of being linked to existing theories of foreign policy.

7. How do cultural differences lead nations to predictable patterns of interaction, whether those patterns be hostile, cooperative, or neutral in nature? Under what conditions would we expect culture to play a more important role in internation interactions?

The answers to these questions would represent a significant empirical breakthrough in the development of a culture/foreign policy research agenda. If there are cultural syndromes, leading to predictable cultural propensities of thought, reaction, and action, scholars should be able to theoretically "simulate" the interaction between two or more of them and investigate the consequences thereof. If China is enacting script X and the United States is enacting script Y, what will be the result? How will each interpret the other's intentions? It should be possible to engage in this type of theory-building exercise now, as a prelude to empirical assessment of such theory. A second part of the theory-building enterprise is to posit under what conditions culture should play a more pivotal role in national behavior. An initial idea that comes to mind is the concept of "cultural insecurity." When a culture becomes threatened internally, a nation may react by attempting to exclude, on cultural grounds, those forces it perceives as threatening. A tighter view of what is culturally acceptable, a return to cultural mores and behavior norms of a period when the threat did not exist, and an insistence on cultural "purity" are all signs that this is taking place. Consider this analysis by Leuchtenberg (1958) of the United States in the 1920s: Large immigrant populations, growing cities, "new intellectual currents of moral relativism," and "the disturbing knowledge that Americans themselves no longer had their former confidence in democracy and religion" caused rural Americans to attempt to impose a "patriotic cult" on the nation. I have argued elsewhere that this type of imposition will be an increasingly common occurrence because of the nature of the post–Cold War world (Hudson, 1994). The emergence of the politics of exclusion may be a clue that the researcher may profitably investigate cultural influences on national direction.

8. Assuming that culture is not static, how does one recognize and evaluate the extent of cultural change? What are the dynamics of cultural change? How, theoretically and practically, can one find traces of cultural change in foreign policy change?

If the culture/foreign policy research agenda is to thrive, it must incorporate from the very beginning a vision of dynamic, not static, culture. Unfortunately, there are few exemplars from the culture studies in other social sciences of how to do this. One way to keep one's finger on the pulse of cultural change is through discursive studies. In the rhetoric of political persuasion will be found those analogies that are contending in the public mind for prominence as guides to national action (see Khong, 1993). In the battle of the editorials can be found the artifacts of popular culture that pervade understanding in the society—"Where's the beef?" "Toughlove for North Korea," "Pizza Hut diplomacy," and so on. However this theoretical task is to be accomplished, it is essential that it be tackled as soon as possible. Chafetz et al. in Chapter 7 illustrate one method of tracking cultural change.

CONCLUSION

It is time to develop a research agenda that explores the effects of culture on national foreign policy. It may be increasingly difficult to understand foreign policy in the post–Cold War world without such research. The existing theoretical structure of foreign policy analysis, actor-specific in nature as it is, is a good place to begin the integration of insights about cultural factors into the study of foreign policy.

Culture studies in other social sciences are progressing. Three foci have emerged: culture as shared meaning, culture as value preferences, and culture as a template for human action. There already exists a small interface of works that combine these three views of culture with the perspective of the foreign policy analyst. While this is an excellent and promising start, it is necessary to raise the broader conceptual and methodological questions that will help define a culture and foreign policy research agenda. The aim of this essay—and of this book—is to bring about the scholarly dialogue required to do just that.

NOTES

1. See Inglehart (1988) for a similar argument with respect to the broader discipline of political science.

2. For a compendium of more than 160 similar definitions of culture, see Kroeber and Kluckhohn (1952).

3. Ruth Benedict (1946, 1949) and Geoffrey Gorer (1943, 1948) were two of the most prominent national character scholars. Although the approach has had many detractors (see Inkeles and Levinson, 1968), it also has had many supporters. Margaret Mead was a supporter, and Lucian Pye has also defended these early efforts. For a good overview, see Terhune (1970). For examples of racial psychology studies in the United States, see Krogman (1945) and Klineberg (1945).

4. The aim of civic culture studies (sometimes also called the study of political culture) is very different from that of the research agenda I am proposing in this essay. Civic culture studies attempt to determine what type of societal characteristics one must have to sustain a pluralist democracy. The culture and foreign policy research agenda, on the other hand, would ask what effect a nation's

culture has on its foreign policy and foreign policy making. Thus, work in the tradition of *The Civic Culture* (see, e.g., Lowery and Sigelman, 1982) is not as directly useful to the culture and foreign policy research agenda as one might think on the basis of the authors' mutual use of cultural variables.

5. However, in my reading of the international negotiation literature, I find scholars easily jump from one conception of culture to another. Thus, there are works on meaning and verbal/nonverbal communication in international negotiation as well as works contrasting the values of various negotiating players (see, for example, Fisher, 1980; Binnendijk, 1987; Druckman et al., 1976).

REFERENCES

Alker, Hayward, Gavan Duffy, Roger Hurwitz, and John Mallery (1991) "Text Modeling for International Politics: A Tourist's Guide to RELATUS." In *Artificial Intelligence and International Politics,* edited by Valerie M. Hudson. Boulder: Westview Press.

Almond, Gabriel A., and Sidney Verba (1963) *The Civic Culture: Political Attitudes and Democracy in Five Nations.* Princeton: Princeton University Press.

Appleby, R. Scott (1994) *Religious Fundamentalisms and Global Conflict.* New York: Foreign Policy Association.

Argyle, M. (1975) *Bodily Communication.* New York: International Universities Press.

Ball, Desmond (1992) "Strategic Culture in the Asia-Pacific Region." Reference Paper No. 189. Strategic and Defence Studies Centre, Research School of Pacific Studies, Australian National University, Canberra, Australia.

Benedict, Ruth (1934) *Patterns of Culture.* Boston: Houghton Mifflin.

Benedict, Ruth (1946) *The Chrysanthemum and the Sword.* Boston: Houghton Mifflin.

Benedict, Ruth (1949) "Child Rearing in Certain European Countries." *American Journal of Orthopsychiatry* 19:342–350.

Binnendijk, Hans, ed. (1987) *National Negotiating Styles.* Washington, DC: Foreign Service Institute.

Bleiker, Roland (1993) "Neorealist Claims in Light of Ancient Chinese Philosophy: The Cultural Dimension of International Theory." *Millennium* 22, no. 3: 401–422.

Booth, Ken (1979) *Strategy and Ethnocentrism.* London: Croom Helm.

Boynton, G. R. (1991) "The Expertise of the Senate Foreign Relations Committee." In *Artificial Intelligence and International Politics,* edited by Valerie M. Hudson. Boulder: Westview Press.

Breuning, Marijke (1992) "National Role Conceptions and Foreign Assistance Policy Behavior: Toward a Cognitive Model." Ph.D. diss., Ohio State University.

Carman, John, and Mark Juergensmeyer (1990) *A Bibliographic Guide to the Comparative Study of Ethics.* New York: Cambridge University Press.

Chan, Stephen (1993) "Cultural and Linguistic Reductionisms and a New Historical Sociology for International Relations." *Millennium* 22, no. 3: 423–442.

Chidester, David (1987) *Patterns of Action: Religion and Ethics in a Comparative Perspective.* Belmont, CA: Wadsworth.

Cohen, Raymond (1991) *Negotiating Across Cultures.* Washington, DC: United States Institute of Peace Press.

d'Andrade, R. G. (1984) "Cultural Meaning Systems." In *Culture Theory: Essays on Mind, Self, and Emotion,* edited by R. Shweder and R. LeVine. Cambridge: Cambridge University Press.

Douglas, Mary, and Aaron Wildavsky (1982) *Risk and Culture: An Essay on the Selection of Technical and Environmental Dangers.* Berkeley: University of California Press.

Druckman, Daniel, A. A. Benton, F. Ali, and J. S. Bagur (1976) "Cultural Differences in Bargaining Behavior: India, Argentina, and the United States." *Journal of Conflict Resolution* 20:413–448.

Ehrenhaus, P. (1983) "Culture and the Attribution Process: Barriers to Effective Communication." In *Intercultural Communication Theory: Current Perspective,* edited by W. B. Gudykunst. Beverly Hills: Sage.

Esherick, J. W., and J. N. Wasserstrom (1990) "Acting Out Democracy: Political Theater in Modern China." *Journal of Asian Studies* 49, no. 4:835–865.

Etheredge, Lloyd (1992) "On Being More Rational than the Rationality Assumption: Dramatic Requirements, Nuclear Deterrence, and the Agenda for Learning." In *Political Psychology and Foreign Policy,* edited by E. Singer and V. M. Hudson. Boulder: Westview Press.

Fisher, Glen (1980) *International Negotiation: A Cross-Cultural Perspective.* Yarmouth, ME: Intercultural Press.

Gaddis, John Lewis (1992) "International Relations Theory and the End of the Cold War." *International Security* 17, no. 3:5–58.

Gaenslen, Fritz (1989) "On the Consequences of Consensual Decision Making: 'Rational Choice' in Comparative Perspective." University of Vermont.

Geertz, Clifford (1973) *The Interpretation of Cultures.* New York: Basic Books.

George, Alexander L. (1969) "The 'Operational Code': A Neglected Approach to the Study of Political Leaders and Decision-Making." *International Studies Quarterly* 13:190–222.

George, Alexander L. (1994) "The Two Cultures of Academia and Policy-Making: Bridging the Gap." *Political Psychology* 15, no. 1:143–171.

Golan, Daphna (1994) *Inventing Shaka: Using History in the Construction of Zulu Nationalism.* Boulder: Lynne Rienner.

Gorer, Geoffrey (1943) "Themes in Japanese Culture." *Transactions of the New York Academy of Sciences,* ser. 2, no. 5:106–124.

Gorer, Geoffrey (1948) *The American People.* New York: W. W. Norton.

Gorer, Geoffrey, and John Rickman (1949) *The People of Great Russia.* London: Grosset

Gottlieb, Gidon (1993) *Nation Against State.* New York: CFR Press.

Gray, Colin (1986) *Nuclear Strategy and National Style.* New York: Hamilton Press.

Green, Ronald M. (1978) *Religious Reason: The Rational and Moral Basis of Religious Belief.* New York: Oxford University Press.

Gurr, Ted Robert, and Barbara Harff (1994) *Ethnic Conflict in World Politics.* Boulder: Westview Press.

Haftendorn, Helga, and Christian Tuschoff, eds. (1993) *America and Europe in an Era of Change.* Boulder: Westview Press.

Hermann, Margaret G. (1979) "Who Becomes a Political Leader? Some Societal and Regime Influences on Selection of a Head of Government." In *Psychological Models in International Politics,* edited by Lawrence Falkowski. Boulder: Westview Press.

Hermann, Margaret G. (1987) "Foreign Policy Role Orientations and the Quality of Foreign Policy Decisions." In *Role Theory and Foreign Policy Analysis,* edited by Stephen Walker. Durham, NC: Duke University Press.

Herskovits, M. J. (1955) *Cultural Anthropology.* New York: Knopf.

Hofstede, Geert (1980) *Culture's Consequences.* Beverly Hills: Sage.

Hofstede, Geert (1991) *Cultures and Organizations.* London: McGraw-Hill.

Holsti, Kal J. (1970) "National Role Conceptions in the Study of Foreign Policy." *International Studies Quarterly* 14:233–309.

Hudson, Valerie M. (1994) "International and Domestic Security: System Deconcentration in the Asia Pacific." Paper presented at the thirty-fifth annual conference of the International Studies Association, Washington, DC, March 28–April 1.

Hudson, Valerie M., with C. Vore (1995) "Foreign Policy Analysis Yesterday, Today, and Tomorrow." *Mershon Studies International Review* 39, no. 2:209–238.

Huntington, Samuel (1992) *The Clash of Civilizations? The Debate.* New York: Council on Foreign Relations Press.

Inglehart, Ronald (1988) "The Renaissance of Political Culture." *American Political Science Review* 82, no. 4:1203–1230.

Inkeles, Alex, and D. J. Levinson (1968) "National Character: The Study of Modal Personality and Sociocultural Systems." In *Handbook of Social Psychology,* vol. 2, edited by G. Lindzey. Cambridge, MA: Addison-Wesley.

Kahn, Herman (1993) "The Confucian Ethic and Economic Growth." In *Development and Underdevelopment: The Political Economy of Inequality,* edited by Mitchell A. Seligson and John T. Passe-Smith. Boulder: Lynne Rienner.

Klineberg, Otto (1945) "Racial Psychology." In *The Science of Man in the World Crisis,* edited by Ralph Linton. New York: Columbia University Press.

Kluckhohn, Clyde (1951) "The Study of Culture." In *The Policy Sciences,* edited by Daniel Lerner and Harold D. Lasswell. Stanford: Stanford University Press.

Khong, Yuen Foong (1993) *Analogies at War: Korean, Munich, Dien Bien Phu, and the Vietnam Decisions of 1965.* Princeton: Princeton University Press.

Kroeber, A. L., and Clyde Kluckhohn (1952) *Culture: A Critical Review of Concepts and Definitions.* Cambridge: Harvard University Press.

Krogman, W. M. (1945) "The Concept of Race." In *The Science of Man in the World Crisis,* edited by Ralph Linton. New York: Columbia University Press.

Kurtz, L. (1986) *The Politics of Heresy.* Berkeley: University of California Press.

Leites, N. (1951) *The Operational Code of the Politburo.* New York: McGraw-Hill.

Leuchtenberg, W. E. (1958) *The Perils of Prosperity: 1914–32.* Chicago: University of Chicago Press.

Levine, Robert A. (1973) *Culture, Behavior, and Personality.* Chicago: Aldine.

Linton, Ralph (1945) *The Cultural Background of Personality.* New York: Appleton-Century-Crofts.

Little, David, and Sumner B. Twiss (1978) *Comparative Religious Ethics: A New Method.* San Francisco: Harper and Row.

Lowery, David, and Lee Sigelman (1982) "Political Culture and State Public Policy: The Missing Link." *Western Political Quarterly* 35 (September): 376–384.

Luker, K. (1984) *Abortion and the Politics of Motherhood.* Berkeley: University of California Press.

McDaniels, T. L., and R. S. Gregory (1991) "A Framework for Structuring Cross-Cultural Research in Risk and Decision-Making." *Journal of Cross-Cultural Psychology* 22, no. 1:103–128.

Millennium (1993) Special issue on Culture in International Relations. Vol. 22, no. 3 (winter).

Motokawa, Tatsuo (1989) "Sushi Science and Hamburger Science." *Perspectives in Biology and Medicine* 32, no. 4:489–504.

Pickering, A. (1984) *Constructing Quarks: A Sociological History of Particle Physics.* Edinburgh: Edinburgh University Press.

Pye, Lucian (1968) *The Spirit of Chinese Politics: A Psychocultural Study of the Authority Crisis in Political Development.* Cambridge: MIT Press.

Pye, Lucian (1988) *The Mandarin and the Cadre: China's Political Cultures.* Ann Arbor: Center for Chinese Studies, University of Michigan.

Pye, Lucian (1991) "Political Culture Revisited." *Political Psychology* 12, no. 3 (September):487–508.

Root-Bernstein, Robert (1989) "How Scientists Really Think." *Perspectives in Biology and Medicine* 32, no. 4:472–488.

Sampson, Martin (1987) "Cultural Influences on Foreign Policy." In *New Directions in the Study of Foreign Policy,* edited by Charles F. Hermann, Charles W. Kegley, and James N. Rosenau. Boston: Allen and Unwin.

Sampson, Martin, and Stephen Walker (1987) "Cultural Norms and National Roles: A Comparison of Japan and France." In *Role Theory and Foreign Policy Analysis,* edited by Stephen Walker. Durham, NC: Duke University Press.

Seeger, Joseph (1992) "Towards a Theory of Foreign Policy Analysis Based on National Role Conceptions: An AI/IR Approach." Master's thesis, Brigham Young University.

Sen, Amartya (1982) *Choice, Welfare, and Measurement.* Cambridge: MIT Press.

Sen, Amartya (1987) *On Ethics and Economics:* New York: Basil Blackwell.

Shih, Chih-yu (1993) *China's Just World: The Morality of Chinese Foreign Policy.* Boulder: Lynne Rienner.

Skinner, B. F. (1981) "Selection by Consequences." *Science* 213: 501–504.

Solomon, Richard (1971) *Mao's Revolution and Chinese Political Culture.* Berkeley: University of California Press.

Solomon, Richard (1992) "Political Culture and Diplomacy in the Twenty-First Century." In *The Political Culture of Foreign and Area Studies: Essays in Honor of Lucian W. Pye,* edited by R. J. Samuels and M. Weiner. New York: Brassey's.

Swidler, Ann (1986) "Culture in Action: Symbols and Strategies." *American Sociological Review* 51:273–286.

Sylvan, David A., S. Majeski, and J. Milliken (1991) "Theoretical Categories and Data Construction in Computational Models of Foreign Policy." In *Artificial Intelligence and International Politics,* edited by Valerie M. Hudson. Boulder: Westview Press.

Terhune, Kenneth W. (1970) "From National Character to National Behavior: A Reformulation." *Conflict Resolution* 14, no. 2:203–263.

Thompson, Michael, Richard Ellis, and Aaron Wildavsky (1990) *Cultural Theory.* Boulder: Westview Press.

Triandis, Harry C. (1994) *Culture and Social Behavior.* New York: McGraw-Hill.

Tse, David K. et al. (1988) "Does Culture Matter? A Cross-Cultural Study of Executives' Choice, Decisiveness, and Risk Adjustment in International Marketing." *Journal of Marketing* 52:81–95.

Tunander, Ola (1989) *Cold Water Politics: The Maritime Strategy and Geopolitics of the Northern Front.* London: Sage.

Vertzberger, Yaacov (1990) *The World in Their Minds: Information Processing, Cognition, and Perception in Foreign Policy Decisionmaking.* Stanford: Stanford University Press.

Walker, Stephen G. (1977) "The Interface Between Beliefs and Behavior: Henry A. Kissinger's Operational Code and the Vietnam War." *Journal of Conflict Resolution* 21:129–168.

Walker, Stephen G. (1987) "The Correspondence Between Foreign Policy Rhetoric and Behavior: Insights from Role Theory and Exchange Theory." In *Role Theory and Foreign Policy Analysis,* edited by Stephen Walker. Durham, NC: Duke University Press.

Weber, Max (1930) *The Protestant Ethic and the Spirit of Capitalism* (translated by Talcott Parsons). New York: Scribner.

Weber, Max (1951a) *The Religion of China* (translated by H. Gerth). Glencoe, IL: Free Press.

Weber, Max (1951b) *The Religion of India* (translated by H. Gerth). Glencoe, IL: Free Press.

Weber, Max (1963) *Sociology of Religion* (translated by E. Fischoff). Boston: Beacon Press.

Whorf, B. L. (1956) *Language, Thought, and Reality* (edited by J. B. Carroll). New York: Wiley.

Wildavsky, Aaron (1987) "Choosing Preferences by Constructing Institutions: A Cultural Theory of Preference Formation." *American Political Science Review* 81, no. 1:3–21.

Wish, Naomi B. (1980) "Foreign Policy Makers and Their National Role Conceptions." *International Studies Quarterly* 24:532–534.

Wuthnow, R. (1987) *Meaning and Moral Order: Explorations in Cultural Analysis.* Berkeley: University of California Press.

Yee, Albert S. (1996) "The Effects of Ideas on Policies." *International Organization* 50, no. 1 (winter):69–108.

PART 1

CULTURE AS THE ORGANIZATION OF MEANING

2

The Cultural Logic of National Identity Formation: Contending Discourses in Late Colonial India

Sanjoy Banerjee

Banerjee's piece is a good example of discourse analysis in the service of cultural study, used to deconstruct how national identities are formed in opposition to alternative identities. Banerjee deconstructs the rhetoric used by Nehru and Jinnah to determine the foundational dispute over Indian national identity. He is careful to lay a strong empirical basis for his deconstruction, opening the way for discourse analysis to be falsifiable.

—Editor

It is extremely difficult to appreciate why our Hindu friends fail to understand the real nature of Islam and Hinduism. They are not religions in the strict sense of the word, but are, in fact, different and distinct social orders. It is a dream that Hindus and Muslims can ever evolve a common nationality. . . . The Hindus and Muslims belong to two different religious philosophies, social customs, and literature. They neither intermarry, nor interdine together, and indeed they belong to two different civilizations which are based mainly on conflicting ideas and conceptions. . . . Hindus and Mussalmans derive their inspiration from different sources of history. They have different epics, their heroes are different, and they have different episodes.

—Mohammed Ali Jinnah (Quoted in Pirzada, 1970:337–338)

Partition means a patent untruth. My whole soul rebels against the idea that Hinduism and Islam represent two antagonistic cul-

*tures and doctrines. To assent to such a doctrine is for me a denial
of God. For I believe that the God of the* Quran *is also the God of
the Gita, and we are all, no matter by what name designated, children of the same God. I must rebel against the idea that millions
of Indians, who were Hindus the other day, changed their nationality on adopting Islam as their religion.*

—Mahatma Gandhi (Quoted in Merriam 1980:70)

Jinnah, president of the All-India Muslim League, spoke the words quoted
above to the league's historic Lahore session in March 1940, when the
league committed itself to the creation of Pakistan through the partition
of the Indian subcontinent. Gandhi responded as quoted the next month.

The two quotes exemplify two rival emergent cultures of state making in late colonial India. I contend that these cultures were based on national identities, understandings of the national self and of others embedded in a construction of history. I reconstruct these national
identities using a model in which nations derive their inspiration in
many different ways from the same history. I shall emphasize the acts of
derivation, the variety and structures of possible inspirations from the
same history, and the implications of selecting among them.

This chapter examines not so much cultures of foreign policy as cultural policies about what is foreign. It examines the logic of alienation
and hegemony in national identities by which the Indian subcontinent
was partitioned and by which new international boundaries, and new relations across them, were created. The organization of meaning in some
Indian National Congress and Muslim League rhetoric is analyzed to
uncover their constructions of nationhood and proper international
order.

Although this chapter examines national movements before they
achieved statehood, it develops a theory that has implications for foreign
policy analysis. National identities are shown to be constructions of the
historical contexts in which nations must act. Such constructions create
strong biases toward certain courses of foreign policy action. In the particular instance of India and Pakistan, cultural constructs of the other,
and of the foreign, served to greatly influence the subsequent foreign
policies of these states toward each other and toward other countries.

CULTURE AND FOREIGN POLICY

A constructivist definition of culture rejects an essentialist view of culture in which characteristics that persist in certain cultures over long periods determine what happens in those cultures. For example, Confucian

culture as such cannot be the root cause of the East Asian economic boom, since under varieties of Confucianism, China has been rich, then poor (for which some blamed Confucianism), and will perhaps be rich again. Constructivism views culture as an evolving system of shared meanings that governs perceptions, communications, and action (Geertz, 1973). I treat culture as a grammar, as an evolving fund of semantic elements that can be combined in certain ways and not others to define situations, motivate and plan actions, or release emotions. Culture shapes practice in both the short and long term. At the moment of action, culture provides the elements and grammar that define the situation, that reveal motives, and that set forth a strategy for success. If the strategy is successful, that strategy is repeated in similar situations with similar motives. The perception of similarity of situations and motives is a product of the culture. Over historical time, culture distributed among many agents animates and coordinates interdependent practices. Cultures and practices reproduce together.

It is through culture that anything we might call "interests" is constructed. Some—for example, Goldstein and Keohane (1993)—assume interests to be idea-free, transmitted without cultural mediation to actors by the realities of international power. "Clearly," Woods (1995:161) objects, "a state perceives its economic interests on the basis of a set of ideas or beliefs about how the world economy works and what opportunities exist within it." And the equivalent can be said of noneconomic interests as well. I treat culture as the basis on which recurring motives and strategies of action—interests—emerge.

A theory has emerged in the social sciences that the meanings in communication are constitutive of much of the psychological structure of the communicants. Vygotsky (1962) has argued there is an intimate connection between the development of thought and language in childhood and in adult learning. Harre, Clarke, and de Carlo (1985) have argued that emotions and subjecthood itself are constructed through communication. Moscovici (Farr and Moscovici, 1984) has highlighted the roles of "social representations" in psychological functioning. And, of course, Geertz (1973) has elaborated on the role of culture as meaning in emotion, judgment, perception, actions, and other areas of cognition and behavior. What emerges from this literature is that meanings have psychological force. Emotions are the product of a subject's particular construction of the meaning of an event. Alterations of the semantic structure of beliefs and identity of a subject will alter the subject's pattern of emotional responses and other psychological performances. Beyond producing particular psychological responses, patterns of meaning are constitutive of subjectivity itself. Subjects take in symbolic and other inputs, interpret them according to their inventory of concepts, and produce communications and actions. These inventories of concepts are products of discourse—subjects reside in the texts of discourses. The role of political discourse analysis then lies in the reconstruction of historical subjects.

I use two forms of meaning representation to describe national identities. One is a story framework. People, including national leaders, often think and talk in stories. Boynton (1991) reviews the literature to demonstrate the pervasive structuration of human cognition as narratives to foreign policy analysis. He analyzes U.S. Senate hearings on a mission to protect Kuwaiti oil tankers in 1987 as a play of narratives. I analyze national identity as a story with a certain kind of plot. The discourse method required is the search for story fragments in national speech acts that conform to elements of the designated plot. The second form of meaning representation is semantic tropes, especially oppositions, which often appear in national identity stories. I show that the polarized elements of national identity plots are expressed as oppositions in national discourse. As in paleontology, the finding, or not, of text fragments fitting these criteria becomes the basis for certain inferences.

International discourse is a valid source for reconstructing international subjects, including states. Governments, of course, often act in secrecy or give insincere accounts of their actions. Nonetheless, political leaders must for the most part publicly instruct their functionaries and supporters on what they must do, why they must do it, and how they will know if they are doing the right thing. The size and complexity of political action requires a wide dissemination of knowledge. Thus, political action entails a massive public instructional discourse, which is available for analysis.

The method of discourse analysis employed here starts with a semantic model of national identity reconstructed on the basis of theory. The search is for text fragments that fit certain semantic elements. In paleontology, theories about the course of evolution can be supported by the right fossil discoveries. In the text analysis method here, if the right fragments are found, the hypothesized subject model receives support, otherwise not. The method is not to take a fixed body of text and interpret it; certainly not all the semantic elements of a national identity will be present in a single document, speech, book, or standard text package.

A paleontological approach requires explicit criteria of textual evidence. The semantic elements in the national identity must be clarified to the point where they can be recognized in text. There are two criteria for recognizing a text fragment as an expression of an element of national identity: The fragment should come from an appropriate speech act, and it should contain the required semantic elements. The speaker, in exhorting nationals to do something, should appeal to the nationality with which both speaker and audience identify. Other valid speech acts from which identity expressions may be drawn are a speaker describing his or her nation to a national audience, or representing that nation in an appeal to a foreign audience. The model of identity comprises semantic elements, and they must be demonstrated to be signified by the text.

Two approaches to the analysis of discourse are rejected here. One is a positivist critique exemplified by Fischer (1992). The other is a poststructuralist stance, advocated by Ashley (1989) and others, that suggests that a scientific approach is unnecessary. Fischer argues that not every discourse is associated with a corresponding practice. However, one is left with the possibility, which Fischer fails to refute, that every practice has a corresponding discourse. Discourse is the great conversation going on throughout society at all times. The totality of discourse is, of course, impossible to study with known methods. But the thoughts and decisions of all persons are heavily influenced by society's discourse, by the communications they receive and emit. For this reason, such communications, in a wide variety of media, are of great interest in understanding the activities of persons, groups, and, in particular, states.

The line of justification Ashley has advanced for a poststructuralist school is that it is opening up the thinking space of the field but not establishing a superior scientific paradigm. Ashley (1989:259) denies that it is his "intention to hint that in poststructuralism we find a promise of a new and powerful perspective that occupies its own firm ground, that overcomes the limits of other perspectives, and that surpasses them in its ability to answer the questions they readily ask. As we shall see, poststructuralism eschews heroic promises such as these." Instead he claims to show "how and why poststructuralism expands the agenda of social theory, posing questions that other discourses must refuse to ask."

This stance abdicates from scientific debate in its refusal to offer an alternative theory. Poststructuralists as a group do not eschew empirical description and explanation. Der Derian (1987), Weber (1989), and others attempt alternative explanations and historical descriptions. If scholars committed to scientific international studies are to take this literature seriously, as I believe they should, they must ask some of the same types of questions about poststructuralism as they would about any other school.

NATIONAL IDENTITY

The topic of identity has been pushed to the fore of the international relations literature by the metatheory of Wendt (1992). He argues that international anarchy can engender either a self-help system or a more cooperative order, depending on the contents of state identities. Drawing on the social constructionist literature, Wendt defines identity as "role-specific understandings and expectations about self," examples being "sovereign," "leader of the free world," and "imperial power." Identities as well as interests (action motives) emerge from the way actors define their situations. Identity-based interaction leads to each actor assigning each other actor into some type. Interaction on the basis of identities yield self-reproducing institutions, which may be cooperative or conflictual (Wendt, 1992:397–405). Wendt identifies some parts of the social cognitive processes he posits to occur but does not elaborate an empirical process-tracing model.

Banerjee (1991) offers a process-tracing computational model of state subjects and their interaction that meets each of the metatheoretical criteria for identity given above. Examining the empirical case of U.S.-Soviet interaction in Europe during 1945–1949, the model specifies a reflective logic by which the subjects perceive acts, construct situations, characterize the self and others, compare their situation constructions with their prior identities, form emotions and action motives, act, and monitor for results—updating the semantic elements of the subject process. These subject processes yield and require reproducing historical structures, what Wendt calls institutions.

Mercer (1995) has issued a spirited rejoinder to Wendt (1992). He contends that the workings of identity will maintain the international order envisaged in realist theory. Drawing from much of the same literature as Wendt, Mercer argues that the division of humanity into groups is inevitable, and given the need for a positive group identity among members, each group will contrast the others unfavorably to itself, diminishing the motive for cooperation with other groups. Further, he rejects Wendt's (1992) suggestion that states can accurately achieve empathy, because this is not consistently possible. Mercer concludes that these phenomena ensure the continuity of an anarchic international system where states must help themselves and not others, even if a world of larger, fewer states and identities emerges. Yet while drawing this last inference, Mercer (1995) lacks an argument on why humanity must remain divided into states, which are groups of a very special kind. His premises actually do not exclude even the possibility of a worldwide democracy with rival transethnic parties merrily hurling invective at each other, fulfilling their supporters' need for a superior identity. This gap in Mercer's logic flows from his limited treatment of identities. I reconstruct *national* identity to reveal its implication of the just and inevitable partition of humanity into states.

The theoretical reconstruction of national identity that follows is supported by readings of Geertz, Anderson, and Antonio Gramsci. Geertz (1973:240–249) has identified "essential" and "epochal" meanings in nationalist ideologies. The former define the nation's origins, the latter the needs of the present age. Anderson (1983) observes that one of the conditions of the rise of modern nationalism is the transformation of the cultural conception of historical time from a cyclical to a unidirectional one. History comes to be regarded as a one-way progression. Gramsci (Forgacs, 1988:423) draws our attention to ideological hegemony exercised by historical blocs—networks of alliances among dominant social classes.

Banerjee (1994) examines how the dominant Indian national identity gained credibility and generated orientations toward other states during the careers of Indira Gandhi and her son Rajiv. That identity based the nation in the ancient Hindu civilization and highlighted parallel elements in strands of Muslim thought as evidence of a composite culture uniting the two religious communities. It projected that the nation would recover and attain autonomy from, and ultimately coequality with, the West; this would be achieved under the leadership of a new professional class, which would diminish the dependence upon the West inherited from the colonial period. Various events across the globe were interpreted as confirmations of the beliefs underlying this identity. Other states were characterized in categories derived from this historical drama. Pakistan was projected as a degenerate state that failed to recognize the common heritage of Hindus and Muslims in the Indian subcontinent. The United States was characterized as disinclined to acknowledge or cooperate with the attainment of Indian civilizational autonomy, while the USSR was cast as having a parallel interest in India's autonomy.

National identity can be reconstructed as a story with a certain plot structure. Actually, it is less like a traditional one-track story and more like an interactive story whose plot has more than one branch or track, and the one taken depends on the action of the reader/player. The national identity story is rarely put into words all at once, but rather it is told in bits and pieces as the situation warrants; but always much more of it is invoked than told. The story is invoked to interpret situations and to produce decisions and motivate actions in response. The story is retold in new situations to construct a rigged array of choices available to the nation. It matches alternative courses of action to unequally favorable tracks. The favored track of the national identity story is one of unidirectional historical and moral progression. The disfavored track is one of regression and degeneration. National identities are not invulnerable. The story cannot be fitted to each new situation with equal credibility. The national identity story does provide categories and logics for its own verification but is not an elaborate tautology.

The generic plot structure of a national identity story entails a *heritage* that traces the nation's cultural and ethnic genesis. The heritage identifies the nation as the heir of critical strengths and foundations for exclusive unity, but also the heir of distinctive weaknesses and vulnerabilities. There is an achievable *destiny* for the nation that constitutes a redemption of its heritage. Those who acknowledge that heritage and aid the nation's progress to its destiny are friends, and those who deny that heritage and obstruct it are rivals. Progress toward the destiny is not assured—the nation faces a distinct *danger* if it fails to take the right action and degenerates along the lines of weakness that figure in its heritage. There is a contemporary *vanguard* segment of the national society projected as those who are most fully aware of the nation's true heritage and have most absorbed its strengths—and thus are most able and deserving to lead the nation to its destiny. The national rivals of the vanguard are an atavistic *laggard* segment—those who are ignorant of the nation's true heritage, who have most inherited the weaknesses figured in the heritage, and who would lead the nation down the path of danger if given the chance.

The heritage construction corresponds to the "essential" meanings on nationalist ideology (Geertz, 1973:240–429). The definition of the nation's heritage entails the projection of contemporary sociopolitical hierarchies and boundaries into the past. It is an argument for the naturalness, inevitability, and rightness of those hierarchies and boundaries. It is also an appeal for confidence among nationals that the contemporary national endeavor will succeed. In the national identity story, historical examples of contemporary value orientations are found. The claim is: We have always been this way. Heritage, which criticizes the nation and elements within it, may also include instances of injustice against the nation, highlighting those committed by predecessors or ancestors of contemporary agents outside the boundaries of the nation. Heritage subplots recognize certain failings incipient in the nation—failings that generate specific atavistic fears in the narration of the present. These also generate focused sensitivities to shame and insult. In situations where others are seen to act as though the nation had not overcome its incipient failings, insult is taken.

Heritage constructions change, even while referring to the same past events. Nasserite Egypt's heritage was Arab, whereas Sadat's heritage for Egypt was phaeronic, which is to say distinctively Egyptian, stretching back beyond the Arab period. If there is a conflict over national identity, the nation's heritage may be a point in dispute. The secularist identity of India fixes the nation's heritage as a mixture of Hindu and Muslim. This is symbolized in the colors of the national flag, with saffron for Hindu and green for Muslim. The Hindu nationalist identity constructs the Indian heritage as exclusively Hindu. Clearly, the heritage itself is part of a logic of hegemony. If the heritage discriminates among contemporary ethnic groups, there will be privileged groups. If the heritage is consciously nondiscriminatory, it still establishes a hierarchy that privileges those whose personal identities transcend ethnic boundaries and marginalizes those who identify more intensely with their ethnic groups.

Just as the past of a nation is captured in its heritage, its destiny is the favored future track in the national identity plot. Destiny is a future that is on the fulcrum between the achievable and the inevitable and is a redemption of the nation's honor as well as a payment of what is owed to the nation. A destiny is not cast as inevitable but is held as an achievement of the nation's agency. But that agency is the result of the nation's heritage and of contemporary repositories of excellence within it, and these combined bring the destiny to the verge of inevitability. The Nasserite destiny for Egypt was to lead the Arab world, while for Sadat, it was to bridge the Muslim and Christian civilizations. But because the destiny is not inevitable, there is a disfavored future track in the plot by which the nation fails to recognize its true heritage, reiterates its inherited failings, and falls into danger. This track entails a fear of atavism. For the Pakistan movement, the danger was the submergence of Muslim culture in a united India dominated by Hindus.

All national societies to date have been class-divided. Certain social classes and institutions have been dominant. Successful national identities have encoded and embedded the social, economic, and political hierarchy within the definition of the nation itself. National identities that project the dominant classes and institutions as a vanguard serve as a hegemonic ideology for that dominant coalition. National identities justify and require the patience of those outside the dominant coalition. They are asked to postpone the realization of equality so that the nation as a whole can progress toward its destiny. National identities delegitimize counterhegemonic discourses and practices as the work of laggard elements ignorant of the nation's true heritage and dragging it toward danger.

Several elements of a national identity are structured in oppositions—for example, the heritage of the self versus an other, destiny versus danger, inherited strengths versus weaknesses, vanguard versus laggard agents. To understand national identities, it is vital to understand oppositions. I proceed from certain premises about the internal logic of oppositions. An opposition proclaims more than a difference: Bringing two concepts into opposition entails the assertion that they are mutually exclusive, exhaustive of a relevant space, and somehow unequal. One side of an opposition is always set up to lose. An opposition presumes a turf battle between two opposed concepts, with one in favor. The turf that is the object of the battle is almost never explicit in the expression of oppositions. The reconstruction of that turf is a key methodological step.

Oppositions then are pyramidic—they are triads, not dyads. The semantic structure of national identity, as a plot with a system of oppositions, is graphed in Figure 2.1. The larger category is at the apex, and the two opposed concepts are at the base. That apex must be a meaningful larger category that is partitioned by the two opposed concepts. It would

Figure 2.1
Oppositions and National Identity

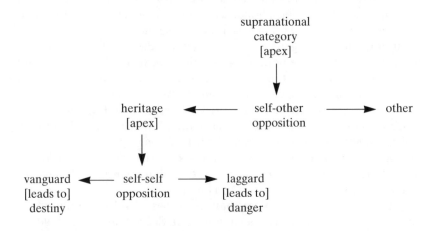

be of little use to say that the larger category is simply the union of the pair of opposed concepts. A meaningful category, semantically autonomous from the opposed concepts, must be uncovered. The construction of the apex concept must provide premises leading to the conclusion that the two opposed categories are mutually exclusive and that one is superior.

There are two kinds of oppositions of interest here: self-other and self-self. Self-other oppositions are pairs where one positive character is ascribed to the self while a negative character is ascribed to the other. Self-other oppositions help subjects divide the social world into discrete agents. In national identities, these semantic formations acknowledge and partition transnational communities; characterize, domesticate, yet alienate foreigners; and resist the infiltration of subversive identities. National identities formed with oppositions of this kind have a chance to reproduce themselves and thus to support national states in international and transnational society. Self-self oppositions contrast the virtues and dishonorable temptations to which the self is prone. These oppositions are internal to the heritage and mark the strengths and weaknesses to which the nation is heir. These serve to discipline the members of the group self.

NATIONAL IDENTITIES AND OPPOSITIONS
IN THE INDIAN PARTITION STRUGGLE

Gandhi's quote at the beginning of this chapter expresses the ideal of unity in diversity. The ideal evolved in Hinduism as a way of reconciling the numerous forms of worship within it. It is adapted to the situation by casting Islam as another system of religious symbols that refers, ultimately, to an integral divinity that transcends any symbols by which humans may refer to it. This ideal of transcendence was at the core of Gandhi's rhetoric and provided the foundations of a unified Indian heritage construction. It was an answer to the problem of diversity that presented itself on a vast scale to the independence movement.

Yet the Indian national identity reached its mature state not in Gandhi's rhetoric but in Jawaharlal Nehru's. Chatterjee (1986) divides the evolution of Indian nationalist discourse into three historical "moments." The first is the "departure" of the nineteenth century, when the nation recognizes that the ascendance of the West necessitates internal reform. The second moment, which emerges in Gandhi's rhetoric, is one of "maneuver," when the nation recognizes its internal capacity for reform and rejects the industrial rationality of the West. The third moment, Nehru's, is "arrival," when the nation learns to combine internal reform with an industrial-bureaucratic rationality. Gandhi's oppositions exemplified in the quote under discussion are between truth and untruth, godliness and godlessness. He used these oppositions not to characterize political groupings, but rather as ideals to strive for. It was left to Nehru to develop character oppositions that could be used to legitimize relations of dominance and exclusion, the stuff of national identities.

For Nehru, a central self-self opposition for his Indian heritage was between the wise ancient civilization on the one hand, and the violent, ignorant, intolerant mob on the other, which was his understanding of the secular and the communal, respectively. This opposition was central to the appeals he issued to people in riot areas in the violent period prior to the partition. He said in a speech in the predominantly Muslim northern town of Meerut in 1946:

> The happenings in Bengal and Bihar and parts of U.P., including Meerut, are not only attacks on innocent men, women, and children, but attacks on the ancient culture and civilization of India. The people should resist such cowardly onslaughts with all the force at their command, or else the country's proud heritage will be wiped out.... I concede that the perpetrators of the crimes have been swayed by the prevalent communal passions. They are good and simple village folk. (Gopal, 1984:95–96)

The speech act here is an appeal to Muslims and Hindus to stop themselves or their coreligionists from rioting. Nehru is desperate, and he is relying on his words to connect with the beliefs of his mainly Muslim target audience in Meerut while preserving the integrity of his message to all audiences. Several elements of Nehru's heritage narrative are visible here. The heritage, and thus the apex category of his self-self opposition, is "Indian," of course, but constructed in a specific way. India is connected to an "ancient culture and civilization" that bequeaths to the living, Hindu and Muslim, a "proud heritage" vulnerable to being "wiped out." This construction contains the premises needed to establish the unequal opposition at the base of the Indian:secular/communal pyramid, which define vanguard and laggard, destiny and danger in the identity.

In framing the opposition, Nehru conflates violence by Hindus (in Bihar) and Muslims (in Bengal and Meerut) and appeals to the secular conscience of both groups to uphold their common "proud heritage." He projects the "perpetrators" as part of the Indian self, "good and simple village folk," but as fallen from grace, being "swayed by the prevalent communal passions." Nehru awards the secular conscience, invoked by "the people," the mantle of guardian of the ancient Indian heritage, and indicts the communal ethos, represented by "cowardly onslaughts," as that which would wipe out that heritage. Implicit in Nehru's constructions are the hierarchies Indian/Hindu and Indian/Muslim. These hierarchies are meant to order the elements of personal and local identities. Nehru asserts the primacy of Indian civilization over religion in those identities.

At the same time, there is another hierarchy, where "simple village folk" are marginalized and persons more like Nehru are privileged as a vanguard. This semantic hierarchy recapitulates a social hierarchy nascent in that period—between a modernizing secular elite and the "simple village folk"—that Nehru was seeking to establish. This self-self opposition lay part of the foundation of ideological hegemony in the independent Indian state.

The heritages require the presence of an "other." One is present in a speech of Nehru's in Bihar in 1946: "It is all the more astonishing and astounding . . . that such things [violence], which made the common foe of all the communities—British Imperialism—laugh in unholy glee, should have at all happened. This frenzy has delayed the whole scheme of Swaraj [independence]" (Gopal, 1984:59). Again Nehru is speaking in a riot-torn area, exhorting to maintain the unity of the independence movement. The British imperialists are the other, to the self of "all the communities"—India. A self-self opposition is being used to discipline elements of the group self through the specter of the other. Nehru's heritage construction is diagrammed in Figure 2.2.

In stark contrast, the excerpt from Jinnah's speech to the Lahore session of the Muslim League sets out the Muslim/Hindu self-other opposition plainly. A central theme in Jinnah's rhetoric and reasoning was the all-encompassing nature of both Hinduism and Islam. As such, he inferred, the separation they imposed on their respective religious communities was total. Jinnah emphasized the separation of the two religious communities to a British writer in 1943: "You must remember that

Figure 2.2
Nehru's Heritage Construction

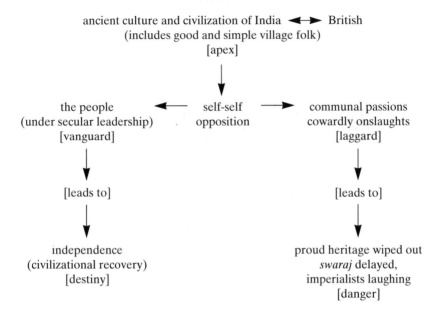

Islam is not merely a religious doctrine but a realistic and practical Code of Conduct. I am thinking in terms of life, of everything important in life. . . . In all these things our outlook is not only fundamentally different from but often radically antagonistic toward the Hindus. We are different beings. There is nothing in life which links us together" (Merriam, 1980:90). This statement highlights the mutual exclusivity of the opposed categories. Separation and antagonism are held to flow from religion itself. Muslims and Hindus of India are constructed as two homogeneous groups. But the opposition itself is possible and necessary only because of the common category—Indian—uniting the opposition.

Jinnah constructed this common category of "Indian" in contradistinction to "Western" in a manner similar to that of British imperialist thinking. Jinnah wrote an article in a British newspaper in 1940 in which he sought to stop the move, under discussion in Britain at the time, to transform India into a single dominion with an electorate that would include persons of both religions. Jinnah said that the "bulk" of the prospective voters were "totally ignorant, illiterate and untutored, living in centuries-old superstitions, . . . thoroughly antagonistic to each other" (Bolitho, 1954:125). Note that Jinnah was not speaking of Hindus alone but of all the electorate, both Hindu and Muslim.

Jinnah cited British imperial accounts of Indian society approvingly in the article. In rejecting the option of dominion status, Jinnah quoted a conservative British lord's statement that the "fur coat of Canada" was unsuited to the "extremely tropical climate of India" (Bolitho, 1954:125). He also quoted a report by a British parliamentary committee in 1934 defending imperialism on the basis of what it considered the intrinsic disunity of India:

> India is inhabited by many races . . . often as distinct from one another in origin, tradition and manner of life as are the nations of Europe. . . . They [Hindus and Muslims] may be said, indeed, to represent two distinct and separate civilizations. Hinduism is distinguished by the phenomenon of its caste, which is the basis of its religious and social system, and, save in a very restricted field, remains unaffected by contact with the philosophies of the West; the religion of Islam, on the other hand, is based upon the conception of the equality of man.

Jinnah commented, "Perhaps no truer description of India has been compressed into a paragraph" (Bolitho, 1954:126). Jinnah elaborated his own explanation to the British audience:

> The British people, being Christians, sometimes forget the religious wars of their own history and today consider religion as a private and personal matter between man and God. This can never be the case in Hinduism and Islam, for both these religions are definite social codes which govern not so much man's relation with his God, as man's relation with his neighbor. They govern not only his law and culture but every aspect of his social life, and such religions, essentially exclusive, completely preclude that merging of identity and unity of thought on which Western democracy is based. (Bolitho, 1954:126–127)

Note the common structure Jinnah attributes to both Indian religions. The central inference here is that both Indian religions, as in the Western past, are all-encompassing social codes, and therefore nationhood should be based on common religion. He also constructs the Hindus as a familiar other. He claims to know the essential nature of Hinduism and projects a weariness of association rather than a rejection of the mysterious.

What emerges from Jinnah's construction of Indian society represented here is a pyramidic semantic structure. At the apex is the supranational category of Indian, and this entails a society characterized unalterably by religious control of social relations and by backwardness relative to Western society. This category is then divided into the two opposites of Muslim and Hindu. The internal structure of the apex concept is crucial to the opposition at the base of the pyramid. The construction of the apex concept yields the premises of the argument for mutual exclusivity of the opposites. For Jinnah, it is precisely the all-encompassing nature of religion in India that precludes coalitions between Hindus and Muslims and thus makes the two groups polar opposites.

Self-other oppositions homogenize both the self and the other. In the case of the Pakistan movement, both forms of homogeneity are apparent. The word *Pakistan* means "land of the pure" in Urdu. This purity connotes an essential homogeneity of the Muslim citizens of the land, in spite of their differentiation in ethnic and linguistic terms. This name was a key factor in galvanizing supporters of the movement in the British Indian empire. Jinnah's presumption that a state with a three-fourths Hindu majority would necessarily oppress Muslims implied the existence of a stable all-Hindu political coalition and excluded, presumptively, the possibility of a majority coalition that would include Hindus and Muslims. Jinnah's opposition is diagrammed in Figure 2.3.

Jinnah's supranational category of Indian, constructed as it was, had implications that gave rise to an international ethic. In 1937, after his party fared badly in provincial elections, Jinnah said of the nature of politics: "An honourable settlement can only be achieved between equals; and unless the two parties learn to respect and fear each other, there can be no solid ground for any settlement. Offers of peace by the weaker party always mean a confession of weakness, and an invitation to aggression. . . . Politics means power and not relying only on cries of justice or fairplay or goodwill" (Singh, 1987:28).

The statement reads like a realist text in international relations theory. It serves as a cognitive basis of the anarchical international order that was to emerge from the British Indian empire. There is a presumption of permanent separation and antagonism between the "two parties"

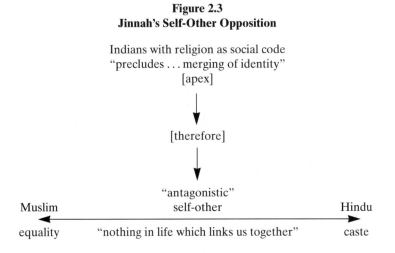

Figure 2.3
Jinnah's Self-Other Opposition

Indians with religion as social code
"precludes . . . merging of identity"
[apex]

[therefore]

"antagonistic"
Muslim   self-other   Hindu
equality   "nothing in life which links us together"   caste

at hand. Under this assumption, the "confession of weakness" is "an invitation to aggression" and is thus proximate cause of aggression. Jinnah asserts the incapacity of moral appeals to overcome antagonism.

At the 1938 session of the Muslim League in Patna, Bihar, Jinnah refuted Congress charges of being an ally of imperialism. Pirzada's (1970:309) rendition reads: "I say the Muslim League is not going to be an ally of anyone, but would be an ally of even the devil if need be in the interest of Muslims." A pin-drop silence suddenly appeared to seize the house at this stage. Mr. Jinnah paused for a moment and then continued: "It is not because we are in love with Imperialism; but in politics one has to play one's game on a chess-board. I say the Muslims and the Muslim League have only one ally; and that ally is the Muslim nation; and the one and only one to whom they can look for help is God." [Applause]

In this excerpt, Jinnah articulates the doctrine of self-help and places it at the pinnacle of the hierarchy of moral values. His reference to the devil implies the absolute moral supremacy of "the interest of Muslims." The silence in the audience reflects its realization of the importance of that statement. This construction excludes the possibility of a common morality linking Muslims and Hindus to which both are obligated to conform. That exclusion again implies the permanent separation of the two groups and a realist understanding of the protonational self-agent. In the political context of the speech, Jinnah, while denying that he is in alliance with the British, is claiming the right to make that alliance. The doctrine of self-help, construed in realist literature as a root condition of the anarchic international system, is projected as political and moral ideology prior to the creation of Pakistan. Central to the principle of self-help is the immutability of motivation of the other, and even of the self. The other is considered to permanently define itself to exclude the subject and is held impervious to dialogue and moral reasoning that will dissolve the boundaries and create a composite self whose interest can be collectively pursued. These views were consistent with Jinnah's thesis that Indian religions were total and exclusive social orders.

What emerges from this analysis of League and Congress discourse is that Nehru and Jinnah both held Indian identities but differed radically on the constitution of those identities. It is not exactly that Jinnah was a Muslim before he was an Indian. Rather, for him, India was not what it was for Nehru. Jinnah's India was a continent, a social geographical zone, and a benighted one in relation to the West. Jinnah's India was a periphery of the West and of the Muslim Middle East. For Jinnah the best things came only from outside India—Islam from the Middle East and enlightenment from the West. As for the latter, it was impossibly superior in relation to India's capacity—both Muslim and Hindu—for moral absorption. For Nehru, India was an interconnected civilization and a center unto itself. It was civilizationally self-sufficient and morally enlightened in comparison with the West. The elements of moral backwardness Nehru perceived in India—communalism and casteism—he viewed as contingent and remediable phenomena, and no worse than the racism and violence of the West.

In Jinnah's India there was nothing left to do but for the self to separate itself from the other. There were no common moral resources to draw upon because all the moral resources were imported. The one source that could be consumed by Indians—Islam—had been consumed only by Muslims, of course, and the other—Christianity—could not be consumed.

CONCLUSION

The purpose of this analysis has been to develop a method of reconstruction and use it to represent the nascent Indian and Pakistani national identities that engaged in the partition struggle. National identities are modeled as narratives with a typical plot structure whose elements are organized in oppositions. These are cultural systems that are circulated in discourse and generate motives and strategies of action. The discursive evidence lends support to the hypothesis that the national identities of the two states were plots consisting of a heritage, vanguard and laggard elements in the nation, and a destiny or danger awaiting the nation, depending on its action.

This analysis has implications for the emerging debate on identity in international relations theory. It develops a representation of national identity more elaborate than heretofore constructed (see Wendt, 1992; Mercer, 1995) and gains greater explanatory power through explaining the logic by which identities can serve as a guide to action. The forked structure of identity here frames situations as offering two unequal action choices (destiny and danger). The importance of national self-criticism is recognized in this conceptualization of identity; here self-criticism lays the ground for the claim to vanguard status of dominant classes and institutions. Furthermore, heritage is central to the unity of a nation. Developing a more precise semantic model of national identity makes possible an examination of how identity influences national practices, internation relations, and foreign policy.

REFERENCES

Anderson, Benedict (1983) *Imagined Communities.* Ithaca: Cornell University Press.

Ashley, Richard (1989) "Living on Border Lines: Man, Poststructuralism, and War." In *Intertextual/International Relations,* edited by J. Der Derian and M. Shapiro. Lexington, MA: Lexington Books.

Banerjee, Sanjoy (1991) "Reproduction of Subjects in Historical Structures: Attribution, Identity, and Emotion in the Early Cold War." *International Studies Quarterly* 35, no. 1.

Banerjee, Sanjoy (1994) "National Identity and Foreign Policy." In *The Indira-Rajiv Years: The Indian Economy and Polity, 1966–1991,* edited by N. Choudhry and S. Mansur. Boulder: Westview Press.

Banerjee, Sanjoy (1995) "Tropes in Statist-Nationalist Discourse: Examples from the Pakistan Movement and the USSR." Paper presented at the meeting of the International Studies Association, Chicago.

Bolitho, Hector (1954) *Jinnah: Creator of Pakistan.* New York: Macmillan.

Boynton, G. R. (1991) "The Expertise of the Senate Foreign Relations Committee." In *Artificial Intelligence and International Politics,* edited by Valerie Hudson. Boulder: Westview Press.

Chatterjee, Partha (1986) *Nationalist Thought and the Colonial World: A Derivative Discourse.* Minneapolis: University of Minnesota Press.

Der Derian, James (1987) *On Diplomacy: A Genealogy of Western Estrangement.* Oxford: Basil Blackwell.

Dessler, David (1989) "What's at Stake in the Agent-Structure Debate?" *International Organization* 43, no. 3 (summer):441–473.

Farr, R., and S. Moscovici (1984) *Social Representations.* Cambridge: Cambridge University Press.

Fischer, Marcus (1992) "Feudal Europe: Discourse and Practices." *International Organization* 46, no. 2 (spring):427–466.

Forgacs, D. (1988) *An Antonio Gramsci Reader: Selected Writings, 1916–1935.* New York: Schocken Books.

Geertz, Clifford (1973) *Interpretation of Cultures.* New York: Basic Books.

Goldstein, Judith, and Robert O. Keohane (1993) *Ideas and Foreign Policy: Beliefs, Institutions, and Political Change.* Ithaca: Cornell University Press.

Gopal, S., ed. (1984) *Selected Works of Jawaharlal Nehru,* 2d series, vol. 1. Delhi: JN Memorial Fund.

Harre, Rom, David Clarke, and Nicola de Carlo (1985) *Motives and Mechanisms.* London: Methuen.

Mercer, Jonathan (1995) "Anarchy and Identity." *International Organization* 49:229–252.

Merriam, A. (1980) *Gandhi vs Jinnah: The Debate over the Partition of India.* Columbia, MO: South Asia Books.

Pirzada, S. S. (1970) *Foundations of Pakistan: All-India Muslim League Documents: 1906–1947; 1924–1947* (2 vols.). Karachi: National Publishing House.

Singh, Anita Inder (1987) *Origins of the Partition of India 1936–1947.* Delhi: Oxford University Press.

Vygotsky, Lev (1962) *Thought and Language.* Cambridge: MIT Press.

Weber, Cynthia (1989) "Representing Debt: Peruvian Presidents Balaunde's and Garcia's Reading/Writing of Peruvian Debt." *International Studies Quarterly* 34, no. 3.

Wendt, Alexander (1987) "The Agent-Structure Problem in International Relations Theory." *International Organization* 41, no. 2 (summer):383–392.

Wendt, Alexander (1992) "Anarchy Is What States Make of It: The Social Construction of Power Politics." *International Organization* 46, no. 2 (summer):391–425.

Woods, Ngaire (1995) "Economic Ideas and International Relations: Beyond Rational Neglect." *International Studies Quarterly* 39:161–180.

3

Change, Myth, and the Reunification of China

Lawrence C. Katzenstein

Katzenstein's contention is that the most influential cultural elements with respect to a specific foreign policy issue are the most difficult to ascertain methodologically. This is so because since all of the members of the culture are cognizant of the element, they find no need to mention it or debate its applicability. He illustrates his point with the "Koxinga myth" that he feels has guided PRC-Taiwan relations. It is only as consensus on the applicability of the myth has eroded that we find, post hoc, how influential that myth has actually been.

—Editor

Conventional wisdom would not anticipate a growing level of economic and cultural interdependence between the competing communist and anticommunist regimes of the People's Republic of China (PRC) and Taiwan after a costly civil war and more than forty years of acrimony. Indeed, both sides still contend that there is only one sovereign China, and that their side is the legal representative of that China. Thus, Taiwan continues to call itself the Republic of China (ROC) and, more important, the rulers of the PRC oppose any attempt by the island leadership to declare Taiwan an independent sovereign state.

While a study of the role of U.S. military deterrence in the establishment of the ROC would explain the continued political existence of Taiwan, it would not explain the actions of recent Taiwan authorities in permitting its nationals to visit families, vacation, and invest in manufacturing in the PRC. Nor would it explain why the PRC continues to include the integration of a peripheral island as a key priority on its political agenda. Taiwan Chinese could certainly find investments in newly industrializing countries (NICs) such as Thailand or Indonesia that would prove to be as lucrative as those in Guangdong or Fukien provinces. They could also find vacation spots with better accommodations than those on the mainland.

Similarly, rational actors in the PRC could choose to focus their energies on new economic zones like Shenzhen or pending acquisitions like Hong Kong rather than become entangled in the complexities of a new popular front with the Guomindang. While Taiwan might look very much like an "economic Hong Kong," from Beijing there must also be some awareness that it would most certainly be a "political Tibet" to administer.

Even the most casual observer will thus observe that economic rationality or even realist political rationality misses the point. The PRC leadership has prioritized the integration of Taiwan because it believes that Taiwan is part of China. Similarly, the Taiwan leadership and business community feel that it is appropriate for Chinese to have a broad range of contacts with other Chinese.

THE DEVELOPING THEORY AND METHOD
OF CULTURE, SYMBOLISM, AND POLITICAL ACTION

While political actors may make rational choices to advance their interests, the utility they assess and are trying to maximize is framed in a set of cultural meanings and understandings. Indeed, to the extent that such meanings evoke feelings toward political action, we are forced away from the elegance of rational-choice models. It is when the individual mind becomes aware of its own feelings that individuals become interested, focused, and committed to action (Dittmer, 1977:569). Emotional stimulation and commitment serve as the touchstone for prior life experiences and societal myths that inform action through mechanisms of analogy and metaphor.

It is precisely this distinction between secondary process rational thought and the primary process thinking of deep consciousness that has provided continuity in the literature on symbols, myths, and political action. Thus, Bennett informs us that such thinking is characterized by "projection, fantasy, the incorporation of nonverbal imagery, a high emotional content, the easy connection of disparate ideas, the failure to make underlying assumptions explicit, and the generation of multiple levels of meaning" (Bennett, 1983:41). In Cassirer (1972:100–101), we also see a link between social cooperation and myths of good and evil. Geertz similarly seeks to "connect action to its sense rather than behavior to its determinants" and uses, among others, the framework of theater for understanding human action (Geertz, 1980b:178).

Emotions not only produce commitment and action, but serve to draw the mind to the disparate and often contradictory myths that enter the subconscious throughout life. Thus, in the United States, we may draw upon a historical mythic store as diverse as those dealing with the Pilgrims, the American Revolution, the Great Depression, and Martin Luther King.

A U.S. citizen could understand the role of the Vietcong as analogous to that of the Minutemen or conversely to that of Quisling (albeit in service to communists). Similarly, the issue of brotherhood could be seen in the context of cooperation by reference to the gift of corn by which the Indians prevented the starvation of the Plymouth colony, or conversely in the confrontational efforts of black and white freedom riders.

The Chinese have similarly made frequent allegorical reference to such diverse fictional and historical sources as the Warring States period, the conflict between Confucians and legalists, the Red Chamber, the Mongol conquests, Czarist imperialism, British imperialism, the Anti-Japanese War, various model citizens, and a broad range of imperial court intrigues. Indeed, it is fair to say that given the historical depth of the Chinese experience and the frequent use of political allegory, the Chinese store of myths and symbols is considerably richer than our own. This may serve to blind the United States to the salience and intricacies of myths and allegories in Chinese political discourse.

The emotional meaning of political events to participants may color "national" assessments of these events. Thus, Dittmer offers that the ABM debate of the late 1960s not only evoked mass concerns about nuclear annihilation or defense employment, but also framed elite concerns about the technical details and deterrence value of the system (Dittmer, 1977: 569). While this observation stops short of saying that the mass symbolic understandings came to tinge "rational" technical judgments, such distortions were clearly evident. In the ABM debate of the 1960s, as in the later SDI debate, supporters often refused to acknowledge the vulnerabilities of BMD technologies, while opponents often refused to recognize working subsystems. Indeed, like many symbolic debates, the latter debate became a ritualistic replay of the former, with each side adhering to positions rooted in symbolic rather than purely technical calculations (Katzenstein, 1989:103–114).

The link between politics, myth, and primary process thinking is most often made at the level of individual consciousness and cognition. Yet this obscures another dominant theme of the literature: the manner in which culture in the form of symbolic systems functions as a dynamic link between levels of analysis. The semiotic theoretical position that supports the link offers one of the few conceptual frameworks that explain both political equilibrium and political change. It notes that culture and mythic systems are public collective entities rather than simply an additive collection of individual beliefs, and thus symbols and myths are useful precisely because they are multivocal: They form a common framework of meaning, but may also be interpreted in different ways by different factions or subgroups.

The link between structure and political culture is best seen by the enigma posed by Pye. He noted that "if the concept of political culture is to be effectively utilized, it needs to be supplemented with structural analysis, but the difficulty is that political structures can be seen on the one hand as products reflecting the political culture, while on the other hand they are also 'givens' which shape the political culture" (Dittmer, 1977:555). It should be noted that many of Pye's late 1960s SSRC colleagues were prone to examine political culture through attitudinal surveys that measured psychological phenomena rather than the social structures that may have stimulated these phenomena.

Culture and Foreign Policy Analysis

Indeed, Pye's quandary has parallels in the development of foreign policy analysis. Snyder, Bruck, and Sapin (1969) expressed a concern with interplay of structure and function as well as with thought and meaning evoked within foreign policy decision settings. However, until recent years research has avoided the question of interaction and has instead proceeded on two tracks. The positivist influence of the 1960s and early 1970s produced a body of events data research that focused on the link between national attributes and foreign policy behavior, while avoiding mediating variables dealing with cognition or culture (East, Salmore, and Hermann, 1978). At the same time, a broad range of descriptive and anecdotal case studies emerged that provided insights into bureaucratic politics, crisis decisionmaking, and group dynamics, which emphasized rich detail at the expense of generalizable findings (Hermann, Kegley, and Rosenau, 1987).[1] More recent work has emphasized the analysis of text to find hidden themes, but still gives little thought to either the political context or structures that may have generated these themes. However, recent work in artificial intelligence and foreign policy (Hudson, 1991), as well as the work assembled in this book, have focused precisely on the question of finding rigorous methods by which to forge generalizations about the links between structure, culture, cognition, and action.

How is this to be done? Two approaches merit discussion here. Geertz begins by noting the limited instinctual but considerable signing and language capacities of humans (Geertz, 1973a:45–46). He then argues that as a result of this combination, humans need to learn cultural formulas for living from their societies—"cultural templates" (Geertz, 1973b:75). Culture surrounds and envelops societal structure. Culture is both transmitted and changed by the reciprocal relations between people in society and the meanings they transmit by these relations. Since these Weberian "webs of meaning" by which man defines himself are composed of public systems of symbols (Geertz, 1973c:5), understanding how symbols work and arouse action is central for Geertz. Thus, he sees ideology as a cultural system of symbols rather than as a belief system in which one's self-interest or place in the structure is the sole determinant of action. In such a framework, it is as much the ability of leaders to present or adopt metaphorical or metonymic appeals that draw on key expressive symbols that come to determine one's emotional valence toward a political issue (Geertz, 1973d:Chap. 8).

Berger and Luckmann (1966) similarly proceed from a core belief that man has weak instincts, well-developed signs and language attributes, and therefore an open and malleable consciousness. Habitual behavior serves to provide direction, specialize activity, and limit choices. Such action taken collectively becomes institutionalized. Societal institutions that exist before the birth of an individual are then accepted through socialization not as social constructions, but as obdurate reality. Social structure is thus created in a three-point dialectical process: Individuals collectively involved in habitual behavior externalize, typify, and hence objectify the behavior into an external institution. Then this new institutional order is internalized by the next generation through socialization.

Legitimation and transmission of these institutions apart from the immediate conditions that gave rise to them requires pretheoretical "knowledge" presented through language. Maxims, myths, and other expressions of "what everybody knows" form a symbolic canopy of both cognitive and normative interpretation. Such knowledge also includes institutional "programs" similar to Geertz's "templates" for correct behavior, which may need to be reaffirmed through symbolic ritual behavior for purposes of reinforcement among participants.

Tensions arise when differential changes in some segments of society cause them to find the existing interpretations inadequate. A similar process occurs when a new generation finds that "wisdom" that emerged under different conditions no longer meets current needs. In the former condition, broad symbolic universes of meaning are constructed to integrate various fragmented subuniverses. In the latter circumstance, the creation of durable subgroups with counterdefinitions might emerge and initiate change in existing structure (Berger and Luckmann, 1966:Chaps. 1, 2).

Esherick and Wasserstrom demonstrate how Chinese subgroups subvert ritual forms into political theater. They draw a distinction between ritual and theater. Following Geertz, they construct ritual as "traditionally prescribed cultural performances that serve as models of and models for what people believe," and as a "sort of all-purpose social glue." While ritual has a limited creative domain for participants, derivative theatrical forms have more creative autonomy to take issue with traditional practices, mock elites, and reveal actual social conditions. Elites can also counter through the use of political theater to defend their positions, as has been the case in regime-sponsored campaigns in China (Esherick and Wasserstrom, 1990:844–845). For example, the original May 4, 1919, student protest against imperialism and warlord corruption emerged as a script for student protests. Later, both the Chinese Communist Party (CCP) and the Guomindang turned May 4th into a safe revolutionary festival in which the script replays the events of 1919 with praise for the protesters. Speakers then attempt generational conciliation by asserting that since the regime is working in the May 4th tradition, there is no division between the government and its youth. Government speakers then claim that it is the duty of students to build this new China, and the students show their loyalty by clapping and singing patriotic songs. However, as the Guomindang found itself among antiparty May 4th student protests in Shanghai in 1947, so the students in Beijing in 1989 simply upstaged the CCP's festival to resume the roles of their 1919 ancestors. The theater subversion of the festival included banners that stated that the ideals of the May 4th movement remained unsatisfied and needed to be reclaimed through struggle (Esherick and Wasserstrom, 1990:848).

In all of these frameworks, public and collectively received symbols constructed into myths and reinforced through rituals serve to provide recipes for stability or action in social life. Societal myths are central to one's reality and provide programmed or templated recipes for action. Moreover, it is necessary to decode these public ritual forms because such myths are not necessarily articulated, *precisely because they are taken for granted as part of reality by the political actors.*

The use of myth as explanation presents some problems, however. First, one must ask how much elites are captives of belief systems and how much they manipulate them. Some observers like Edelman (Edelman, 1971; see also Chapter 4 of this book) would have us believe that elites are more manipulative than captive. However, this is by no means clear. Aronoff notes that a political culture is unquestioned to the extent that it meets existential and societal needs, and conversely that it becomes undermined when it fails to do so. When a political culture becomes other than immutable, becomes rationally evaluated and manipulated for political purposes, the more it is likely to be questioned and changed (Aronoff, 1983:7). Dittmer in addressing this point also notes that elites can be constrained as well as aided by legitimating symbolism. Thus, elites seeking to expand social welfare relative to defense appropriations will be constrained by the lack of potent legitimating symbols. In addition, mass movements as well as elites can coopt symbols and myths for their own purposes (Dittmer, 1977:562), as we have seen in our discussion of political theater. Such movements mark some failure in the symbolic legitimation of the accepted order and contention over what was formerly seen as taken for granted. This then returns us to the position that the most salient symbolic and mythic structures for elite foreign policy analysis are those that are accepted as part of an unquestioned and obdurate reality. But this leaves us with obvious epistemological and methodological problems.

The epistemological problem is that while symbols or myths may be observed because they are public, the individual or subgroup interpretation of a necessarily vague and multivocal myth is not. Thus, these mental constructs that actually orient and direct action are more likely to be understood by participant observation and interpretation than by measurement of attitudes or behavior.[2] In fact, the most important myth systems, which are perhaps not often discussed because of their centrality and acceptedness, are precisely the ones that may have the most explanatory power. Thus, myths that orient us in time and space, or in the life cycle, are powerfully rooted in our cultures and psyches but often come up only at the margins of political discourse. It is difficult to know not only how to find them, but also how to figure out how to measure their salience and relationship to other myths and to measure and generalize their appeal across space and time.

The current state of the art is thus strong on explanation and prediction, but weak on measurement, rigor, and generalizability. Others who have been trained in the positivist tradition or are sensitive to its concerns have pondered the question of how to bring culture into the positivist agenda. Early SSRC studies of political culture (Almond and Verba, 1963) and even more current work dealing with culture and postindustrial society (Inglehart, 1988) and culture and pollution (Douglas and Wildavsky, 1982) have depended primarily on attitudinal surveys to measure cultural variations. The recent tradition has moved more in the direction of semiotics but stops short of the linkage between the interpretive and the methodologically generalizable (Dittmer, 1977:583). For example, in an earlier attempt at a generalizable synthesis, I employed an artificial intelligence expert system of Chinese negotiations based on reductionist psychology to explain negotiations over Taiwan (Katzenstein, 1990).

Dittmer, whose excellent theoretical contribution is in using semiotics to separate a specifically cultural sphere from both political culture and political psychology, does offer some methodological hints. First, he acknowledges the reductionist political psychology contribution of surveys because, at the very least, this work identifies the mass effectiveness of manipulative symbols used by the elites. Yet he searches for key symbols, like flags or icons, that condense a whole range of meanings within a political system and analyzes the political system for value orientations, attitudes towards authority, and hierarchical patterns. He also suggests that we identify in a system objects that seem to attract special interest, see what participants find interesting in them, and then examine their use and elaboration in various group contexts (Dittmer, 1977:555, 583).

These methodological hints thus point us in the direction of key symbols or objects. However, unless we have some link between symbols and values, we return to the very reductionism that has limited culture studies and foreign policy analysis. Unless we also have some filter for categorizing myths and symbols both within and across political systems, we return to simple case-by-case interpretation. Of course, there are those who, like Geertz, feel that cumulation is case-by-case interpretation (Geertz, 1973c:25); but I think we can do better.

What I propose is a classification of myths based not on logic or meaning (like the binary oppositions of Lévi-Strauss), but rather on their relationship to human cognition and perception. Although myths and symbols cannot be reduced to a psychological phenomenon, it is certainly true that they operate on, develop, and ultimately are generated by collective human cognition. Indeed, this is a central explanatory appeal of this approach.

Following Rokeach's model of cognitive organization (Rokeach, 1960:40–51), we could categorize myths that relate to central core orientations like time and space, myths that relate to value orientations that are less central but key to personality development, and, finally, myths of lesser impact that relate to volatile constructs like attitudes. Such a framework, while not reductionist, would also allow us to know and eventually to measure the impact of myths and therefore their salience in determining political action. It would also provide a map for the interaction of effects, because myths dealing with the meaning of time and space or other primitive beliefs would ripple through other myths and thought processes (Figure 3.1).

To be more specific, Rokeach held that primitive beliefs were those that a person had acquired early in life about physical reality and social reality. Physical reality includes beliefs about color, space, and time as well as the relationship of the sun and the heavens. Mathematical beliefs would also be included. Social beliefs would include, for example, whether authority figures or people generally were to be trusted or feared. Beliefs about the self would deal with orientation in physical space, beliefs about autonomy and dependence, and general self-worth. The central or primitive region is equivalent to the unexamined axioms of a mathematical system and involves beliefs that are preideological.

The intermediate region deals with beliefs that are ideological and involve adopting values from religious or political authorities, and I think it is safe to refer to beliefs in this region as values concerning authority and derived through authority. Such values are less durable than primitive beliefs but more durable than attitudes.

The peripheral region contains attitudes and beliefs derived from the intermediate region. Thus, a belief about abortion may be derived from religion; or a belief about a public policy might come from party affiliation. But not all of these attitudes are equally weighted and may vary from person to person (Rokeach, 1960:35–50).

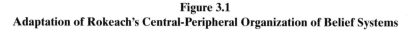

Figure 3.1
Adaptation of Rokeach's Central-Peripheral Organization of Belief Systems

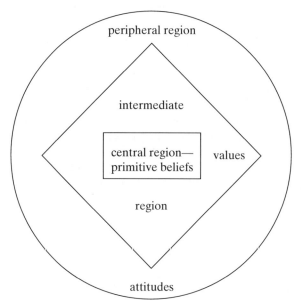

In terms of foreign policy analysis or even political analysis generally, one can look to primitive beliefs derived from myths and find ripple effects through values and attitudes. Thus, if one has primitive beliefs about time that make the past seem closer, ancient political authorities and connected ancient myths will be seen as analogies more relevant to current situations than if ancient history was seen only as relevant to the past. Presumably other primitive beliefs about space or beliefs about autonomy/dependence would have consequences for selecting authorities and values and eventually lead to attitudes about key policies.

In this essay, I examine how a primitive myth about the organization of time supports the relevance of an ancient myth about Taiwan. The Chinese myth about the origins of time orients Taiwan Chinese on a time horizon closer to the historical past and further from the future than would be the case for contemporary Western observers. This orientation allows the use of much older historical analogies by the Chinese than would be deemed relevant by Westerners.

After discussing Chinese temporal orientation, I then demonstrate how the use of Taiwan as a base of operations for Ming dynasty supporters holding out against the new Qing political order has served as a historical myth guiding the post-1949 PRC and ROC generation of leaders in their ensuing negotiations. Next, I discuss how the profound economic and material changes in Taiwan and the PRC have reconfigured this "Koxinga myth" and have led some to even question the value of reunification. In Taiwan, economic reform and growth have overturned an authoritarian Leninist structure with real political pluralism. Growing out of this pluralism are voices calling for Taiwan independence from China as a way of securing economic progress and democracy. In other words, this new generation has become closely attuned to the Western myth of linear progress—the "Science and Democracy" clarion call that motivated their revolutionary ancestors such as Yen Fu. Curiously, the adoption of the myth of progress by some younger elements of the PRC leadership has led to their admiration of the Taiwan economic miracle and to their desire for closer functional integration. Indeed, this generational shift includes some of the same social forces that motivated the events of spring 1989.

THE MYTHS

The Mandate of Heaven and Conceptions of Time and Change

The two main forces involved in ancient Chinese cyclical theories of change were the *yin* and the *yang*. The *yang* was seen as the active or male force, while the *yin* was seen as the passive or female force. *Yang* corresponded to the heavens, the repository of the seminal essence, and *yin* corresponded to the earth, the repository of the germinal essence. *Yin* and *yang* met in the autumn and spring to make the world fertile. The monarch, or son of heaven, was delegated power by heaven—the "mandate of heaven"—to regulate human activities in accordance with the natural order. He did this by propagating a calendar to show the inhabitants of his domain how to conform to the course of natural things. A good year, synonymous with a good harvest, would come through the proper regulation of *yin* and *yang* demonstrated by seasonal rains and favorable weather (Granet, 1977:48, 64–65; Ronan, 1977:158). Since heaven was seen as being endowed with intellect, purpose, virtue, and benevolence, it followed that the ruler should be similarly endowed. If the ruler engaged in evil acts of will, he would destroy order and harmony and would cause natural catastrophes and anomalies. If no change were forthcoming in the rule of the state, ruin and destruction would prevail (Liu, 1967:164).

Articulated by the Han Confucian scholar Tung Chung Shu in *Spring and Autumn* (Liu, 1967:164), and considered a central feature of Chinese political morality from its first appearance in the early Han Book of History (*Shu Ching*) until the early twentieth century, the mandate of heaven has been central to the beginning and end of regnal cycles. Heaven ended the "bad last" and installed the "good first" monarch in the dynastic cycle (Stover and Stover, 1976:28). However, the mandate of heaven conception does not stand alone but is rather, as Tung's title implies, the political extension of the naturalist religion conception of time.

However, in addition to the mandate of heaven myth, the Chinese also had strong elements of linearity built into their temporal framework. Historians measured time in terms of regnal periods but also devised a scheme for single-track history to include events in minor dynasties and overlapping kingdoms (Needham, 1965:11). Continuous history evolved into great historical narratives, some covering as many as thirteen centuries, which helped the Chinese overcome the compartmentalization of naturalist conceptions of time (Needham, 1965:13). The efforts involved in the construction of such histories and the centrality accorded history by the state would not have been forthcoming had the Chinese not believed time to be linear (Needham, 1965:51).

The resulting Chinese synthesis is therefore best explained when the naturalist conception is fit back into a linear framework. It is proposed that a reconciliation between the start of dialectical zigzag time at the start of each reign and the longer cumulative linear time can lie only in an accordion conception of time in which the years of a regnal cycle exist in a horizontal oppositional zigzag along a straight line and are contiguous with the years of such arrangements in previous regnal cycles (Figure 3.2).

This compressed conceptualization of past time in comparison to the Western conceptualization of time renders the past closer to someone standing in the Chinese present than in the Western present. In addition, the Chinese see the future as more protracted. In largely agricultural societies, the repetitive nature of agricultural tasks and the short-term seasonal planning required lead to a belief that the future is largely a continuation of the present (Goody, 1968:40–41). There is some additional support for this protracted future time conception in a linguistic study of a grammatical form known as the counterfactual theoretical mood. In the simplest form, this mood may be expressed by the

Figure 3.2
Conceptions of Time

CHINESE		T2.	T4.	
	T1.	T3.		T5.
WESTERN	T1. ——	T2. ——	T3. ——	T4. —— T5.

statement "X is not the case, but if X then Y" (Bloom, 1979:59). Because such a mood seems to be absent from the Chinese language, it is hypothesized that related cognitive structures dealing with such theoretical schemas would also be absent (Bloom, 1979:55, 61; see also Katzenstein, 1987).[3]

As a result of the myth of the mandate of heaven and related cultural constructs in Chinese temporality, it is held that the Chinese give unusual salience to analogies or myths from deep historical time. In addition, their protracted sense of future time makes them more tolerant of protracted negotiation. Both points are relevant to our discussion of PRC-Taiwan integration.

The Ming Presence on Taiwan
After the Qing Takeover of the Mainland

In all of the discussion of CCP-Guomindang rivalry, very little discussion has been raised about a historical analogy that could serve as a reference. Yet there is every reason to believe by the *behavior* of the principals that a particular historical analogy is being followed while not being publicly articulated.

During the fighting between the Ming loyalists and the Qings (Manchus), who were consolidating their power over the empire in the mid-1600s, a naval warrior, Koxinga, emerged on the Ming side. A member of the powerful Zheng family, Koxinga continued to support the Ming even after his father went over to the Qings in 1646. His well-armed fleet kept Qing forces at bay along the coast and permitted his control of a base at Xiamen in Fujian province. This base became an international entrepôt and a center for ten trading companies controlled by Koxinga.

This profitable arrangement was eventually ended by a successful Qing attack on Xiamen. However, Koxinga survived and extracted a considerable fortune later through exploits against Dutch coastal colonists. Despite the fact that he eventually died from a series of self-destructive acts, his sons and later his grandsons established a base and an extensive trading empire on Taiwan. This dramatic commercial success permitted a population of more than 100,000 Chinese to flee the mainland and live profitably on the island. Two attempts by the Qing court to attack the Zhengs by naval warfare failed, and Taiwan was simply allowed to develop temporarily as a commercial enterprise.

Qing emperor Kangxi finally became disgusted with the Ming loyalists and hired Shi Lang, a senior admiral and disgruntled former employee of Koxinga, to conduct a massive naval attack on Taiwan. After Shi's victory, Kangxi graciously ennobled certain members of the Zheng family and permitted some to move to Beijing. Taiwan troops were not executed but rather integrated into the Chinese army. Finally, the rights of the aboriginal Taiwan population, such as to their hunting lands, were respected after the island was consolidated into the empire (Kristof, 1987:E3; Spence, 1990:54–57).

In broad terms, this account has an almost eerie relationship to contemporary history between Taiwan and the mainland. One could easily substitute the Guomindang for the Zhengs; postwar Shanghai or even current Hong Kong for the Xiamen entrepôt; the emergence of Taiwan under the Guomindang for Taiwan under the Zhengs as a commercial success and refuge for those who would want to restore the old regime; and the CCP for the Qings as those who would give the opposition some role in the government.[4] Such analogies would make a very strong case for either historicism or decisionmaking by historical myth. The analogy becomes even stronger if one realizes that elements of the old Ming bureaucracy were able to ultimately coopt the Mongols into Chinese methods of governance in much the same way that the Guomindang would like to coopt the communists through traditional Chinese culture and history as well as economic development. Moreover, since Taiwan did not really enjoy much interaction with China until around 1620, it is clearly transitional Ming-Qing China that is relevant for analogy. Yet, despite the common threads, the analogy to this prior case is not a commonly articulated theme in either the mainland or Taiwan press, though foreign press observers have noted the behavioral parallels. Moreover, individual Chinese on both sides of the Taiwan Strait note the analogy as a matter of course (Arkush, 1996; Lin 1996).[5] Thus, we have a myth that is so taken for granted that it needs no articulation.

Finally, it should also be noted that recent movement by younger and non-Guomindang political leaders in Taiwan to forget about return and control of the economically backward mainland, and a related move for Taiwan independence, may be seen as a generational shift initiated by material conditions that are not addressed by the myth system (Kristof, 1989:4). This last point is crucial precisely because it creates fertile ground for new uses of the old myths or the generation of new myths to justify Taiwan independence and termination of the quest to retake or integrate with the rest of China.

PRC-TAIWAN RELATIONS AND THESE MYTHS

"China has a long history—4,000 years, 5,000 years," Deputy Foreign Minister John H. Chang said. "Forty years is just a second. We can wait. We are patient" (Chang, 1986:14).

On December 7, 1949, Chiang Kai-shek ordered the remnants of his Guomindang regime to withdraw to Taiwan from Chengdu, its last seat of power on the mainland. The Chinese Communist Party soon declared its intention to "liberate" Taiwan in order to bring closure to a civil war that both sides formally see as still unfinished. To this end, the newly formed East China Command of the new communist government constructed new airfields, began construction of new motor launches, and began training in amphibious warfare in preparation for an invasion in the summer of 1950. Indeed, given PLA successes against KMT forces on the mainland and on Hainan Island, it appeared that "liberation" would have been quite probable. However, the beginning of the Korean War brought with it a shift in U.S. policy that was now unwilling to tolerate the capture of Taiwan by communist forces. The Seventh Fleet was positioned in the Taiwan Strait to prevent any invasion.

U.S. intervention served to quell the invasion threat and change the PLA deployment opposite Taiwan from an offensive one to a defensive one. The defensive configuration on the mainland was linked to a belief that the United States might encourage ROC operations against the mainland as part of the general operations arising from Korea. However, while the U.S. presence led to a cessation of hostilities between the two sides, sporadic episodes of violence continued.

In 1954, the PRC either bombed or shelled ROC-held islands, including Quemoy and the Ta Chen group. The ROC forces retaliated at this time by bombing gun emplacements on the mainland. In 1955, the PRC bombed and later occupied some of the offshore islands while the ROC bombed shipping in some mainland ports. In 1958, a crisis erupted over PRC attempts to isolate Quemoy and Matsu with artillery barrages, but these proved unsuccessful. Eventually, however, these hostilities have given way to tacit understandings about the use and location of each side's air, naval, and reconnaissance forces. There have not been major violent exchanges since the withdrawal of the U.S. Seventh Fleet destroyer patrol that occurred as part of the U.S.-PRC rapprochement (Huebner, 1987). Yet, as noted below, when the PRC became concerned about the independence movement on Taiwan in 1995, they staged an amphibious assault on a nearby island. Thus, it is fair to conclude that from preparations for a naval invasion in 1950 to the amphibious assault in 1995, the PRC is invoking the historical memory of Shi Lang's successful naval invasion to their obvious strategic advantage.

Proposals for Unification

The PRC and the ROC both adhere to a "one China" policy and each claims legitimate authority over that China. To this end, the ROC legislature was districted to have representatives from each province of China, drawn from 1949 mainlander émigrés rather than from each section of Taiwan. Similarly, the PRC has in recent years encouraged participation of Taiwan-born PRC nationals and overseas Chinese to represent "Taiwan province" in sporting events and other forums (Clough, 1978:Chap. 4).

After the Korean War and the attacks on the offshore islands in 1954–1955, the PRC opened the question of a peaceful resolution of the Taiwan question. At the 1956 National People's Congress meetings, Zhou Enlai proposed that KMT leaders begin talks to discuss the "peaceful liberation of Taiwan." He outlined a series of assurances designed to encourage KMT leaders to enter the process. He pledged that those KMT leaders who supported reunification would not be punished for prior misdeeds, but rather would be given appropriate positions to help in the reconstruction of China. During the envisioned negotiations, KMT officials would also be allowed to visit with friends and relatives on the mainland and send representatives to inspect mainland conditions. Both they and their representatives would be guaranteed safe passage. Moreover, later that year, during a press conference, Zhou said that Chiang Kai-shek would be offered a post above the ministerial level if unification were to occur (Clough, 1978:136).

The lack of success of this diplomatic initiative may have led to the PRC's return to military action against the offshore islands in 1958. This military action was followed by a PRC appeal to the leaders of Taiwan warning them not to become dependent on the United States, which PRC leaders claimed only sought to isolate Taiwan and forge it into a trusteeship. The PRC must have assumed that the ambassadorial-level talks begun between themselves and Washington in 1955 would lend credence to this fear.

The ROC leadership resisted all negotiations, but also agreed with the PRC in rejecting U.S. initiatives to create a separate status of "two Chinas" or "one China, one Taiwan" in order to resolve the question. Indeed, the adherence of both the senior leaders of the KMT and the PRC to the "one China" position made both hostile to the Taiwan independence movement. However, the PRC accused the United States and Japan of financing the movement, while the ROC contended that the PRC had secretly done so to foster dissension in Taiwan.

In the wake of the Nixon visit in 1972, Taiwan saw its diplomatic position erode. The loss of its UN seat and its Security Council permanent membership to the PRC, and the clear indication that the United States was moving toward full relations with the PRC, undercut the ROC's claim to be the only legitimate government of China. Beijing used its improved status to try once again to convince people on Taiwan of the predestined move toward "liberation."

The post-1972-era PRC campaign for "peaceful liberation" was directed more toward Taiwanese than toward the mainlander ruling elite of Taiwan. It was felt that the younger Taiwanese would eventually inherit the mantle of authority and needed to be courted into the "one China" framework (Chiu, 1973:275). Prominence was given to the Taiwan Democratic Self-Government League on the mainland and to the February 28, 1947, revolt of Taiwanese against the new mainlander government. However, this latter event was cast as being part of the more general uprising by all Chinese against KMT oppression. Persons of Taiwanese origin were elected to the Central Committee, PRC tourist services encouraged Taiwan people to visit adjacent Fukien, and, as mentioned earlier, the PRC fielded teams of Taiwanese from the United States, Canada, and Japan to participate in national, Asian, and other sports competitions.

The new overtures to Taiwan also included more tolerance by the PRC for the Taiwan independence movement. They were now cast as simply misguided by their separation from the mainland rather than as foreign agents. Zhou Enlai encouraged them to visit the mainland, stressed that he had peaceful intentions, and guaranteed that the living standard of Taiwan would not drop with reunification. Zhou at this time offered Tibet's autonomous region status as a possible model to guarantee that Taiwan would retain a high degree of self-government. The PRC also reiterated their earlier offer of amnesty and high government office to mainland elites in return for their help in achieving reunification (Clough, 1978:135–136).

In 1974, Deng Xiaoping began to take over many of Zhou's state responsibilities because of Zhou's terminal cancer. In speaking to a group of overseas Chinese, Deng was somewhat more provocative in that he simply prioritized peaceful methods for reunification over "nonpeaceful" methods. But he refused to rule out the use of "patriotic forces" that could play a part in using the "nonpeaceful" method. He did, however, characterize liberation efforts as requiring a long period of work that, while not producing great results initially, would accumulate "little by little" to produce an effect (Clough, 1978:137–138). Interestingly, this appraisal was echoed by the Taiwan government in a slightly different context some fifteen years later. Concerning the Chinese-Taiwan open-door cultural exchanges and eventual friendship after the Tiananmen massacre, ROC Deputy Foreign Minister John H. Chang said, "We Chinese say that if you can keep the water on the ground the ditch will come out by itself" (Jones, 1989).

Despite these new overtures and threats, Chiang's son, then-Premier Chiang Ching-kuo, opposed negotiations. He held to the government's long-standing policy of not establishing contacts with communists. ROC President C. K. Yen held at this time that negotiations with the PRC would be possible only if it ceased to be communist (Clough, 1978:142).

However, just how communist the PRC would be seemed precisely at issue after Deng increased his power and initiated the Four Modernizations in 1978. The growth of Shenzhen and other special economic zones, the expansion of joint venture enterprises with U.S., Japanese, and other foreign interests, and the general opening of the PRC to the outside world bode well for meaningful reform. In the early 1970s, many Taiwan Chinese who were now nationals of the United States and Japan were anxious to visit the PRC. As reforms progressed, understandings emerged between the PRC and the ROC that allowed ROC nationals to visit their relatives and former villages on the mainland.

Indeed, during my own visit to the PRC in 1988, there were genuine signs of warm regard for Taiwan. Some wines produced in Taiwan were in evidence on banquet tables. Some students from fishing or merchant families owned European-style racing bikes constructed in Taiwan. But, more important, middle- to upper-level party officials made a point of telling me how much they would like to integrate KMT officials into the Chinese government because of their economic acumen and success in running the Taiwan economy. One former provincial governor even made a point of showing me Chiang Kai-shek's former summer home near the beach in Qingdao, which is now a popular tourist attraction.

During this period of warming ties, Deng introduced the formula of "One Country, Two Systems," which in the Taiwan case would have exceeded even the autonomy permitted Hong Kong by the Sino-British agreements of 1984. Under this formula, the ROC would be allowed to keep its capitalist system, its own provincial government, and even its own army (Deng, 1987:48–52; Weng, 1987). Indeed, while political structures have not joined, economic and cultural integration has moved quickly. Beijing offered condolences at the death of Chiang Ching-kuo in 1988. These feelings were apparently sincere because Chiang had permitted real trade to begin between the PRC and the ROC. In 1988, trade reached a level of $2 billion a year resulting in Taiwan ranking as China's sixth-best trading partner and China ranking as Taiwan's fifth-best. In addition, more than two hundred thousand Taiwan citizens visited the PRC in 1988. That same year saw Deng Xiaoping's artist daughter's pictures hanging in a gallery in Taipei, Taiwan doctors training and sitting for exams in traditional medicine in the PRC, and undertakers in Taipei arranging for ashes to be sent to family burial sites on the mainland (Frye, 1988; Southerland, 1988:27; Hoon, 1988:28).

Yet problems remain on the political integration front. In response to the Deng "One Country, Two Systems" scheme, ROC representatives called for reunification with the implementation of the ROC constitution on the mainland and adherence by Beijing to the KMT's "Three Principles of the People": dignity, democracy, and free enterprise (Weng, 1987:202–203). Beijing naturally did not accept this proposal for a KMT takeover of the mainland. However, somewhat more curiously, Beijing has also rejected confederation plans and economic confederations of codevelopment that seem close to their own formulation (Li, 1989).

More recently, while people who have visited the mainland came to fear the PRC after Tiananmen, condemnation has been muted for fear of provoking an attack, and economic and cultural ties have continued. But, while the PRC continues to seek reunification and has even made a point of reaching out to Taiwanese again, younger Taiwanese have begun to move away from the sacred principles of their fathers in recapturing the mainland. Many have now seen the poverty that abounds in the mainland and would not like responsibility for its development. While many of the older KMT legislators continue to hold to the old position, many of the younger political leaders are just as happy with their profitable status quo (Public Opinion Research Foundation, 1990).

MATERIAL CONDITIONS, GENERATIONAL CHANGE, AND MORE RECENT DEVELOPMENTS ON REUNIFICATION

It is certainly the case that the old analogy from Ming-Qing times has some merit as a formula for the current situation. Since the 1950s, the PRC has offered the KMT some role in the mainland government. They have continued, like their Qing predecessors, to adhere to the position that the political and social life of people on Taiwan would not be altered. Moreover, since many of the mainland's historical treasures were destroyed during the Cultural Revolution, many of the historical works remaining on Taiwan could add to the national identity. Finally, since the leaders on Taiwan have had considerably more experience with the type of heavily export-based economy that the PRC is trying to develop, one would think that the introduction of KMT advisers or ministers in ministries of commerce or trade could be quite helpful.

However, aside from the obvious animosities between older communist and anticommunist elements, the usefulness of this analogy has been undermined by the very dynamics that have formed the two states. As of the mid-1990s it would appear that Taiwan's political system has changed from a military-authoritarian state to a truly pluralistic democratic state. Similarly, despite its communist trappings, the PRC has evolved from a radical, mass-based, one-party system to a mobilizing military-authoritarian one. This has had consequences for the values of the new leadership replacing the postwar leadership and, more important, for the ultimate outcome of the negotiations.

Taiwan—The Development Model That Actually Worked

It was common among development theorists of the 1950s and 1960s to hold that as underdeveloped states acquired surplus capital and moved from primary to secondary production that a development "syndrome" would take hold. This syndrome would be marked by urbanization, increased investments in education and infrastructure, and increased political pluralism. As the economy or division of labor became more complex and cities became more populated, interest groups would emerge to represent these interests. Some variants on this theme included the belief that if the interest groups mobilized before state institutions could handle these interests, political instability would result. Another variant was that an alliance between foreign capital, the military, and the state bureaucracy would conspire to suppress participation as a means of maximizing stability for investment. Nevertheless, the dominant message was one of industrialization and growth linked to pluralistic democracy.

Both the PRC and the ROC could be looked upon, then, as alternative methods of development that were held by their partisans as a means for providing China with the industrial base and competitive dynamism that were sorely lacking during the decaying Qing empire. The story of modern China is simply one of political and economic experimentation by both the KMT and the CCP to provide the state with the wealth and power to prevent subjugation to any future hegemon. In keeping with this, the experiment on Taiwan has worked, and the experiment on the mainland has been altered to make it work.

The Taiwan miracle has been written about extensively, especially since the lifting of martial law and the legalization of opposition parties like the Democratic Progressive Party (DPP) in 1987. First, land reform redistributed wealth, while such classic strategies as import substitution, monetary stabilization, and protective tariffs worked to establish new industries, including many with lucrative products for export. The average economic growth rate from 1951 to 1987 was 8.9 percent—and 11.2 percent in 1987 alone. In addition, not only has GNP and GNP/per capita risen, but only ten nations in the world rank higher than Taiwan in terms of distribution or disparity of income. The number of registered interest groups has grown markedly from 2,560 in 1952 to 11,306 in 1987.

The beginning of this new era of multiple parties was really marked by the generational change from Premier Chiang Kai-shek to his son Chiang Ching-kuo, and subsequently to Premier Lee Ten-Hui. This generation of leadership realized that the basic tenets of Chiang's program were now obsolete and that the pressures for increased representation were far more pressing. Thus, while the senior Chiang continued to maintain a national Chinese legislature with aging representatives of their former provinces, the junior Chiang and, later, Lee arranged to pension these unrepresentative leaders off and replace them with a more representative elected legislature. Similarly, the new order lifted martial law in 1987 and permitted the legalization of opposition parties, since an invasion from the mainland was no longer imminent.

The PRC and the Near-Term Status Quo

While it is not clear what positions the PRC will take on Taiwan when Deng dies, it could be argued that the critical shift was actually the one from Mao to Deng. For it was with the inception of the Four Modernizations that China began seriously to open to the outside world and to foreign investment and information. The post-Tiananmen movement from an alliance with reformers to an alliance with the Chinese military simply marked a movement to the military-authoritarian road to accomplish these modernizations. The continued diversification and growth of the Chinese economy should bode well for the forces of pluralism in the long term, but in the near term, the result is likely to be continued authoritarianism and economic growth.

Following these trends of increasing pluralism in Taiwan, and authoritarianism in the PRC, it should serve as no surprise that the greater variation will occur in the PRC's policy toward Taiwan. Indeed, we have seen a marked increase in belligerent rhetoric and military maneuvers by the PRC on the eve of Taiwan's general elections, regarded by many as a mandate on Taiwan's movement toward a separatist stance. These developments, in turn, adhere in some ways to the ancient Ming-Qing analogy. These include:

1. *The use of force.* The PRC has refused to renounce the possible use of force in unifying Taiwan as recently as Foreign Minister Qian Qichen's pronouncement in September 1994. Qian warned that any declaration of independence by Taiwan would lead to an immediate invasion. Large-scale Chinese amphibious assault exercises on Dongshan Island between Fujian and Taiwan during this period were clearly designed to underscore this position (Baum, 1994:24). As noted, these trends have worsened recently.

2. *External relations.* The PRC opposes any formula that treats Taiwan as a national entity. This includes any informal diplomatic ties or membership in any international organizations.

3. *Taiwan's status.* The PRC sees Taiwan as a province and its government as a "local authority." It seeks to use the Hong Kong model of Taiwan as a SAR. This will permit international economic contacts and the retention of its current political system and military, but these must ultimately follow orders from Beijing. National symbols would be removed.

4. *Negotiations.* The CCP promotes direct negotiations on unification or bilateral relations with representation of other minor parties on the mainland and Taiwan.

By contrast, the ROC's current policies are much more textured and reflect the new dynamism of their political system. Especially noticeable is the effect of parties like the DPP, which actually favor independence, and the countervailing position of the Socialist Party, which is pressing for reunification.

The ROC positions include:

1. *Use of force.* President Li's termination of "The Period of National Mobilisation for Suppressing the Communist Rebellion" in 1991 was an attempt by the KMT to move the discourse away from the use of force.

2. *External relations.* The ROC seeks to reestablish diplomatic ties and join intergovernmental organizations whenever possible under a "one China" principle.

3. *Taipei-Beijing relations.* The ROC proposes "one country, two areas, two political entities" as a pragmatic formula with enough ambiguity for both sides.

4. *Negotiations.* The ROC opposes direct negotiations between the two sides during the first stage of national unification but favors technical talks between unofficial intermediary groups. These include the Straits Exchange Foundation for the ROC and the Association for Relations Across the Taiwan Straits for the PRC. Both were founded in 1991 and held meetings to arrange postal regulations; regulations on certificates of adoption, birth, death, and inheritance; school records; and youth exchanges. The PRC also made commitments to improve the investment environment for Taiwan investors (Wu, 1995:65–97; *Beijing Review,* 1993:7). Taiwan holds that transportation, trade, and postal links will remain indirect during the current stage of negotiations. They will become direct when trust has been established, when the use of force has been renounced, and when Taiwan has been recognized as a political entity.

CHANGING CONDITIONS AND THE USE OF MYTHS

In the earlier discussion of Geertzian approaches and political theater, it was shown that the subversion of mythic rituals was possible because myths can be multivocal and speak to different constituencies with different agendas. Here the location of the mandate of heaven myth in the primitive core of Chinese culture guarantees that ancient myths will be invoked by both sides to justify views ranging from Taiwan independence through economic confederation to integration through force. The Koxinga myth, as we shall see, has some relevance on each of these points. However, one may see the use of other ancient myths and the development of modern myths to justify other positions as well. One can only speculate on how this mythic pantheon will emerge in the context of political contention. However, it is clear that the material and political changes outlined above will fuel a spirited discourse. There will be those who seek closer ties for economic gain, those who seek independence to avoid the economic discomfort with the PRC that the West Germans have experienced in unifying with the East, and those who will still seek to impose the political system of one side on the other. However, since the PRC has rapidly changed from a communist state to a bureaucratic authoritarian one, and the ROC has changed from an authoritarian state to a polyarchy, it is not clear what sort of system we are talking about in either case.

However, the outlines of some possible myth formulations have begun to emerge from the margins of discussion. One ancient myth that had been used to herald a Nationalist victory in the 1960s could be used by both Nationalist ideologues and those in the PRC who want more of a Nationalist role in China's economic planning. This myth was accompanied by the slogan *"Wu wang zai Ju"* or "Never forget the time in Ju." This refers to events in 284 B.C. when the kingdom of Yan had taken all of the territory of the kingdom of Qi except for Ju. The Qi general, Tian Tan, was able to reverse the progress of the war and save Qi and its lands and grain. Clearly this upset victory, couched in a hierarchical reversal, could be invoked by Nationalists and their allies at some future time in the negotiations (Keightley, 1996).

Similarly fertile new ground for a Taiwan independence myth comes from the current political conditions on Taiwan and scholarship concerning Taiwan in the 1940s. Since KMT leaders are now the moderates between the conservative New Party and the pro-independence DPP, and the populace now sees Taiwan as separate from the PRC, it is possible that Taiwanese could draw from arguments that neither the CCP nor the KMT viewed Taiwan to be part of China proper until the 1940s (Sullivan, 1996). One modern myth that could be created for this position is Edgar Snow's account of Mao saying that while Manchuria is part of China and must be regained, "we do not include Korea, formerly a Chinese colony [sic] . . . the same thing applies to Taiwan. As for Inner Mongolia . . . we will struggle to drive Japan from there and help Inner Mongolia to establish an autonomous state" (Snow, in Clifford, 1996).

The Koxinga myth will likely continue to play a key role even if subverted by any of the key political groupings on either side. The strength of this myth emerges from the striking parallels of the two historical situations. The Nationalists used the Koxinga myth in 1949 as a myth of conciliation to link new immigrants and people on Taiwan to the destiny of all of China. In effect, the Nationalists usurped the provincial hero traditionally honored by Taiwan's rulers by observing April 29, the date of Koxinga's landing, as a holiday. His Confucian temple and Shinto shrine were covered with Chiang Kai-shek's calligraphy saying *"Chen*

Hsing Chung-hua" or "revive China." Through the 1970s he was commemorated in calendars, street names, and even television melodramas. Like the official museum display noted by Arkush above, there was a myth promoted by the Guomindang that linked Koxinga to Sun Yat-sen's revolution through two centuries of resistance through secret societies. Thus, the Chinese revolution was posed as coming full circle in returning to Taiwan for regeneration. But the Guomindang also stopped short of explicit analogy with Koxinga because, in the end, he lost. Thus, the link with Sun Yat-sen, the strategic importance of the islands, and other points of positive change are emphasized. They even dedicated a new temple on Quemoy in the late 1960s to link Koxinga's old military base to a KMT return to the mainland (Croizier, 1977:63–70).

The Koxinga myth has also been adopted from time to time by the communists, despite the role accorded it by the Nationalists. The communists in Maoist years have made much of Koxinga's loyalty to the Ming regime over his loyalty to his father and of the support both Chinese and Taiwan aborigines gave him in his anti-imperialist conquests against the Dutch colonizers. They stress both the fraternal unity of Chinese nationality groups and the role of superior strategy and bravery over technology. While he fell into neglect because of upper-class origins during the Cultural Revolution, he was still never repudiated because anti-imperialism was seen to take priority over class contradictions. As relations with Taiwan have warmed, Koxinga's image has received less attention. But he could be invoked in the cause of national defense or anti-imperialism if armed liberation were deemed necessary (Croizier, 1977:70–74).

Finally, there is some reason to believe that Koxinga could be used as a symbol of independence. While some independence leaders in the past saw him as an ancient Chiang Kai-shek who only used the Taiwan people to attack the mainland, others have seen him as the leader of the most ancient ancestors of present Taiwanese. A third of schoolchildren questioned in 1970 in towns that were primarily native Taiwanese saw him among the three greatest historical heroes. He was honored as a deity in a large number of local temples on Taiwan, but was seen as only a minor hero in Singapore, and had almost no visibility among children questioned in Hong Kong (Croizier, 1977:74–78). Thus, it is quite possible that these Taiwan schoolchildren who are now twenty-five years older could adopt Koxinga for his bravery and independence by subverting commemorations held by the Guomindang.

CONCLUSION

In this research, we have seen variations of a historical myth used to guide foreign policy. Precisely because such cultural myths are so widely applied, there is little trace of their application in empirical artifacts. Yet careful study can demonstrate not only the effect of an unarticulated myth, but also how the myth's relevance can be undermined or reinterpreted by succeeding generations. Although pluralism and free enterprise are changing the face of PRC and ROC politics, any change may well require elaboration through traditional mythic allegory to capture a wide base of public support precisely because of the importance of distant history in the Chinese belief system.

NOTES

1. The opening chapter of this book provides a good overview of the development of this literature.

2. This is why Geertz relies on "thick description."

3. While space precludes the entire body of evidence and the entire argument, those interested may consult Katzenstein (1987).

4. Some high-ranking educational officials and party members suggested this as a viable scenario during my trip to the PRC in November and December 1988.

5. There is substantial, if anecdotal, evidence of cognitive framing in accord with this myth. Thus, David Arkush of the University of Iowa by Internet communication recalls seeing "an official Taiwan museum exhibition on Koxinga which posited a direct connection between Ming loyalists on Taiwan, through secret societies, and the 1911 revolution, understood as Guomindang connected, overseas-based, and successful in toppling the Mainland government." He continues, "The analogy to the present was unstated, but crystal clear."

Chau-Yi Lin, a Syracuse University graduate student, reports by Internet that Professor Chuang Wu-yua used this analogy in a seminar to Taiwan policymakers concerning the China-Taiwan relationship as reported in late 1995 in the *Independence Weekly Post* on Taiwan. He compared the Qing attempts to isolate the Ming loyalists on Taiwan both economically and politically with current practices of the PRC. The report indicated that he received "echos" from the Taiwan-China policymakers present.

Croizier (1977:Chap. 5) describes how Koxinga has been adopted periodically as a mythic hero by the Nationalists, the communists, and even the Japanese (owing to his Japanese mother). According to historical context, the myth has been adapted to Nationalist, communist-anti-imperialist, Japanese-Asian, and even Taiwan independence agendas.

REFERENCES

Almond, Gabriel, and Sidney Verba (1963) *The Civic Culture: Political Attitudes and Democracy in Five Nations.* Princeton: Princeton University Press.

Arkush, David (1996) Discussion of the link of Koxinga to the Guomindang and Chinese Revolution through secret societies as viewed at an official museum exhibition. Internet communication from the University of Iowa.

Aronoff, M. J. (1983) "Conceptualizing the Role of Culture and Political Change." In *Culture and Political Change,* edited by M. J. Aronoff. New Brunswick, NJ: Transaction Books.

Baum, Julian (1994) "Fear of Falling." *Far Eastern Economic Review* 157, no. 41 (October 13):24.

Beijing Review (1993) "Across-Straits Symposium on Law," September 27, vol. 36, no. 39, p. 7.

Beijing Review (1994) "New Talks Boost Across-Straits Ties," August 15, vol. 37, no. 33, p. 4.

Bennett, W. Lance (1983) "Culture, Communication, and Political Control." In *Culture and Political Change,* edited by M. J. Aronoff. New Brunswick, NJ: Transaction Books.

Berger, Peter L., and Thomas Luckmann (1966) *The Social Construction of Reality.* Garden City, NY: Doubleday.

Bloom, Alfred H. (1979) "The Role of Chinese Language in Counterfactual/Theoretical Thinking and Evaluation." In *Value Change in Chinese Society*, edited by R. W. Wilson, A. A. Wilson, and S. L. Greenblatt. New York: Praeger.

Cassirer, Ernst (1972) *An Essay on Man.* New Haven: Yale University Press.

Chang (King Yuh), John (1986) *A Framework for China's Unification.* Taipei: Kwang Hua.

Chiu, Hungdah (1973) *China and the Question of Taiwan.* New York: Praeger.

Chiu, Hungdah (1993) "The Koo-wang Talks and the Prospect of Building Constructive and Stable Relations Across the Taiwan Straits." *Issues and Studies* vol. 29 no. 8, pp. 29–36.

Clifford, Nick (1996) Discussion of Mao and Snow's *Red Star Over China*, indicating that Mao did not regard Taiwan as part of China in the 1940s. Internet communication from Middlebury College.

Clough, Ralph N. (1978) *Island China.* Cambridge: Harvard University Press.

Clough, Ralph N. (1993) *Reaching Across the Straits: People to People Democracy.* Boulder: Westview Press.

Croizier, Ralph (1977) *Koxinga and Chinese Nationalism, History, Myth and the Hero.* Cambridge: Harvard University Press.

Deng Xiaoping (1987) "One Country Two Systems in Deng Xiaoping." In *Fundamental Issues in Present Day China.* Beijing: Foreign Languages Press.

Dittmer, Lowell (1977) "Political Culture and Political Symbolism, Toward a Theoretical Synthesis." *World Politics* 29, no. 4 (July):552–583.

Douglas, Mary, and Aaron Wildavsky (1982) *Risk and Culture.* Berkeley: University of California Press.

East, Maurice, Stephen Salmore, and Charles Hermann, eds. (1978) *Why Nations Act.* Beverly Hills: Sage.

Edelman, Murray (1971) *Politics as Symbolic Action: Mass Arousal and Quiescence.* New York: Academic Press.

Esherick, Joseph W., and Jeffrey N. Wasserstrom (1990) "Acting Out Democracy: Political Theater in Modern China." *Journal of Asian Studies* 45, no. 4: 835–866.

Frye, Alton (1988) "For Both Taiwan and China the Courtship Gets Serious." *Los Angeles Times,* December 5.

Geertz, Clifford (1973a) "The Impact of the Concept of Culture on the Concept of Man." In *The Interpretation of Cultures,* edited by Clifford Geertz. New York: Basic Books.

Geertz, Clifford (1973b) "The Growth of Culture and the Evolution of Mind." In *The Interpretation of Cultures,* edited by Clifford Geertz. New York: Basic Books.

Geertz, Clifford (1973c) "Thick Description: Toward an Interpretive Theory of Culture." In *The Interpretation of Cultures,* edited by Clifford Geertz. New York: Basic Books.

Geertz, Clifford (1973d) "Ideology as a Cultural System. "In *The Interpretation of Cultures,* edited by Clifford Geertz. New York: Basic Books.

Geertz, Clifford (1980a) "Blurred Genres: The Refiguration of Social Thought." *American Scholar* 49:165–179.

Geertz, Clifford (1980b) *Negara: The Theater State in Nineteenth Century Bali.* Princeton: Princeton University Press.

Goody, Jack (1968) "The Social Organization of Time." *International Encyclopedia of the Social Sciences.* New York: Free Press.

Granet, Marcel (1977) *The Religion of the Chinese People.* New York: Harper and Row.

Hermann, C. F., C. W. Kegley, Jr., and J. N. Rosenau, eds. (1987) *New Directions in the Study of Foreign Policy.* Boston: Allen and Unwin.

Hoon, Shim Jae (1988) "Just a Little Bit Closer." *Far Eastern Economic Review* 141 (September 15):28.

Hudson, Valerie M. (1991) *Artificial Intelligence and International Politics.* Boulder: Westview Press.

Huebner, Jon W. (1987) "The Abortive Liberation of Taiwan." *China Quarterly* 110 (June):256–275.

Inglehart, Ronald (1988) "The Renaissance of Political Culture." *American Political Science Review* 82, no. 4:1203–1230.

Jones, Clayton (1989) "China Killings Spark Muted Outcry." *Christian Science Monitor,* June 19.

Katzenstein, Lawrence (1987) *Great Disorder Under Heaven: Social Time, Conflict and the Origins of the Strategic Triangle.* Ph.D diss., Rutgers University.

Katzenstein, Lawrence (1989) "Controlling the Political Arrival of Ballistic Missile Defense." *Journal of Legislation* 15:103–114.

Katzenstein, Lawrence (1990) "An AI Model of Chinese Decision Making on the Question of Taiwan Integration." Paper presented at the annual conference of the International Studies Association, Washington, DC, August 24.

Keightley, David N. (1996) Discussion of the Ju analogy and reference to Burton Watson (1969), *Records of the Historian: Chapters from the Shi Chi and Ssuma Ch'ien* (New York: Columbia University Press). Internet communication from the University of California at Berkeley.

Kristof, Nicholas D. (1987) "A Mellowing Taiwan Sees a Different Mainland." *New York Times,* October 18, p. E3.

Kristof, Nicholas D. (1989) "Taiwan's Longing to Recover Mainland China Is Dwindling." *New York Times,* February 5, p. 4.

Li, Jianquan (1989) "More on Reunification of Taiwan with the Mainland." *Beijing Review* 32, no. 3 (January 16–22).

Lin, Chau-Li (1996) Discussion of Professor Chuang Wu-yua and Ming Loyalists. Internet communication from Syracuse University.

Liu, Wu-Chi (1967) "Tung Chung-shu." *Encyclopedia of Philosophy,* vol 7. New York: Free Press.

Needham, Joseph (1965) *Time and Eastern Man.* Glasgow: Royal Anthropological Institute.

Public Opinion Research Foundation (1990) "The Results of a Survey of Opinions Toward the June 4 Tienanmen Incident on the Part of General Residents of the Taiwan Area and Residents of the Taiwan Area Who Have Visited Relatives on the Mainland." Taipei: China Reunification Alliance.

Rokeach, Milton (1960) *The Open and Closed Mind.* New York: Basic Books.

Ronan, Colin (1977) *The Shorter Science and Civilization in China,* vol 1. Cambridge: Cambridge University Press.

Snyder, Richard, H. W. Bruck, and Burton Sapin (1969) "The Decision-Making Approach to the Study of International Politics." In *International Politics and Foreign Policy,* edited by James N. Rosenau. New York: Free Press.

Southerland, Daniel (1988) "Beijing, in Message of Condolence to Taiwan, Praises Chiang Ching-kuo." *Washington Post,* July 15, p. A27.

Spence, Jonathan D. (1990) *The Search for Modern China.* New York: W. W. Norton.

Stover, Leon E., and Takeo K. Stover (1976) *China: An Anthropological Perspective.* Pacific Palisades, CA: Goodyear.

Sullivan, Michael (1996) Discussion on work of Larry Sullivan and Frank Hsiao indicating the CCP and KMT to be part of China Proper or very important until the 1940s. Internet communication from University of Wisconsin–Milwaukee.

Tien, Hung-Mao (1989) *The Great Transition: Political and Social Change in the Republic of China.* Stanford, CA: Hoover Institution Press.

Weng, Byron S. J. (1987) "The Hong Kong Model of 'One Country, Two Systems': Promises and Problems." *Asian Affairs* 14, no. 4.

Wu, Hsin-hsing (1995) "The Dynamics of Cross-Strait Political Interaction: Compromise and Confrontation." *Issues and Studies* vol. 31 no. 6, pp. 65–97.

4

Myth and NAFTA: The Use of Core Values in U.S. Politics

Hellmut Lotz

How did Americans ever acquiesce to NAFTA? Polling data show that the Gore-Perot debate was crucial in swaying American public opinion on NAFTA. Mexico, to most Americans, is "foreign"; traditionally, it would not be seen as either possible or desirable to link U.S. economic fate and U.S. laws to such an alien culture. By analyzing the rhetoric of the Gore-Perot debate, Lotz is able to show how Gore successfully outmaneuvered Perot and recast the American Dream to make NAFTA seem a natural extension of it.

—Editor

This is a choice between the politics of fear and the politics of hope. It's a choice between the past and the future. It's a choice between pessimism and optimism. . . . We're not scared.

—Al Gore (*Larry King Live,* 1993)

Looking at the *Congressional Record* on NAFTA, as well as the public debate, one will quickly identify myth as an important means of communication. Politicians use stories to illustrate their points of view. When stories evoke historic memories pertaining to values and symbols, I classify them as myth. Note that this meaning does not require a myth to be fictitious. Neither, of course, must myth be true. The significance of myth is rather that it helps the members of a society to produce a common interpretation of the world in a situation where many individuals possess little information. My thesis is simple: Politicians who are rivals for public approval will resort to myths in order to capitalize on a society's core values. They attempt to define an issue by relating commonly understood symbols to the problems in question. Successful politicians wield symbols that represent the core beliefs of a society, thus shaping public opinion. The outcome of these attempts to shape public opinion in turn have a great impact on the available policy options.

In this context, the debate started by the U.S. ratification process of NAFTA deserves special attention because of the vast cultural differences, the different levels of industrial and infrastructural development, and the historical conflicts between Mexico and the United States. The complexity of the issue provides special opportunities for the user of myth. As NAFTA is not the result of a typical Cold War power-politics decision, but an attempt to improve the economic situation of Canada, Mexico, and the United States, the agreement is linked more closely to domestic concerns than many foreign policy decisions. To be more precise, since the focus of the dispute over NAFTA was its impact on U.S. workers, voters perceived a strong personal interest in the agreement.

On the other hand, NAFTA is an attempt to resolve very complicated problems that relate to global trends in the international economy and are far removed from the daily experience of "average" citizens in the United States. The tension thus evolved from tangible, clear-cut interests, and a complicated environment that created difficulties for politicians who needed to explain their reasoning to constituents. Compounding the circumstances was that NAFTA is the first free trade agreement ever to involve G7 and developing nations, and this involvement contributed to the contentious atmosphere of the NAFTA dispute. Whether those unprecedented arrangements were perceived to be advantageous or detrimental was a question of the understanding individuals used to interpret the world. Thus, the evaluation of NAFTA became very controversial. This conflict culminated in the TV debate between Vice-President Al Gore and Ross Perot on the *Larry King Live* show on November 9, 1993.

In their effort to reach out to the broad public during the NAFTA ratification process, proponents as well as opponents of the agreement employed myths. These myths must be analyzed both as cognitive maps and as instruments to recruit political support in order to understand the efforts of a nation adjusting to a rapidly transforming world. The identity of a people determines its initial perception of other cultures, peoples, and states. Such myths as American Exceptionalism, Manifest Destiny, the American Dream, and the values of the Declaration of Independence, the Constitution, and the Bill of Rights constitute in large measure the social and political identity of the United States (Smith, 1978: vii–xiv). In the process, they contribute to a collective understanding of the United States' international environment. Consequently, I pursue the following questions:

- Which myths were used by the disputants to appeal to the "American people's" understanding of the international environment in general and their Mexican neighbors in particular?
- How were those myths applied and altered to suit the situation and the interests of the political actors?
- Why was one disputant's use of myth more successful than his opponent's?

This chapter is roughly divided into four sections, which are dedicated to (1) the explanation of the theory of myth as developed in philosophy, anthropology, history, and the humanities; (2) U.S. myths; (3) a description of the Gore/Perot debate on *Larry King Live;* and (4) an analysis that explains the impact of the debate on public opinion.

This essay shows how cultural legacy determines our attempts to make sense of our environment. Investigating the role of myth with reference to NAFTA allows me to illustrate the merits and the limitations of myth as an explanatory variable, while observing its interaction with other variables (Vaughan, 1992:174). Most important, focusing on myth as an independent variable is an elegant way to study the role of culture in foreign policy because I can avoid the methodological and ideological traps that limit national character studies. An analysis of something like the "essence of American character" would have to be guided by intuition. Consequently, the underlying standards would be subject to a great degree of variance. In contrast, the analysis of rhetoric pertaining to an issue like an international treaty is clearly focused. The object of investigation is identified and observable as myths manifest themselves in communication. Further, it is not necessary for my purposes to analyze the origins of a culture or a myth. Rather, it is sufficient to identify the existence of a myth in order to evaluate its effects on foreign policy.

THE THEORY OF MYTH

Myths are a system of human understanding (Cassirer, 1964b). Constituted socially, they are vital to the cohesiveness of a group. They explain the position of the individual in relation to his physical and social environment. In the process, myths provide simplified models or *cognitive maps* to understand a complex environment. By merging "concept and emotion," myths are powerful historical memories that help maintain the values of a community.

Myths are communicated as narratives that pertain to values. Every myth is supported by a large variety of stories that are commonly accepted by a society if they relate to historic experience. The relevance of myths lies in their ability to gain broad acceptance by a community, rather than their degree of rationality or realism. It is irrelevant whether the myth is true or false.

Since myth is used to explain the world on the basis of shared meaning, it is a cultural variable. A society's myths are obviously not the results of a natural process. Yet myths naturally foster the understanding of the world we live in. The community's perception of its own role and its environment is constituted by its myths. Every myth is one possible, but not necessary, interpretation of our perception. Since myth fosters the creation of a system of meaning, myth is one foundation of culture.

Myth is a concept that is commonly applied in anthropology, the study of ancient cultures, and throughout the humanities. It is commonly used to analyze premodern societies and their cultural heritage. But Griswold (1994) and Cassirer (1945) point out that myth is not restricted to premodern societies.[1]

Griswold explains that myths as stories shared orally by narrators were the dominant form of communication across time and space before the invention of the phonetic alphabet (Griswold, 1994:140–141). As literacy became more prevalent with the invention of the phonetic alphabet, the influence of narrators diminished. However, myth was not completely eliminated. On the contrary, radio and television provide a new forum for narrators today. Thus, the influence of myth increases in the postmodern telecommunications society, as Cassirer witnessed as a victim of Nazi propaganda.

Cassirer's Philosophy of Understanding and Myth

Myth became a central element of Ernst Cassirer's (1874–1945) philosophy, which he developed to interpret the political events of his lifetime. As a Kantian,[2] Cassirer held a positive attitude toward modernity. For a long time, he was convinced that science was an unconquerable bulwark against superstition and that myth and its phenomena were reserved for premodern societies. Witnessing the efficiency of national-socialistic propaganda, Cassirer reevaluated his concept of myth and pointed out that myth is always present in human understanding.

Symbol is the foundation of Cassirer's philosophy. He assumes language, art, and myth as symbolic forms. Thus, they are intellectual spheres[3] that ultimately pertain to physical reality. Further, he points out that to understand their environment, which is necessary for accessing reality, individuals depend on symbolic forms (Cassirer, 1964c:3). Symbols are the medium between understanding and reality. A study of symbols will therefore explain how we assign meaning to our perceptions. Cassirer's concept of meaning is not supposed to be an extension of epistemology. Rather, epistemology is a component of understanding.

Myth is a symbolic form that precedes scientific understanding. It is irrational, unreflected, and uncritical, but it is a necessary level in the process of understanding. According to Cassirer, science has to understand that myth is not its external opponent but rather its historical predecessor in an organic sense. Only this understanding enables science to fulfill its mission to eliminate myth and replace it with knowledge (Cassirer, 1964b:x–xii).[4]

Originally, the challenge as Cassirer perceived it was to overcome myth by exposing our natural understanding of the world to critical thought. Having experienced the skillful application of myths by the national-socialist government, he came to realize that mythical understanding was able to overpower scientific understanding even in modern times. Cassirer concluded that myth could only be counterbalanced by *logos,* but it could not be destroyed in human culture (Cassirer, 1944a: 246). Applying Karl Bühler's language theory, Cassirer explained that ordinary speech always has both descriptive and emotional functions that compete and cooperate with each other. The modern magician-politician manages to destroy this equilibrium and places the whole emphasis on the emotional side. "The descriptive and logical word was transformed into the magical word" (Cassirer, 1944a:255–256).

According to Cassirer, myths always have two characteristics. First, they are the outgrowth of collective wishes. If central desires of a community cannot be fulfilled by rational means, the modern human might abandon rationality in favor of myth (Cassirer, 1944a:251). Second, myths are both an outgrowth of despair and confidence. The attitude may best be described as, "We may have failed, but a higher power will succeed on our behalf."

Myth and Contemporary Epistemology

This interpretation of national-socialism illustrates only the complete abandonment of rationality. But the power of myth is also present in times of relative stability. The dual character of ordinary language, including descriptive and emotional elements, suggests that the emotional component includes a potential for myth at all times. For example, applying Kuhn's explanation of scientific knowledge as conventionalist, one may deny that the elimination of myth in science is possible. Kuhn's definition of science as a social rather than an objective enterprise (Kuhn, 1970) illuminates why science is only an extension of myth. Both science and myth rest on the convention of a society. While myths need to be shared by society—a nation or a tribe, for example—the principles of science must be accepted by the scientific community. Even if one were to concede that science emancipates itself from myth by establishing explicit, rigorous standards, the conclusion is clear. The difference between science and myth is not dependability but the critical quality of science, which questions results and rests on explicit standards. Therefore, the difference is a matter of degree; it is not fundamental. From a pragmatic point of view, this difference in degree changes the world dramatically, but it does not produce certainty. Science retains its power to reduce—but not eliminate—the mythical components of human understanding. According to Cassirer, our understanding of the world is always somewhat mythical.

Structuralism and Deconstruction

Structuralism, a theory developed by the linguist Ferdinand de Saussure (1857–1913), explains our inability to escape myth with a theory of symbols.[5] According to Saussure, it is language that guides our discovery and interpretation of reality. Language is a system of signs related to each other. This system makes sense of the world and is handed down through socialization.[6] "Whatever we perceive or experience must happen in relation to our sign systems (like language) or they mean nothing" (Cowles, 1994b:88). In other words, we do not see the physical world but rather signs that belong to a system.

The sign system in use is one possible, but not necessary, interpretation of the world. Colors, for example, are a straightforward physical phenomenon. Yet Latin designates gold, red, saffron, and turquoise as *rufus* (Eco, 1985:158–159), while contemporary English finds at least four terms for this group of colors. Another impressive example that supports structuralism is delivered by Gestalt psychology. Dual-image pictures contain two exclusive images. Two observers can look at the same sheet of paper, examine the same lines, and yet see two different images. The object identified depends on the signs the observer recognizes.

Structuralism is commonly used to interpret art objects and literature. It is also used by anthropologists, who base their interpretation on the analysis of the sign systems used by the society under scrutiny. Claude Lévi-Strauss, probably the most prominent anthropologist to apply structuralist theory, argues that the opposition between history and myth is constructed. In his analysis of Canadian Indian myths, he concludes that the telling of myth is very much like writing history. In his view, a study of mythical structures will lead to a better understanding of what history is all about. He insists that the historian, just like the myth- or storyteller, is subject to such influences as individual interests, tribal or national bonds, different intellectual traditions, etc. Thus, different historians may produce written historical records on the same issue with different content. Lévi-Strauss asks why one should demand consistency among different myths if historical accounts cannot meet this standard. Thus, he concludes that history is not a separation from myth, but rather a continuation of myth (Lévi-Strauss, 1979:40–43). His explanation of myth as a precursor of history matches Cassirer's concept of mythical understanding as a precursor of science.

Considering that both science and history maintain mythical elements, it is comprehensible that even democratic nations bound to law and justice cannot do without myths. Myths are needed because they are the means that consume the least amount of resources in an attempt to rally a people behind a common cause. Democracies employ symbols, such as flags, patriotic songs, the robes of judges, and freedom shrines, that are demonstrated ritually in parades and the like. Constitutions assume the role of "holy writ" (Robertson, 1994:65). Pure rationality would not be strong enough to produce the sacrifice every state must enforce on the individual in order to survive a crisis such as war. Thus, it is not surprising that U.S. society has hosted and fostered a number of myths from its colonial genesis to the present.

THE UNITED STATES AND MYTH

Many U.S. values are closely connected to the nation-building process, while others are rooted in more recent experiences, such as the Vietnam War. U.S. values have been commented on by both residents and foreigners since the Revolutionary War (1774–1783). While the origin of a U.S. social identity is disputed, there is considerable agreement on the core of U.S. values: individual liberty and equality of opportunity (Almond, 1960). Since I evaluate the consequences of political rhetoric, an analysis of values is necessary (though an explanation of their origin is not).

Early publications about the North American colonies were often promotional pamphlets that attempted to attract settlers. They promised a better life by contrasting the shortcomings of the Old World with the promises of the New World. On the other hand, Puritan preachers or humanist philanthropists provided philosophy they considered necessary to ensure the success of their experiments to create a better world in America. Dolan points out that the Puritan settlement of North America needs to be interpreted as part of the Protestant movement. After the Bible had become accessible to the public through translation into the vernacular, one was able to learn the will of God directly. Emulating the biblical example, a covenant people could be reestablished in a new, empty world that was not tainted as Europe was (Dolan, 1994:12–30).

Whether the settlers came for religious or other reasons, they left Europe to improve their situation. They perceived America as the New World, ready to be transformed according to their own wishes. New was better than old, and if one believed in the restoration of God's people constituted by covenant—as John Winthrop explained in his famous speech on the *Ar-*

bella in 1630—then these people were morally superior. The covenant also implied a minimalist educational standard. The ability to learn God's will by reading the Bible is sufficient for individuals to make their own choices.

The sense of a new beginning was probably strongest for those who had gone to America for religious reasons. The emigration of religious groups, such as the Quakers and Puritans, to North America was intended to produce a better, if not ideal, society. "Wee shall be as a Citty upon a Hill," admonished John Winthrop (Boorstin, 1958:3). From the very beginning, America was to set itself apart from the Old World—to be exceptional. At the same time, it was to be an example to the world of God's might, furthering the obedient elect and destroying those that violate God's ways.

Works by revolutionary authors like Crèvecoeur, Thomas Paine, Benjamin Franklin, and Thomas Jefferson sought to establish standards for a New World, as well as proclaim the ethical foundation that justified their war against England. They referred to the ideas of Enlightenment philosophers, most prominently Locke, Montesquieu, and Rousseau. For example, Rousseau's doctrine of the superiority of nature reinforced the sense of exceptionalism, since a new society was closer to the natural state than the Old World. Benjamin Franklin helped to secularize exceptionalism by providing for a success ethic that perceived wealth as the fruit of individual virtue. He also made appeals to common sense popular, implying that the truth was accessible to anyone and not reserved for elites. Populism later postulated the superiority of the man on the street's common sense over the elaborate education of elites.

The Declaration of Independence explained that governmental power needs to derive from citizen consent and stressed individual rights, particularly life, liberty, and the pursuit of happiness. This emphasis was reinforced by including in the Constitution a list of guaranteed civil liberties: the Bill of Rights. The attempt to establish a government according to rational and democratic principles redefined the country's mission. Thus, the Puritan religious experiment had evolved into an Enlightenment project either in the name of rationality or secular democracy.

While this description is not complete, it is clear that central U.S. values can be traced to the colonial and early national period. Individualism, the freedom to make choices, opportunity, the association of new with progress, and American Exceptionalism were all present. Most of these values were subject to more or less fundamental change throughout U.S. history. For example, the prescriptions of what the country ought to be became much more secular and focused on individual opportunity rather than on religious obligations, thus furthering the development of the contemporary American Dream.

Ever since the Revolutionary War, American ideals have been used as an agent of change to challenge U.S. power structures in behalf of underprivileged segments of the society. Such was the case in the struggle for a universal white male franchise, women's rights, and racial issues. During the nineteenth century, this was a matter of political rhetoric and private initiative. Since World War II, we have witnessed a number of cases where the judiciary would protect and, in a sense, create civil rights for African Americans and women. Thus, the American Dream became a self-fulfilling prophecy for many, legitimizing the demands for equality.

The American Dream, consisting of individualism, equal opportunity, and the right to pursue happiness, is a powerful myth because so many families in the United States share the emigration experience. Grandparents tell their offspring how they left Britain, Germany, Poland, Ireland, Italy, Japan, and many other countries[7] to find a better life. They tell stories of hardships and discrimination that were overcome with the healing power of hard work, which eventually bought them their own home and a college education for some of their children. With pride they help make some of their own mayor, governor, or even president of the United States. The hardships of immigrating generations and their success coupled optimism with individualism.

Politicians referring to the American Dream use language like "opportunity for American families," "the man on the street," "jobs," or "standard of living." They like to stress the opportunity for individuals to "make a difference," and to "do better" than their parents. Often politicians like to argue by example rather than in abstract terms when they talk of the American Dream. They tell stories about their own or their friends' families or about people they met on the campaign trail to illustrate how their policies would further opportunities for Americans.

For the philosophically minded, American Exceptionalism was originally linked to the promotion of ideas. America was to establish a divine, later rational or democratic, political order. Considering the practical consequences, we can observe a close relationship between the American Dream and American Exceptionalism. The common element is the individual who is to have opportunity, according to the American Dream, and who possesses rights, under the Constitution. The American Dream set America apart from the rest of the world. For many decades, America was unique because it offered unprecedented opportunities to the individual. In a way, American Exceptionalism is a derivative of the American Dream.

When politicians use American Exceptionalism, they refer to the unsurpassed power and greatness of the United States. They list the nation's successes, such as World War II, or technological innovations, like flying to the moon. They stress the universality of democracy, the rule of law, and the inalienability of human rights and claim that nowhere else are individual rights as well protected as in the United States. By relating personal experiences, U.S. greatness is contrasted with the shortcomings of other nations, or their moral indebtedness to the United States. Superlatives are an important rhetorical means. "The greatest nation in the world," "the greatest economy in the world," "the people that enjoys the most freedom," "nowhere else on the face of the earth," and "the only remaining superpower" are phrases that are commonly used to appeal to an audience by the use of American Exceptionalism.

However, Exceptionalism has two contradictory versions: Isolationism and Leadership. Isolationism fears the vulnerability of America's uniqueness through exposure to an alien and corrupt environment. On the other hand, American Exceptionalism also justifies American Leadership in the world by proclaiming a mission for the United States. Proponents of Leadership focus on America's moral strength and political power to spread and protect the American way of life, including democracy, market economy, and individualism, in less fortunate areas of the world. Like the American Dream, Leadership is optimistic and assumes equality among humans, while Isolationism is pessimistic and makes a qualitative distinction between Americans and foreigners.

One last American myth must be mentioned. Almond and Verba (1963) identified the Democratic myth. According to them, the Democratic myth is the belief that an attentive constituency controls its political representatives with a threat to remove them from office if they do not perform according to the expectations of the people. In a broader sense, the Democratic myth refers to the will of the people as the source of legitimate rule. It appeals strongly to the value of equality. Populism, a more radical form of this myth, interprets democracy to be literally the rule of the people. Populists are quick to detect a conflict between a constituency and its representatives or other elites. In the opinion of populists, common sense and experience are superior to the knowledge of specialized elites.

There are other American myths, like Manifest Destiny, that were powerful in the past but are outdated today because their aims have been achieved or abandoned. The myth of the Frontier still has a strong appeal. It is associated with innovation in technology, social reform, and enterprise. However, in the NAFTA debate, the Frontier played no role, while the American Dream, American Exceptionalism, and Populism were invoked often.

The Gore/Perot debate is an example of politicians who manipulate public opinion with arguments that appeal to the core beliefs of their society. While both debaters used American myths to make their point, Gore is clearly the winner over Perot and gains the support of the viewers. The use of myth alone does not guarantee victory for Perot. This raises the question of whether there are myths that are more powerful than others and whether different mythical arguments are compatible with one another.

FOREIGN POLICY AND PUBLIC OPINION

To determine the significance of the Gore/Perot debate, it is necessary to outline the role of public opinion in U.S. foreign policy. Ideally, politicians derive a policy mandate from public opinion. The corresponding prescription of a representative democracy demands politically informed rational-active citizens who vote on the basis of issues. A coherent set of policy preferences is matched with an accurate perception of the candidates' stands on issues. Rational-active citizens cast their votes in favor of the candidate who best reflects the "voter's issue preferences" (Erikson, Luttberg, and Tedin, 1991:14–15). According to this concept, politicians will realize their private interests if voters do not exercise control over their political representatives with their votes.

Almond and Verba (1963) derived from their comparative study the conclusion that even the United States, a country with a long democratic history, lacks rational-active citizens. They explained that a democratic government must have both the power to govern and the dependency to be responsible to the governed. If every person were a rational-active citizen, governmental power would soon be lamed. Nonetheless, the awareness by both the elite and citizens that a potential of participation may be realized produces power enough to guarantee responsive, efficient government. This awareness rests on two pillars: It is supported by values that are shared by the elite and the citizens; and participation is frequently witnessed to be successful in altering government output. In other words, governmental accountability rests rather on potential than on actual voter behavior (Almond and Verba, 1963:480–487). This implies that policymakers have some space to maneuver before they will be punished by the electorate for ignoring public opinion.

In foreign policy, that space is often considerably greater than for many domestic issues because of the low level of information sought by the electorate. A Times Mirror Center study determined in 1990, for example, that only 8 percent of those in the age group 18–29, 12 percent in the age group 30–49, and 17 percent of those 50 and older followed the news about the political changes in the Soviet Union (Times Mirror Center, 1990:7). While the age group 30–49 pays considerable attention to domestic issues, their interest drops sharply when it comes to international news (Times Mirror Center, 1990:4). Edelman (1974:6–7), who used structuralism to interpret politics, points out another consequence of an information deficit—it leads to a more emotional response by the public.

Almond (1960:54) calls public opinion in the United States that pertains to foreign policy "mood . . . essentially an unstable phenomenon." He found that U.S. citizens perceive less of a personal interest in international issues. Rather than developing "views and opinion resting on some kind of intellectual structure," opinion concerning foreign policy is subject to "frequent alteration in response to changes in events" (Almond, 1960:53). He attributes the lack of attention to foreign policy issues to the preoccupation of the U.S. public with private affairs. Nonetheless, interest increases dramatically if a crisis is perceived. Consequently, Almond finds sudden increases of attention when threatening events occur in the international theater. However, as the Cold War persisted, Almond recorded a change in public opinion. U.S. citizens during the Cold War attributed more importance to foreign policy independent of particular crises (Almond, 1960:xxii).

In a post–Cold War study, Almond's findings are supported. Aldrich, Sullivan, and Borgida (1993) point out that voters have strong attitudes about foreign politics in general, in spite of the low level of information they possess about specific international issues. Foreign issues have been mentioned by voters as "among the most important problems facing the nation" in all elections for which appropriate data are available. General foreign policy attitudes were successfully exploited by Ronald Reagan in the Republican primaries for president in Florida, for example (Aldrich, Sullivan, and Borgida, 1993:179–181).

Public Opinion in U.S. Foreign Policy: The Controversy over Contra Aid (Sobel, 1993) aims to explain how a gap between public opinion and actual foreign policy can persist without a voter backlash. Between 1981 and 1990, Reagan provided aid to the Nicaraguan contras in spite of disapproval rates that were higher than the approval rate among the U.S. public at any time during that period. As the public became more aware, the disapproval rose from 32 percent in 1981 to 66 percent in 1982, according to Gallup opinion polls. Until 1990, disapproval remained high, between 43 percent and 64 percent (Roth and Sobel, 1993:21–24).

Sobel concludes that public opinion cannot determine foreign policy but does place restrictions on it that must be heeded. He defines public opinion as a composite of partisanship, ideology, the climate of opinion, presidential popularity, and support or opposition to specific policies, which is "the system of guidance and constraint on policy" (Sobel, 1993:275). Presidential approval rates may enable the president to enforce his policies in the legislature in spite of public opposition to a specific policy. Legislators may also be free to ignore national sentiments as long as they heed public opinion in their districts. Further, Sobel explains that disapproval as expressed in an opinion poll puts constraints on a policy because the legislators will be very careful not to cross the line that may activate the rational-active citizen potential. While the legislature did not stop Reagan, its support was limited. Congress never formally endorsed President Reagan's Nicaraguan policy, it passed declarations of qualified disapproval, and it did not provide sufficient funding for the contras. Ronald Reagan's administration was forced to come up with unconventional money sources that eventually led to the Iran-Contra affair.

While public opinion plays a role in curbing foreign policy, the president can also use public opinion to wrest consent for his foreign policy from Congress (Dahl, 1950:108). In the case of NAFTA, however, Clinton had to first gain public approval for the trade agreement. He had profited somewhat from the labor opposition against NAFTA during his presidential campaign but was generally in favor of a free trade accord with Mexico. After gaining the presidency, his administration complemented NAFTA with side agreements targeting the environmental and labor opposition. Nonetheless, labor resistance did not decline but rather was joined by Ross Perot's publicity campaign against NAFTA. USA-NAFTA, an alliance of corporations, tried to offset Perot's efforts but did not achieve the desired results. On the contrary, as disapproval for NAFTA rose from 33 percent to 41 percent in September 1993 (Harbrecht and Garland, 1993:34), Richard Gephardt, House majority leader, turned publicly against the agreement. It became evident that President Clinton had to fight for every vote in Congress to realize his policy preference.

Attempting to reverse the tide against the trade accord, USA-NAFTA sought to recruit prominent business leaders such as Lee Iacocca to debate Ross Perot on television. Apprehensive of possible labor retaliation against their corporations, Iacocca and others refused. Because the vote on the implementation legislation was close in the House of Representatives, the White House decided to challenge Perot to a TV debate with the vice-president, Al Gore. The debate took place on November 9, 1993, nine days before Congress voted on the ratification. It was assumed that President Clinton was more than thirty votes short of the necessary majority in the House (Lambro, 1993) to pass the implementation legislation for NAFTA, but he was narrowing the gap. Thus, the outcome of the ratification vote was very uncertain on November 9.

ANALYSIS OF THE GORE VERSUS PEROT DEBATE

I conducted a content analysis of the Gore/Perot debate using a transcript CNN provided on Lexis-Nexis (*Larry King Live,* 1993). Coding mythical rhetoric is challenging insofar as myths are ideas that pertain to abstract values, but the rhetoric argues with examples. This means that one can talk about the American Dream that is about individualism, equality, and opportunity without ever using the words *individualism, equality,* or *opportunity.* The challenge is to find out which explicit language invokes implicit myths. In the case of the Gore/Perot debate, I classified an argument as belonging to the American Dream whenever there was a reference to the availability of jobs to U.S. workers or a reference to the standard of living. To both Gore and Perot, jobs are the means that provide opportunity. All three of Perot's statements that I assign to the American Dream category assert that U.S. workers will lose jobs. When Gore attributes an increase in jobs to NAFTA or free trade, I classify the event as use of the American Dream myth. I also included stories into the American Dream category, such as those Gore uses to illustrate that Mexicans have the same aspirations as U.S. citizens and admire them as well as their products. Gore's account of a shopping frenzy in the world's largest Wal-Mart store in Mexico City is such a case.

When Perot connected the vulnerability of the United States and job loss with conditions in Mexico or elsewhere abroad, I categorized the argument as the Isolationism version of American Exceptionalism. This includes stories about slums created by the investment of U.S. corporations and about the birth of brainless children because of U.S. toxic waste in Mexico. Arguments that appealed to U.S. strength as a means to remedy deficiencies were assigned to the American Leadership category of American Exceptionalism. For example, Gore acknowledges problems with the Mexican political system but promotes NAFTA as an institution that will allow the United States to exercise more influence in behalf of democratization and environmental protection there.

Populism was the relevant category if there was a reference to the democratic process or an elite versus the people antagonism. Perot's claim to be the outsider who cannot buy network advertising time for his cause, his accusation of foreign lobbyism to conspire in behalf of NAFTA, and his threat of voter retaliation are cases of appeal to Populism. Gore's populist stories usually discredit Perot's populist claims by attacking Perot personally as a rich hypocrite who has not disclosed his anti-NAFTA campaign's finances and who owns his private free trade zone, etc.

Applying these coding rules, I found that Gore and Perot both appealed to an almost identical set of myths, which included the American Dream, American Exceptionalism, and Populism (see Figure 4.1). Note, however, that Isolationism, a branch of American Exceptionalism, is Perot's most frequently used myth, while Gore does not use it at all. Also, Gore uses the American Dream eight times, whereas Perot uses it only three times. The numbers suggest that the American Dream is Gore's main myth and Isolationism Perot's. Since the American Dream, being the original and core myth of the United States, is more powerful than its derivation Isolationism, we can attribute the difference of focus to be the primary source of Gore's success and Perot's defeat. Isolationism is but one version of American Exceptionalism, which is, in turn, one aspect of the central myth, the American Dream. Further, Leadership was used by Gore four times and once by Perot. Since Leadership

Figure 4.1
Occurrences of Myth

| | Primary Myth | Secondary Myth | | |
| | American Dream | American Exceptionalism | | Populism |
		Isolationism	Leadership	
Gore	8	0	4 (2)*	4
Perot	3	6	1	5

*Gore referred twice to American strength without linking it to America's mission.

is positive and inclusive, it is compatible with the American Dream. While Isolationism is supposed to protect the American Dream, it is negative and exclusive and therefore incompatible with the American Dream. A detailed analysis will demonstrate that the antagonism becomes obvious when Isolationism is opposed with the American Dream. Before undertaking this analysis, it is useful to note (see Figure 4.2) the results of a panel study conducted by Gallup on the reaction of the audience to the debate (Gallup, 1993b).[8]

Job Creation Versus Job Loss

Perot and Gore both employed American Dream stories and arguments. A comparison, however, reveals major differences. Gore's stories are about job creation, while Perot talks about job loss (see Figure 4.3). While Gore is optimistic, Perot talks about a negative future with NAFTA. Perot's emphasis on pessimism, combined with the fact that he referred to the American Dream only three times, reveals that the American Dream was only a platform to support Isolationism. Gore, on the other hand, concentrated on the American Dream and repeated his most important message—NAFTA creates jobs—eight times. I believe the conceptual opposition between the American Dream and Isolationism is a major reason 60 percent of the respondents in the panel study said that Gore communicated better with them (Perot, 34 percent).

Heroes Versus Victims

Gore's American Dream stories were about American heroes. He shared how the organized labor worker Gordon Thompson would profit from the removal of tariffs and the sale of additional cars to Mexico. Gore could also cite the testimony of archetypical heroes of the

Figure 4.2
Who Is Doing a Better Job?

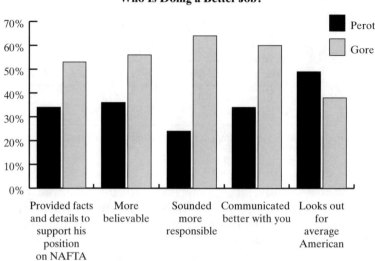

Figure 4.3
American Dream Versus American Dream

Gore	Perot
• 8 occurrences	• 3 occurrences
• Main emphasis	• Platform to Isolationism
• Positive/optimistic	• Negative/pessimistic

Figure 4.4
American Dream Versus Isolationism

Gore	Perot
• American heroes, man on the street, and prominent Americans	• Mexican victims (condescending and repugnant)

American Dream—former presidents, Nobel Prize winners in economics, Lee Iacocca, and Colin Powell—in favor of NAFTA.

Perot's Isolationism leads him to focus on Mexican victims (see Figure 4.4). The most radical statement was Perot's interpretation of the Mexican Dream: to have an outhouse and running water. Even though Perot asserted that he had an interest in the improvement of Mexican living and human rights standards, he appears to be condescending. The stories he shares are so repugnant that they "feel" incredible whether they are true or not. Consequently, 53 percent of the panel respondents were of the opinion that Gore had provided facts and details better than Perot, who had the support of only 34 percent of respondents.

Strength Versus Vulnerability

Gore attacked Perot's Isolationism with Leadership, which was especially effective because both Isolationism and Leadership are versions of Exceptionalism. As Isolationism dwells on vulnerability, Leadership stresses America's mission (see Figure 4.5). The message that America's strength working through NAFTA is the remedy for the problems Perot mentioned was positive and therefore more pleasant. Further, Perot's message was divisive, since the villains who oppressed Mexican victims included corporate America. Gore's leadership solution avoided alienating important segments of the U.S. population, thereby keeping the audience united as U.S. citizens. With Leadership, Gore offered an alternative that addresses the same issues as Isolationism, while allowing American Exceptionalism to be compatible with the American Dream.

The Struggle to Claim Experience and Common Sense

Perot's claim to be the political outsider naturally led him to the use of Populism. He used Populism almost as often as Isolationism (five times, see Figure 4.6). Anticipating Perot's appeal to Populism, Gore claimed Populism for himself in the debate before his opponent could. He explicitly appropriated Perot's language appealing to "experience" and "common sense." Gore used "experience" to link free trade with jobs and Perot with the Great Depression. Thus, Gore simultaneously depreciated

Figure 4.5
Leadership Versus Isolationism

Gore	Perot
• Mission	• Vulnerability
• Strong united America	• Divisiveness

Figure 4.6
Populism Versus Populism

Gore	Perot
• Experience	• Outside image
• Common sense	• The people know best

the value Populism may have had for his opponent and associated his own position with opportunity and the American Dream and Perot's with the Great Depression. When Perot chimed in on "experience" and "common sense," he came in second. Nonetheless, in the course of the debate, he managed to style himself as the champion of the U.S. worker's interest. Perot attacked past trade agreements and lobbyism. The fact that NAFTA was unpopular was a more valid evaluation of the agreement according to Perot than the judgment of economists, politicians, and celebrities. Perot's appeal to common sense and his interest in job security for average U.S. workers were convincing. Gore was on the defensive with reference to Populism but exercised effective damage control by pointing out Perot's personal inconsistency with his message—his billionaire status, and so forth. In the end, 49 percent of the viewers sampled granted Perot the edge on looking out for average U.S. citizens, while 38 percent believed Gore did a better job in this category.

Threats Versus Optimism

In his closing statement, Perot referred to Populism and threatened legislators who would vote for NAFTA. Gore took the opportunity to contrast once again Perot's pessimism with Gore's own message of hope and self-confidence (see Figure 4.7). Gore used the inclusive first person plural, while Perot segregated between the people (good, owners of the country) and legislators (morally corrupt, unfaithful servants). Gore explicitly labeled his own view a message of hope and Perot's a message of fear. Thus, Gore managed to confront Populism with the stronger American Dream myth. Populism is an appealing argument in U.S. politics, but an insider/outsider dichotomy must necessarily be divisive and aggressively critical and therefore antagonistic to the primary myth of the American Dream, which is egalitarian, optimistic, and inclusive.

Political Consequences

Gallup tracked public opinion about NAFTA over several months. In a poll taken between November 2 and November 4, 46 percent of the population opposed NAFTA, while only 38 percent supported the agreement (Gallup, 1993a:11).[9] The debate was crucial for the White House to gain momentum for the recruitment of additional votes in the House of Representatives. In the panel study that sampled viewers of the debate, favorability of NAFTA increased among viewers from 34 percent before the debate to 57 percent after the debate. Opposition stayed stable at 38 percent before and 36 percent after the debate. "No opinion" answers decreased from 28 percent to 7 percent (see Figures 4.8 and 4.9). While there had been little or no change among supporters and opponents of

Figure 4.7
American Dream Versus Populism

Gore	Perot
• Contrasts U.S. qualities such as optimism and strength with Perot's defeatism	• Is threatening, revengeful, negative

Figure 4.8
Opinion of Viewers Before Debate

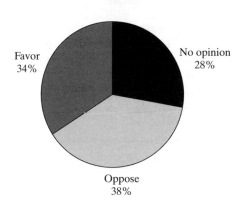

Figure 4.9
Opinion of Viewers After Debate

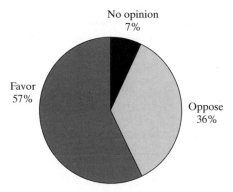

NAFTA, *almost three out of four undecided viewers had followed Gore's argumentation.* The impact on the entire U.S. population was considerably less, but the president had regained the momentum in public opinion. Most members of Congress who announced their support of NAFTA after November 9 specifically referred to Gore's convincing performance. Gore had provided an example of how to defeat the opposition should their voting record on NAFTA become an issue in the 1994 elections. After his defeat, Perot's threat seemed less menacing. In this positive climate, the president was able to employ more traditional means to recruit support in Congress, such as providing exemptions for certain agricultural regions and crops or compensation for the negative impact of NAFTA in key congressional districts.

CONCLUSION

Al Gore's successful use of myth and Ross Perot's failure demonstrate that myth alone does not guarantee convincing mass communication. Both debaters employed the American Dream but in different ways. While the American Dream was the centerpiece of Gore's argument, for Perot it only served as the link to American Isolationism. Perot's Isolationism focused on values that were incompatible with elements of the American Dream. Perot might have been able to persuade a majority if he had not been opposed with a myth that was closer to the core beliefs of the U.S. public.

Different myths need not be consistent with one another even if they are shared by the same society. The underlying values of myths can exclude one another to some degree. Therefore, it is imperative for the political actor who attempts to manipulate public opinion to identify those myths that are the core of a society's beliefs, which in this case was the American Dream myth in the United States. Politicians who choose to employ a peripheral myth, such as American Isolationism, which contains elements inconsistent with the core myth, expose themselves to the danger of being countered with the more powerful core myth. The struggle to define an issue in one's own terms is a race to link the issue to the core values of a society. It is imperative to beat opponents to the high ground of core beliefs.

On the other hand, Gore's effective application of American Leadership illustrates the conditions for a successful use of a peripheral myth. First, the peripheral myth should be embedded into a grand scheme of the core myth. The central argument should rest on a core myth, while additional arguments can be supported by peripheral myths. Second, while myths are not necessarily coherent with one another, an argument should be consistent. Therefore, the politician must determine whether a peripheral myth is compatible with the main argument and its corresponding myth. Gore was particularly fortunate, because American Leadership is a branch of American Exceptionalism in the same way as American Isolationism is, so it was especially suited to off-balance his opponent's argument.

Typically, myths are shared by a society and serve to unite that society. Hence, it is dangerous to use myths in a divisive way. Prerequisite for successful divisive application of myth is an already divided society, such as the Weimar Republic. However, this prerequisite was not present in the United States of 1993. For example, in the context of NAFTA, it is interesting that neither race nor Hispanic ancestry was a significant predictor of popular opinions of NAFTA (Times Mirror Center, 1993),[10] while African American leaders were in opposition to NAFTA and Hispanic members of Congress supported the agreement. This fact raises the question whether the U.S. public is really as divided as our leaders believe. Suffice it to say that Perot's use of divisive populist rhetoric, though persuasive to many, simply did not carry the day. His divisiveness, in the end, was not a useful instrument of manipulation.

A correlation between opinions on NAFTA and partisanship points to the limitations of myth as a concept in foreign policy analysis. While the majority of Democratic members of Congress voted against NAFTA, Democrats and Independents leaning toward the Democratic Party are more likely to support NAFTA than their Republican counter parts. Anti-NAFTA sentiments of Democrats prevail only among union members. The fact that most Democratic members of Congress follow organized labor rather than the opinion of their general constituency is better explained by the existing theories on special interest than on myth. Myth, on the other hand, illuminates Republican vulnerability to Perot and his third-party movement. While a majority of Republicans support free trade, Perot's point of view appeals to enough Republicans to spoil the party's chances for a national majority.

Most important, however, myth explains how President Clinton could win the ratification vote on NAFTA by the convincing performance of his vice-president, Al Gore. In conclusion, the exploration of political manipulation through myth is a promising avenue for theoretical and methodological advance in the study of culture and foreign policy.

NOTES

1. The interested reader may turn to Sahlins (1981), who applied structuralist theory to explain how myths change. Slotkin (1993) and Robertson (1994) applied the concept of myth to explain U.S. history.

2. Note that Cassirer perceived himself as a Kantian but did not share many of the neo-Kantian teachings as held by the Marburger Schule, associated with the term *neo-Kantian* (Krois, 1985:xvii).

3. Cassirer uses the German term *geistige Gestaltungsformen. Gestaltungsform* means a sphere in which objects may be shaped and recreated but not necessarily originated. *Geistig* can mean intellectual, spiritual, or philosophical; in its broadest sense it is understood as nonmaterial.

4. This knowledge is not true in a positive sense but is the result in Kant's sense of critical reflection, which is not satisfied until the perception of pictures (symbols) coincides with rational ideas (Cassirer, 1964c:7). Thus, it remains hypothetical, as Karl Popper teaches explicitly.

5. Edelman (1974) applied structuralism to produce a theory of politics that rests on the perception of symbols.

6. While myth is a memory shared by many individuals across a society, it has nothing to do with C. G. Jung's archetypes, but rather is transmitted by socialization.

7. The exception seems to be African Americans. Also, it is not clear yet whether Hispanic immigrants will participate successfully in the American Dream.

8. The population consisted of viewers over the age of eighteen. The sample was 357 adults. The sampling error was determined at plus or minus 6 percent in a confidence interval of 95 percent.

9. The population consists of U.S. citizens over eighteen years of age. The size of the sample is 1,003 respondents and was weighted according to the demographic averages of the last census. The sampling error was plus or minus 3 percent in a confidence interval of 95 percent.

10. *America's Place in the World* consisted of a weighted sample of 2,000 adults representing the U.S. population. The sampling error was estimated at plus or minus 2 percent in a confidence interval of 95 percent.

REFERENCES

Aldrich, John H., John L. Sullivan, and Eugene Borgida (1993) "Foreign Affairs and Issue Voting: Do Presidential Candidates Waltz Before a Blind Audience?" In *Controversies in Voting Behavior,* 3d ed., edited by Richard G. Niemi and Herbert F. Weisberg. Washington DC: *Congressional Quarterly.*

Almond, Gabriel (1960) *The American People and Foreign Policy.* Praeger: New York.

Almond, Gabriel A., and Sidney Verba (1963) *The Civic Culture: Political Attitudes and Democracy in Five Nations.* Princeton: Princeton University Press.

Boorstin, Daniel J. (1958) *The Americans: The Colonial Experience.* New York: Random House.

Boorstin, Daniel J. (1973) *The Americans: The Democratic Experience.* New York: Random House.

Cassirer, Ernst (1944a) "Philosophy and Politics." In *Symbol, Myth, and Culture—Essays by Ernst Cassirer,* edited by Donald Phillip Verene. New Haven: Yale University Press, 1979.

Cassirer, Ernst (1944b) "Judaism and Modern Political Myth." In *Symbol, Myth, and Culture—Essays by Ernst Cassirer*, edited by Donald Phillip Verene. New Haven: Yale University Press, 1979.

Cassirer, Ernst (1945) "Reflections on the Concept of Group and the Theory of Perception." In *Symbol, Myth, and Culture—Essays by Ernst Cassirer,* edited by Donald Phillip Verene. New Haven: Yale University Press, 1979.

Cassirer, Ernst (1964a) *Philosophie der Symbolischen Formen—Erster Teil: Die Sprache.* Darmstadt: Wissenschaftliche Buchgesellschaft.

Cassirer, Ernst (1964b) *Philosophie der Symbolischen Formen—Zweiter Teil: Das Mythische Denken.* Darmstadt: Wissenschaftliche Buchgesellschaft.

Cassirer, Ernst (1964c) *Philosophie der Symbolischen Formen—Dritter Teil: Phänomenologie der Erkenntnis.* Darmstadt: Wissenschaftliche Buchgesellschaft.

Cassirer, Ernst (1985) "Das Symbolproblem und seine Stellung im System der Philosophie." In *Symbol, Technik, Sprache: Aufsätze aus den Jahren 1927–1933, Ernst Cassirer,* edited by Ernst Wolfgang Orth and John Michael Krois. Hamburg: Meiner.

Cowles, David (1994a) "Deconstruction and Poststructuralism." In *The Critical Experience: Literary Reading, Writing, and Criticism,* edited by David Cowles. Dubuque, IA: Kendall/Hunt.

Cowles, David (1994b) "Structuralism." In *The Critical Experience: Literary Reading, Writing, and Criticism,* edited by David Cowles. Dubuque, IA: Kendall/Hunt.

Dahl, Robert (1950) *Congress and Foreign Policy.* New York: W. W. Norton.

Destler, I. M. (1994) "Foreign Policy Making with the Economy at Center Stage." In *Beyond the Beltway: Engaging the Public in U.S. Foreign Policy,* edited by Daniel Yankelovich and I. M. Destler. New York: W. W. Norton.

Dolan, Frederick (1994) *Allegories of America: Narrative, Metaphysics, Politics.* Ithaca: Cornell University.

Eco, Umberto (1985) "How Culture Conditions the Colours We See." In *On Signs,* edited by Marshall I. Blonsky. Baltimore: Johns Hopkins University Press.

Edelman, Murray (1974) *The Symbolic Uses of Politics.* Urbana: University of Illinois Press.

Erikson, Robert S., Norman R. Luttberg, and Kent L. Tedin (1991) *American Public Opinion: Its Origins, Content, and Impact,* 4th ed. New York: Macmillan.

Flanigan, William H., and Nancy H. Zingale (1994) *Political Behavior of the American Electorate,* 8th ed. Washington, DC: CQ Press.

Gallup (1993a) "The Battle Over NAFTA." *Gallup Poll Monthly* (November): 10–12.

Gallup (1993b) "Perot Losing Public Support." *Gallup Poll Monthly* (November):13–15.

Griswold, Wendy (1994) *Cultures and Societies in a Changing World.* Thousand Oaks, CA: Pine Forge Press.

Harbrecht, Douglas, and Susan B. Garland (1993) "Will NAFTA's Big Brass Band Ever Get in Step?" *Business Week,* October 4.

Kroeber, Alfred L., and Clyde Kluckhohn (1952) *Culture: A Critical Review of Concepts and Definitions.* Cambridge: Harvard University Press.

Krois, John Michael (1985) "Einleiung." In *Symbol, Technik, Sprache: Aufsätze aus den Jahren 1927–1933, Ernst Cassirer,* edited by Ernst Wolfgang Orth and John Michael Krois. Hamburg: Meiner.

Kuhn, Thomas (1970) *The Structure of Scientific Revolutions,* 2d enl. ed. Chicago: University of Chicago Press.

Lambro, Donald (1993) "NAFTA's Chances Brighten; White House Sees Progress in Push." *Washington Post,* November 11.

Larry King Live (1993) *NAFTA Debate: Gore vs. Perot.* November 9, Washington, DC, CNN. Source: Lexis/Nexis, Transcript #961-1.

Lévi-Strauss, Claude (1979) *Myth and Meaning.* New York: Schocken Books.

Moran, Robert T., and Jeffrey D. Abbott (1994) *NAFTA: Managing the Cultural Differences.* Houston: Gulf.

Moravcsik, Andrew (1993) "Introduction: Integrating International and Domestic Theories of International Bargaining." In *Double-Edged Diplomacy: International Bargaining and Domestic Politics,* edited by Peter B. Evans, Harold K. Jacobson, and Robert D. Putnam. Berkeley: University of California Press.

Popper, Karl (1989) *Logik der Forschung,* 9th ed. Tübingen: Mohr.

Putnam, Robert D. (1993) "Diplomacy and Domestic Politics." In *Double Edged Diplomacy: International Bargaining and Domestic Policy,* edited by Peter B. Evans, Harold K. Jacobson, and Robert D. Putnam. Berkeley: University of California Press.

Pye, Lucian W. (1965) "Introduction: Political Culture and Political Development." In *Political Culture and Political Development,* edited by Lucian Pye and Sidney Verba. Princeton: Princeton University Press.

Pye, Lucian W. (1991) "Political Culture Revisited." *Political Psychology* 12, no. 3 (September):487–508.

Richwine, Lisa (1993) "Administration Tactics Won NAFTA Fight." *Washington—States News Service,* November 19.

Robertson, James Oliver (1994) *American Myth, American Reality,* 7th print ed. New York: Hill and Wang.

Roth, John K. (1976) *American Dreams—Meditations on Life in the United States.* San Francisco: Chandler and Sharp.

Roth, Kathryn, and Richard Sobel (1993) "Chronology of Events and Public Opinion." *Public Opinion in U.S. Foreign Policy: The Controversy over Contra Aid,* edited by Richard Sobel. Lanham, MD: Rowman and Littlefields.

Sahlins, Marshall (1981) *Historical Metaphors and Mythical Realities: Structure in the Early History of the Sandwich Islands Kingdom.* Ann Arbor: University of Michigan Press.

Slotkin, Richard (1993) *Gunfighter Nation: The Myth of the Frontier in Twentieth-Century America.* New York: Harper Perennial.

Sobel, Richard (1993) "What Have We Learned About Public Opinion in U.S. Foreign Policy?" In *Public Opinion in U.S. Foreign Policy: The Controversy over Contra Aid,* edited by Richard Sobel. Lanham, MD: Rowman and Littlefields.

Smith, Henry Nash (1978) *Virgin Land—The American West as a Symbol and Myth.* Cambridge: Harvard University Press.

Tancer, Shoshona (1994) "The NAFTA Challenge." In *NAFTA: Managing the Cultural Differences,* edited by Robert T. Moran and Jeffrey D. Abbott. Houston: Gulf.

Times Mirror Center for the People and the Press (1990) *The Age of Indifference: A Study of Young Americans and How They View the News.* Washington, DC: Times Mirror Center.

Times Mirror Center for the People and the Press (1993) *America's Place in the World.* Washington, DC: Times Mirror Center.

Vaughan, Dianne (1992) "Theory Elaboration: The Heuristics of Case Analysis." In Charles C. Rayin and Howard S. Becker, *What Is a Case? Exploring the Foundations of Social Enquiry.* Cambridge: Cambridge University.

Verba, Sidney (1965) "Conclusion: Comparative Political Culture." In *Political Culture and Political Development.* edited by Lucian Pye and Sidney Verba. Princeton: Princeton University Press.

Yankelovich, Daniel, and John Immerwahr (1994) "The Rules of Engagement." In *Beyond the Beltway: Engaging the Public in U.S. Foreign Policy,* edited by Daniel Yankelovich and I. M. Destler. New York: W. W. Norton.

PART 2

CULTURE AS SHARED VALUE PREFERENCES

5

Culture, History, Role: Belgian and Dutch Axioms and Foreign Assistance Policy

Marijke Breuning

Breuning wrestles theoretically and methodologically with applying culture to foreign policy analysis. Theoretically, she links culture with national role conception, and shows how to develop a focused comparison case study that allows her to rule out competing explanations. To demonstrate her technique, she performs a content analysis of statements by Belgian and Dutch leaders concerning development assistance policy. She persuasively shows how one can marshal empirical evidence to trace the effect of differing historical experiences on present foreign policy.

—Editor

The cultural values that shape a society constrain the foreign policy choices of its leaders. How cultural values do so, and where the origins of such values can be found, has not been studied extensively in the field of international relations (Hudson, Chapter 1 of this book; Goldstein and Keohane, 1993). Nevertheless, the notion that values matter, embedded in culture or otherwise, is not new. Leites's (1953) *Study of Bolshevism,* for example, is an early attempt to show that the Soviet Union, collectively, perceived the world differently from the United States (see also Pye, 1991). Subsequent work following Leites's lead has focused mostly on individual perception (e.g., Hermann, 1980; George, 1979; Walker, 1977) and on small-group dynamics (e.g., Janis, 1983). The impact of the broader social context or of cultural values on foreign policy decisionmaking that Leites discussed has mostly been ignored (Farnham, 1990). However, foreign policy decisionmaking does not take place in a vacuum. Decisionmakers are both products and representatives of their society. If decisionmakers were influenced solely by their role as foreign policy makers, constraints produced by a state's position in the international environment ought to explain its foreign policy. If, on the other hand, states that are similarly positioned pursue different foreign policies, other explanations must be sought (Elkins and Simeon, 1979).

Belgium and the Netherlands are such similarly positioned states: Both are small, Western European states, both are heavily dependent on international trade, and both are former colonizers; yet they pursue very different foreign assistance policies. Parliamentary debates concerning the foreign assistance of these two states have been investigated elsewhere, and their content covaries with foreign policy behavior (Breuning, 1995 and 1992). Moreover, the cross-national differences in rhetoric cannot be attributed to party politics or the role individual ministers played in the foreign assistance decisionmaking in these two states (Breuning, forthcoming and 1995).

In sum, the themes addressed in the Dutch and Belgian parliaments with regard to foreign assistance differ and are not easily attributable to individuals or parties. What then makes the Dutch and the Belgians express themselves differently when they discuss and make foreign assistance policy? This essay investigates the proposition that differences in cultural values between the two states constitute one plausible explanation for the differences in decisionmaker rhetoric. It will adopt a cognitive approach to the study of culture's impact on foreign policy decisionmaking. It will view culture as "the collective construction of social reality" (Sackmann, 1991:33) or, in Hudson's terms (Chapter 1, this book), a shared system of meaning that shapes the values and preferences of a collectivity of individuals.

CULTURE AND SHARED COGNITION

That collectivities of individuals can share cognitions has been well documented (Klimoski and Mohammed, 1994; Levine, Resnick, and Higgins, 1993; Resnick, 1991; Sackmann, 1991; Wildavsky, 1987). Although many studies focus on small groups or organizations, the concept of shared cognition can be applied to societies or states as well (Cole, 1991 and 1988). Research on the shared cognitions of small groups or on culture in organizations acts here as a heuristic device for studying the impact and origins of cultural values in societies or states.

There are certainly many differences between small groups or organizations and societal culture. However, in both cases there is a founding, there is transmission of cultural values, and there is an organizational or institutional structure that affects the processes by which values are transmitted and individuals are selected to top decisionmaking positions. As a result, there are bounds on what sorts of goals can be conceived and what sorts of behaviors are engaged in to reach those goals.

In short, despite the very real differences between small groups, organizations, and societies, in each there are shared cognitive mechanisms.

An investigation into the manner in which sociocultural values shape the predispositions of foreign policy decisionmakers requires further definition of the rather broad and inclusive concept of culture. Culture will here be defined in terms of the common inheritance of a society. I am using the term *inheritance* rather than *history,* because the emphasis here is on the meanings that are communicated through national history rather than a more objectivist notion that has the "facts speak for themselves." The messages embedded in the tales of one's ancestors' exploits contain information about a society and the common values the society seeks to instill in its next generation (Levine, Resnick, and Higgins, 1993; Carlsnaes, 1993 and 1992; Vertzberger, 1990; Farr and Moscovici, 1984). Also, institutional structures are an inheritance and constrain policy behavior as well (Koelble, 1995; March and Olsen, 1984). First, they represent a political bargain struck at a particular time and generally reflect conditions and power configurations of that time (Koelble, 1995; Sackmann, 1991). Second, institutions become vehicles of value transmission as they socialize a next generation into their practices, expectations, and basic assumptions (Sackmann, 1991; March and Olsen, 1984; Feldman, 1984). Third, institutional practices shape decisionmaking processes (March and Olsen, 1984).

In other words, history has an impact in at least two ways: (1) It provides us with stories of who we are, where we came from, and what we value, and (2) it gives us certain institutional arrangements that organize decisionmaking processes in terms of both content and structure. Neither is etched in stone, but neither will change without strong reason or incentive (Sackmann, 1991; Hermann, 1990). Both produce constraints on decisionmaking—the first through socially shared values and practices, the second through institutional constraints. The past does not deterministically shape foreign assistance policy but influences shared conceptions of the role the state is perceived to play in international politics and debate about the policy direction most appropriate to that role—or the desired modification of it.

SOURCES AND IMPACT OF CULTURE

Culture is here defined in cognitive terms, because it is through the mediation of cognitive mechanisms that the common inheritance of a society influences the content and structure of decisionmaking processes. Sackmann has defined culture in organizations as "a social construction of rules that guide perceptions and thinking." These constructions "emerge in a process of social interaction that is primarily oriented toward problem solving. Over time a body of cultural knowledge is being created that is passed on to other generations" (Sackmann, 1991:22). In other words, the genesis of culture is in the practices individuals within an organization develop as they confront problems that need to be solved. Once in place, these practices are transmitted to new members of the organization. Indeed, individuals may be selected on the basis of their perceived compatibility with the organization's practices (Sackmann, 1991). Although citizens are not, on the whole, selected into citizenship of a particular state, one could argue that selection into positions of leadership, responsibility, and power does indeed favor individuals who have been determined to possess valued traits and qualities.

New members generally are not aware of the cognitions they have in common among themselves and with older or previous members of the organization. This presents some difficulty for the study of culture, because individuals may implicitly act on values they cannot explicitly verbalize (Sackmann, 1991; Levine and Moreland, 1991; Diamond, 1991). To conclude that this means culture cannot be studied empirically is to admit defeat too readily, however. What it does mean is that culture and its impact on foreign policy decisionmaking is best studied comparatively. If the assumptions that form the basis for action are not constant across states, this is best shown through cross-national comparison. Decisionmakers in different states must be shown to proceed from different premises. Doing so requires indicators that are observable.

However, observable indicators must be grounded in a framework that hypothesizes about the relationship between cultural values and their consequences. The interrelation between culture and foreign policy behavior is here conceptualized as consisting of four distinct elements: national role conception or identity, institutional frameworks, the envisioned or desired future, and conceivable strategies to attain that future. Each of these elements requires further elaboration.

National Role Conception/Identity

The notion of a national role conception or identity, the least easily observed element, consists of axiomatic beliefs. Beliefs can be termed "axiomatic" when they cannot be further reduced, but instead constitute the basic premises that organize all other knowledge. The term is set in context by Sackmann (1991), who describes four kinds of knowledge that together constitute cultural knowledge: descriptive and definitional knowledge, causal attributions, normative attributions, and enduring beliefs that become axiomatic—the first three being derived from and reducible to the fourth. While axiomatic beliefs are implicit in the other three forms of knowledge, it is the latter beliefs that find more ready expression in statements and debates.

Nonetheless, just as the same scientific axioms are at the heart of several different formulas, individuals proceeding from the same or very similar axiomatic beliefs may derive different visions and political strategies from them. But axiomatic beliefs do not provide total freedom, but instead make certain visions and strategies inconceivable and thus set parameters on what it is possible to envision. The axiomatic beliefs, hypothesized to be shared, form the glue that binds a society together.

This hypothesis contains both an explanation of cross-national variance and within-state variability. Sociocultural values are assumed to be axiomatic beliefs that members of a society hold in common, even if the opinions they derive from these beliefs vary greatly. Members of different societies are expected to proceed from different cultural value axioms, which accounts for cross-national variability. If ideology can be held constant cross-nationally and there remain differences in policy behavior, a cultural explanation is a credible contender in the quest to explain those differences.

In sum, culture is a residual explanation rather than a catch-all theory. Culture is the explanation one resorts to after other explanatory variables have been found either not to account for the observed differences in policy behavior or to leave much of the variance unexplained.[1] Furthermore, both the content and the origin of cultural values can be understood only with reference to axiomatic beliefs (Sackmann, 1991: 52–53). A key to such axioms can be found in the messages and meanings embedded in national history. What counts is not so much the literal events as the "lessons learned" and the "moral of the story." Meanings of such an identity-building, identity-altering, or identity-maintaining sort are most likely to be found in events that mark turning points in the state's history: events surrounding the founding of the state, major events that shock the system, and leaders that perform heroic acts either in response to or precipitating such events.

The collective sense of identity that is hypothesized to result from such events is taught to new generations, who are socialized to perceive their state in terms of it. This national role conception or identity affects foreign policy behavior in two ways: It has an impact through the institutional frameworks that are negotiated by founders and altered at subsequent turning points, and it shapes the parameters of the conceivable visions of desired futures.

Institutional Frameworks

The institutional frameworks and processes that determine the structure of incentives within the political system constitute the second element of the framework. Both formal rules and informal practices affect the behavior of individual actors in a system (Searing, 1991; March and Olsen, 1984). The former do so because they set the parameters within which policy choices are made (Koelble, 1995). However, Searing (1991:1242) points out that "informal rules are extremely effective in shaping the behavior of politicians and therefore cannot be overlooked." This means that the practices that develop within formal frameworks, and that are not fully specified by codes or statutes, are as important in shaping behavior as the formalized rules themselves (Searing, 1991; Turner, 1987; Knowles, 1982). Organizations cannot be fully understood without taking both the formal and informal rules into account.

Both formal and informal rules can be regarded as the outcomes of political struggles that, once in place, shape how subsequent political struggles are played out and potentially how the rules are modified across time (Koelble, 1995:242; see also Rose, 1980). Though socialization constrains individuals within such systems, they are not robots merely playing out roles, but add their own individual contributions (Searing, 1991). This implies that institutional frameworks can change in an evolutionary manner (Sackmann, 1991), as opposed to the shocks that are hypothesized to alter axiomatic beliefs. This change is expected to be slow and to take place within the bounds of the basic assumptions that are at the heart of the axiomatic beliefs.

Envisioned/Desired Future

Axiomatic beliefs and institutions, which together influence the goals or desired or potential futures that can be envisioned, constitute the third element of the framework (Markus and Nurius, 1986). However, such futures are not deterministically shaped. Socially shared cognition does not demand that individuals hold identical beliefs (Klimoski and Mohammed, 1994; Sackmann, 1991). Nonetheless, it does suggest that the cultural explanation becomes credible only when political ideology cannot fully explain cross-national differences.

Conceivable Strategies

Strategies for bringing the state closer to the envisioned future is the fourth element of the framework. Like the visions themselves, the strategies that can be conceived are consistent with and constrained by the axiomatic beliefs and institutional frameworks and are observable as foreign policy behavior. A variety of strategies might be consistent with any set of axiomatic beliefs. Thus, observed foreign policy behavior Y does not straightforwardly entail axiomatic belief X, or vice versa. Rather, observed patterns of behavior across time and cross-nationally can lead to the conclusion that state A's foreign policy behavior is bounded in one way, while state B's is constrained in another way.

Culture/Foreign Policy Model

In sum, the relation between culture and behavior consists of four elements, which interrelate as shown in Figure 5.1. The model recognizes that axiomatic beliefs do not determine, but instead influence, the other elements. Other factors may account for cross-national or across-time differences, such as the political color of the party (or coalition) in power or the individual agenda of a minister. The cultural explanation of foreign policy behavior must be applied with caution.

BELGIUM AND THE NETHERLANDS: AN ILLUSTRATIVE COMPARISON

The framework outlined above explains how cultural values influence foreign policy behavior. It also explains that shared cultural values are both pervasive and elusive. They leave their mark on institutional frameworks, shape visions of the future, and constrain the choice of strategies. The degree to which they do so is an empirical question. In attempting to find empirical answers, it is important to consider alternative explanations before resorting to cultural values. A comparison of Dutch and Belgian foreign assistance policies illustrates this point.

Belgium and the Netherlands are both small states located in Western Europe. Both are heavily dependent on international trade, and both are former colonizers. Their size and economic vulnerability put them in comparable situations internationally. Their history as colonial powers might predispose them to provide relatively higher levels of foreign assistance

Fig. 5.1
Culture and Foreign Policy

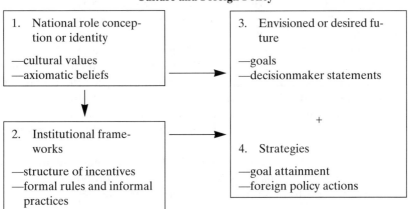

than they might otherwise have allocated. While all these factors lead one to expect similarities in foreign assistance policy behavior (Keohane, 1986; East, 1978 and 1973), the policies of these two states differ (Breuning, 1995 and 1992).

In terms of the framework, the two states pursue different strategies. If the cultural explanation were to be taken as preeminent, the argument might be that having similar positions in the international system is irrelevant and that expecting similarities in policy behavior is therefore unrealistic. Instead, the different cultures of the two states would logically lead to different foreign assistance policies. This argument is not acceptable, because it ignores the relevance of the international environment to the conduct of foreign policy in favor of dynamics internal to the state. In short, differences in foreign assistance policy behavior alone can never support a cultural explanation. They merely make such an explanation a possibility.

Thus, the fact that Belgium and the Netherlands pursue different foreign assistance policies has ruled out one potential explanation but not provided an alternative. An investigation of parliamentary debates has shown that the decisionmakers of the two states stress different themes (Breuning, 1995 and 1992). On the basis of these differences in rhetoric, one could argue that Belgian and Dutch decisionmakers hold different visions of their state's current and future role, certainly as it relates to foreign assistance.

Again, culture might provide an easy explanation. However, the visions of a desired future that motivate policy behavior are shaped not only by cultural values, but by political ideology as well. The axiomatic beliefs at the heart of cultural values can translate into different political values and visions. Therefore, differences in rhetoric may merely reflect differences in party politics or even individual ministers. The relative frequency with which various themes are addressed in the foreign assistance debates in Belgium and the Netherlands is, however, not explained by party politics or individual ministers. There is relative consistency across time within each state, coupled with cross-national differences (Breuning, forthcoming and 1995).

Rather than ruling in cultural explanations, this has ruled out some alternative explanations. Party politics or individual ministers cannot fully account for the differences in the foreign assistance rhetoric found in Belgium and the Netherlands. Since institutional frameworks may constrain the futures that decisionmakers can envision and the policy strategies they devise, a comparative assessment of those structures is in order.

Belgium and the Netherlands are both parliamentary democracies with constitutional monarchies. Moreover, both use proportional representation systems to determine the allocation of seats in parliament. In both cases, this leads to multiple parties and coalition governments. Also in both countries, the coalition generally includes Christian Democrats and either a labor/socialist party or a liberal party. These institutional similarities do not extend to the factual role of the minister for development cooperation in the cabinet, however.

There is no separate ministry for development cooperation in the Netherlands. Instead, the Directorate General for International Cooperation (DGIS) is housed within the Ministry of Foreign Affairs. The Dutch minister for development cooperation, officially a minister without portfolio, is charged with the administration of development cooperation and heads the DGIS within the Ministry of Foreign Affairs. The first appointment of such a minister, in 1965, did not reflect the desire to elevate the importance of this issue area as much as it constituted a tactic in the formation of a new coalition government (Everts and Walraven, 1989; Maas, 1986).

The official authority of the minister of development cooperation is limited (Kruijssen, 1986; Maas, 1986). This makes the ability of this minister to establish positive working relationships with his or her colleagues in other departments important. For instance, international monetary policy, including relations with the World Bank and associated agencies, is formally within the jurisdiction of the Ministry of Finance.

The importance of the appointment has increased over time, however, mostly because the individuals who occupied the post played an active role within successive cabinets (Maas, 1986; Wels, 1982). Wels argues that this not only elevated the status of the minister of development cooperation, but it also increased the importance of the Ministry of Foreign Affairs more generally. This coincides with an increasing importance in the Dutch political debate of relations with the Third World and of human rights issues (Wels, 1982:142).

In comparison, the Belgian Administration for Development Cooperation (BADC) is part of the Ministry of Foreign Affairs, Foreign Trade, and Development Cooperation. The formal institutional structure of an administrative unit within the ministry is similar to the Dutch institutional framework. The difference is that the Belgian ministry includes foreign trade, which may indicate the importance foreign economic relations have for this state. However, the Belgian minister of development cooperation has never attained the kind of political influence his or her Dutch counterpart has gained. Although this is sometimes blamed on the frequent changes of minister (Vandommele, 1982; Serlon, 1985), it is more easily explained by coalition politics. According to Vandommele (1982:500), the office of minister of development cooperation is the "small change" that rounds out a coalition. An office used as a testing or training ground, it is often the first ministerial post an individual holds—a situation that has its roots in the colonial era (Coolsaet, 1987).

This suggests that the institutional configuration in Belgium will not easily yield a high-profile development cooperation policy. Junior ministers are likely to be more concerned with impressing, or at least not antagonizing, those within and outside politics who can help further their careers (Serlon, 1985). They may be new both to the subject matter of development cooperation and to running a ministry, which makes their position within the cabinet weak.

In sum, formal institutional similarities coincide with differences in informal political practices *and* differences in foreign aid performance. The Belgian rhetoric focuses more often on the need to have foreign assistance pay off for its economy. This is matched by a relatively lower percentage of GNP spent on aid and a moderate to high level of bilateral aid tying. The Dutch rhetoric stresses social justice and empowerment as a means to greater stability in the international environment. This coincides with relatively higher foreign assistance spending and bilateral aid and with a low level of tying. The difference between foreign aid spending and the tying status of bilateral aid is consistent and significant, as illustrated by the difference of means test for Belgian and Dutch data for 1975–1990 in Table 5.1 (see also Breuning, 1995).

The formal institutional similarities between the Belgian and Dutch foreign policy bureaucracies—a development cooperation agency housed within the Ministry of Foreign Affairs—are coupled with different informal practices. The similarities in formal institutional frameworks do not support a cultural explanation. However, the practices do, because the differences in practices cannot be explained by either international or domestic structures. These different practices, moreover, can help explain the differences in foreign assistance policy behavior.

How did these different informal practices develop within Belgium and the Netherlands? This question is at the heart of a cultural explanation. It asks not only what the content of axiomatic beliefs is, but how they came to be, how they are maintained, and how they change.

CULTURE'S ORIGINS

Taken together, the differences in informal practices, in goals expressed in decisionmaker rhetoric, and in the foreign assistance policy behavior of Belgium and the Netherlands point to the plausibility of a cultural explanation. As indicated above, the differences between these two states on each of these measures is not easily attributed to structural, institutional, party, or individual explanations. Moreover, the elements covary in a logical manner: There is consistency to the cross-national differences. However, showing that such differences exist does not provide any indication as to why they exist, where they came from, how they are maintained, and how they might change.

Table 5.1 Foreign Assistance Spending and Tying Status (1975–1990)

	The Netherlands			Belgium				
	N	Mean	SE	N	Mean	SE	T	Sign.
ODA as percentage of GNP	16	.94	.023	16	.52	.016	15.02	.000
Tying status (percentage of bilateral aid)								
Tied	11	16.6	3.20	9	63.78	5.54	−7.71	.000
Partially tied	11	30.6	2.95	9	.00	.00	9.33	.000
Untied	11	52.7	2.83	9	36.22	5.54	2.81	.012

Source: OECD (various years). *Development Co-Operation: Efforts and Policies of the Members of the Development Assistance Committee.* Paris: OECD.

I have defined culture in terms of the common inheritance of a society. This definition allows for the exploration of the roots of current practices. This facilitates the formulation of hypotheses regarding the axiomatic beliefs held by the decisionmakers of Belgium and the Netherlands. It is assumed here that national history provides citizens with a shared identity and common values. Not every event in a nation's history has significance in this regard. Those elements of national history that are particularly relevant in shaping axiomatic beliefs are expected to be (1) the existence of a "heroic history," which may or may not be associated with (2) the founding of the state; (3) the extent and nature of the colonizing experience, in the context of foreign assistance policy in particular; and (4) other turning point events.

Heroic History

A heroic history is a memory of a time when the state was a powerful or significant actor in international affairs (Breuning, forthcoming). I expect that such a memory leads decisionmakers to hold the axiomatic belief that they can make a difference in the international environment. The absence of such a history would be hypothesized to lead to a belief that the fate of the state is subject to forces beyond the control of the decisionmakers. In short, a heroic history leads to an actor orientation, whereas the absence of such a history leads to a subject orientation.

Founding of the State

The founding of the state may have taken place as a result of heroic acts on the part of national leaders and their supporters. Conversely, the attainment of statehood may have depended on outside forces. The lessons learned about the nation's role in the international environment parallel those learned through the existence or absence of a heroic history. In other words, if heroic founding experiences and a heroic history coincide, the state's decisionmakers are likely to perceive their state as a capable actor in international affairs. If the state's founding depended on outside forces and no particular moment of power and significance is part of the national inheritance, decisionmakers are likely to perceive their state to be at the mercy of forces beyond their control. Such forces might be traditional great power machinations, but may also consist of the need to accommodate transnational corporations or other economic measures to secure the state's precarious economic well-being. In short, the founding experiences and presence or absence of a heroic history are likely to reinforce each other if they point in the same direction. If not, then a heroic history may modify the common inheritance to alter shared axiomatic beliefs in the direction indicated by that history. A comparison of Dutch and Belgian history illustrates the different lessons these two societies are hypothesized to have learned.

The Dutch achieved national independence in 1648, after having been at war with their Spanish rulers since 1568 (Voorhoeve, 1985). The war overlaps with the Dutch success as a commercial-maritime power during the seventeenth century, which accounts for their eventual ability to win their political independence (Kennedy, 1987). The Dutch pride themselves on having won their freedom by means of their own resources. Both the history of the Eighty Years' War and the riches of the seventeenth century are featured prominently in Dutch history.

Belgian independence, on the other hand, was brokered by the great powers of the time. Although the Belgians themselves initiated the revolt against the rule and policies of the Dutch king, William I, independence was not secured through military means. Rather, the London Conference decided that a neutral and independent Belgium was the most feasible solution to the Belgian Revolt (Witte, Craeybeckx, and Meynen, 1990; Fishman, 1988; Vermeersch, 1970). In sum, the Belgian state lacks a heroic history: Its founding was brokered by outsiders, and its forced neutrality constrained its potential for action in international relations. Although this does not prove that the Dutch have an actor orientation and the Belgians a subject orientation, it suggests that such axiomatic beliefs might exist.

The Colonizing Experience

The duration and nature of the colonial experience of a state is important regarding foreign policy in general but has specific importance for development cooperation policies (Breuning, forthcoming). The further the colonial experience extends back in time, the more likely it is that a sense of responsibility or mission developed. The length of colonization alone does not explain its nature, although in the Belgian and Dutch cases, the difference can be explained in those terms.

Although the Belgian king, Leopold II, acquired possession of Zaire in 1885, the Belgian state was not involved in its administration until the colony was transferred to it in 1908 (Pakenham, 1991; Van Bellinghen, 1990; Witte, Craeybeckx, and Meynen, 1990). In the aftermath of World War I, Belgium acquired mandates over Rwanda and Burundi. The Belgian colonial era ended in the early 1960s when first Zaire and then Rwanda and Burundi acquired independence (Bouveroux, 1994; Luykx and Platel, 1985). Thus, Belgian colonialism was short-lived and initially driven by monarchial ambitions.

In contrast, Dutch colonialism has roots extending back to the 1600s, when merchant marine companies established trade connections in both Southeast Asia and the Americas (Kennedy, 1987; Voorhoeve,

1985; Wels, 1982). Although the initial focus was on trade rather than the acquisition of territory, during the nineteenth century the Dutch did establish territorial control over Indonesia, Suriname, and the Netherlands Antilles (Voorhoeve, 1985; Wels, 1982). Although the Dutch reluctantly gave up control of Indonesia in 1949, they retained control of a portion of the archipelago. West New Guinea was finally incorporated into the Indonesian state in 1962 (Lijphart, 1966). The end of the Dutch colonial era came more slowly in the Western Hemisphere: Suriname did not acquire independence until 1975, and the Netherlands Antilles remain an "overseas territory."

Although Dutch relations with the colonies were initially driven by trade rather than by a monarch's personal ambitions, as territorial control tightened, the Dutch perceived themselves as being on a "civilizing" mission as well. The notion of a "white man's burden" supports not only an actor orientation, but also a universalistic value orientation. It entails a vision of a colony's future that includes reshaping its society in terms of the colonizer's value system. This means that the universe is seen as ordered and that this order is knowable to human beings. In a more generalized context, Voorhoeve (1985) views Dutch policy as infused with "Calvinist" features, which for him entails a foreign policy driven by moral principles rather than practicality.[2]

This view of the world can be contrasted with one that is particularistic or situational. The latter entails a more relativistic attitude guided not by fixed principles but by a situational ethic. Such an attitude focuses on "getting by," given the practical circumstances. Coolsaet (1987) has charged that Belgian foreign policy was at times superseded by short-term commercial expediency. Dewachter (1992) describes Belgium as a loyal alliance partner and accepting of international political and economic structures (see also Dewachter and Verminck, 1987). Both imply that Belgian foreign policy is driven by the desire to satisfy Belgian interests rather than to wage moral crusades. In other words, behavior is results oriented rather than intent based.

Again, these descriptions do not prove anything, but they do suggest that the axiomatic beliefs of Belgian and Dutch decisionmakers are apt to differ. The latter appear to proceed from a universalistic view of the world, coupled with intent-based policy. The former appear to proceed from a particularistic ethic, coupled with results-oriented policy. Such principles about the world and how to behave are axiomatic.

Turning Point Events

Turning point events are the shocks that prompt a society to reevaluate itself (Hermann, 1990; Auerbach, 1986). Such major events lend dynamism to a cultural explanation: As new events reshape socially shared

Figure 5.2
Axiomatic Beliefs Regarding Foreign Policy

State's relation to the international environment	ACTOR ORIENTATION (can make a difference)	◀ vs. ▶	SUBJECT ORIENTATION (subject to forces beyond control)
Nature of the international environment	UNIVERSALISTIC WORLDVIEW (universe is ordered in some fixed way)	◀ vs. ▶	PARTICULARISTIC WORLDVIEW (situations must be dealt with on their own terms)
Rules of behavior	INTENT BASED (behavior is based in principles)	◀ vs. ▶	RESULTS ORIENTED (behavior depends on opportunities presented by the situation)

beliefs about the nation and its role in international affairs, earlier historical influences are modified. Turning point events may either reinforce or alter axiomatic beliefs.

Taken together, the existence of a "heroic history," perhaps concurrent with the founding of the state, other turning point events, and an experience as colonizers are hypothesized to shape socially shared axiomatic beliefs. The common inheritance of a society predisposes its decisionmakers to accept certain commonly shared values about whether the state makes a difference in the world, how that world is viewed, and what strategies the state can most fruitfully pursue. Figure 5.2 summarizes these three dimensions. Such socially shared values do not exhaust the domain of politically relevant cultural values. The purpose here, however, is not to be exhaustive, but to illustrate that propositions about the origins and content of cultural values can be studied systematically.

A FRAMEWORK FOR EMPIRICAL INVESTIGATION

The expectations derived from the histories of Belgium and the Netherlands provide an avenue through which culture's origins and impacts can be studied empirically. Doing so requires that the hypotheses about the axiomatic beliefs of Belgian and Dutch decisionmakers be tested systematically. This is best done by analyzing the examples and stories decisionmakers utilize to support their foreign policies. Cross-national differences would have to be shown with regard to an actor versus subject orientation, a universalistic versus particularistic worldview, and an intent-based versus results-oriented approach to behavior. The proposed strategies for evaluating each of these dimensions consist of the following.

The *actor versus subject orientation* is expected to manifest itself in the relative use of active versus passive language (Akmajian, Demers, and Harnish, 1984). The predominant use of transitive verbs in the active voice is regarded as evidence for an actor orientation, while the predominant use of the passive voice reflects a subject orientation. Intransitive verbs are coded as active if the subject engages in an action, and passive if the sentence regards a condition or state of being. It is expected that both types of verbs will be used, and the measure therefore has to take into account the relative use of either type of verb. It is expected that Dutch debate will include a greater proportion of active language use than Belgian debate. The latter is expected to have a relatively higher proportion of passive language.

A content analysis strategy targeted to evaluate the substantive content of rhetoric supplements this approach. It focuses on the sort of actions decisionmakers say they will pursue: Do they say they hope to convince their international counterparts of some principle or strategy, or do they merely promise to discuss the matter? The relative strength of the rhetoric is coded into high and low categories. The expectation is that the Dutch will tend to use stronger language than the Belgians.

The *universal versus particularistic worldview* is evaluated through the use of rule-based versus case-based modes of reasoning. The former are based on logical arguments that can be stated in the form of if . . . then propositions or production rules (Sylvan, Ostrom, and Gannon, 1994; Mefford, 1991). Such reasoning proceeds by deduction from general principles. Knowledge acquired in one context can be used to understand others. Such a view can be contrasted with case-based reasoning, which proceeds inductively. Lessons learned in one context may or may not apply in another. Whether a lesson applies depends on a positive assessment that the situations share sufficient commonalities. The possibility of a cultural component to reasoning styles is illustrated by a study of how individuals in different cultural settings perceive the self in relation to others (Markus and Kitayama, 1991). Each sentence is categorized on the basis of its reference to general principles or to a specific case or situation. The expectation is that the Dutch will exhibit a universalistic worldview, whereas the Belgians will exhibit a particularistic one.

The *intent-based versus results-oriented approach* to political behavior is assessed through a content-analytic scheme that evaluates whether ministers tend to be criticized or praised more frequently for either their motives or their accomplishments. Do members of parliament question the minister about the motives or the intent of his or her policies or, conversely, about policy results or failings? To the degree that there is a focus on motives, an intent-based approach could be argued to prevail. To the degree that there is a focus on accomplishments, a results-oriented approach could be argued to exist. The expectation is that the Dutch will focus to a greater degree on intent and the Belgians on results.

On all measures, the relative emphasis indicates the degree to which particular axiomatic beliefs guide decisionmakers. The presence of an actor versus subject orientation, a universalistic versus particularistic worldview, and an intent-based versus results-oriented approach to behavior are each likely to reflect extremes on dimensions rather than clear-cut categories. This makes cross-national evaluation especially important: It is only by contrasting the axiomatic beliefs that are shared within societies that we can evaluate what is cultural—or specific to a society and its leaders.

A content analysis of a systematic random sample of sentences from one Dutch and one Belgian debate for the 1986–1987 parliamentary year was employed to evaluate the hypothesized relationships. That year was chosen because debates were available for both states and both were governed by center-right coalitions. The latter ensures that any differences between the two states are unlikely to be an artifact of party politics. A systematic random sample was drawn on the basis of an estimate of the total number of sentences for each debate, with the intent of drawing samples of a hundred sentences for each state (Manheim and Rich, 1995). Some of the sentences selected through this process were statements of procedure or other nonsubstantive sentences. The N sizes reported in the analyses that fall below 100 reflect the fact that some of the sentences did not contain sufficient information to make the necessary judgments. For the Dutch sample, all sentences were in the Dutch language. The Belgian sample yielded primarily Dutch (or Flemish) sentences, although a few French-language sentences were part of the sample. The proportion of Dutch and French sentences reflects the proportion of Dutch and French in the debate from which the sample was drawn.

The coding process involved a series of separate judgments to be made about each sentence in the sample. In each case, the value mentioned first in the examples below is coded 0 and the second is coded 1. There are two measures for the actor versus subject orientation. The first concerns the active or passive voice of the verb and the second regards the strength of the proposed action. The following sentences serve to illustrate the coding of the active and passive voice:[3] "Minister Schoo took the initiative to reduce the market disturbing EC food aid to a minimum." This sentence contains a transitive verb in the active voice and is hence coded as active.

The following sentence contains a verb in the passive voice and is therefore coded as passive: "The .7 percent of GNP is a justified demand of public opinion." The active voice is used as an indicator of an actor orientation, while the passive voice indicates a subject orientation. The strength of the language used was also coded, as an additional measure to evaluate actor versus subject orientation. The expectation is that stronger action verbs are reflective of an actor orientation, whereas verbs reflecting less strong or forceful actions are reflective of a subject orientation. For example, "The development of the rural infrastructure demands expertise regarding the local situation" was coded as containing a high-strength verb, because it demands action. In contrast, because the assertion in the following sentence that something is possible is not a very forceful one, the sentence is coded as low-strength: "It would be possible to raise the funds intended for the cofinancing of NGO projects, which currently come to about 1 billion."

Whether a universalistic or a particularistic worldview predominates is judged on the basis of the mode of reasoning employed: Does the speaker's argument have a basis in general principles or is reference made to specific cases or situations? If the former is the case, the sentence is coded as reflecting a universalistic worldview. If the latter is the case, the sentence is judged to reflect a particularistic worldview. For example, "Like the Task Force also argues: Growth alone is insufficient to eliminate poverty" is judged to be evidence of a universalistic worldview, because it makes reference to a general principle.

The following sentence makes reference to a specific situation and is therefore coded as evidence of a particularistic worldview: "In twenty-five years' time we have succeeded to charge no fewer than seventeen different state secretaries, hailing from the most diverse political parties including even the FDF, with the management of development cooperation."

Last, whether behavior is judged on the basis of its intent or its results is judged by coding whether sentences focus on the minister's intended policy or the results achieved by his department. A focus on the minister's plans and intentions supports an intent-based approach to behavior, whereas a focus on policy results and outcomes supports a results-oriented approach. "How does the minister intend to deal with the debt problems of the Third World?" literally asks the minister about an intended action and is thus coded as intent based. By comparison, "The recognition of the NGOs and the associated government support has been achieved step by step in the course of twenty years" focuses on a policy result and is therefore coded as results oriented.

Each sentence in the sample was coded for each of the four measures. Sentences that provided insufficient information to make a judgment regarding a particular measure were coded as missing for that measure.

PRELIMINARY FINDINGS

Analysis of the data obtained through the coding procedures described above shows that these four measures differentiate between the Dutch and Belgian sentences. Moreover, the differences are consistently in the hypothesized direction, and all are statistically significant. The results of the tests are reported in Table 5.2.

It was hypothesized that the Dutch would use a greater proportion of active language than the Belgians. In fact, the Belgians tend to use passive language significantly more often than the Dutch. The means regarding the relative use of passive language for the two are .46 and .16, respectively. This supports the contention that the Dutch see themselves as playing an active role in foreign affairs, whereas the Belgians do not have such aspirations.

Second, it was hypothesized that the Dutch would tend to use stronger language than the Belgians. This is borne out by the data. The Belgians tend to avoid strong or forceful language. Although the Dutch do not use forceful language predominantly, they use strong wording relatively more frequently than the Belgians. The means for low-strength language are, respectively, .88 for the Belgians and .64 for the Dutch. Although both of these measures are in the hypothesized direction, the first more strongly supports an actor orientation for the Netherlands and a subject orientation for Belgium.

Third, it was hypothesized that the Dutch would exhibit a universalistic worldview, whereas the Belgians would exhibit a particularistic one. Indeed, the Belgian sentences reflect specific cases or situations much more frequently than the Dutch: The means for case-based language are .69 and .38, respectively. Conversely, the Dutch make reference to general principles quite frequently. Again, this difference is in the hypothesized direction. The Dutch do indeed appear to hold a more universalistic worldview, whereas the Belgians view the world in particularistic terms.

Last, it was expected that the Dutch would focus to a greater degree on intent, whereas the Belgians were expected to focus more strongly on results. The Belgians do indeed focus on the accomplishments—or lack thereof—of their foreign aid policy to a much greater degree than the

Table 5.2 Difference of Means Tests for Measures of Actor/Subject Orientation, Universalistic/Particularistic Worldview, and Intent-Based/Results-Oriented Approach

	The Netherlands			Belgium				
	N	Mean	SE	N	Mean	SE	T	Sign.
I. Actor versus subject orientation								
a. Use of passive language	100	.16	.037	94	.46	.052	-4.73	.000
b. Use of low-strength action words	100	.64	.048	94	.88	.033	-4.10	.000
II. Particularistic worldview language use	63	.38	.062	70	.69	.056	-3.67	.000
III. Results-oriented language use	72	.28	.053	77	.62	.056	-4.48	.000

Dutch. The respective means for emphasis on results are .62 and .28. In other words, the Dutch more frequently question the minister about intended policies and actions, while the Belgians emphasize specific policies and accomplishments. Again, this difference is in the hypothesized direction.

In sum, all four measures show a significant difference between Dutch and Belgian axiomatic beliefs. Moreover, in each case, the differences are in the hypothesized direction. The findings indicate that the Dutch perceive themselves as actors who can make a difference, proceed from a universalistic worldview, and have a strong interest in the intent rather than the results of policy. The Belgian decisionmakers, on the other hand, exhibit a subject orientation, coupled with a particularistic worldview and an emphasis on policy results. This supports the notion that decisionmakers of the two countries hold different axiomatic beliefs. Since the empirical study represents only a small sample, a larger study would be needed to provide further confirmation of these results. However, the results reported here indicate that the strategy outlined above can be regarded as a promising avenue for the empirical study of culture.

CONCLUSION

Axiomatic beliefs do not straightforwardly covary with policy behavior. How useful is it, then, to embark on the long and arduous journey to empirically measure those beliefs? Cultural explanations are not suited to point predictions. Rather, axiomatic beliefs define the parameters within which the decisionmakers of a state operate. Such insights are not just academically interesting, but they are significant for foreign policy decisionmakers as well (George, 1993). Decisionmakers who understand the cultural values and implicit assumptions of the foreign leaders they deal with are in a position to communicate and negotiate more effectively.

The study reported here provides only preliminary data. More important, however, it provides a framework for empirical study that includes fairly straightforward measures that are not difficult to apply to sentences in different languages. The data provide a reliable method that can be used to measure those aspects of culture that help explain differences in conceptions of a state's national role, which in turn affect policy preferences.

Nevertheless, culture as an explanation of foreign policy behavior needs to be applied with caution. It should not be employed as a generic, catch-all explanation; it should be used only if other explanations have been found wanting. Yet cultural variables provide a valuable complement to other explanations. Cultural variables can shed light on the premises and axioms at the heart of a state's foreign policy behavior.

NOTES

1. Using cultural explanations after other explanations have been exhausted emphasizes human commonality over difference. While, in the final analysis, difference probably matters in an explanation of foreign policy behavior, undue emphasis on difference impedes understanding far more than undue emphasis on commonality: Whereas the latter leaves a residual unexplained, the former feeds prejudice.

2. The intent versus results orientation relates to Weber's argument regarding the contrast between an ethic of ultimate ends versus an ethic of responsibility. The former stresses good or pure intentions, while the latter takes into account human circumstances and frailties (Weber, 1946).

3. All sentences presented here, which were translated by the author, were coded in their original language.

REFERENCES

Akmajian, Adrian, Richard A. Demers, and Robert M. Harnish (1984) *Linguistics: An Introduction to Language and Communication,* 2d ed. Cambridge: MIT Press.

Auerbach, Yehudit (1986) "Turning-Point Decisions: A Cognitive-Dissonance Analysis of Conflict Reduction in Israel–West German Relations." *Political Psychology* 7:533–550.

Bouveroux, Jos (1994) *België uit Afrika? Rwanda, Boeroendi, en Zaire* [Belgium out of Africa? Rwanda, Burundi, and Zaire]. Antwerp: Standaard.

Breuning, Marijke (1992) "National Role Conceptions and Foreign Aid Policy Behavior: Toward a Cognitive Model." Ph.D. diss., Ohio State University.

Breuning, Marijke (1994) "Why Give Foreign Aid? Decision Maker Perceptions of the Benefits to the Donor State." *Acta Politica* 29:121–145.

Breuning, Marijke (1995) "Words and Deeds: Foreign Assistance Rhetoric and Policy Behavior in the Netherlands, Belgium, and the United Kingdom." *International Studies Quarterly* 39:235–254.

Breuning, Marijke (Forthcoming) "Configuring Issue Areas: Belgian and Dutch Representations of the Role of Foreign Assistance in Foreign Policy." In *Problem Representation in Political Decision Making,* edited by D. A. Sylvan and J. F. Voss.

Carlsnaes, Walter (1992) "The Agency-Structure Problem in Foreign Policy Analysis." *International Studies Quarterly* 36:245–270.

Carlsnaes, Walter (1993) "On Analysing the Dynamics of Foreign Policy Change: A Critique and Reconceptualization." *Cooperation and Conflict* 28:5–30.

Cole, Michael (1988) "Cross-Cultural Research in the Sociohistorical Tradition." *Human Development* 31:137–157.

Cole, Michael (1991) "Conclusion." In *Perspectives on Socially Shared Cognition,* edited by L. B. Resnick, J. M. Levine, and S. D. Teasley. Washington, DC: American Psychological Association.

Coolsaet, Rik (1987) *Buitenlandse Zaken* [Foreign affairs]. Louvain: Kritak.

Dewachter, Wilfried (1992) *Besluitvorming in Politiek België* [Decisionmaking in Belgian politics]. Louvain: Acco.

Dewachter, Wilfried, and Mieke Verminck (1987) "De Machtsbases van België in the Internationale Politiek" [The powerbases of Belgium in international politics]. *Res Publica* 29:21–27.

Diamond, Michael A. (1991) "Dimensions of Organizational Culture and Beyond." *Political Psychology* 12:509–522.

East, Maurice A. (1973) "Size and Foreign Policy Behavior: A Test of Two Models." *World Politics* 25:556–557.

East, Maurice A. (1978) "National Attributes and Foreign Policy." In *Why Nations Act,* edited by M. A. East, S. A. Salmore, and C. F. Hermann. Beverly Hills: Sage.

Elkins, David J., and Richard E. B. Simeon (1979) "A Cause in Search of Its Effect, or What Does Political Culture Explain?" *Comparative Politics* 11: 127–145.

Everts, Philip, and Guido Walraven (1989) *The Politics of Persuasion: Implementation of Foreign Policy by the Netherlands.* Brookfield, VT: Avebury.

Farnham, Barbara (1990) "Political Cognition and Decision Making." *Political Psychology* 11:83–111.

Farr, Rob, and Serge Moscovici (1984) "On the Nature and Role of Representations in Self's Understanding of Others and Self." In *Issues in Person Perception,* edited by Mark Cook. London: Methuen.

Feldman, Daniel C. (1984) "The Development and Enforcement of Group Norms." *Academy of Management Review* 9:47–53.

Fishman, J. S. (1988) *Diplomacy and Revolution: The London Conference of 1830 and the Belgian Revolt.* Amsterdam: CHEV.

Franck, Christian (1987) "La prise de décision belge en politique extérieure" [Belgian foreign policy decisionmaking]. *Res Publica* 29:61–84.

George, Alexander L. (1979) "The Causal Nexus Between Cognitive Beliefs and Decision-Making Behavior: The 'Operational Code.'" In *Psychological Models in International Politics,* edited by L. S. Falkowski. Boulder: Westview Press.

George, Alexander L. (1993) *Bridging the Gap: Theory and Practice in Foreign Policy.* Washington, DC: United States Institute of Peace.

Goldstein, Judith, and Robert O. Keohane (1993) *Ideas and Foreign Policy: Beliefs, Institutions, and Political Change.* Ithaca: Cornell University Press.

Hermann, Charles F. (1990) "Changing Course: When Governments Choose to Redirect Foreign Policy." *International Studies Quarterly* 34:3–21.

Hermann, Margaret G. (1980) "Explaining Foreign Policy Behavior Using Personal Characteristics of Political Leaders." *International Studies Quarterly* 24:4–46.

Holsti, Kal J. (1970) "National Role Conceptions in the Study of Foreign Policy." *International Studies Quarterly* 14:233–309.

Janis, Irving L. (1983) *Groupthink: Psychological Studies of Policy Decisions and Fiascoes,* 2d rev. ed. Boston: Houghton Mifflin.

Kennedy, Paul (1987) *The Rise and Fall of the Great Powers.* New York: Random House.

Keohane, Robert O., ed. (1986) *Neorealism and Its Critics.* New York: Columbia University Press.

Klimoski, Richard, and Susan Mohammed (1994) "Team Mental Model: Construct or Metaphor?" *Journal of Management* 20:403–437.

Knowles, Eric S. (1982) "From Individuals to Group Members: A Dialectic for the Social Sciences." In *Personality, Roles, and Social Behavior*, edited by William Ickes and Eric S. Knowles. New York: Springer-Verlag.

Koelble, Thomas A. (1995) "The New Institutionalism in Political Science and Sociology." *Comparative Politics* 27:231–243.

Kruijssen, H.A.J. (1986) "Ontwikkelingssamenwerking als Rijksoverheidsdienst" [Development cooperation as a governmental department]. In *De Volgende Minister* [The next minister], edited by A. Melkert. The Hague: NOVIB.

Leites, Nathan (1953) *A Study of Bolshevism*. Glencoe, IL: Free Press.

Levine, John M., and Richard L. Moreland (1991) "Culture and Socialization in Work Groups." In *Perspectives on Socially Shared Cognition*, edited by Lauren B. Resnick, John M. Levine, and Stephanie D. Teasley. Washington, DC: American Psychological Association.

Levine, John M., Lauren B. Resnick, and E. Tory Higgins (1993) "Social Foundations of Cognition." *Annual Review of Psychology* 44:585–612.

Lijphart, Arend (1966) *The Trauma of Decolonization*. New Haven: Yale University Press.

Luykx, Theo, and Marc Platel (1985) *Politieke Geschiedenis van België* [Political history of Belgium], vol. 2. Antwerp: Kluwer Rechtswetenschappen.

Maas, P. F. (1986) "Kabinetsformaties en Ontwikkelingssamenwerking 1965–1982" [Coalition formations and development cooperation 1965–1982]. In *De Volgende Minister* [The next minister], edited by A. Melkert. The Hague: NOVIB.

Manheim, J. B., and R. C. Rich. (1995) *Empirical Political Analysis: Research Methods in Political Science*, 4th ed. New York: Longman.

March, James G., and Johan P. Olsen (1984) "The New Institutionalism: Organizational Factors in Political Life." *American Political Science Review* 78:734–749.

Markus, Hazel R., and Shinobu Kitayama (1991) "Culture and the Self: Implications for Cognitions, Emotion, and Motivation." *Psychological Review* 98:224–253.

Markus, Hazel R., and Paula Nurius (1986) "Possible Selves: The Interface Between Motivation and the Self-Concept." In *Self and Identity: Psychological Perspectives*, edited by Krisia Yardley and Terry Honess. New York: Wiley.

Mefford, Dwain (1991) "Steps Toward Artificial Intelligence: Rule-Based, Case-Based, and Explanation-Based Models of Politics." In *Artificial Intelligence and International Politics*, edited by Valerie M. Hudson. Boulder: Westview Press.

Pakenham, Thomas (1991) *The Scramble for Africa*. New York: Random House.

Pye, Lucian (1991) "Political Culture Revisited." *Political Psychology* 12: 487–508.

Resnick, Lauren B. (1991) "Shared Cognition: Thinking as Social Practice." In *Perspectives on Socially Shared Cognition*, edited by L. B. Resnick, J. M. Levine, and S. D. Teasley. Washington, DC: American Psychological Association.

Rose, Richard (1980) "Governments Against Sub-governments: A European Perspective on Washington." In *Presidents and Prime Ministers*, edited by Richard Rose and E. N. Suleiman. Washington, DC: American Enterprise Institute.

Sackmann, Sonja A. (1991) *Cultural Knowledge in Organizations: Exploring the Collective Mind*. Newbury Park, CA: Sage.

Searing, Donald D. (1991) "Roles, Rules, and Rationality in the New Institutionalism." *American Political Science Review* 85:1239–1260.

Serlon, Paul (1985) "L'AGCD: Vingt-cinq années d'enlisement" [The BADC: Bogged down for twenty-five years]. *La revue nouvelle* 41:529–542.

Sylvan, Donald A., Thomas M. Ostrom, and Katherine Gannon (1994) "Case-Based, Model-Based, and Explanation-Based Styles of Reasoning in Foreign Policy." *International Studies Quarterly* 38:61–90.

Turner, Ralph (1987) "Articulating Self and Social Structure." In *Self and Identity: Psychological Perspectives,* edited by K. Yardley and T. Honess. New York: Wiley.

Van Bellinghen, Jean-Paul (1990) "Belgium and Africa." In *Modern Belgium,* edited by Marina Boudart, Michel Boudart, and R. Bryssinck. Palo Alto, CA: Society for the Promotion of Science and Scholarship.

Vandommele, Mark (1982) "Twintig Jaar Belgisch Ontwikkelingsbeleid" [Twenty years of Belgian development cooperation]. *Internationale Spectator* 36: 499–506.

Vermeersch, Arthur J. (1970) *Vereniging en Revolutie: De Nederlanden 1814–1830* [Union and revolution: The Netherlands 1814–1830]. Bussum, Netherlands: Fibula–Van Dishoeck.

Vertzberger, Yaacov Y. I. (1990) *The World in Their Minds: Information Processing, Cognition, and Perception in Foreign Policy Decisionmaking.* Stanford: Stanford University Press.

Voorhoeve, Joris J. C. (1985) *Peace, Profits and Principles: A Study of Dutch Foreign Policy.* Leiden: Martinus Nijhoff.

Walker, Stephen G. (1977) "The Interface Between Beliefs and Behavior: Henry Kissinger's Operational Code and the Vietnam War." *Journal of Conflict Resolution* 21:129–168.

Walker, Stephen G., ed. (1987) *Role Theory and Foreign Policy Analysis.* Durham, NC: Duke University Press.

Weber, Max (1946) "Politics as a Vocation." In *From Max Weber: Essays in Sociology,* edited by H. H. Gerth and C. Wright Mills. New York: Oxford University Press.

Wels, C. B. (1982) *Aloofness and Neutrality: Studies on Dutch Foreign Relations and Policymaking Institutions.* Utrecht: HES Publishers.

Wildavsky, Aaron (1987) "Choosing Preferences by Constructing Institutions: A Cultural Theory of Preference Formation." *American Political Science Review* 81:3–21.

Witte, Els, Jan Craeybeckx, and Alain Meynen (1990) *Politieke Geschiedenis van België van 1830 tot Heden* [Political history of Belgium from 1830 to present], 5th ed. Antwerp: Standaard.

6

Cultural Influences on Foreign Policy Decisionmaking: Czech and Slovak Foreign Policy Organizations

John F. Zurovchak

Zurovchak builds a theoretical bridge to the discipline that has most fur-thered research on the effects of group structure, process, and choice—organizational behavior. He does so by adopting the approach and method of Geert Hofstede, the leading researcher in this field. Zurovchak asks whether the type of cultural analysis Hofstede performs on business corporations would be equally applicable to foreign policy departments of national governments. Using Hofstede's rankings of Czech and Slovak culture on four dimensions, Zurovchak then conducts in-depth interviews with foreign ministry officials of these two countries. Zurovchak is able to show that Hofstede's rankings can predict the structure and functioning of these two ministries, and hence, arguably, their foreign policy preferences as well.

—Editor

Are foreign policy organizations interchangeable across cultures? To what degree are differences in foreign policy decisionmaking among states reflections of cultural distinctiveness as opposed to products of issue area, bureaucratic processes, or elite personalities? Put simply, how must culture, defined as the socially created and learned values that influence human interaction, be factored into the foreign policy decisionmaking equation? These are provocative questions. Although many foreign policy analysts agree that culture is an integral aspect of decisionmaking, very few efforts have been made to study it systematically. Instead, as Hudson points out in her introduction to this book, culture is all too often used as a residual catch-all category: When all is said and done, those differences in foreign policy decisionmaking that remain to be explained are usually attributed to some amorphous notion of culture.

This project is an attempt to examine the impact of culture on foreign policy decisionmaking.[1] More specifically, I hope to explore in greater detail the nature of the relationship between cultural values and the structures and processes within foreign policy decisionmaking organizations. The ultimate goal is to provide a better understanding of how culture influences the foreign policy process, which in turn might provide more accurate predictions of foreign policy choice and behavior.

Given the paucity of empirical research in political science linking culture to foreign policy decisionmaking, I employ a framework borrowed from cross-cultural organizational psychology. Specifically, I use a dimensional framework developed by Geert Hofstede (1980, 1991). According to Hofstede, placement on each of the dimensions is correlated with differing structural and procedural attributes in various IBM subsidiaries found in more than fifty countries. His conclusion is that national culture, defined as the unique combination of placements on the four dimensions, systematically affects the organizational characteristics found in these subsidiaries.

I apply Hofstede's framework to another type of organization, the foreign policy organization. In an attempt to mirror his controlled comparison of subsidiaries of a single corporation, I employ the framework in a unique instance in which two foreign policy organizations coexisted simultaneously within a single state. Within postcommunist Czechoslovakia,[2] the emergence of a Slovak foreign policy organization alongside the federal foreign ministry and the subsequent simultaneous evolution and development of these two organizations set up a natural experiment that allows evidence of cultural differences to be examined more effectively than is normally possible in a "most similar cases" design. Furthermore, given the long-standing notion that Czechs and Slovaks are culturally very similar, if not identical,[3] this site becomes pivotal in determining both the applicability of Hofstede's framework to foreign policy decisionmaking organizations and, more important, for demonstrating the explanatory power of this variable in that even small differences in culture may affect organizational structures and processes.

I have divided this chapter into two parts. The first presents a detailed examination of my conceptualization and operationalization of culture in terms of a dimensional framework. Specifically, I examine each of the four dimensions and demonstrate how placement on a dimension correlates with particular structural and procedural attributes within the foreign policy organization in question. The second part tests the framework and hypotheses by applying them to the case of postcommunist Czechoslovakia.

BRINGING CULTURE INTO THE EQUATION:
A DIMENSIONAL FRAMEWORK

This essay represents the initial steps of an effort to overcome the obstacles that have thus far hindered incorporation of cultural variables into the decisionmaking equation. The ultimate goal is to determine empirically whether or not culture has an important influence, although not an exclusive influence, on foreign policy decisionmaking. The challenge is to create a compelling and tenable cultural framework that promotes empirical investigation.

Two conditions must be satisfied: (1) Culture must be (re)conceptualized so as to facilitate rigorous empirical research, and (2) the conceptual distance between the independent variable and the dependent variable must be reduced, since "the smaller the conceptual distance between cultural variables and what one wishes to explain by them, the more compelling a cultural explanation is likely to be" (Gaenslen, 1986:82).

The first step is to remove culture from its traditional role as a nebulous, catch-all category and to infuse it with more analytical power. As Hudson points out in her introductory chapter, typical definitions of culture are simply too broad to successfully support hypothesis generation, testing, or verification. Nearly any behavior, thought, or perception would fall within the boundaries of such definitions, thus making empirical research virtually impossible. In contrast, Hofstede constructs a model in which culture is depicted as a series of concentric circles with values at the center and rituals, heroes, and symbols arrayed as if they were the remaining layers of an onion, with the direction of influence being much stronger from the center outward rather than vice versa (Hofstede, 1991:3–18). Concentrating on the innermost circle, the model depicts a direction of influence whereby values constrain, and even periodically determine, the rituals (behaviors) performed within a given community. Values also are the linchpin in my effort to incorporate culture into foreign policy decisionmaking (FPDM) frameworks. As such, my conceptualization clearly falls within Hudson's second category of cultural frameworks.[4]

The Four Dimensions

This section details the operationalization of my independent variable in the form of Hofstede's four dimensions. In addition to describing each value dimension, I review related cross-cultural research that links each of them to various structural configurations and behavioral patterns.

Individualism/Collectivism.   One of the most widely utilized value constructs is the Individualism/Collectivism (IC) dimension. The ideal typical poles of this dimension are labeled Individualism and Collectivism, with the primary difference lying in the degree to which persons within a society feel dependent on other persons and groups that surround them. In essence, individualists define the self as independent of such persons and groups, whereas collectivists view the self as an interdependent part of society. According to Harry Triandis (in Gudykunst and Young, 1984: 296), the differences between the two may be summarized as follows: "Collectivistic cultures emphasize the goals, needs, and views of the in-group over those of the individual; the social norms of the ingroup, rather than individual pleasure; shared ingroup beliefs, rather than unique individual beliefs; and cooperation with ingroup members, rather than maximizing individual outcomes." Furthermore, "in addition to subordinating personal to collective goals, collectivists tend to be concerned about the results of their action on members of their ingroups, tend to share resources with ingroup members, feel interdependent with ingroup members, and feel very involved in the lives of ingroup members" (Hui and Triandis, 1986:509).

Several studies have utilized the IC dimension. For example, Leung and his colleagues conducted a study focusing on the preference for methods of conflict resolution prevalent in individualist and collectivist societies. In comparing two collectivist cultures, one from the East and one from the West, to two individualist cultures investigated in a previous project, they found that indeed both of the collectivist cultures had similar preferences for harmony-enhancing procedures and "clearly compared with the two individualist cultures, the two collectivist cultures ... preferred negotiating and complying more, both of which may be regarded as harmony-enhancing; and threatening, accusing, and ignoring less, all of which may be regarded as basically confrontational" (Leung et al., 1992:207).

In a closely related vein, Mann carried out research focusing on children's use of decision rules to resolve competing claims by group majorities and minorities. According to Mann (1986:319),

> The prediction that the cultural dimension of collectivism-individualism (Hofstede, 1980) influences the rules and principles children follow in determining majority versus minority rights and allocations is supported by classroom experiments in Australia, New Zealand, Japan, and Israel. Children in collectivist cultures are more likely to use the equal say or turn taking rule in resolving majority and minority claims. Children in individualist cultures are more likely to follow majority rule or self-interest in resolving majority and minority claims.

Thus, IC appears to be an important factor to consider when speaking of preferences for particular decision rules found in a given culture; it therefore may be an essential ingredient to understanding how conflicting majority and minority claims are resolved in a foreign policy organization.

Finally, Hofstede (1980, 1991) also offers some hypothesized differences that should appear in workplace interactions between societies preferring either individualist or collectivist values. He postulates that in a collectivist culture, employees will act according to the interest of the in-group, which may not always coincide with his or her individual interest (Hofstede, 1991:63). Also, in collectivist societies, the relationship between superior and subordinate is more often perceived in moral terms; it is even viewed as a family link complete with mutual obligations of protection and loyalty. Finally, he predicts that a focus on social relationships prevails over a concentration on the task in collectivist societies (Hofstede, 1991:67), a hypothesis similar to one offered by Gaenslen (1986) that contends decisionmakers in collectivist cultures are often overly reactive to the behavior of fellow participants and therefore tend to concern themselves with the social aspects of the group rather than with the task environment.

On the other hand, "employed persons in an individualist culture are expected to act according to their own interest" (Hofstede 1991:63). Superior/subordinate relationships are most often viewed as a contract based on mutual advantage, with promotions being based on performance. Finally, a focus on task prevails over a focus on relationships in individualist cultures (Hofstede, 1991:67).

Not only do behavioral processes appear to be affected by IC, but decision structures in the organization also seem to be constrained by a community's placement along the IC continuum. Gaenslen (1986) proposes that an emphasis on either individualist or collectivist value orientations will affect the level of attention given to the structural aspects of group composition and forum of decisionmaking. He asserts that individualists will pay less attention to such aspects, often even leaving them to chance, whereas collectivists should pay greater attention to such details and expend much more time and energy on making sure they uphold the expected cultural norms.

Table 6.1 summarizes the expected organizational attributes associated with Individualism/Collectivism.

Gender Differentiation. The second cultural value dimension affecting the characteristics of foreign policy decisionmaking organizations is one that attempts to distinguish between behaviors that are considered to be either "feminine" or "masculine"—that is, "tender" or "tough." Although this dimension has been labeled Masculinity (MAS) by Hofstede (1980, 1991), I have chosen to call it Gender Differentiation (GD) and label its ideal-typical poles strong and weak GD. Before proceeding with

Table 6.1   The Implications of IC for Decisionmaking

Individualism	*Collectivism*
1. Decision procedures, group composition, and forum of decision-making are often left to chance.	1. Much attention is given to design procedures, composition of decisionmaking group, and forum of decisionmaking.
2. Task prevails over relationship.	2. Relationship prevails over task.
3. Advancement is supposed to be based on skills and performance.	3. Advancement takes group obligations into account.
4. Conflict is resolved through competition and/or majority rule since group harmony is not a priority.	4. Conflict is resolved through negotiation and/or bargaining since group harmony is a high priority.
5. Superior/subordinate relations are based on mutual advantage.	5. Superior/subordinate relations are family-like and include protection and loyalty.

Source: Adapted from Gaenslen (1986) and Hofstede (1991).

a description of this dimension and its implications for organizational structures and processes, a brief word on the underlying reasons for this change is necessary.

According to Hofstede, the reason for labeling this dimension MAS, with polar ends identified as masculine and feminine, lies in the simple fact "that this dimension is the only one on which the men and the women among the IBM employees scored consistently differently" (Hofstede, 1991:82). Yet, as he points out (Hofstede, 1991:82–83), the labels masculine and feminine seem inappropriate and do not appear to capture what the dimension measures. For example, he states,

> Based on all the information about the distinctions between societies related to this dimension, it can be defined as follows: *masculinity* pertains to societies in which social gender roles are clearly distinct (i.e., men are supposed to be assertive, tough and focused on material success whereas women are supposed to be more modest, tender and concerned with the quality of life); *femininity* pertains to societies in which social gender roles overlap (i.e., both men and women are supposed to be modest, tender, and concerned with the quality of life). [Emphasis in the original]

Instead, I argue that the dimension should be labeled Gender Differentiation, with strong and weak the names of the ideal-typical poles at either end of the continuum. In cultures labeled weak GD, the values of men and women will overlap to a high degree. Conversely, in a culture with strong GD, I hypothesize that values and social gender roles will not overlap among men and women and their value preferences will be quite distinguishable.

In terms of specific organizational configurations and traits, I hypothesize weak GD cultures to be correlated with organizations in which leaders strive for consensus. Furthermore, I expect such cultures to stress equality, solidarity, and quality of work life. Decisions should be a "group" effort in which many members are consulted and cooperation is the defining norm. On the other hand, in cultures where a strong GD prevails, I predict leaders will be decisive and assertive. Unlike the weak GD culture, the stress will likely be on equity, performance, and the competition of views among colleagues. Organizations in this type of culture "stress results, and want to reward it on the basis of equity, i.e., to everyone according to performance" (Hofstede, 1991:93). Decisions, rather than being group efforts, will tend to be individual events. In other words, individual decisions are viewed as being better than group decisions since a social orientation does not prevail in strong GD countries (Hofstede, 1991:96–103).[5]

Table 6.2 outlines the differences in organizational structures and processes that are correlated with strong and weak GD.

Power Distance.   The third value dimension is one that focuses on the preference for equality or hierarchy within a given society. Hofstede labels this dimension Power Distance (PD) and bases it on the research of Mulder (1976, 1977), who defines it as the "emotional distance that separates subordinates from their bosses" (Hofstede, 1991:24). More specifically, this dimension is a measure of the willingness among members of a culture to accept an unequal distribution of power in society, most prominently in groups and organizations. Power Distance not only encompasses such attitudes toward authority, and authority-subordinate relations, it is also related to conformity and its opposite, encouragement of intellectual independence and a readiness to challenge alternative interpretations.

Cultures that are characterized by small PD emphasize egalitarianism. There is some degree of hierarchy between superiors and subordinates; however, it is neither the primary focus nor is it rigidly enforced. Within organizations, authority tends to be decentralized, and hierarchies that do exist are broad and flat. In such organizations, democratic ideals are encouraged and conflicts are often resolved through disagreement and competition—in other words, through the expression of multiple opinions. In terms of the implications for decisionmaking processes, the emphasis in small PD cultures is on consultative decisionmaking in organizations. Members are viewed as peers and a more collegial atmosphere

Table 6.2   The Implications of GD for Decisionmaking

Strong Gender Differentiation	*Weak Gender Differentiation*
1. Superiors are expected to be decisive and assertive.	1. Superiors strive for consensus.
2. Stress is on equity, performance, and the competition of colleagues.	2. Stress is on equality, solidarity, and quality of work life.
3. Recognition and achievement are highly valued.	3. Benevolence and service are admired.

Source: Adapted from Hofstede (1991).

tends to prevail. Within this atmosphere, there is more give and take by superiors with respect to subordinates, with superiors often even willing to grant limited autonomy to subordinates. Not only are superiors willing to grant such autonomy, subordinates are also willing to accept responsibility for decisionmaking. Overall, this type of culture reflects a willingness among both superiors and subordinates to accept a high level of participation and responsibility in decisionmaking (Hofstede, 1991; Gaenslen, 1986).

Cultures that fall more toward the large PD end of the spectrum stress rigid configurations of authority. Centralization and autocracy are high and strict hierarchies of superior/subordinate relations predominate. Hierarchies are steep, vertical pyramids that demand strict adherence. The implications for decisionmaking processes connected with this ideal type are obviously quite different from those associated with cultures characterized by small PD. In cultures characterized by large PD, decisionmaking is a product of strictly enforced patterns of authority. Within such organizations, democratic ideals are weaker, and there is little encouragement for subordinates to express disagreement. Conflicts are not resolved through competition but rather are suppressed—or, better still, simply not expressed. Instead of a collegial atmosphere prevailing, pecking orders are established and equality is an alien thought. Superiors, rather than seeking to solicit opinions from subordinates and viewing them as peers, often seek to control subordinates. Subordinates likewise fear expressing disagreement with leaders and actually prefer an autocratic or paternalistic leadership style. In acting on this preference, subordinates often attempt to avoid decisionmaking responsibility (Hofstede, 1991; Gaenslen, 1986).[6]

Table 6.3 presents the organizational characteristics identified with large and small PD.

Table 6.3   The Implications of PD for Decisionmaking

Small Power Distance	*Large Power Distance*
1. Less centralization and autocracy exist throughout organization.	1. High degree of centralization and autocracy exists throughout organization.
2. There is more give and take by superiors with respect to subordinates.	2. Subordinates fear expressing disagreement with leaders, while superiors desire to control subordinates.
3. Superiors are willing to grant some autonomy to subordinates, while subordinates are willing to accept responsibility.	3. Subordinates want to avoid responsibility.
4. Subordinates are willing to participate in decisionmaking and even expect to be consulted.	4. Subordinates are reluctant to participate in decisionmaking.

Source: Adapted from Gaenslen (1986) and Hofstede (1991).

Uncertainty Avoidance.   The final dimension is labeled Uncertainty Avoidance (UA). It is a measure of the degree of discomfort with ambiguity, nonconformity, and uncertainty within a society and ranges along a continuum from weak UA to strong UA. The UA dimension gauges how different cultures solve the universal problem of dealing with an uncertain future and the anxiety that accompanies such ambiguity and uncertainty. The basic distinction is between cultures that tolerate ambiguity in a variety of situations, organizations, institutions, and social relations and those that do not. Hofstede borrows the term UA from the research of Cyert and March (in Hofstede, 1980:156), who maintain that organizations in specific societies avoid uncertainty in the following way: "They avoid the requirement that they anticipate future reactions of other parts of their environment by arranging a negotiated environment. They impose plans, standard operating procedures, industry tradition, and uncertainty-absorbing contracts on that situation."

Turning to the implications that such a dimension has for the characteristics of an organization, the two ideal typical poles are associated with different structural and procedural configurations. In a society in which a preference for weak UA prevails, organizations are expected to have few rules and regulations, or standard operating procedures (SOPs). In fact, "in countries with very weak uncertainty avoidance there rather seems to be an emotional horror of formal rules. Rules are only established in case of absolute necessity" (Hofstede, 1991:121).

Even those rules that do exist will be very general in nature, with extensive room for interpretation and maneuvering. Societies that are located at the opposite extreme have quite different organizational characteristics. In general, authority is vested in complex and comprehensive systems of rules and regulations. These SOPs, both formal and informal, are often many and precise with little room for interpretation, maneuvering, or neglect. This is because rules "try to make the behavior of people predictable" (Hofstede, 1980:158). In strong UA cultures there exists a societal norm to create very structured environments. This norm may be so strong in cultures at the extreme end of the continuum that "the emotional need for laws and rules . . . often leads to the establishing of rules or rule-based behaviors which are clearly nonsensical, inconsistent, or dysfunctional" (Hofstede, 1991:121).

Table 6.4 is a comparative summary of the differences in the attributes of foreign policy organizations in societies that are characterized by either a weak UA or a strong UA.

THE RESEARCH DESIGN AND SOURCES OF DATA

The foreign policy organizations of postcommunist Czechoslovakia from January 1990 to December 1992, as well as the organizations found in its subsequent independent parts, the Czech Republic and the Republic of Slovakia, serve as the vehicles for testing the hypotheses proposed in this project. As sites for data collection, both the joint state and its offspring are quite distinctive,[7] as the two foreign policy organizations coexisted simultaneously within the same state for a period of two and a half years. In addition to the federal foreign policy organization, the Ministry of Foreign Affairs,[8] there also evolved an ethnically based Slovak foreign policy organization, the Ministry of External Relations. The net result is that the concurrent existence of these two organizations, and their subsequent parallel development and evolution within the independent states of Slovakia and the Czech Republic, provide a veritable laboratory setting for examining the effects of culture on structures and processes within foreign policy decisionmaking organizations. Essentially, cultural influences are more readily isolated since the system and regime variables are largely held constant.

The site is also important in that postcommunist Czechoslovakia imposes quite rigorous demands on the framework since the two cultures being compared are so similar. Many comparative studies focus on cultures perceived to be quite different, such as Gaenslen's (1986) research comparing Japanese, U.S., Chinese, and Russian interpersonal relations. In contrast, this project attempts to demonstrate that even small differences in culture may have a profound impact on organizational structures and processes.

Table 6.4   The Implications of UA for Decisionmaking

Low Uncertainty Avoidance	*High Uncertainty Avoidance*
1. Few and general rules and SOPs characterize organization.	1. Authority is vested in rules and SOPs that are many and precise throughout the organization.

Source: Adapted from Hofstede (1991).

The first step in carrying out this comparative research is to measure the independent variable, culture. To this end, the independent variables are defined as the unique set of numerical ratings on all four dimensions for each culture. The ratings are then linked to the hypothesized structures and processes given in Tables 6.1 through 6.4, which, in turn, are compared with the actual structures and processes (as perceived by foreign policy officials) that characterize the foreign policy organizations in Prague and Bratislava. Data measuring the dependent variables are both quantitative and qualitative and consist of interview responses of foreign policy decisionmakers from the respective foreign policy organizations in Prague and Bratislava. These interviews were conducted during two periods, April/May 1994 and September/October 1994. They included officials from all levels of each organization, from first deputy ministers to desk officers to supporting staff personnel. These interviewees acted as informants, providing descriptions of the predominant structures and processes within their respective organizations. Content analysis of the interview responses provides both a quantitative measure, in the form of frequency counts, etc., and a qualitative measure, in the form of descriptive analysis. The object is to determine whether the predicted structural configurations and behavioral patterns actually prevail in the ministries in Prague and Bratislava.[9]

Since I rely on a series of subjective responses to describe ostensibly objective structures and processes, a brief word on my standards of interpretation is necessary. Each interviewee was asked largely the same questions. Since my aim is to uncover differences in the responses given by Czechs and Slovaks about the structures and processes that characterize their foreign policy organizations, my confidence is highest for those dimensions that meet two criteria: (1) Czech and Slovak respondents give different answers to the same questions, and (2) a large number of respondents within a ministry give the same or similar responses. In other words, if a question is asked about a particular structure or process within the organization, two answers that are similar are better than one, three are better than two, etc. Likewise, whenever Czechs and

Slovaks give similar answers to questions pertaining to structures and processes, I report it. Furthermore, contradictory answers from individuals within the same foreign policy organization are also presented. In both the latter instances, confidence in the hypothesized association between a specific dimension and organizational structures and processes decreases. Finally, in some cases I expect the data to be too sparse to make any intelligible interpretation.

The Dimensional Ratings: Czechs Versus Slovaks

Beginning in December 1993 and continuing through 1994, the Dutch consulting firm DHV, in cooperation with Charles University, conducted a survey using Hofstede's (1980) methods and translations of his questionnaire. The questionnaire was administered to 200 Czechs and 150 Slovaks. Out of 200 Czech respondents, 60 were managers holding general administrative positions in various industries who ranged between twenty-five and sixty-five years of age. The remainder of the respondents were employees of a variety of industries. According to DHV, the two sets of respondents are comparable and possess no significant differences.[10]

Table 6.5 presents the results of the DHV survey and gives the dimensional ratings for Czechs and Slovaks. Each index has a range from approximately zero to one hundred; scores higher than fifty denote the following: Individualism, large Power Distance, high Uncertainty Avoidance, and strong Gender Differentiation; scores below fifty indicate Collectivism, small Power Distance, low Uncertainty Avoidance, and weak Gender Differentiation.

Comparing Czech and Slovak Foreign Policy Organizations

This section examines whether or not the hypothesized foreign policy structures and processes associated with these ratings (given in Tables 6.1 through 6.4) actually prevail in the two foreign ministries. The data for examining these organizational attributes are the product of the in-depth interviews described previously. I restricted the interviews to personnel in the "bilateral" and the "multilateral" sections within each organization, in order to focus on the departments that would have the most influence over foreign policy formulation and implementation.

The bilateral sections are divided into territorial departments that are responsible for all aspects of bilateral relations, with a limited number of countries grouped into geographical regions. The multilateral affairs section in each ministry includes departments responsible for security, international organizations, foreign aid, and economic cooperation. Interviews in both sections included officials from the level of first and

Table 6.5   Dimensional Ratings for Czechs and Slovaks

	PD	UA	IC	GD
Czech Republic (N = 200)	40	75	55	5
Slovak Republic (N = 150)	55	75	40	25

second deputy minister down to staff persons working in specific departments. In Prague, twelve interviews were conducted; in Bratislava, the
number was ten.[11] The average interview lasted 43.44 minutes, with the
shortest being 27 minutes and the longest 75 minutes. Demographically,
the Czech and the Slovak respondents were similar in many ways.
Roughly 33 percent of the Czechs and 30 percent of the Slovaks indicated some connection with the foreign ministry under the communist
regime. Likewise, 50 percent of the Czech officials and 40 percent of the
Slovak informants were younger than fifty. Approximately 20 percent of
the Slovaks reported a background in business, with 15 percent of the
Czech interviewees reporting similar backgrounds. Gender appeared to
be the only category on which the two sets of respondents differed significantly, as only three out of twenty-two respondents were female, all
three Czech. All interviews were conducted in English according to a set
protocol, with some deviations occurring due to the flow and temper of
each conversation.[12]

The following section describes the evolution and development of
each of the foreign policy organizations that came to represent the
Czechs and Slovaks following the dissolution of the common state in
January 1993. It presents the formal structure of each organization and
specifies the sections and departments that are included within them.
Later in the chapter I introduce and analyze the interview data and compare the responses of Czechs and Slovaks to verify whether the structural configurations and behavioral patterns reported by interviewees
conform to those hypothesized by the framework.

Continuity and change in Czech and Slovak foreign policy organizations.
In discussing the Czech and Slovak foreign policy organizations in the
postcommunist era, it is impossible to understand their evolution, development, and reform without acknowledging the institutions that preceded them. These organizations were built on the existing remnants of
the institutions from the former regime, as one Czech official acknowledged was the case of the foreign ministry in Prague, stating, "The new
Czech Ministry of Foreign Affairs is patterned after the former Federal
Ministry of Foreign Affairs."[13] Another official echoed this perception,

noting, "The foreign ministry has taken over the rules and regulations of the communist and federal eras."

However, as many of the respondents pointed out, although the formal structural arrangements, such as number of sections and departments, territorial divisions, etc., are nearly the same in both the communist and postcommunist ministries, the actual operation of the new institution is based on a more democratic ideal as opposed to a communist one. In practice, this means more freedom at all levels of the ministry to affect foreign policy formulation and implementation. As one official noted, "No longer is foreign policy the domain of a few top-level party officials." Thus, qualitative differences in operation are evident between the communist foreign policy organization and its postcommunist successor, even if the section and department names and jurisdictions remain largely the same.

As Figure 6.1 shows, the Ministry of Foreign Affairs in Prague is a multilevel, multisection organization. The ministry consists of a hierarchy in which the foreign minister (*Ministr*) is at the apex of the organization. He is assisted by two deputy foreign ministers, a first (I. *náměstek*) and a second (II. *náměstek*). Below these deputy ministers are the heads, or directors-general (*vrchního ředitele*) of the various sections. Within each section there are from four to five departments, each directed by a department head or director (*ředitele*), and within these departments are the various staff personnel. Each department numbers approximately eight to ten members, although some of the larger departments, such as the second territorial department, which includes the United States and some European countries, may include up to twenty-five members. The schematic organization of the Czech Ministry of Foreign Affairs is depicted in Figure 6.1.[14]

The Slovak Ministry of Foreign Affairs (Ministerstvo zahraničných vecí) formally came into existence only with the emergence of an independent Slovakia following the dissolution of the common state at midnight on December 31, 1992. However, traces of its roots can be found as early as August 1990. As the new state struggled with its postcommunist identity, leaders in Slovakia contended that Slovak interests were being overlooked and even disregarded. As a result of this perception among Slovaks, a new organization took shape in late 1990 in Bratislava and was introduced as the Ministry of External Relations. The aim of this new institution was to safeguard and advance Slovak foreign policy priorities, which were seen as differing from Prague's foreign policy agenda. As the dissolution of the joint state became a fait accompli in late 1992, the Ministry of External Relations was formally designated as the new Ministry of Foreign Affairs of the Slovak Republic.

Like the foreign ministry in Prague, the Slovak foreign policy organization is a multilevel, multisection organization. Figure 6.2 depicts the

Figure 6.1
Ministry of Foreign Affairs, Czech Republic

Minister

	1st Deputy Minister				2nd Deputy Minister		
Ministry Cabinet	**EuroAtlantic Section**	**Section of Multilateral Affairs**	**Section of Asia, Africa, and Latin America**	**Section of Law and Consuls**	**Section of Information and Culture**	**Administrative Section**	**Service Section**
Ministry Spokesman	Slovak Dept.	Dept. of European Security	4th Territorial Dept.	Diplomatic Protocol	Press Dept.	Personnel Dept.	Finance Dept.
General Inspection	1st Territorial Dept.	Dept. of European Community	5th Territorial Dept.	Int'l Law Dept.	Dept. of Cultural and Scientific Relations	Dept. of Wages	Investment Dept.
Dept. of Analysis and Planning	2nd Territorial Dept.	Dept. of UN Organizations	6th Territorial Dept.	Consular Dept.	Dept. of Czechs Living Abroad	Dept. of Upper Administration	Dept. of Building Management and Security
Office of Special Affairs	3rd Territorial Dept.	Dept. of Int'l Economic Cooperation	7th Territorial Dept.	Dept. of Human Rights and Migration	Central Czech Dept.	Dept. of Legislative Law	Service Dept.
Institute of Int'l Affairs						Dept. of Technical Matters	Dept. of Special Liaison
							Diplomatic Service

140

Figure 6.2
Ministry of Foreign Affairs, Slovak Republic

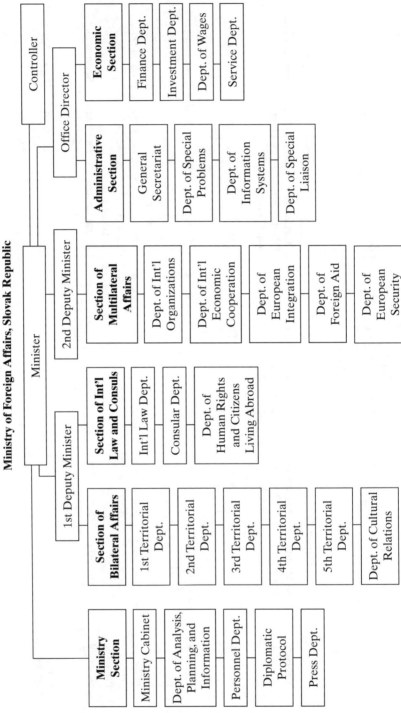

schematic organization of the ministry. The first point to note is how strikingly similar the Slovak organization is to the Czech ministry in terms of its formal structures. This is not surprising considering that, as one official from Bratislava reported, the Slovaks "are following the same general plan of organization that the Czechs have adopted." This perception is supported by another official who was previously employed in the federal foreign ministry until the dissolution of the common state. He related: "The structure we now have in this ministry reminds me of the structure of the Federal Ministry of Foreign Affairs."

As Figure 6.2 illustrates, the Slovak foreign policy organization also consists of a hierarchy in which the foreign minister (*minister*) is at the apex of the organization. He, too, is assisted by two deputy foreign ministers, a first (I. *štátny tajomník*) and a second (II. *štátny tajomník*).[15] As in the case of Prague, the heads or directors of the sections are below the deputy foreign ministers. The Slovak ministry consists of nearly the same division of labor as that in Prague, with one major exception: The Slovak ministry has only one bilateral section instead of two. Within this section, the territorial departments are also fewer, numbering only five. The Slovak organization is therefore more centralized with respect to the bilateral affairs section, as all territorial departments are within one section, and thus under one director.

Although a comparison of Figure 6.1 (Czech Ministry of Foreign Affairs) and Figure 6.2 (Slovak Ministry of Foreign Affairs) shows similar institutions, differences in organizational hierarchy as well as lines of authority are clearly evident. In the Czech ministry there are no well-defined lines of authority between the second-level deputy ministers and the various departments, nor in terms of intra- and interdepartmental relations. In sharp contrast, Figure 6.2 depicts a clearly defined hierarchy with distinct lines of authority emanating from the minister, the two deputy ministers, and even the various sections and departments. This visual evidence conforms to expectations given the respective dimensional ratings for Czechs and Slovaks on PD and IC and is further corroborated by the interview responses presented below.

Comparing Expected and Actual Structures and Procedures

As we have seen, Czech culture is characterized by Individualism (IC=55), weak Gender Differentiation (GD=5), small Power Distance (PD=40), and high Uncertainty Avoidance (UA=75). Slovak culture, on the other hand, may be described by the following attributes: Collectivism (IC=40), weak Gender Differentiation (GD=25), large Power Distance (PD=55), and high Uncertainty Avoidance (UA=75). Thus, differences in structure and process between the two ministries should appear on the IC and PD dimensions, while the two organizations should be relatively similar along the GD and the UA dimensions. The question asked in this section is: Do the structures and processes of the Czech and Slovak foreign ministries exhibit the characteristics we would expect given their respective cultural orientations? The following discussion attempts to answer this question for each of the four dimensions.

Individualism/Collectivism. The first two hypotheses are stated as follows:

- IC-1. Within individualist societies decision procedures, group composition, and forum of decisionmaking will be left to chance, whereas much attention will likely be given to them in collectivist societies.
- IC-2. Cultures with an individualist orientation should emphasize task in contrast to collectivist orientations, in which an emphasis on social relationships prevails.

As a way of tapping the information related to these first two hypotheses, I asked each respondent the following question: "You have just described some problems/issues which you said were significant, and which stand out in your mind. Could you describe, in as much detail as possible, what went on in the decisions you mentioned above?" This general question was then supplemented with more pointed questions that sought to probe the level of attention given to decision procedures, group composition, and decision forum.

Most Czech respondents began by discussing formal decisionmaking, mentioning either the routine briefings that take place every morning at the highest level, or the weekly meetings that occur at the section and department levels. Their responses indicate that the weekly meetings held across all levels of the Czech foreign policy organization serve as important forums in which to convey information and to discuss policy problems. They vary in frequency from section to section and from department to department, but all seem designed to facilitate the flow of information among and between levels of this large and complex organization.[16]

More important, in addition to these formal weekly decision forums, evidence also surfaced of an informal decisionmaking process in which group composition and decision forum seemed to be situationally specific. For example, one high-level official maintained that "although formally structured decision forums do exist for routine decisionmaking in the form of weekly meetings occurring on Mondays and Thursdays, the *real* decisionmaking takes place in very small groups that are ad hoc . . . these decisions are done orally and not so much in written form, either with memos or minutes." Another official added, "Such ad hoc sessions *occur at the request of the section or department in question in order to deal with a specific topic or problem.* They nearly always consist of only two, three, or four individuals ... never more than five" (emphasis added).

Decisionmaking in the Czech organization appears multifaceted. For routine problems and issues there are references to weekly meetings at all levels. In this type of decisionmaking, attributes such as group composition and decision forum are fixed in order to expedite information flow and to ensure the smooth operation of the ministry. In informal decisionmaking, however, it seems that such aspects are not (pre)determined. Instead, decision forum and group composition are products of the situation at hand. In other words, there does not appear to be a specific group that must be convened or consulted on all nonroutine occasions in order to make decisions. Instead, who is included and where they shall meet are a function of the problems or issues that arise.

Dovetailing with the tendency to leave decision procedure, group composition, and decision forum to chance in informal decisionmaking is an emphasis on task rather than on social relationships. This task orientation is evident in the fact that ad hoc decisionmaking seems to be dictated by situational determinants rather than group relationships. Two officials summarized these tendencies concisely with nearly identical words. One stated, "We rarely have meetings for meetings' sake, that is, have regular meetings week to week or every other day. If issues come up, then we address them." The other stated, "We have regular meetings once or twice a week, if the situation demands it. We meet in order to solve problems."

Officials in the Slovak foreign ministry were also asked to describe the processes that characterize decisionmaking in their organization. Interestingly enough, these officials gave responses similar to those of the Czechs when speaking about routine, formal decisionmaking. According to many of the respondents, weekly meetings are also the norm in the Slovak organization. In fact, according to the responses from both Czechs and Slovaks, it appears that in terms of the formalized, routine decisionmaking processes that involve information transfer and assignment of daily tasks among the sections and departments, the two foreign policy organizations are nearly identical.

What is interesting, however, is how both organizations deal with informal and nonroutine problems and issues. Unlike the Czechs, Slovaks appear to deal with unexpected problems and issues by using different strategies. Although several Slovak respondents used the term *ad hoc* to describe nonroutine decisionmaking procedures, their use of the term differed from that of the Czechs. In the most detailed reference to informal decisionmaking given by a section head in Bratislava, the evidence appears to suggest that special attention is given to group composition and forum of decision when unexpected problems arise. As this section head reported:

> We have ad hoc meetings concerning various matters. They are quite often held on Saturdays because everyone is free ... we usually have them on the weekend or late in the evening, six or seven o'clock, because it is quite clear that nobody will disturb us. At these meetings, we discuss important matters. These meetings are usually attended by a quite narrow circle, the minister plus three or five people. They are a kind of "brain trust" of the ministry.

As this response seems to indicate, meetings are held on specific days so that a particular group of individuals may be present. I interpret this to indicate that at least in these situations, attention is paid to the forum of decisionmaking (Saturdays) in order to allow a specific group to attend (group membership). Furthermore, this group is referred to as the "brain trust," which appears to indicate that such meetings are not one-time affairs but instead are part of an ongoing group that convenes to address nonroutine issues and problems. In addition, I found no references among the Slovak respondents, such as the following Czech response, that revealed how the problem or issue helped in determining who was included in a decision group. When speaking about a decision involving a crisis in a region relevant to a particular department, one member of that department related that the decision group consisted of "the section chief, the vice-ministers, and other department heads from the whole division, in all, six to eight people together discussing the decision." When asked directly, "Does it always have to be this set group of people included in every decision?" this official replied:

> No, no, no. For example, if we are trying to be a nonpermanent member of a regional cooperative organization, then this decision is very big. It involves a meeting of all the section chiefs in the ministry. There will be a vote, then a decision, and we will send a letter to the organization. However, it [who is involved] depends on whether or not we are the only decisionmakers involved, or if there are more departments involved. In one case it involved the European department, and the UN organizations departments. In another case, we found ourselves cooperating with the second territorial department. Sometimes, it is just me and my section chief, or it might also include the vice-minister. It depends on the problem.

Given the evidence presented above, I believe both the Czech and Slovak foreign policy organizations appear to conform to the expectations of hypotheses IC-1 and IC-2, but only in the case of informal decisionmaking dealing with problem solving, as opposed to information exchange. In the Czech organization, the evidence points to decisionmaking procedures that are left to chance, coupled with an emphasis on task rather than on social relationships. In contrast, within the Slovak organization, the style of dealing with unexpected problems or issues appears to be one in which more attention is given to decisionmaking character-istics such as decision forum and group composition, with social relation-ships playing an important role in the decision process.

The third and fourth hypotheses deal with aspects of the relation-ship between superiors and subordinates. The propositions summarizing these next two hypotheses are:

- IC-3. Superior/subordinate relations are based on mutual advan-tage where Individualism is prevalent; however, where Col-lectivism is the inclination, superior/subordinate relations are characterized as family-like and include mutual and recipro-cal obligations of protection and loyalty.
- IC-4. Advancement should be based on skills and performance in societies bearing an individualist orientation, whereas in soci-eties characterized by Collectivism, advancement in the orga-nization will take group obligations into account.

According to responses from Slovak officials, it appears that personal connections play a role at all levels of their organization. Positions usually viewed as civil service jobs, such as department heads and section heads, also involve connections. This evaluation seems to be borne out in an anecdote told by a department head. This official related how, with each new foreign minister that was appointed (there have been four in the past three years alone!), wholesale changes occurred throughout the foreign ministry. This was even the case when the new minister and the old minis-ter belonged to the same party. This respondent's answer seems to be a clear instance of not only how promotion and advancement (or demotion and firing) involve group obligations, but also how superior/subordinate relations are characterized by protection and loyalty. He stated: "For some time, when Mr. Y was the minister of foreign affairs, he was com-pletely ignoring those people who were here under Minister X, even though they were in the same party. Not only that, we had many, many people here fired or called back from their posts because they worked for Minister X. And Minister Y wanted most of his people."

This evidence is further corroborated by two other officials who spoke in differing ways of how the Slovak foreign policy organization appears to be characterized by family-like relationship patterns. In the first instance, a department head spoke about how he could bypass his immediate superior (the section chief) and two deputy ministers and go directly to the foreign minister himself. In speaking of this special rela-tionship, this official said, "I can go to the minister whenever I want be-cause I have known Mr. Minister for a long time. He is a personal friend of mine. Because I have good contacts and good relations with Mr. Min-ister, I have no problems."

The second official, also a department head, focused on the relationship between and among sections in the organization. In his opinion, relations were sometimes strained between sections because officials in other sections did not have a similar background, or had not been long-time ministry employees. This official commented, "As you may know, the balance of our section graduated from Moscow. We know each other very well. We worked together in Prague. The problem is with the directors of the other sections. They are new and are without experience. So that's the main problem in cooperation between these sections. I think that people in our section are more experienced than people in other sections."

Unlike responses from Slovak officials, Czech respondents provided very little evidence to either confirm or disconfirm an inclination toward promotion based on individual skills and performance or relational patterns among bosses and their subordinates that are based on mutual advantage. Therefore, the evidence appears to suggest that while hypotheses IC-3 and IC-4 hold for the Slovak organization, the evidence pertaining to the Czech foreign ministry is ambiguous.

Finally, with regard to methods of conflict resolution, the fifth IC hypothesis states:

- IC-5. If an individualist orientation prevails, conflict will be resolved through competition and/or majority rule since group harmony is not a priority; in contrast, if a collectivist orientation predominates, conflict resolution strategies will focus on negotiation and bargaining in an effort to preserve or restore group harmony.

To uncover evidence pertaining to the style of conflict resolution in each foreign policy organization, I asked respondents the following question: "When opinions differ in your section (department) with respect to a specific problem, how would you characterize the ways in which these differences are resolved?" As the following quotations indicate, none of the respondents speaks about conflict resolution strategies per se. Instead, interviewees talk about the presence or absence of conflict or disagreement in their departments.

For example, several Czech interviewees alluded to a conflictive or a competitive aspect of their foreign policy organization. As one staff person stated, "It is only my personal view that sometimes people from other departments feel that we interfere in their jobs. They feel we are their competitors, or rivals even, or that we hide something from them." Another official at the staff level commented in a similar, although much more diplomatic way, noting that "the departments are parochial to an extent and do vie with each other for resources and for attention."

Finally, the competitive nature of the process surfaced in the comment of a respondent who said, "What you put into a file, into a document, or into a position is a matter of constant review and argumentation among ourselves."

These responses indicate the presence of competition in the Czech foreign policy organization. This conforms to expectations, since group harmony is not a priority within an individualist orientation. Instead, individuals are free to act as advocates for positions, and conflict resolution should occur through argumentation, persuasion, and the competition of contending viewpoints.

When speaking to Slovak officials, such references to disagreements were curiously absent. In fact, when asked the question above, many simply could not recall having conflicts of opinion. One official even declared, "Disagreement does not occur. I cannot recall any instances in which I disagreed with the minister or with the deputy foreign ministers."

I am not sure how to interpret this apparent tendency to downplay the level of conflict or disagreement in the Slovak organization. It is plausible that the unsettled domestic political situation made Slovak respondents more cautious when discussing this topic.[17] Perhaps it is the case that conflict and disagreement among members of a department or section is headed off by a period in which the policy in question is up for commentary and debate. A department head in the Slovak organization seemed to refer to such a process, commenting, "A lot of time is spent gaining a single understanding of the problem. We rely on paper as well as the phone quite a bit. This is because we want to discuss with each other our views before we present them to the section head."

Although I am reluctant to interpret this evidence as supporting hypothesis IC-5, I do think it implies that within the Czech foreign ministry, conflict is an accepted aspect of decisionmaking and is often resolved through argumentation and the competition of views. On the other hand, in the case of the Slovak foreign ministry, it is plausible that this downplaying of conflict and the references to the "commenting period" reflect an emphasis on harmony within the organization that is consistent with a collectivist value orientation.

Power Distance. The second dimension along which Czech and Slovak scores differ is Power Distance, defined as the extent to which "the less powerful members of institutions and organizations within a country expect and accept that power is distributed unequally" (Hofstede, 1991:28). Furthermore, this dimension is associated with the degree of centralization and hierarchy found in an organization, as well as the level of conformity and its opposite, a willingness to express disagreement.

The first characteristic, degree of centralization, is summarized in the following hypothesis:

- PD-1. Organizations in societies characterized by small Power Distance should be less centralized, with hierarchies being broad, flat, and flexible. In contrast, organizations in large Power Distance societies will likely have a high degree of centralization throughout the organization, with hierarchies being steep and rigid.

To obtain data pertaining to the level of centralization within each organization, I examined responses to a general question on decision-making as well as other questions, such as, "Do you have the flexibility to go above the department (section) head?" or "How strict is the hierarchy of decisionmaking?" or, finally, "Does your boss have to approve everything that leaves the department or do you ever send out information to departments that doesn't necessarily need his/her approval?" As would be expected given their different Power Distance ratings, Czech and Slovak responses to these questions differed markedly.

Before considering the responses of Czech and Slovak officials, from our previous comparison of the formal structures of the two ministries from Figures 6.1 and 6.2, it is immediately apparent that in the Slovak organization there is a higher degree of centralization. This is consistent with the higher PD score of Slovaks as compared to Czechs.

Turning to the interview data, responses from Czech officials seem to indicate that although a hierarchy exists in their foreign policy organization, it is neither a steep one nor is it so rigidly enforced that circumventing superiors results in severe penalties. As one director-general related, "There is a hierarchy, but it is not a strict one. Each section must know what the others are doing. For instance, a section head of multilateral affairs must know a lot of information about the various countries with which the Czech Republic is dealing. Therefore, the hierarchy must not be so strict as to hinder or prevent communication."

Similarly, in nearly all of the interviews of officials from the ministry in Prague, one word continually surfaced as a description of the organizational hierarchy: flexibility. For example, one official noted, "Of course, you must know that there is an organizational order in the ministry. And all the functions we are talking about are subject to this organizational structure. Basic issues and the basic organizational scheme have to be conducted according to the organizational structure, but this is, as far as I know now, quite flexible. So, in many respects, one has to follow the organizational structure, but there is flexibility." Such a description is in accordance with the expectations of hypothesis PD-1: In a culture with small Power Distance, the organizational hierarchy includes a degree of flexibility that would not be apparent in an organization with a large Power Distance.

In a more revealing response, a staff member in one of the departments suggested that the organizational hierarchy was not flexible *enough* and at times proved to be an obstacle. In fact, this individual argued that the hierarchy should be made flatter, with horizontal ties between departments strengthened. He explained,

> When you have a multilateral department, you may need to cooperate with your partners in the so-called territorial departments and other functional departments. However, there is an obstacle in the rules and in the hierarchy of the ministry since it is divided by section and there are many departments. I think a system that could enable us to initiate teams and that would have horizontal outreach would let us take more initiative. Although it is not part of the organizational structure, it's being done. But it would help if these things were institutionalized; because sometimes when a person in a certain other department needs assistance with what he or she is doing, we can encounter problems. Such an arrangement would be much more beneficial than the present pattern which is, you have to convene a briefing, or common meeting of representatives of various departments. And it's up to the head of the department who he or she is going to send to that meeting. Sometimes you have different people coming for the same subject and it doesn't help the situation.

Another official, this time a director-general, portrayed the organizational hierarchy within the Czech foreign ministry in yet another way. In particular, this respondent argued that the hierarchy apparent in Figure 6.1 is a formal structure and that informally, in the daily operation of the ministry, it is not rigidly enforced. Specifically, when queried about the chain of command and accessibility to officials one level removed, this respondent noted that all directors-general could bypass the first and second deputy foreign ministers to directly contact the minister. This he called the "rule of direct access."

In a similar way, department heads within the organization report that horizontal communication with personnel from departments in other sections is also relatively unhindered. Lower-level personnel note that intersectional communication and cooperation is a common practice even though it may not be formally advocated. In one such case, an official noted, "Well, the hierarchy of decisionmaking in the ministry is such that on a working basis you can contact almost any official in the ministry up to the level of department director. Although formally, if you are working on a subject and something leaves the department, then it needs to be approved either by the director or if he is not present, by myself." This flexibility conforms to the expectations posited in hypothesis PD-1.

These Czech responses differ from the responses given by Slovaks when queried about their organizational hierarchy. Specifically, Slovak foreign policy officials depict their ministry as a stricter hierarchy. In fact, one section head advocated centralizing the organization even further by merging the single bilateral section with the multilateral section to create one large division under a single official! In a discussion of the present organizational structure, this individual intimated, "We should integrate the section of bilateral cooperation with the section of multi-lateral cooperation. We should have one very strong political division and have this fully staffed with several deputy directors, departments, and I don't know what else. . . . But we should try to find some better model; I would prefer a very large structure, a very effective structure."

Although most respondents were not ready to increase the central-ization to this extent, many interviewees did seem to describe the present structural configuration as a rigid hierarchy in which jurisdictions are clearly demarcated. Evidence of this rigidity in the organizational hierar-chy may be found in two particular responses. In the first, a staff member of a department described how communication between departments in differing sections is hindered by the centralization of authority and the pecking orders that accompany it. In particular, this staff member told how communications must first go through the department head and then through the section head to the other section head and then back down again to the department head; for the response, the sequence must be reversed. In frustration, this lower-level official lamented, "According to our routine, I should communicate with a colleague of the bilateral section or division through my boss. He will in turn address his colleague and back down. This is nonsense."

In still another episode, a department head related the story of how he was placed in charge of a special delegation for a specific issue of pri-ority to Slovak foreign policy. On the one hand, he stated, "As head of the delegation, I'm responsible to the minister, and I will communicate directly with the minister, of course." On the other hand, whenever he returned, he said, "I am here as the director of one department, which means I should report, being the director, to the head of the division. So if I am abroad, I am independent, when I come back . . . I, according to the book, am to address my colleagues [in the delegation] through my boss. This cannot work."

In sum, with respect to the organizational hierarchy in the Czech and Slovak foreign ministries, it seems that the evidence presented above supports hypothesis PD-1. Czech organizational structure is viewed as a necessary evil and is neither rigid nor strictly enforced but rather flexible. As one official succinctly put it, "I think the organiza-tional hierarchy is as free as possible to enable good ideas to surface as quickly as possible." In contrast, the Slovak responses indicate that their organization is more centralized and has a hierarchy in which vertical connections are emphasized more than horizontal connections. Further-more, unlike the Czech ministry in which the formal structure may be circumvented in both formal and informal ways, the Slovaks adhere much more to their hierarchy and do not mention bypassing their superiors through a "rule of direct access."

Hypothesis PD-2 addresses the willingness of subordinates to express disagreement with their superiors.

- •PD-2. In organizations characterized by small PD, there will be more give and take by superiors with respect to subordinates, with subordinates willing to express disagreement. On the other hand, in organizations with large PD, subordinates fear expressing disagreement.

To obtain data, I asked the following question: "Have you ever disagreed with your immediate superior? What was the result of this disagreement?" In the Czech case, the responses appeared to conform to expectations associated with a small PD as they indicate both willingness and ability to express disagreement with their superiors. For example, in response to the question above, one department head answered, "I can say what I think to my chief or to the vice minister . . . I can voice my own opinion openly." Another respondent recalled an instance in which a critical decision was preceded by a discussion involving many different officials. According to this department head, "There was a big discussion here in the ministry. I gave my opinion, and then another point of view concerning our current policy was expressed. This one focused on the interests of our allies that differed from ours. The result was that I was told to go out and make the argument for us that we would vote with our allies. That became the policy. *But I personally voted against all the people in the department*" (emphasis added).

According to these responses, expression of disagreement seems to be unhindered, with many of the interviewees concurring with the staff member who claimed, "I could present my views freely on every occasion." Even in cases where disagreements had not surfaced, respondents expressed confidence that they would be at ease expressing disagreement. Such was the case for one staff-level official who confided, "Up until now, I haven't had any big conflict or even conflicts at all with him [the boss], but if I have and I think I have good arguments, then I will express them."

Contrast these Czech responses with Slovak answers to the same questions. Most striking in the Slovak responses is the absence of any mention of disagreement between subordinates and their superiors. In fact, many of the Slovak respondents replied with some variation of the statement that disagreements never, or very rarely, occurred. According to one department head, "Disagreement does not occur in this department. I cannot recall instances in which we disagreed." Another department head who was asked a similar question responded, "You know, I have only been in this position for two months, but I haven't had any such problems [disagreements with a superior]. I have good relations with my bosses, so I haven't had any disagreements."

I find these Slovak responses difficult to interpret. They are ambiguous with regard to actual expression of disagreement with superiors or even the willingness to express such disagreement. Several possibilities seem plausible. First, it may be the case that these respondents actually have not encountered instances in which they disagreed with their superiors, although this is unlikely. On the other hand, it may be the case that their responses reflect a reluctance to express disagreement to their bosses, which would be consistent with a large PD orientation. Finally, it may simply be the case that the socially desirable answer is to not admit to such instances of conflict or disagreement, which would also conform to expectations of large PD.

In the end, what can be said with regard to hypothesis PD-2 is that Czech and Slovak responses differ in their willingness to express disagreement to superiors within their respective foreign policy organizations. The Czechs are much more forthright in their admission that disagreements occur, and, even more important, they feel comfortable expressing disagreement with their superiors. Slovaks, on the other hand, do not mention instances in which they disagree with their bosses, nor do they mention a willingness to express such disagreement even if it should occur. Such patterns are consistent with the expectations associated with the existence of a large Power Distance orientation in the Slovak foreign policy organization and a small Power Distance orientation in the Czech organization.

The third and fourth hypotheses deal with the level of responsibility given to subordinates by their superiors within the organization and the level of participation in decisionmaking based on such responsibility. They are as follows:

- PD-3. In small PD cultures, superiors should be willing to grant some autonomy to subordinates, while subordinates should be willing to accept such responsibility. In contrast, in large PD cultures, superiors seek to control subordinates who in turn want to avoid responsibility.
- PD-4. In organizations characterized by small PD, subordinates are willing to participate in decisionmaking and even expect to be consulted. However, in organizations with a large PD, subordinates are reluctant to participate in decisionmaking.

In order to secure information on the level of responsibility within the various sections and departments, I asked each respondent the following questions: "How much autonomy do you have in your department? Are you comfortable with this level of responsibility or would you like to see it increased or decreased?" Likewise, to garner information about participation, I asked, "Do you expect to participate in important matters within the department? If not, in which matters do you expect to participate? How often are your expectations met?"

In general, according to the Czech interview data, levels of superior control are low, while levels of subordinate responsibility are high throughout the bilateral and multilateral sections. In particular, one head of a territorial department noted, "It is no longer the case that superiors dictate policies, but there is a 'give and take' tendency toward policy formulation." Another individual concurred, stating, "Before, the pattern was only, 'I have all the information, that means I am the king, and I can rule,' so I can say to my staff 'you are good, you will get more information' or 'you are not so good, which means you get nothing.' But I think increasing the responsibility of the staff is a better way of managing than the kind of leading or management that used to take place."

Such responsibility extends even down to desk officers. As evidence, when queried about the responsibility of subordinates within the department, one territorial department head responded, "Every one of my people here has two or three countries. They manage the things with these countries instead of always coming to consult with me. They no longer say 'what shall we do with this problem.' [Now] they have the responsibility to say what we should do, what the Czech Republic should want to say . . . it is better when everyone is responsible for the decision-making." In fact, this new responsibility is such that one department head claimed that he and his staff "were [now] responsible for 85 to 90 percent of policy formulation" for the territories within their department. Such high levels of responsibility and participation even among the lower levels of subordinates appear to be illustrative of a small Power Distance culture.

Not only do the bosses acknowledge that they have extended a larger responsibility for decisionmaking to subordinates, these subordinates also recognize and accept such responsibility. As one low-level official responded, "He [the section head] gives us a lot of freedom and, in my view, he instigates us to use the freedom not as anarchy, but as responsibility." And still another confided, "I guess, you know, my boss is trying to give us, not only to me, but to other[s], autonomy." Finally, one staff member simply stated, "I believe the level of responsibility is quite acceptable." Such sentiments appear to confirm that superior/subordinate relations in the Czech Ministry of Foreign Affairs are characterized by a certain degree of give and take, with bosses seeking to loosen control and subordinates willing to accept increased responsibility and participation, all of which would indicate the existence of a small Power Distance orientation in the Czech foreign policy organization.

In contrast to the patterns described by the Czech respondents, Slovak answers to the questions above provided mixed evidence. In some instances, interviewees alluded to a strong desire to control subordinates among the leading officials of the organization, along with a corresponding desire among subordinates to avoid both decisionmaking responsibility and participation in decisionmaking. On the other hand, other section and department heads described how they preferred to delegate more responsibility to subordinates who in turn accepted such responsibility and actively participated in decisionmaking. As evidence of the controlling pattern, one official offered the following lengthy explanation:

> We do have an organizational structure in this ministry; what we don't have is competence in practice in our decisionmaking processes. . . . We rely on our bosses too much. For example, it is not normal, but when I took over this department, it was up to me what style of policy I would use. If I wanted my staff to sign in every morning, or arrive before 7:45 and sit here until after working hours, it depended on me. That is not good. . . . Every director can influence the style of life of his department. This is extremely problematic.

In contrast, another department head offered a description in which it appears the degree of control exercised by him over his staff members is quite low. According to this individual, "When I took over this department, I completely restructured it. Instead of structuring it vertically, I made it horizontal. This change provides more flexibility for my department and does not leave only one or two people who know what is going on. In other words, no longer do only one or two people have a large proportion of power in this department, which I did not like, because when they leave, nobody else knows what is going on." These two quotations are the best examples of the contrasting evidence that surfaced among Slovak respondents regarding PD-3 and PD-4. Thus, although hypotheses PD-3 and PD-4 seem to hold for the Czech foreign policy organization, the Slovak respondents supplied data consistent with both a small and a large PD value orientation for both hypotheses.

Gender Differentiation.   Even though a full twenty points separates the Slovaks from the Czechs, they both remain in the weak GD classification. Thus, differences in interview responses should be differences of degree, not of type. According to Table 6.2, the following hypothesized behavioral patterns are expected to prevail in each organization:

- GD-1. Superiors strive to achieve consensus in the management of their departments rather than to be assertive and directive.
- GD-2. Stress is on equality, solidarity, and quality of work life rather than equity of performance and competition against colleagues.

- GD-3. Benevolence and service are admired rather than recognition and achievement.

The interview data on these three hypotheses present mixed impressions with regard to both the Czech and the Slovak foreign policy organizations. The data from the Czech respondents are less problematic and indicate some conformity to the expectations associated with a weak GD; however, the Slovak respondents supply answers associated with both a strong GD and a weak GD.

Czech officials portrayed the decisionmaking tendencies of their superiors in the following ways:

> The section chief was very good at soliciting opinions from all interested parties. It was his practice to ask all individuals to participate in making a decision and to give their opinions wherever possible. The discussion would take a long time and then a decision would be taken as to what to do. This system took a long time to reach a decision. The section chief was very open and was always ready to discuss a variety of opinions.

> My boss always seemed to look for more information by asking everybody what they thought. He never simply told us this is the order. Because of this way of making decisions, meetings are longer and more drawn out. This is a very time-consuming process, but I think it is worth it.

> He [my boss] gives us some ideas and he says, "I think it's possible to do it this way." And then you have to make up your mind if that is the way you want to do it.

> If he [the department head] needs something, he calls us and we discuss the problem with him. Let's say, for example, as did happen, he goes to a meeting at which he should recommend a Czech position on the new situation involving the "Pact of Stability." He called me and asked me what the newest development was and he presented me with informal proposals that he thought he would present at the meeting. He asked me, "Do you agree with them or do you disagree with them? Or are they inconsistent?"

These quotations show an inclination toward including all individuals in the decisionmaking process and soliciting multiple opinions in the pursuit of consensus.

Likewise, evidence emerged in some Slovak responses that decisionmaking tendencies among superiors also conformed to expectations along this dimension. In three different instances, Slovak officials described a decision process in which the role of consensus played a major part. One individual depicted a decision process as follows: "My boss spends a great deal of time gaining a common understanding of a problem." In another example, a Slovak respondent describing the mode of decisionmaking he employed himself stated, "I want to have a dialogue, not issue orders, because I don't like orders. I think it is much more useful to have a dialogue to discuss problems, to discuss guidelines, to discuss practically everything with them. Of course, I must know about everything my diplomats are dealing with, so the control must be there. I try to control them, but very softly. There is no need to give them strong orders and to be hard on them."

Yet another department head characterized similar decisionmaking tendencies, stating, "Here in [my] department, I must make the decisions. It is my personal preference to find consensus with those under me. It makes no sense to develop a process in which I always say, 'This is no good . . . send this paper back . . . I don't agree.'"

It seems that these individuals are describing a decision process in which consensus and dialogue play large roles, as would be expected in a society with a weak GD orientation. However, other evidence contradicts such a view. In particular, two respondents described decisionmaking preferences in the Slovak organization that did not seek consensus. For example, one department head related, "There are departments and directors who just make decisions. They do not ask for opinions or what their people think." In another case, perhaps the most revealing, a section head asserted, "I meet with my department heads, not to ask them what they think, but to give them tasks and information. I tell them what to do and they should do what they are told. Orders come from above and are passed down; no department must run this division. It must be the other way around." Considering these Slovak responses, it is unclear whether the prevailing norm among superiors in the Slovak organization is one that seeks consensus or one that is directive.

With regard to the second and third hypotheses, the question I designed failed to solicit the desired information. Since the questions I asked failed to yield adequate information concerning Gender Differentiation, I turned to an ancillary indicator of GD in organizations. As Hofstede points out, there is "a positive correlation between a country's femininity [weak GD] score and the participation of women in higher-level technical and professional jobs" (Hofstede, 1991:95; 1980:292, 306). If Hofstede's hypothesis is correct, support of the assertion that the Czech foreign policy organization is characterized by a weak Gender Differentiation surfaced in the form of women occupying higher offices in the Czech foreign ministry. Out of the total number of twenty-two respondents, only three were women. As it turns out, all three female respondents were Czechs. More important, of these three women, two were department heads in the Czech foreign policy organization. In contrast, no women respondents came from the Slovak organization. In fact, the only women I encountered in Bratislava held lower-level positions as secretaries and administrative assistants. The women department heads in the Czech ministry add confidence to our assertion that Czech society has a weak Gender Differentiation.

In summary, in comparing the Czech organization to the Slovak ministry, expectations of weak GD are largely met in the former (particularly with regard to GD-1), while in the latter the evidence is contradictory and difficult to interpret.

Uncertainty Avoidance. The Czechs and the Slovaks each received a dimensional rating of seventy-five on the UA dimension. This score places both societies among the countries labeled high in Uncertainty Avoidance. Therefore, the expectation is that both the Ministry of Foreign Affairs in Prague and in Bratislava will be characterized by the attributes associated with high UA. The interview data, however, do not demonstrate any correlation between the Czech or the Slovak UA score and the tendency toward a reliance on rules and regulations. Instead, the opposite seems to be true: Both the Czech ministry and the Slovak ministry operate as if their respective ratings were low.

The core of the UA dimension is the existence and reliance on sets of rules, regulations, and SOPs throughout the organization as a method for reducing uncertainty. UA-1 summarizes the expected relationships between high and low UA and the rules and regulations found within a particular organization:

- UA-1: Organizations with a low UA orientation will be characterized by few and general rules and SOPs, while in organizations with a high UA orientation, authority is vested in rules and SOPs, which are many and precise throughout the organization.

To uncover evidence pertaining to this hypothesis, I asked the following questions: "Would you characterize your section (department) as having too many rules and regulations? Are the rules and regulations applicable to all levels of decisionmaking and all issues, or are they applied only to routine, noncritical situations?" Or, "If a problem arose that you had to address, would your boss approve of your solving the problem even if it went against the normal rules, or would your boss rather that you follow the rules in order to solve the problem?" Or finally, "Would you ignore the rules of your department in order to solve a problem that arose or would you follow proper regulations for achieving a solution?"

According to nearly every Czech respondent, the foreign ministry is not characterized by extensive rules and regulations. Instead, problems are addressed on a situational basis in a very pragmatic way. Again, organizational rules exist and are even codified into a manual that I was shown several times. However, these rules serve as general guidelines. In the most telling quote, a department head in the bilateral affairs section stated, "Maybe we have a lot of rules, but I do not know them. No, we are really flexible. At least, we are trying to be flexible." Such a cavalier attitude toward the rules and regulations that govern the operation of the organization is contradictory to the expectations associated with a high Uncertainty Avoidance.

In another example of the less than rigid attitude toward rules and regulations, one department head indicated that SOPs for each department are determined by the official in charge. This department head, who had held the position for only a short time, commented that development of the organizational structure was in the hands of department heads and did not therefore necessitate rigidly binding general systems of rules and regulations for the entire organization. According to this individual, "It is in my hands. . . . It is up to me how I organize the operation of my department . . . and this is what I am working on just now, since I have been appointed to this office only recently." Thus, it does not appear that the Czech foreign policy organization is constrained by an extensive system of rules, regulations, and bureaucratic SOPs and therefore does not appear to conform to the expectations associated with high UA cultures.

The Slovak interview data also do not conform to expectations along this dimension. As in the Czech case, there is little correspondence between the Slovak UA score and a propensity toward the reliance on rules and regulations. On the contrary, the Slovak organization, reminiscent of the Czech case, performs as if it were the product of a low UA culture. Evidence of a low Uncertainty Avoidance in the Slovak interview data, while not as extensive as that in the Czech data, does appear in the form of responses that characterize the overall operation of the ministry as being flexible. According to one department head, within the ministry there is a "large degree of flexibility and autonomy within which to work." Although there are rules and regulations, they are not the primary authority within the organization. Another official concurred, stating that there are SOPs, but they "are not suffocating," and can in fact be violated in case of emergency.

Although both the Czech and the Slovak foreign policy organizations possess structural configurations corresponding to a lower UA than their dimensional ratings would seem to forecast, the implications of this UA score are different for both organizations. In particular, the low UA in the Czech case is combined with a low PD. This results in a decision process that is largely ad hoc in nature and very task oriented. In sharp contrast, the low UA in the Slovak organization is combined with a high PD so that personal power dominates the decisionmaking process. This is consistent with Hofstede's (1980:318–319) expectations regarding the joint effects of PD and UA on organizations. As he argues,

> Where PDI is high, power is the leading principle which keeps the organization together and which protects it against uncertainty. In cultures where PDI is low, there are two possibilities. If people have an inner need for living up to rules [high UAI], the leading principle which keeps the organization together can be formal rules. If people do not have an inner need for living up to rules [low UAI], the organization has to be kept together by more ad hoc negotiation, a situation which calls for a larger tolerance for uncertainty from everyone.

Nowhere is this more evident in the Slovak case than in one official's response that rules and regulations are unnecessary, because "we know each other well, we have worked together in Prague for a long time, *so we do not need rules*" (emphasis added).

In sum, the interview data do not appear to support characterizing either the Czech Ministry of Foreign Affairs or the Slovak Ministry of Foreign Affairs as a high UA organization. The opposite seems to be the case; responses from individuals in both ministries seem to indicate that the rules and regulations are flexible and that even though they may exist on paper, they are not followed diligently; in some cases they are not even known by department heads![18]

Rival Hypotheses

In summary, this chapter has demonstrated that different structures and processes in the Czech and Slovak foreign policy organizations are associated with differing dimensional ratings for each of the societies under examination. Specifically, the Czech foreign ministry is characterized by structures and processes associated with Individualism and small Power Distance. On the other hand, the Slovak foreign policy organization is characterized by structures and processes associated with Collectivism and large Power Distance.

Two rival hypotheses come to mind as explanations for the findings presented above. In particular, differences between Czech and Slovak responses may be a product of lingering communist culture or the result of differing levels of experience. Addressing the former first, it seems plausible that the differences between Czechs and Slovaks may be the product of a higher holdover rate of former communist officials in the Slovak foreign ministry. The responses given by Slovaks, characterized by a reliance on personnel relations, an orientation toward the collective, and the neglect of rules and regulations, conform to behavior patterns consistent with those that prevailed in the former communist regime. In addition, since the Czech law on lustration (the exclusion of former communist officials from state posts) prevented many former communist officials from retaining office, it is possible that these findings are merely the product of more communist-era holdovers in the Slovak foreign ministry. Thus, the discrepancy is not one of general societal or ethnic culture, but rather one of a communist versus postcommunist culture. Wolchik (1995:171) expresses a similar argument:

> The legacy of the communist past is [similarly] alive in the bureaucracies at higher levels, where it also proved to be impractical to replace large numbers of individuals. The continuity of personnel has in many cases resulted in a continuation of the style of operation that prevailed during the communist era, and there is still a need to reorient many bureaucrats' and officials' style of work and attitude toward citizens.

Two factors undermine this type of argument. First, the demographic characteristics of both sets of interviewees contain similar percentages of officials who indicated an affiliation with the foreign ministry under the former communist regime. There were no significant discrepancies in the background characteristics of the set of respondents pertaining to communist background. Furthermore, of the officials that did indicate some affiliation with the foreign ministry under the communist regime, only two individuals gave answers that could be construed as consistently depicting a typical communist mentality. Of these two individuals, one was Czech and one Slovak. With the remainder of the respondents, answers did not conform to any consistent pattern that may be considered communist.

A second explanation is that Slovak foreign policy officials lack the experience of the Czech officials and thus rely more on personal relationships and less on institutionalized rules and regulations, as would be the case with more experienced officials. Again, however, the demographic data indicate that both Czech and Slovak respondents have mixed backgrounds, some with long-term service in the foreign ministry, others with business backgrounds, still others with only minimal experience in the ministry; and, finally, some lower-level officials hold first-time positions following graduation from higher education. Therefore, socialization patterns and levels of experience seem to be similar in both foreign policy organizations, once again undermining support for the hypothesis associating differences in structures and processes to the level of experience of officials in the Czech and Slovak organizations.

CONCLUSIONS

This project has attempted to provide a framework for incorporating culture into the foreign policy decisionmaking equation. We can only

hope that it will begin to build a foundation for rigorous empirical research linking culture to foreign policy decisionmaking. As pointed out
in the introduction to this book, such research has been sorely lacking in
the FPDM literature for several decades. To overcome the obstacles that
often hinder cultural research in FPA, I have offered a framework based
on four value dimensions, with the intent (1) to provide a basis for distinguishing one culture from another, and (2) to demonstrate that a country's location on these value dimensions is associated with particular foreign policy structures and processes. In general, this chapter shows that
even though Czechs and Slovaks existed in a joint state for more than
seventy years, and each adopted nearly the same formal structures for
their respective ministries, the structures and processes in those organizations differed in ways largely consistent with the ratings of each country on the four dimensions. My conclusion, therefore, is that culture plays
a role in the foreign policy decisionmaking process by influencing, to
some degree, the structure and functioning of the foreign policy organization in a particular state.

More specifically, in two out of four dimensions, namely the Individ-
ualism/Collectivism and Power Distance dimensions, a strong association surfaced between the dimensional ratings and the hypothesized
structural configurations and behavioral patterns in both the Czech and
Slovak foreign policy organizations.[19]

The findings in this chapter also offer some initial hypotheses with
regard to these "cultural characteristics." In particular, location on the
Individualism/Collectivism dimension is associated with group composition, the decisionmaking forum, the emphasis placed on social relationships within the organization, and the nature of superior/subordinate relations. Likewise, placement on the Power Distance dimension appears
to be related to the willingness to express disagreement with leaders and
levels of participation in decisionmaking. All of the above may be seen
to affect informational inputs in various ways. For instance, the nature of
superior/subordinate relations and the willingness to disagree with leaders, as determined by placement on the PD dimension, may affect the
flow of discrepant information across levels of the organization. Similarly, the reluctance of subordinates to participate in decisionmaking
may preclude the use of the full informational resources of the organization, thereby contributing to defective decisionmaking.

Another implication of these findings concerns the quality of information—in particular, "information that comes from within the decisionmaking system and flows to another part of it." As Vertzberger
(1990:78) notes, "The policymaker's orientation toward an external
source could become crucial in their choosing among alternative interpretations of the situation. The source's rank in the bureaucratic and political hierarchy also has an effect: elite sources are more liable to be ac-

cepted as dependable and their information as important than lower-ranking sources, even if the latter are in a position to obtain more relevant and accurate information." Location on the Power Distance and Individualism/Collectivism dimensions would seem to be important factors in "choosing among alternative interpretations of the situation." They are associated with the degree of centralization within the foreign ministry and the steepness of the organizational hierarchy and therefore may influence the distance between elite and lower-ranking levels, influencing in turn the potential bias toward the dependability and importance of the information in question.

One avenue of possible future research is to examine the role of cultural variables in influencing the quality of decisionmaking by constructing research designs to test the hypothesized relationships offered by Vertzberger and others (Janis, 1972). One way of examining the relationships between cultural variables and quality of decisionmaking and information processing is to construct detailed comparative case studies using George's (1979) process tracing methodology. Such a method would highlight links between dimensional ratings and decisional outputs. Another possibility is to conduct detailed comparative case studies of foreign policy successes and fiascos in much the same way as Janis (1972) and t'Hart (1990) have done, but with an eye toward isolating cultural variables instead of personality variables. The goal would be to link cultural variation in Czech and Slovak foreign policy organizations to foreign policy outcomes and outputs in specific successes and fiascos.

In summary, this initial effort provides some insights into the influences of cultural variables on foreign policy decisionmaking in the Czech Republic and Slovakia. It is possible to discern how cultural value orientations affect the structures and processes of foreign policy organizations in these two countries. The next step is to determine whether these structures and processes can be linked to foreign policy outputs and behaviors through future research projects such as those described.

NOTES

1. This research was supported by a grant from the National Science Foundation (DIR-9113599) to the Mershon Center Research Training Group on the Role of Cognition in Collective Political Decision Making at The Ohio State University.

2. The Czech and Slovak Federated Republic ceased to exist at midnight on December 31, 1992. Where appropriate, I will refer to the joint state as Czechoslovakia, particularly in the time period from 1989 to 1992. When referring to the states that emerged following the dissolution of the joint state in 1992, I will use the common names of each new entity: the Czech Republic and Slovakia.

3. For example, the notion of "Czechoslovakism" held that Czechs and Slovaks were not two distinct ethnic groups but rather "two branches of the same family tree." For a more detailed elaboration of this view, consult Johnson (1985); Leff (1988); and Wolchik (1991).

4. Let me present four caveats concerning culture: (1) Culture is not immutable. Even though this framework operationalizes culture by assigning numerical ratings on four dimensions to specific societies, these ratings must be viewed only as "snapshots" in time. It remains an empirical question as to the rate and degree of cultural change in any specified time period and something to be studied in the future. (2) Culture is a multilayered concept. As social identity literature points out, individuals and, by extension, societies exist in a web of overlapping and at times conflicting "cultures" such as societal culture, ethnic culture, organizational culture, occupational culture, gender culture, elite culture, mass culture, and a host of other types of cultural identities that individuals deem salient at any given time. In this project, I concentrate largely on societal-level culture in the Czech Republic and Slovakia. One additional cultural identity is considered: the communist culture. (3) Culture and institutions are interrelated. Although I focus on culture as the independent variable and institutional structures and processes as the dependent variables in this project, I do not posit causal priority in either one. Instead, they are mutually interdependent and reinforcing.

5. For more details on additional studies, see Hofstede (1980:286–298).

6. For more details on additional studies relating to PD, see Hofstede (1980:95–105); (1991:20–30).

7. Since it is the research opportunity that is unique and not either the Czech or Slovak foreign policy organization, the findings of this project and the implications these findings have for FPDM in general are not so unique as to preclude generalization to other foreign policy organizations.

8. I am asserting that the Ministry of Foreign Affairs in Prague is culturally Czech, whereas the Ministry of External Relations and its successor, the Ministry of Foreign Affairs in independent Slovakia, are culturally Slovak. Taking the latter first, the Ministry of External Relations consisted only of Slovak officials who sought to pursue Slovak national interests and therefore should be considered culturally Slovak. Furthermore, upon the dissolution of the common state in January 1992, officials of the Ministry of External Relations, in conjunction with a large percentage of Slovak officials from the federal ministry, combined to form the core of the new Ministry of Foreign Affairs in Bratislava. Again, pursuing Slovak national interests, representing the newly independent Slovakia, and possessing no Czech members, the organization should be considered culturally Slovak. In contrast, the federal Ministry of Foreign Affairs in Prague is a more difficult case. Throughout the years following the Prague Spring in 1968 and until the collapse of the communist regime in December 1989, the federal Ministry of Foreign Affairs actively recruited Slovaks to lessen the dominance of the Czechs. However, the percentage of Slovaks consistently remained quite low, at less than 10 percent. Given this extremely low percentage of Slovaks in the federal ministry, I contend that a more prevalent Czech culture completely dominated the minority Slovak culture, so much so that the ministry could be considered culturally Czech. This is true to an even greater extent following the dissolution of the common state, because a large percentage of those Slovaks who were employed in the federal ministry departed for Slovakia in late 1992, thereby making the federal ministry even more "Czech" than before.

9. I have chosen to utilize interview data from informants within the two organizations to assess the nature of the structures and processes that prevail in each of them on a daily basis. In other words, I am using informants' representations of what goes on rather than measuring such information more objectively. Alternative measures, such as declassified transcripts of meetings, memoranda, and other written communications, memoirs, etc., are often available in older, more established institutions. For both the Czech and the Slovak foreign policy organizations, such "paper trails" were not yet available; however, these measures will be important to use in future examinations of the two foreign policy organizations.

10. The DHV respondents contained managers and employees from a variety of industries, while Hofstede's respondents were employees and managers of only IBM subsidiaries. These differences may pose some problems in comparability across the DHV survey and Hofstede's data set. However, it is arguable that the DHV data may be more reflective of a society's culture, since the respondents were not solely from one industry. In the end, the nature and degree of such comparability problems is not apparent at this time due to the lack of information regarding the types of industries in which the managers were employed.

11. Although the number of interviews in each ministry appears small at first, I believe it is an adequate sampling, for several reasons. First, many of the departments in each ministry have very limited staffs, averaging only eight persons, including department heads. Furthermore, turnover rates are extremely high at present, leaving even a smaller number of persons with enough experience for interviewing. Therefore, interviewing all department heads and staff members of an acceptable tenure from each department produced a pool consisting of approximately thirty-six persons in each foreign ministry. Thus, in Prague, my interviewees represented 33 percent of possible interviewees, while in Bratislava, 30 percent of potential interviewees were included. Finally, the interviewees are informants rather than respondents; therefore, the number of interviews is less important than the quality of information they convey.

12. There were two reasons for conducting the interviews in English: (1) Fiscal constraints prevented me from hiring a translator for the field work, and (2) my Czech and Slovak language skills were not sophisticated enough to conduct the interviews in the native language of the respondent. Fortunately, all my informants possessed an extremely good command of the English language, at a level advanced enough that little was lost in the interview process. This is not to say that my interviews conducted in English did not lose some of the nuance and flavor that Czech- and Slovak-language interviews would likely have contained; however, the interview transcripts attest to the richness of the detail provided by all respondents even though they were speaking in a foreign tongue. Finally, in conducting the interviews in English, I at least omitted the potential for errors of translation and misunderstanding between the translator and the informant and between the translator and myself. Although the English interviews were not the best possible option in an ideal world, they were certainly the best possible option available to me.

13. All quotations without notation in the following sections are taken from the interviews of Czech and Slovak foreign policy officials. Names have been withheld to protect the anonymity of the respondents at their request.

14. This structural configuration is an English-language translation of the actual diagram produced by the Ministry of Foreign Affairs in January 1994 and therefore represents a Czech conceptualization of their ministry in Prague.

15. Figure 6.2 is likewise an English-language translation of the actual diagram produced by the Ministry of Foreign Affairs in Bratislava in October 1994. It is interesting to note that until early September 1994, the Slovak organization had only one deputy minister to assist the foreign minister. However, following this date, a second deputy was added, thus bringing the Slovak organization even more in line with the Czech organization in terms of formal structures.

16. For more information on these formal meetings, see Zurovchak (1995: Chap. 5).

17. The political atmosphere in Slovakia was unsettled in both March and September 1994. In March 1994, the former foreign minister, Josef Moravcik, became the prime minister after a vote of no confidence removed Vladimir Meciar from that office. A new foreign minister, Eduard Kucan, was subsequently appointed. These personnel changes at the highest ministerial level were accompanied by wholesale replacements throughout the Ministry of Foreign Affairs in Bratislava. Similarly, in the last week of September 1994, an election returned Meciar to the prime minister's office and once again foreshadowed changes in the foreign ministry staff at all levels. This volatility in the political realm may have created an atmosphere of caution among respondents regarding some of my questions.

18. A rival hypothesis concerning the discrepancy between predicted and observed levels of UA in both foreign policy organizations contends that low UA levels are due to the newness of the foreign policy organization. This hypothesis seems plausible with regard to the ministry in Bratislava, as many interview respondents cited the "newness of the ministry" and the lack of "historical experience" and "minimal institutionalization" as factors affecting the operation of the ministry. To a lesser degree, the Czechs also contend that reform of the foreign ministry has given it a new character in which rules, regulations, and SOPs are not institutionalized and therefore do not affect the structure and functioning of the ministry in predicted ways. This explanation would seem to be a confirmation of Anthony Downs's classic hypothesis that newly created bureaucracies lack institutionalization of a standard set of rules and regulations and therefore do not exhibit the levels of rigidity found in older bureaucracies. One way of testing this hypothesis is to continue to track the development of these organizations across time and to replicate this study on each organization at different times.

19. Interestingly enough, these dimensions seem to parallel the two dimensions found in the work of Thompson, Ellis, and Wildavsky (1990), cited by Hudson in her introduction to this book.

REFERENCES

Gaenslen, Fritz (1986) "Culture and Decision Making in China, Japan, Russia, and the United States." *World Politics* 39, no. 1:78–103.

George, Alexander L. (1979) "Case Studies and Theory Development: The Method of Structured, Focused Comparison." In *Diplomacy: New Approaches in History, Theory, and Policy,* edited by P. B. Laurent. New York: Free Press.

Gudykunst, William B., and Yun Kim Young (1984) *Communicating with Strangers: An Approach to Intercultural Communication.* Reading, MA: Addison-Wesley.

Hofstede, Geert (1980) *Culture's Consequences: International Differences in Work-Related Values.* Beverly Hills: Sage.

Hofstede, Geert (1991) *Cultures and Organizations: Software of the Mind.* London: McGraw-Hill.

Hui, C. H., and H. Triandis (1986) "Individualism/Collectivism: A Study of Cross-Cultural Researchers." *Journal of Cross Cultural Psychology* 17: 225–248.

Janis, Irving (1972) *Victims of Groupthink: A Psychological Study of Foreign Policy Decisions and Fiascoes.* Boston: Houghton-Mifflin.

Johnson, Owen (1985) *Slovakia 1918–1938: Education and the Making of a Nation.* New York: Columbia University Press.

Leff, Carol Skalnik (1988) *National Conflict in Czechoslovakia: The Making and Remaking of a State, 1918–1987.* Princeton: Princeton University Press.

Leung, K., Y. Au, J. Fernandez-Dols, and S. Iwawaki (1992) "Preference for Methods of Conflict Processing in Two Collectivist Cultures." *International Journal of Psychology* 27, no. 2:195–209.

Mann, Leon (1986) "Cross-Cultural Studies of Rules for Determining Majority and Minority Decision Rights." *Australian Journal of Psychology* 38, no. 3: 319–328.

Mulder, Mauk (1976) "Reduction of Power Differences in Practice: The Power Distance Reduction Theory and Its Applications." In *European Contributions to Organization Theory*, edited by G. Hofstede and M. S. Kassem. Assen, Netherlands: Van Gorcum.

Mulder, Mauk (1977) *The Daily Power Game.* Leiden: Martinus Nijhoff.

t'Hart, Paul (1990) *Groupthink in Government: A Study of Small Groups and Policy Failure.* Rockland, MA: Swets and Zeitlinger.

Thompson, Michael, Richard Ellis, and Aaron Wildavsky (1990) *Cultural Theory.* Boulder: Westview Press.

Vertzberger, Yaacov (1990) *The World in Their Minds: Information Processing, Cognition, and Perception in Foreign Policy Decisionmaking.* Stanford: Stanford University Press.

Wolchik, Sharon L. (1991) *Czechoslovakia in Transition: Politics, Economics and Society.* New York: Printer.

Wolchik, Sharon L. (1995) "The Czech Republic and Slovakia." In *The Legacies of Communism in Eastern Europe,* edited by Zoltan Barany and Ivan Volgyes. Baltimore: Johns Hopkins University Press.

Zurovchak, John F. (1995) "Cultural Influences on Foreign Policy Decision Making: Comparing the Structures and Processes of Czech and Slovak Foreign Policy Organizations." Ph.D. diss., Ohio State University.

PART 3

CULTURE AS AVAILABLE TEMPLATES FOR ACTION

7

Culture and National Role Conceptions: Belarussian and Ukrainian Compliance with the Nuclear Nonproliferation Regime

Glenn Chafetz, Hillel Abramson, and Suzette Grillot

Chafetz et al., like Breuning, adopt the theoretical position that national role conception (NRC) is the best conceptual device to trace the influence of culture on foreign policy. Chafetz et al., however, focus not on the origins of NRCs but on their effects on foreign policy choice. They are able to demonstrate that the NRCs of Belarus were incompatible with the possession of nuclear weapons, while the NRCs of Ukraine demanded such possession. Chafetz et al. are also able to show, through longitudinal analysis, the process of role redefinition that Ukraine underwent in order to comply with the Lisbon Protocol.

—Editor

"A Russian, a Ukrainian and a Belarussian enter a railway carriage. Each sits down on a pin. The Russian throws his out of the window. The Ukrainian puts his in his pocket. The Belarussian puts his pin back on the seat—because that is where it is supposed to be."[1] To understand the joke, one must not only recognize some truth in the idiosyncratic

An earlier version of this chapter appeared in the December 1996 issue of *Political Psychology*.

behaviors it attributes to three Eastern Slavic nations, but must also accept the essence of culture: the idea that individual behavior can be predicted to some degree on the basis of beliefs, attitudes, and values common to the groups to which they belong (Vertzberger, 1990:260). The essence of cultural theories of foreign policy is that the behavior of groups organized into states can also be predicted on the basis of these shared beliefs, attitudes, and values (Gaenslen, 1986). There are a number of ways to approach the effects of culture on foreign policy behavior, as manifested in the diversity of approaches in this book. This chapter tackles the problem from the perspective of role theory.

We contend that the national role concept is useful for understanding how states translate national cultural characteristics into foreign policy content. We argue that specific foreign policy behaviors follow from the roles states play in the world (leader, ally, revolutionary, mediator, isolate, etc.). Roles in turn are a product of internally and externally generated, culturally influenced expectations. Put another way, foreign policy outputs can be understood as the meshing of national and international norms of behavior. We demonstrate this hypothesized relationship among culture, role, and policy by examining Belarussian and Ukrainian nuclear proliferation policy.

Our specific claim is that the initial divergence in Belarussian and Ukrainian policies—Belarus immediately signed the Nuclear Non-Proliferation Treaty (NPT) as a nonweapons state, while Ukraine wavered between compliance and defiance—can be explained by different role conceptions. Ukraine's vision of its role was complex, with some role conceptions such as regional and global systems leader conforming to nuclear status. Belarus, on the other hand, consistently viewed itself as a collaborator in all relevant international social systems, which militated toward compliance with the NPT. Further, we argue that the differing role conceptions followed in part from cultural differences. The most important of these are Ukraine's greater perceived distinctiveness from Russia and its Cossack (martial) tradition and, as the joke illustrates, the Belarussians' greater willingness to accommodate. Finally, we conclude from Ukraine's eventual compliance with the NPT that the degree to which a specific cultural content will be translated into a role and policy depends on three factors: (1) how central the content-affected role concept is to the given state's overall identity; (2) how consistent the role behaviors generated by the concept are with prevailing international norms; and (3) how much power the international community brings to bear on maintaining international norms.

In the first part of the chapter, because role theory cannot be evaluated without comparison to competing theories, we discuss those theories and their limitations. Next we explicate how role theory addresses these weaknesses and why we expect this theory to better account for nuclear proliferation decisions. We then explain how a quantitative case study methodology using inferential statistics can be used to test the feasibility of role theory. Next we present the results of this comparative case study. In the discussion section, we demonstrate that hypotheses generated by role theory indeed do account for Ukrainian and Belarussian behavior. Finally, we discuss some limitations of the theory, suggest remedies for dealing with them, and conclude by describing how further research can assess the feasibility of these remedies.

PREVAILING THEORIES AND THEIR LIMITATIONS

Neorealism

Neorealism holds that state interests derive from the fundamental anarchy of the international system. Because no sovereign authority exists to guarantee the security of states, states pursue a constant strategy of balancing against the power of other states. They do this either internally or externally depending on available resources. Internal balancing involves relying on domestic increases in either qualitative or quantitative means to increase power. Acquisition of nuclear weapons, according to this theory, is an attractive internal, qualitative means for increasing power. States prefer internal balancing when possible, because it reduces their dependence on potentially unreliable allies for security (Waltz, 1981:2). External balancing entails allying oneself with other states to balance potential adversaries. Accordingly, it makes sense for states to prefer nuclear acquisition or, second best, to seek alliance with a nuclear state.

There are three basic problems with this approach. First is the claim that states' relative power is a sufficient explanation of decisions to proliferate. This claim is problematic because there were also strong ideological, religious, ethnic, or cultural motivations in all the situations in which states chose illegal proliferation: Algeria, Argentina, Brazil, Egypt, India, Iran, Iraq, Israel, Libya, North Korea, Pakistan, South Africa, South Korea, and Taiwan. Moreover, although Argentina and Brazil may have begun nuclear programs because each feared the other's power, both states eventually renounced nuclear weapons despite their continued power inequality. Similarly, Egypt's renunciation and Algeria's pursuit of nuclear weapons adds more doubt to the claim that relative power is a sufficient explanation of decisions to proliferate.

Second is the neorealist prediction that states internally or externally balance on the basis of system polarity (see Hopf, 1991; Wagner,

1993). Polarity refers to the number of clearly dominant states in a given system or subsystem. According to the theory, all states either balance against or ally with one of the poles. Neorealism does plausibly predict that India would balance against China, that Pakistan would balance against India, that Iran and Iraq would balance against Israel and each other, and that North Korea would balance against the United States, Japan, and South Korea. The balancing prediction would also lead one to expect widespread nuclear proliferation or at least a reorganized system of extended deterrence in the multipolar system said to characterize the end of the Cold War (Frankel, 1990:7; Mearsheimer, 1990:12, 37–39). Instead, however, Germany, South Korea, and Japan, rather than acquiring nuclear weapons themselves or realigning, have maintained their alliances with the United States and have expressed strong support for the nuclear nonproliferation regime. Other nuclear-capable states like Canada, Sweden, Switzerland, Italy, and Belgium have also shown no inclination to balance against centers of power like France, Britain, and the United States. Similarly, assuming that Russia is the pole in the Eurasian subsystem, both Ukraine and Belarus should have balanced against it absent a greater threat from another pole. There was no other possible external threat to either state, yet Ukraine chose to balance against Russia only briefly before relinquishing its weapons, while Belarus abandoned its arsenal and proclaimed its neutrality immediately. Belarus and Ukraine are not exceptional. South Africa, Kazakhstan, Brazil, and Argentina all renounced existing arsenals or abandoned active programs despite no change to their respective benefit in the systemic distribution of power (see Holsti et al., 1982).

Third, even in cases in which countries have sought remedy for a local or global power imbalance during the whole of the nuclear era, the claim that states prefer internal to external balancing when possible is not supported empirically. Of the forty-six states with the capacity to acquire nuclear weapons during this period (the forty-one noted earlier in addition to the five legal nuclear states), only six (China, India, Pakistan, Iran, Iraq, and North Korea) have manifested a preference for internal over external balancing. Four (the United States, France, the United Kingdom, and Israel) show no preference, in that they maintain both nuclear establishments and membership in alliances. Thirty states rely on alliances or neutrality. (Soviet and Russian preferences could not be classified.)

In sum, neorealism cannot account for states' voluntary rejection of power and failure to seek balancing alliances. The inclination to balance against power is at best a weak indicator of the decision to acquire nuclear weapons. Moreover, even when countries seem to seek a balance of power, the claim that states prefer internal to external balancing when possible is true for only a small minority of cases.

Liberalism

Liberal democracy does at first appear to be sufficient as a predictor of compliance, and it is measurable. Because of a presumed culture of accommodation, established, liberal democracies tend overwhelmingly to comply with the nonproliferation regime (Doyle, 1986). In fact, of the twenty-one strongly democratic states that the nonproliferation treaty prohibits from possessing nuclear weapons, only Israel has violated the treaty. The experience of Argentina, Brazil, and South Africa further supports the correlation between liberal democracy and nonproliferation. South Africa renounced its nuclear weapons only following its rejection of apartheid, and Argentina and Brazil discontinued their nuclear weapons programs only following their respective transitions to democracy (Spector, 1992). Relying on Gastil's definition and scale of liberalism, of the eight violators and would-be violators, only one, Israel, is strongly liberal. Another, India, is moderately liberal. The remainder are authoritarian (Gastil, 1990; Amnesty International, 1990–1993).

A theory of nonproliferation built around liberalism alone, however, is still lacking *because a significant number of nonliberal states also comply with the nonproliferation regime.* Accordingly, domestic liberalism cannot explain the proliferation decisions of a significant number of states.

Strategic Beliefs Theory

A final theory that has generated support among scholars of proliferation is strategic beliefs theory, rooted in belief systems theory (see Larson, 1994). The central proposition of strategic beliefs theory is that decisionmakers' attitudes about the efficacy of certain weapons or strategies are the deciding factors in explaining proliferation or compliance. As support for this contention, Lavoy (1993) offers the case of Pakistan. Lavoy argues that nuclear acquisition or development is pursued in those states in which strong proponents of the efficacy of nuclear weapons can persuade others of the weapons' utility.

There are problems with this approach as well. First, there is good evidence that the leaders of Western Europe's non-nuclear states were convinced of the net deterrent benefits of nuclear weapons during the Cold War, but they complied with the nonproliferation regime nonetheless (Schwartz, 1983). Second, the leaders of Kazakhstan, South Korea, Egypt, and Taiwan all presumably believed in the deterrent value of nuclear weapons, but they abandoned their programs (or weapons in Kazakhstan's case) not because of a change in strategic beliefs, but because of pressure from the international community. Furthermore, there is no evidence of change in South Africa's beliefs about nuclear weapons to correlate with its decision to abandon its arsenal in 1991. In sum, beliefs about the utility of nuclear weapons do not explain most of the cases of proliferation or compliance.

ROLE THEORY:
A COMPREHENSIVE AND PROMISING THEORY

Overview of Role Theory

Role theory assumes that states are actors that behave consistent with specific roles with which they identify. A role is a much more specific concept than culture, but the two are inextricably interrelated because of their indispensability to actors for perceiving and surviving their environments (Vertzberger, 1990:260–295). Roles, according to Rosenau, are the "attitudinal and behavioral expectations that those who relate to its occupant have of the occupant and the expectations that the occupant has of himself or herself" in given situations (Rosenau, 1990:220; see also Holsti, 1970; Cottam, 1986; Walker, 1987; Wendt, 1992; and Barnett, 1993). Hence, roles are synthesized phenomena, created by the combination of an actor's subjective understandings of what behavior a role requires (role conceptions), society's demands (role expectations), and the particular context in which the role is acted out. Roles are neither deterministic nor infinitely elastic. They are the categories of state identity that states, like individuals, rely on to simplify a complex world and to help guide them through that world. Without roles, individuals cannot impose order on their environment and consequently will experience difficulty functioning socially and may even suffer psychological breakdown (Linville, 1985, 1987; Northrup, 1989:55; Bloom, 1991). The same process is expected to occur within states, albeit with less dramatic consequences.

Though some may question the application of this theory to states, we can apply role conceptions to states and other collectivities, as well as to individuals, for two reasons. First, identities and role conceptions are cultural. They are social phenomena by definition and thus can be shared, even among most of the individuals within a state (Fiske and Taylor, 1991:96–141; Wendt, 1992, 1994; Barnett, 1993:274; Mercer, 1995:237). Second, even when role conceptions are not commonly shared, the individuals who make foreign policy in the name of states do so on the basis of what they think the roles of their states in the world should be and which roles will be acceptable to their constituents (Putnam, 1988). Holsti has identified, and we have modified, the typical roles states play in the international system (for a complete listing of role conceptions, see Table 7.1).

With respect to possession of nuclear weapons, these roles can be divided into three categories: roles indicating a tendency toward illegal possession, roles indicating a tendency away from illegal possession, and roles indicating a tendency neither toward nor away from illegal possession of nuclear weapons. Based on Holsti's role typology and patterns of proliferation, we have identified four roles with a marked tendency toward nuclear acquisition: regional leader, global system leader, regional protector, and anti-imperialist. The reasoning is that most states perceive nuclear weapons to be a symbol of leadership based on the model of legal nuclear weapons states. Moreover, they often consider nuclear weapons helpful or even necessary to undertake special roles to protect others in their region or with whom they otherwise identify. Finally, states for whom an anti-imperialist role is salient regard nuclear weapons as a necessary tool for overturning the status quo—for example, Algeria, Libya, Iran, Iraq, India, and North Korea. Israel is the only illegal nuclear weapons state that does not fit into at least one of the categories.

The following seven roles show a marked tendency away from illegal proliferation: mediator-integrator, example, protectee, regional subsystem collaborator, global system collaborator, bridge, and internal developer. All of these roles except internal developer involve good citizenship either regionally or globally and thus imply compliance with global rules or regional arrangements. The internal developer role is salient to states whose primary purpose internationally is to secure assistance for domestic economic development. Accordingly, the expenditure of scarce resources on an illegal arms program is incompatible with one of their central roles.

If the decision to comply with the nuclear nonproliferation regime is best understood as a function of national role conception, states that see themselves as defenders of international society as a whole, challengers of the status quo, and centers of revolution are more likely to possess or seek to possess nuclear weapons. Because social, nonsocial, and contextual elements constitute states' roles and role conceptions, all these elements are likely to influence the decision to acquire nuclear weapons or not. These elements follow a continuum from the relatively immutable factors of geography and population size, through slowly changeable elements such as ethnic and racial composition and political culture, to relatively malleable social dimensions such as a state's past and current experiences with other countries and its social and economic pressures. Practically speaking, the mutability of factors that constitute a given state's identity means that small states with weak economies are not likely to adopt the role of global or regional hegemon and may be less

Table 7.1 National Roles Evinced by Belarus and Ukraine

Role Type	Major Functions	Tendency Toward Nuclear Status	Examples of States Articulating the Role Conception (Legal and Illegal)
1. Regional leader	Provide leadership in delimited geographic or functional area	Yes	India, Iran, Iraq
2. Global system leader (only relevant post–Cold War)	Lead other states in creating and maintaining emerging global order	Yes	United States, Russia
3. Regional protector	Provide protection for adjacent regions	Yes	United States, France, Russia
4. Anti-imperialist	Act as agent of struggle against imperialist threats	Yes	Iran, North Korea, Iraq, India, Libya
5. Mediator-integrator	Undertake special tasks to reconcile conflicts between other states or groups of states	No	Sweden, Norway, Argentina
6. Example	Promote prestige and influence by domestic or international policies	No	Japan, Sweden, Norway, Argentina
7. Protectee	Affirm the responsibility of other states to defend it	No	Germany, Japan, Egypt, many small states
8. Regional subsystem collaborator	Undertake far-reaching commitments to cooperate with other states in region to build wider communities	No	Denmark, Australia, Chile, Japan, South Africa, Egypt, many other states
9. Global system collaborator (only relevant post–Cold War)	Undertake far-reaching commitments to cooperate with other states to support the emerging global order	No	Japan, Germany, Argentina, many other states
10. Bridge	Convey messages between peoples and states (more passive and vague than mediator-integrator)	No	Switzerland, Austria, Spain, Turkey, Finland
11. Internal developer	Direct efforts of own and other government to internal problems	No	Mexico, many less developed countries

12. Active independent	Shun permanent military or ideological commitments; cultivate good relations with as many states as possible	No	Sweden, Switzerland, Kyrgyzstan
13. Independent	Act for one's own government's interest, narrowly defined	Neither	Almost all states

likely to possess nuclear weapons. Large, powerful states are less likely than small states to accept subordinate roles in international institutions and other social settings and may be more apt to acquire nuclear weapons. However, more malleable social elements may exert a stronger influence on a state's role conception, for two reasons. First, physical attributes may be ambiguous. States of medium size may not know whether to identify with great powers or small states and must rely on other cues like culture and ideology. Second, without the experience of social interaction, physical attributes have no meaning. Race, for example, has no significance as a social category in a state with no experience of colonialism, slavery, or discrimination. Moreover, without a history of social interaction, states lack the experiential basis for judging threats to their domestic arrangements and hence cannot judge whether they should adopt roles consistent with the notion that nuclear weapons are necessary.

Social interaction is particularly likely to produce change when the centrality or salience of given role conceptions is unclear, or when a given state's national role conceptions do not match international expectations of the state's role. In such cases, internal debate, conflict, or indecision may result in gradual changes in cultural attitudes and role conceptions (Barnett, 1993). Changes tend to be gradual because an infinitely malleable role conception would make the world seem random and beyond control and would provoke identity crises with every alteration in the environment (Northrup, 1989:55; Bloom, 1991:35–39; Weary, Gleicher, and Marsh, 1993). As a result, states do not usually abandon role conceptions outright. Instead, they slowly downgrade their centrality. Rapid shifts in role may, however, occur in states undergoing internal upheaval, such as revolution, or in new states such as those formed by the disintegration of the Soviet Union.

Different social settings or contexts also may lead to some variability in states' roles. The social settings may be area or even issue specific. Germany, for example, acts as a leader in European economic affairs, while deferring to the United States and others in European and global military-strategic matters. Because Germany does not view itself as a leader in this context, it would be less likely to seek nuclear weapons.

Given the scope of this theory to take into account social, nonsocial, and contextual elements noted only in part by other theories, and its ability to account for change in policy over time, we expect role theory to have greater ability to predict and explain states' proliferation decisions. Indeed, it is somewhat surprising that given its promise, role theory has never been formally tested.

TESTING THE USEFULNESS OF ROLE THEORY

Part of the difficulty in determining the usefulness of role theory is the low base rate of the behavior in question. Very few states have violated the proscription on acquiring nuclear weapons (Meyer, 1978). Of the two hundred states that constitute the international community, only seventeen—Algeria, Argentina, Belarus, Brazil, Egypt, India, Iran, Iraq, Israel, Kazakhstan, Libya, North Korea, Pakistan, South Africa, South Korea, Taiwan, and Ukraine—either possess or have sought illegal possession of nuclear weapons. Of those, five—Argentina, Brazil, Egypt, South Korea, and Taiwan—renounced active nuclear weapons programs, and three—Belarus, Kazakhstan, and South Africa—relinquished or destroyed existing arsenals. The number of violators is only a small fraction of the entire community. Therefore, if the state is the unit of comparison, statistical comparisons of violators with nonviolators may not be powerful enough to detect predicted differences in expressed roles even if there are any.

One way around this small sample size problem is to choose two countries that were the most opposite in their stance on nuclear proliferation and expand the sample size by making the public statements of the two countries' governments the unit of comparison. The idea would be to use inferential statistics to compare the role statements of the country that initially retained nuclear weapons and then decided to relinquish them with those of the country that consistently wanted to relinquish them; results would support or reject predicted differences and changes in role statements over time. We ask whether the country that illegally retained nuclear weapons initially made more public role statements indicating a tendency toward nuclear proliferation and then decreased those statements as it began to relinquish its nuclear stock. Because role conceptions may be context specific, an additional test of the theory would involve checking role statements of the country that initially retained nuclear weapons for changes with reference to social setting. Self-identification as a regional protector of a region with no extended nuclear deterrence, for example, implies a tendency toward proliferation. By contrast, self-identification as a regional protector of a region with extended deterrence implies a tendency away from proliferation. Particularly coupled with other non-nuclear roles, the latter role conception implies a decision not to proliferate. Using this methodology, a test of the feasibility of role theory is possible.

Ukraine and Belarus are particularly well suited for such a test for four reasons. First, these states fit the criterion of being initially opposite in their stance on possession of nuclear weapons. Whereas the Ukraine retained nuclear weapons and then relinquished them, Belarus from the outset promised to relinquish its nuclear stock. Belarus complied unequivocally, promising to accede to the NPT as a non-nuclear weapons state at Lisbon in May 1992 and following through with formal accession in July the following year. Ukraine, by contrast, promised to join the nonproliferation regime as a non-nuclear weapons state in Lisbon in 1992, in Massandra, Ukraine, in September 1993, and in Moscow in January 1994. It failed, however, to follow through on the first two commitments. It placed after-the-fact conditions on the Lisbon agreement (a protocol of the Strategic Arms Reduction Treaty first agreed to by the United States and the Soviet Union) and renounced the Massandra accords immediately after concluding them. Finally, in November 1994, Ukraine's parliament voted to sign and ratify the NPT. Ukraine's changed position on proliferation provides us with a second reason for choosing these states: They allow for a test of the dynamic aspects of the theory as well.

Third, these states are well suited for a test of the social contingency of role conceptions. Given its initial pro-proliferation stance, Ukraine would be expected to view itself at first as a regional protector of East-Central Europe, but not of the Commonwealth of Independent States (the CIS comprises the states of the former Soviet Union except for the three Baltic states), because Ukraine's exclusion from NATO's nuclear umbrella and self-exclusion from the CIS umbrella provided by Russia implies a need for an independent nuclear deterrent. But consistent with its eventual decision to relinquish its nuclear arsenal, Ukraine would be expected over time to abandon the role conception of regional protector in an unprotected region. Regional protector in a protected region would become possible, however.

Fourth, the similarities of Ukraine and Belarus present nearly controlled experimental conditions (Przeworski and Teune, 1970; Solingen, 1993). Both acquired independence at the same time and were presented with the same choice: whether or not to comply with the international nuclear nonproliferation regime by giving up the weapons left them by the collapse of the Soviet Union. Because both possessed nuclear weapons, both states' eventual compliance resulted from nonmaterial factors rather than material incapacity. Both inhabit a nearly identical geopolitical space. Both abut a powerful nuclear neighbor, Russia. Russian politicians have threatened the territory and independence of both states (see Stankevich, 1992b; Eggert, 1992). Both are in the early stages of democratization and economic liberalization, but neither has stabilized its democratic institutions. Neither is allied with other states. Both are economically and militarily weak.[2] Both have a significant Russian minority population (though Belarussians are more thoroughly and evenly Russified than Ukrainians). Both are predominantly Eastern Slavic. Religiously, both are predominantly Eastern Orthodox, though there are significant Catholic minorities in each as well. Both have nuclear aversions stemming from the continuing negative effects of the Chernobyl reactor accident. Both desire integration into the Western political and economic system (Urban and Zaprudniak, 1993; Marples, 1993; Krawchenko, 1993; Kiselyov, 1994; Tiurina, 1994). Finally, neither state has ever experienced modern statehood (though Ukraine was briefly independent from 1918 to 1919).

One may question the generalizability of conclusions drawn from states that inherited, rather than developed, nuclear weapons. While this difference should not be overlooked, we do not think it crippling for the following three reasons. First, even states that developed the weapons themselves have renounced them. South Africa renounced an existing arsenal, and Argentina, Brazil, Sweden, Switzerland, South Korea, Taiwan, and other industrialized countries terminated nuclear weapons programs that had progressed quite far (Spector, 1992). Second, the impact of sunk costs as a factor in renouncing gains can be overstated. To use money as an analogy: Whether one earns or inherits a million dollars, a vow of poverty is much easier for those already poor than for the rich. Third, the Belarussians and the Ukrainians (and Kazakhs) claim quite plausibly that the Soviet Union relied on their intellectual and material as well as Russian resources in the development and construction of the nuclear arsenal (Skachko, 1993). Thus, how the two states should be classified—as inheritors or developers—is unclear.

There is, however, one feature common to Ukraine and Belarus that should induce caution in generalizing from their experience. Both states are new. Their identities are, therefore, less firmly established and more easily changed. Accordingly, it would be a mistake to infer, for example, that because international pressure swayed Ukraine, such pressure would necessarily work on Israel or India. In both of the latter cases, one could argue that their respective role conceptions as pariah or Third World leader, forged out of decades (or in the Israeli case, centuries) of anti-Semitism could not be subordinated as easily as the uncertain roles competing for salience in Ukraine and Belarus.

The question of the initial divergence in Ukrainian and Belarussian policy also requires attention. What factor or factors could account for the difference between Belarus's quick compliance and Ukraine's indecision? We argue that Belarus was consistently and overwhelmingly culturally predisposed to accommodative roles and thus destined to meet international expectations. For Ukraine, however, decisions were more problematic because certain physical attributes and cultural features impelled it to see itself as a great power modeled after France and Russia. This national role conception in turn justified nuclear status.

The physical differences between Ukraine and Belarus are obvious. The latter is a small state and therefore unlikely to seek international leadership. The former, with a population of fifty million, is as large as two legal nuclear weapons states, France and Great Britain. The cultural differences, however, may better explain the differences in the initial policy approaches of Ukraine and Belarus. Anatoly Rozanov, director of research for the Belarussian Institute for Development and Security, described Belarussians as "calmer, more tolerant Russians" (Rozanov, 1995). The self-professed tolerance of Belarus is supported by the much lower incidence (or absence, if one accepts the claims of the Belarussians) of the virulent anti-Semitism and xenophobia manifested throughout Ukrainian and Russian history (Motyl, 1993:94). Indeed, Belarus conducted a week-long celebration of Jewish cultural contributions to the nation in October 1993. Both the foreign and cultural ministers claimed that Belarussian society was civic and inclusive in nature rather than ethnic and exclusive.[3]

Another reason for Belarus's quick embrace of accommodative roles may be the greater Russification of the Belarussian populace. Though the percentage of the population identifying itself as Russian in Belarus and Ukraine differs by only a percentage point, Zaprudniak (1993) argues that demographic figures incompletely describe the relationship between Belarus and their larger neighbor. Most Belarussians have a cultural affinity with Russia and do not find it threatening in any way to their own.

The situation in Ukraine differs considerably. Ukrainians believe themselves much more distinct from Russians and much greater players on the world stage. Although the presence of a significant Russian minority in Ukraine precluded the formation of a state rooted purely in ethnicity, a distinctive and exclusive ethnicity plays a much greater role in the independent Ukrainian identity than it does for Belarus (Wilson, 1995:269–271; Motyl, 1993:94). Three mythic legs support a more assertive Ukrainian national identity. The first is the belief that Ukraine, not Russia, is the proper inheritor of the greatness of Kievan Rus', the large and powerful medieval state that produced both Ukraine and Russia (Motyl, 1993:88). A second reason for a greater Ukrainian distinctiveness is the place of the Great Famine in the national consciousness. The Ukrainian famine of 1931 was Stalin's deliberate attack on the Ukrainian peasantry for resisting his collectivization of Soviet agriculture (Conquest, 1986). As Motyl writes, "For Ukrainians the famine has assumed mythic proportions. It is the defining moment of their recent history, no less traumatic and portentous than the Holocaust is for Jews. The famine symbolizes the horror of the Soviet experience, the curse of Russian domination, and the necessity of Ukrainian liberation" (Motyl, 1993:14). The third major factor is the Cossack tradition. The Cossacks were landless, free soldiers descended from escaped serfs. Their wanderings, violence, disregard of social constraints, and accomplishments on behalf of Ukrainian statehood became incorporated into the larger Ukrainian culture (Wilson, 1995:271–274; Sysyn, 1991).

The effect of these differences between Ukrainians and Belarussians was a greater feeling of distinctiveness from and antipathy toward

Russia from Ukrainians. This is reflected not only in current jokes and anecdotes, but also in deeply embedded symbols of culture like the poetry of Taras Shevchenko. One well-known Shevchenko poem bemoans the treatment of Ukraine at the hands of Peter I and Catherine II:

Now I understand
It was the First who
crucified out Ukraine
And the Second finished
off the Widowed orphan.
Murderers! Murderers! Cannibals! (Cited in Subtelny, 1994:235)

The apparently strong cultural predisposition of Ukrainians to Russophobia, rebellion, and great power status is consistent with Ukraine's initial postindependence foreign policies of maintaining an independent nuclear arsenal and challenging Russia for inheritance of the Soviet navy. Nevertheless, Ukraine eventually mitigated both its hostility and its presumed policy effects. The question is, Why? Recall from the introduction our assumption that the ability of cultural predispositions to find their way into policy outcomes depends on three factors: the centrality of the culturally loaded role concept to a given state's overall identity, the consistency of the role behaviors generated by the concept with respect to prevailing international norms, and the amount of power the international community brings to bear on maintaining international norms. All three dimensions converged to reduce to the influence of Ukrainian culture in the ultimate policy.

First, Ukrainian attempts to keep its nuclear arsenal encountered strong resistance from the international community, led by the United States. Second, Ukrainian leaders found that a purely ethnic, Russophobic strategy of state legitimation could not provide the level of support necessary to maintain a viable state because of the significant Russian minority in their own population. Accordingly, to keep the state together, Ukraine's leaders had to look to other sources of support (Bremmer, 1994; Solchanyk, 1994). As we show, the Ukrainian perception of itself as a great power rival to Russia was not the only role Ukrainian citizens and politicians could envision. Accordingly, as both internal and external pressures on Ukraine to adopt a less Russophobic, less system-dominant role increased, other role conceptions became more central. By including itself as a (reluctant) partner, rather than contender, of Russia, Ukraine accepted the Russian and Western arguments that Russia was the sole legitimate successor to the Soviet Union's role in providing nuclear security to the region.

Therefore, according to role theory, we should expect Ukraine initially to manifest more statements consistent with possession of nuclear weapons than Belarus. Over time, however, we expect to see differences between the expressed roles of these two countries decrease, with Ukraine making fewer role statements consistent with a tendency toward, and more statements consistent with a tendency away from, proliferation. These changes would occur at specific times during which specific events signified an increase in internal and international pressures for nonproliferation. These events included the final disintegration of the Soviet Union on December 1, 1991; the signing of the Lisbon Protocol to the START Treaty on May 23, 1992; the Massandra Agreement with Russia on September 3, 1993; the Moscow Agreement with Russia and the United States on January 14, 1994; and the Ukrainian national election of July 10, 1994. Finally, these changes would be characterized by concomitant changes in what social settings are being referred to in the role statements. More specifically, we expect to see a broadening of Ukraine's role conceptions to include both CIS and non-CIS states.

METHODS

Study Sample

The study sample consisted of statements of only the highest-level decisionmakers of Ukraine and Belarus on foreign and defense policy and role conception; these statements were published in Russian, Ukrainian, Belarussian, and English-language newspapers and information services.[4] We tried to confine ourselves to the most general statements of role, identity, or purpose, regardless of audience.

For Belarus, the highest-level decisionmakers chosen were the chairman of the Supreme Soviet, Stanislaw Shushkevich; the foreign minister, Petr Kravchanka; the prime minister, Vyacheslav Kebich; and the minister of defense, Pavel Kozlovskiy. In Ukraine, the decisionmakers were the president, Leonid Kravchuk; the foreign minister, Anatoly Zlenko; the defense minister, Konstantin Morozov; and the prime minister, Leonid Kuchma. During the period under investigation, Vitaly Radetskiy replaced Morozov as minister of defense, and Yukhim Zvyahilskyy replaced Leonid Kuchma in Ukraine. After the elections in June 1994, Kuchma replaced Kravchuk as president, Valery Shmarov took over as minister of defense, and Hennady Ukovenko became acting foreign minister. After the period under investigation, Mechislav Hrib replaced Shushkevich as chairman of the Supreme Soviet in Belarus, and Anatoly Lukashenko was elected president.

Of course, others in each state bore responsibility for shaping how the state as a whole conceived of its role, including the respective parliaments and populations. We limited the search to the top policymakers, however, because the individuals occupying those positions were the only ones we could confidently assume could speak with authority on matters of foreign and defense policy. Furthermore, we also assumed that any role conception carrying significant political weight in the country would be reflected in the statements of the highest policymakers. The accuracy of our analysis depended only on finding articulations of identity and purpose that carried enough weight among the highest representatives of the state to figure in their public statements. This approach is consistent with the two-level games approach first posited by Putnam (1988).

We examined almost all Belarussian public statements of national role conception for the period December 1991 to July 1993. Belarus became an independent state in December 1991 and formally acceded to the NPT in July 1993. We used the same starting point with Ukraine but concluded our search in November 1994 upon the Ukrainian parliament's vote of accession.

Classification of Role Statements

Our procedure was to classify the statements collected according to the role categories established by Holsti and modified by us (see Table 7.1 for a complete listing of the categories). We searched for statements indicating a vision of a kind of action or status. Though status is not action, the latter can be inferred from the former. "Great power" is a status but indicates a leadership role. Examples of statement classifications follow.

The chairman of the Belarussian parliament, Stanislaw Shushkevich, promised the Council of Europe "strict compliance with all our undertakings [and] respect for international treaties and agreements" (system and subsystem collaborator). Shushkevich observed that being "situated at the crossroads of Europe, [Belarus] can play an important role in the process of gradually closing the gap between CIS member countries and Europe" (bridge and mediator-integrator) (Kravchanka, 1992; "Shuskevich," 1992).

Some statements were not as straightforward. Ukrainian President Kravchuk frequently portrayed Ukraine as a "big power" (global leader) (Kravchuk, 1992c, 1993a). Kravchuk claimed that Ukraine's purpose was "to set up a zone of stability and security for Central and Eastern Europe" (regional leader) (Kravchuk, 1992f, 1992g; Zlenko, 1993a, 1993c, 1993d). Kravchuk asserted that Ukrainian leaders must "take account of Ukraine's own characteristics and history," and that every state must "choose . . . [its] own position and path . . . [and take into consideration] its own distinctive features" (independent)

(Kravchuk, 1993d, 1993b). Kravchuk also promised that Ukraine "will never tolerate . . . being subordinated" (independent) (Kravchuk, 1992d, 1992a, 1992d).

The following Ukrainian statements indicated a trend away from role conceptions consistent with nuclear proliferation: During a meeting with the U.S. secretary of defense, Les Aspin, Ukraine's defense minister, Morozov, said that Ukraine could "rightfully expect security guarantees from the United States and other powers" (protectee) (Morozov, 1993b). Similar remarks from Foreign Minister Zlenko and President Kravchuk were classified the same way (Kravchuk, 1993e; Zlenko, 1993e). Kravchuk declared that his country "favors the creation of all-embracing international systems . . . and considers participation in them to be a basic component of its own nation" (system and subsystem collaborator) (Kravchuk, 1993a: see also Morozov, 1993a; Zlenko, 1993b). Some statements were obvious, like those of Leonid Kuchma, Kravchuk's successor, forcefully articulating a role conception for Ukraine as an "economic bridge" (bridge) between Russia and the West (Portnikov, 1994; Sokolovskaya, 1994).

We added two categories articulated by both Belarussian and Ukrainian decisionmakers that Holsti had not included: global system collaborator and global leader. We assume that the difference between our and Holsti's system of classification stems from the importance played by the Cold War in his analysis—without the rigid divisions of the Cold War, leaders can conceive of roles on a global systemic, rather than simply subsystemic, scale.

Classification of the statements was performed by six raters who were instructed to place each of the statements in as many categories as they wished. The correlation between categories in most cases was nonexistent. In cases where there was a correlation, it was very low (max. $R=.31$). Mean interrater alpha reliability for the fourteen categories was .70 (range=.44 to .86), which was within acceptable limits for experimental purposes.

Measures of Role Differences

In all, there were fourteen measures of role differences, corresponding to the fourteen role types on which the two states could be compared (Table 7.1). For each statement, if the statement was judged to express a particular role, it was assigned a value of 1 for that role category. In contrast, if it was judged not to express that role, it was assigned a 0 for that category. The resultant measures of role differences consisted of fourteen percentages (average of zeros and ones for each category multiplied by 100) on which the two countries could be assessed for predicted differences in expressed roles.

RESULTS

Role Conceptions of Ukraine and Belarus Across Time

To test the hypothesis generated by role theory that Ukraine would produce more role articulations consistent with nuclear status than Belarus, we first performed a discriminant analysis to test if overall, across the fourteen categories, Ukraine and Belarus differed in their role conceptions. Results indicated that they did reliably differ overall in percentages of expressed roles: $X^2(14) = 47.3$, $p < .0001$. In fact, 84.4 percent of statements were classified correctly when using role type to predict country membership. Accordingly, we performed individual t-tests to determine on what particular roles the two countries differed.

As can be seen from Table 7.2, as predicted, the percentages of three role conceptions that would indicate a tendency toward nuclear proliferation—regional leader, global system leader, and regional protector—were reliably higher for Ukraine than for Belarus. Ukraine also demonstrated a tendency toward the anti-imperialist role absent for Belarus. Likewise, as expected, the percentages of two role conceptions that would indicate a tendency away from nuclear proliferation—mediator-integrator and example—were significantly higher for Belarus than for Ukraine. Results thus supported the hypothesis that Ukraine would express more roles indicating a tendency toward nuclear proliferation and that Belarus would express more roles indicating a tendency away from proliferation.

These differences were detectable despite the fact that expression of roles indicating a tendency toward nuclear proliferation was not common, the total of such roles being only 17.4 percent. That expression of such roles was not common, and was in fact less common than other types of role statements, suggests that countries may be concerned not only about the political implications of making direct statements about their desire to possess nuclear weapons, but even about the implications of expressing roles that run counter to the expectations of the international community as a whole.

Consistency of Role Conceptions of Ukraine and Belarus over Time

To test whether pressure from the role expectations of other countries would also be associated with gradual changes in Ukraine's role conception away from nuclear proliferation, we adopted two methods. (We did not test for changes in Belarus's role conceptions because they tended away from proliferation anyway.) First, to assess for predicted changes in Ukraine's role conceptions, we used a one-way analysis of variance

Table 7.2   Percentages of National Roles Articulated by Ukraine and Belarus

Role Type	Percentage of Ukrainian Articulations (N = 93)	Percentage of Belarusian Articulations (N = 33)
Tendency toward nuclear proliferation		
Regional leader	11.0	0.5[a]
Global system leader	2.9	0.5[a]
Regional protector	1.9	0.0[a]
Anti-imperialist	1.6	0.0[b]
Total	17.4	1.0
Tendency away from nuclear proliferation		
Mediator-integrator	0.9	14.6[a]
Example	5.7	17.2[a]
Protectee	9.5	8.6
Regional subsystem collaborator	20.6	23.2
Global system collaborator	12.3	11.1
Bridge	3.2	7.0
Internal developer	7.0	7.6
Total	59.2	89.2
No tendency		
Active independent	12.0	2.5[a]
Independent	21.5	16.2
Total	33.5	18.7
No role	17.4	20.2

Notes: a. Means significantly differ at p = .05.
b. Using separate variance estimates, mean tended to differ ar p = .06.

(ANOVA). We examined whether differences between the two countries in percentages of role statements of all types gradually decreased over three shared time periods during which the international community increased its pressure on Ukraine to relinquish its nuclear arsenal. As can be seen from Table 7.3, differences between the two countries in percentages of role statements indeed decreased. Moreover, results suggested that the change was gradual in that the number of roles on which the two countries reliably differed did not decrease until the third time period. This was after the Massandra Agreement between Ukraine and Russia.

Second, to examine if only Ukraine experienced shifts in its role conceptions, we used separate one-way ANOVAs to examine the internal consistency of expressed roles by both Ukraine and Belarus over time. More specifically, we attempted to determine if there were any reli-

Table 7.3 Differences in Percentages of National Roles Articulated by Ukraine and Belarus over Time

Role Type	Time 1 (N = 26)	Time 2 (N = 40)	Time 3 (N = 32)
Tendency toward nuclear proliferation			
Regional leader	T	•	•
Anti-imperialist	•		
Tendency away from nuclear proliferation			
Mediator-integrator		•	
Bridge		•	
Internal developer	•		
No tendency			
Active independent	•	•	
Independent	•		

Notes: Time 1 – After Ukrainian independence/breakup of the USSR.
Time 2 = After signing of Lisbon Protocol to START Treaty.
Time 3 = After Massandra Agreement between Ukraine and Russia.
• = Reliable difference in expressed roles between Ukraine and Belarus at p < .05.
T = Tendency to differ in expressed roles.

able shifts in percentages of expressed roles for Ukraine and Belarus over the time periods during which these countries were increasingly pressured to relinquish nuclear weapons. These included three periods for Belarus and five for Ukraine. These analyses also confirmed that although Belarus, whose role statements initially indicated a tendency toward nonproliferation, did not reliably change over time, Ukraine's role conceptions did change. More specifically, Ukraine reliably changed over time in its expression of its role as mediator-integrator, $F(4, 88)=4.14$, $p=.004$, and evidenced clear tendencies of change in expression of its roles of regional protector, $F(4, 88)=2.32$, $p=.06$, bridge, $F(4, 88)=2.25$, $p=.07$, and independent, $F(4, 88)=2.34$, $p=.06$. Hence, results supported the contention that Ukraine, due to pressure from role expectations of other countries, would show less consistency over time in its expressed roles than Belarus.

Social Setting Factors and Ukraine's Changes in Role Conceptions

To determine more precisely the direction of Ukraine's change in role statements over the five time periods, we performed follow-up t-tests.

Results from these tests indicated that while Ukraine did show reliable decreases in percentages of roles consistent with proliferation over the first four time periods, Ukraine unexpectedly manifested a significant increase in its role of regional protector.

There are two possible explanations for this increase. First, perhaps the increase in regional protector role was due to social setting factors. More specifically, if Ukraine had abandoned any hope of supplanting or competing with Russia as the successor to the Soviet Union in providing nuclear security, references to the role of regional protector *in the CIS region* would not show a reliable increase. To test this notion, we used separate one-way ANOVAs to assess for changes over time in role statements that referred to CIS states, either alone or together with non-CIS states, and role statements that referred to non-CIS states alone. As Table 7.4 shows, there was, as predicted, no reliable increase over time in regional protector role statements that referred to CIS states alone or together with non-CIS states. This is consistent with Ukraine's refusal to sign any agreement giving the CIS teeth in foreign and defense policymaking.

A second and complementary explanation is that the role conception of bridge between East and West, which showed dramatic increase in the last time period, became much more central and salient to Ukraine's overall social identity. Also consistent with this possibility is that the largest and most reliable change over time for Ukraine was an increase in percentage of bridge role statements.

Changes in Leadership and Role Conceptions over Time

Although results support the contention that Ukraine changed its envisioned role set, it is still unclear exactly how this change occurred. Did Ukraine's current leaders gradually change their positions on what roles they should play in particular regions, or did the people have to elect new leaders whose envisioned roles happened to coincide more with nonproliferation compliance?

To determine which of these explanations was more probable, we performed separate one-way ANOVAs to see if changes in expressed roles that referred to non-CIS countries or CIS and non-CIS countries together were related to the four changes in Ukrainian leadership that occurred during the study period. Results revealed that whereas changes in expression of other roles did not appear to be reliably related to changes in leadership, changes in bridge role, $F(3, 51)=4.51$, $p<.01$, were. Follow-up t-tests revealed that changes in expression of this role occurred after the election of Kuchma as president, $t(51)=2.69$, $p<.01$. Results thus suggested that while changes in expression of other roles occurred relatively independent of changes in leadership, the change in what is hypothesized to be the most central role in determining Ukraine's nonproliferation

Table 7.4   Changes in Percentages of National Roles Inconsistently Articulated by Ukraine over Time in the CIS Social Setting

Role Type	Time 1 (N = 20)	Time 2 (N = 17)	Time 3 (N = 28)	Time 4 (N = 11)	Time 5 (N = 17)
Tendency toward nuclear proliferation					
Regional protector	1.2	0.0	0.0	0.0	1.7
Tendency away from nuclear proliferation					
Mediator-integrator	1.2	0.0	0.0	8.3	0.0
Bridge	0.0	0.0	2.2	0.0	21.7
No tendency					
Independent	32.1	9.7	30.0	12.5	18.3

Notes: CIS social setting refers to statements made about CIS states either alone or together with non-CIS states.
Time 1 = After Ukrainian independence/breakup of USSR.
Time 2 = After signing of Lisbon Protocol to START Treaty.
Time 3 = After Massandra Agreement between Ukraine and Russia.
Time 4 = After Moscow Agreement.
Time 5 = After Ukrainian presidential election.

stance, the bridge role, was a result of, and probably required, a change in leadership. This interpretation finds support in those analyses of the Ukrainian election that attribute Kuchma's victory to greater willingness to cooperate with the CIS and the support of ethnic Russians not eager to challenge Russia's leading role (Portnikov, 1994; Sokolovskaya, 1994).

DISCUSSION

We have demonstrated that role theory accommodates cultural analysis and plausibly explains compliance with the nuclear nonproliferation regime. The theory generated testable hypotheses about whether differences in national role conception could explain the differences in behavior between Belarus and Ukraine and within Ukraine over time. We found clear support for the hypothesis that Ukraine would initially express more roles indicating a tendency toward nuclear proliferation and that Belarus would express more roles indicating a tendency away from proliferation. Second, as expected, we found that differences between the two states in percentages of role statements decreased over time. Thus, we inferred that Ukraine changed its conceptions of its roles in response to international pressures.

Third, the presence of an unexpected result, an increase in Ukraine's role conception as a regional protector, was consistent with the theory's prediction that roles are sensitive to social settings, as the regional protector role in a non-CIS region and within the CIS implied divergent tendencies. Finally, changes in the articulation of roles were found to be both dependent and independent of changes in leadership. This result indicates the intuitively obvious: Leaders both produce and reflect national role conceptions.

We believe that role theory can explain and predict the proliferation behavior of other states. A cursory examination lends support to this claim. Role theory explains why states like Pakistan and North Korea defy material constraints to challenge the expectations and demands of the international community. North Korea's conception of itself as a rebel against Western imperialism explains its decision to devote scarce resources to a nuclear program. Moreover, its leaders have fostered a cult of self-reliance that is consistent with that role. Pakistan's most salient role is defender of the faith against perceived Indian imperialism. This role conception outweighs both material constraints and Pakistan's desire to act as a collaborator in the larger world political system. Role theory is also consistent with the compliance of poor and technologically less advanced states, because lack of capacity can be viewed as a source of a compliance-consistent role conception without being deterministic.

Of the eight current violators and would-be violators of the regime, seven conceive of roles consistent with proliferation. Iran, Iraq, Libya, and North Korea regard themselves as revolutionary actors. Their perceived role is to undermine or alter the international system, and they regard nuclear weapons as useful, if not necessary, tools for their purposes. India does not envision its roles as quite so radical but nevertheless regards itself as a representative of the colonialized states and thus a challenger of the status quo. India also regards itself as a world system leader on a par with China, just as Ukraine saw itself briefly as a leader on a par with France and Russia. Accordingly, nuclear weapons are both the tools and symbols of their perceived roles. Algeria sees itself as a leader in the Arab-African subsystem of states as well as an absolute equal of other states. Its role conception is driven by a powerful ideology of self-reliance that obviates any subordination in the international system in terms of status or privileges (Basu, 1985; Lassassi, 1988). As long as it refuses to accept any establishment of hierarchy among states, it cannot accept the explicit hierarchy of the NPT.

Role theory explains why wealthy states, like Germany, South Africa, Japan, and others that have demonstrated a technological and economic capacity to "go nuclear" have abjured or renounced nuclear weapons. These states have all expressed role conceptions consistent with good citizenship such as system collaborator, subsystem collaborator, and mediator-integrator. Violation of the nonproliferation regime fails to conform to how these states see themselves.

Role theory explains why significant numbers of larger states respect the regime and why some smaller states do not. Fourteen states as large as or larger than Ukraine abjure nuclear weapons (Germany, Indonesia, Brazil, Japan, Bangladesh, Egypt, Ethiopia, Italy, Mexico, Nigeria, Philippines, Thailand, Turkey, and Vietnam). Smaller states do not necessarily comply either. Israel, Libya, Iraq, and North Korea violate the proscription on weapons or weapons development. Therefore, size not mediated by national role conception is less predictive of behavior.

Role theory, by accommodating culture as a source of national role conception, provides a theoretical apparatus for capturing variables, such as culture, that other frameworks ignore. This facet of the theory explains the one exception among the otherwise universally compliant democracies: Israel. Israel sees itself as a collaborator in the global social setting. Its history of abandonment and struggle, however, has permeated its culture, and this culture separates it from the other liberal democracies. Moreover, because the West, and in particular the United States, identifies strongly with Israel, Israel pays no cost for defying the international community (Quester, 1991; Chafetz, 1995).

LIMITATIONS AND DIRECTIONS FOR THE FUTURE

There are, of course, limitations to the theory. First, any theory that requires such a detailed accumulation of data on so many dimensions to acquire an independent variable presents obvious disadvantages in terms of utility. Future research using correlational or factor analysis needs to be done to determine more precisely if the number of role dimensions can be reduced. These data reduction methods can be used if all statements are rated on a continuum of how much they express each of the fourteen roles rather than on whether each role is present or absent. If fewer dimensions are needed, not only might data collection be easier, but the theory can be more parsimonious and easier to use.

Even if the number of role dimensions can be reduced, a more efficient method of predicting a state's role conception would still prove useful. Working deductively from schema theory and inductively from Belarussian and Ukrainian leadership statements about the source of their respective role conceptions, we hypothesize that policymakers in both states used *analogies* to determine role conceptions. These analogies, once identified, offer powerful clues about perceived national roles (Hybel, 1990; Khong, 1992). The analog is chosen on the basis of availability in recent memory and perceived similarity (Martin and Clark,

1990; Khong, 1992:G1, 35–36; Taber, 1994). Usually the basis for the perception of similarity is quite superficial (Gentner, 1989).

Results suggest that Ukrainian and Belarussian decisionmakers did use analogies to determine their respective role conceptions. Interviews with Belarussian and Ukrainian leaders and casual inspection of the foreign policy statements collected revealed several comparisons to other states as a basis for adopting certain roles. For new states, or states in situations with which they have no experience, other states can serve as analogs, as was the case for Belarus and Ukraine.

Belarussian leaders explicitly compared their state to Finland, Sweden, Belgium, Switzerland, Austria, and other small European states (Kravchanka, 1993; Shushkevich, 1993a; Yegorova and Yuferova, 1992). These states all played roles as bridges, mediators, and assorted other kinds of international good citizens. None aspired to leadership or any other role consistent with nuclear weapons. There is direct, though anecdotal, evidence that modeling of this kind also informed Belarussian conventional force postures. Leonid Privalov, deputy chairman of the Belarussian Parliamentary Commission on National Security in 1992, said that Belarus would model its military after Denmark's; because Denmark maintained a force of twenty-seven thousand out of a population of five million, Minsk would field a force of "54,000 out of its population of ten million" ("Iz Minska," 1992). These examples suggests that role modeling, rather than any rationally calculated utility of nuclear weapons, is the basis for at least some Belarussian defense decisions.

The Ukrainian analogies were less consistent. The Ukrainian role models most evident were France and Russia. The former foreign minister and both the former and current presidents of Ukraine argued that the size and (unspecified) capabilities of their country qualified it to be considered as a, if not the, successor to the Soviet Union along with or instead of Russia (Kravchuk, 1992e; "President Kuchma," 1994; Skachko, 1993; Zlenko, 1993c). Succession to the rights, responsibilities, and obligations of the Soviet Union meant international leadership and legal nuclear weapons status. Russia was an obvious analogical target for Ukraine because it was the most accessible. It was the center of the Soviet empire; it shares a long border with Ukraine; and its history and population are intertwined with those of Ukraine.

France was another Ukrainian role model. Konstantin Hrischenko, head of the Arms Control and Disarmament Directorate of the Ukrainian Ministry of Foreign Affairs, reported that as soon as Ukraine began an independent foreign policy, many officials with responsibility for foreign and defense policy relied on France as a role model for foreign policy and inferred the nuclear course from that model (Hrischenko, 1994). France is not nearly as accessible as Russia as an analogical target, but the similarities were particularly resonant. First, France shared two surface features with Ukraine: It was approximately the same size, and it possessed nuclear weapons. Second, the Gaullist spirit of independence and cultural superiority and history of challenging U.S. political leadership also appealed to a state in search of an escape from Russia's perceived hegemony.[5] Thus, Ukraine initially defied international and domestic political pressures to renounce nuclear weapons, in part because nuclear weapons possession was a salient feature of both its role models. Initially, the legitimacy of French and Russian weapons was irrelevant because only a few common features are sufficient to activate the analogy. Indeed, there is ample experimental, historical, and even physiological evidence to support the contention that decisionmakers stop their search for similarities after matching a few superficial features (Higgins and Bargh, 1987; Miller and Desimone, 1994). Furthermore, the analogy tends to persist once invoked, even in the face of more relevant contrary evidence, because of the analogy's function as a tool to increase cognitive efficiency.

The question arises, then, as to why the initial comparisons to France and Russia faded as a source of role. We infer the analogies faded because of a lack of cognitive consensus. As shown, Ukrainian leaders never articulated a consistent role conception. As one influential member of parliament reported, not all decisionmakers accepted France and Russia as role models. Some considered Germany, Italy, and Canada better models—though there is less documentation for them than for France and Russia (Holovaty, 1993). The inconsistency was resolved, at least temporarily, by the election of July 1994, which reflected the increasing centrality of the bridge role in Ukraine's overall self-concept.

Though the use of leadership analogies offers one possible shortcut to the labor required to find the independent variable, this approach presents its own challenges. The success of the analogical shortcut for determining national role conception depends on finding evidence of analogical reasoning among decisionmakers. In the present study, this evidence was relatively abundant in the Belarussian case but thin for Ukraine. It may vary more extremely in other cases. The issue of centrality is the second weakness. Our approach only weakly suggests which of possibly several articulated roles or analogies is most central and salient.

Despite these difficulties, however, we believe that we have presented a plausible argument that the use of national role conception as both an independent and mediating variable may explain more cases of compliance and noncompliance with the nuclear nonproliferation regime than prevailing theories of proliferation. We believe that the predictive power of the theory, as demonstrated by this study, outweighs its disadvantages and makes role theory an attractive alternative for explaining nuclear proliferation specifically and foreign policy more generally. In particular, our research supports the findings that internal determinants of role differences, such as national culture, will become more salient for powerful and established states in the absence of confining international structures. Accordingly, the collapse of the rigid bipolar structure of the Cold War and the ensuing uncertainty and fluidity should make for a world in which strong and established states manifest cultural dispositions in foreign policies far more often than we saw during the Cold War.

NOTES

1. "In the Slav Shadowlands," *Economist,* May 20, 1995, p. 47.
2. Some might quarrel with this characterization of Ukraine because it did hold nuclear weapons, but with no operational control over weapons, questionable loyalty among officers and troops, erratic fuel supplies, insufficient training time, and poor morale, there is no other way but weak to describe Ukraine's military. See Buida (1993) and Khripunov (1993).
3. G. Chafetz's visit to Minsk, Belarus, October 1993.
4. Sources included *Pravda, Izvestia, Nezavisimaya Gazeta, Rossisskaya Gazeta, Demokratychna Ukraina, Komsomolskaya Pravda, Kievskiye Novosti, Molod Ukrayiny, Femida, New York Times, Washington Post, Foreign Broadcast Information Service,* and *Nexis.* Unless otherwise noted, all translations were provided by Chafetz.
5. We are indebted to Valerie Hudson for pointing out many of the French and Ukrainian similarities.

REFERENCES

Amnesty International (1990–1993) *Amnesty International Reports.* London: Amnesty International Publications.

Barnett, M. (1993) "Institutions, Roles, and Disorder: The Case of the Arab States System." *International Studies Quarterly* 37:271–296.

Basu, A. R. (1985) "National Interests and Objectives in Algerian Foreign Policy." *Africa Quarterly* 21:39–60.

Bloom, W. (1991) *Personal Identity, National Identity, and International Relations.* Cambridge: Cambridge University Press.

Bremmer, Ian (1994) "The Politics of Ethnicity: Russians in the New Ukraine." *Europe-Asia Studies* 46, no. 2:261–284.

Buida, V. (1993) "Prinyata voennaya doktrina." *Nezavisimaya Gazeta,* October 21, p. 3.

Chafetz, G. (1995) "The Political Psychology of the Nuclear Nonproliferation Regime." *Journal of Politics* 57:743–775.

Conquest, Robert (1986) *The Harvest of Sorrow:* New York: Oxford University Press.

Cottam, M. L. (1986) *Foreign Policy Decision Making: The Influence of Cognition.* Boulder: Westview Press.

Doyle, Michael W. (1986) "Liberalism and World Politics." *American Political Science Review* 80, no. 4:1151–1169.

Eggert, K. (1992) "Rossiya v Roli 'Evraziyskogo Zhandarma?'" *Izvestia,* August 7, p. 6.

Fiske, S., and S. Taylor (1991) *Social Cognition,* 2d ed. New York: McGraw-Hill.

Frankel, B. (1990) "An Anxious Decade: Nuclear Proliferation in the 1990s." *Journal of Strategic Studies* 13:1–13.

Gaenslen, Fritz (1986) "Culture and Decision Making in China, Japan, Russia, and the United States." *World Politics* 39:78–103.

Gastil, R. D. (1990) "The Comparative Survey of Freedom: Experiences and Suggestions." *Comparative International Development* 25:24–50.

Gentner, D. (1989) "The Mechanisms of Analogical Learning." In *Similarity and Analogical Reasoning,* edited by S. Vosniadou and A. Ortony. Cambridge: Cambridge University Press.

Higgins, E. T., and J. A. Bargh (1987) "Social Cognition and Social Perception." *Annual Review of Psychology* 38:369–426.

Holovaty, S. (1993) Personal interview with Glenn Chafetz, Minsk, Belarus, October.

Holsti, Kal J. (1970) "National Role Conception in the Study of Foreign Policy." *International Studies Quarterly* 14:233–309.

Holsti, Kal J., et al. (1982) *Why Nations Realign: Foreign Policy in the Postwar World.* London: George Allen and Unwin.

Hopf, T. (1991) "Polarity, the Offense-Defense Balance, and War." *American Political Science Review* 85:475–493.

Hrischenko, K. (1994) Presentation to the meeting of the NIS Nuclear Relations Working Group, Kiev, Ukraine, June.

Hybel, A. R. (1990) *How Leaders Reason: US Intervention in the Caribbean Basin and Latin America.* Cambridge, MA: Basil Blackwell.

IAEA (1993) *Bulletin.* Vienna: IAEA Publications.

"Iz Minska: Pervaya Partiya Yadernogo Oruzhiya Vyvezen Belarus v Rossiyu" (1992) *Krasnaya Zvezda,* January 28, p. 3.

Jervis, Robert (1976) *Perception and Misperception in International Politics.* Princeton: Princeton University Press.

Kebich, V. (1991) London, British Broadcasting Company, October 5.

Khong, Y. F. (1992). *Analogies at War: Korea, Munich, Dien Bien Phu, and the Vietnam Decisions of 1965.* Princeton: Princeton University Press.

Khripunov, I. A. (1993) *Russia's Arms Trade in the Post–Cold War Period.* Paper presented at the conference of the American Association for the Advancement of Science, San Francisco.

Kiselyov, S. (1994) "Ukraine: Not So Western After All." *Bulletin of the Atomic Scientists* 50:32–35.

Kravchanka, P. (1992) Interview with Petr Kravchanka, February 12. *FBIS-SOV-92-029,* p. 80.

Kravchanka, P. (1993) Speech on collective security treaty on Radio Minsk, April 8. From *FBIS-SOV-93-068,* April 12, pp. 56–57.

Kravchuk, L. (1992a) Statement that he will never tolerate subordination. *Vienna Profile,* January, 20, pp. 48–49. From *FBIS-SOV-92-018,* January 27, pp. 60–61.

Kravchuk, L. (1992b) Radio address, Radio Kiev, January 22. From Nexis.

Kravchuk, L. (1992c) Interview on Russian-German ties. *Der Spiegel,* February 3, pp. 155–163. From *FBIS-SOV-92-023,* February 4, pp. 57–61.

Kravchuk, L. (1992d) Discussion of independence. *Wprost,* March 8, pp. 13–14. From *FBIS-SOV-92-055,* March 20, pp. 67–70.

Kravchuk, L. (1992e) Discussion of nuclear weapons, security. *Ukrinform* (Ukrainian diplomatic information service), April 29. From *FBIS-SOV-92-083*, p. 47.

Kravchuk, L. (1992f) More of Kravchuk's final Paris news conference. *Izvestia*, June 19, pp. 1, 5. From *FBIS-SOV-92-119*, June 19, p. 58.

Kravchuk, L. (1992g) Address to German media on Ukraine's role in Europe. *ITAR-TASS*, October 2. From *FBIS-SOV-92-193*, October 5, pp. 36–37.

Kravchuk, L. (1993a) Statements on future relations with Russia. *Interfax*, March 18. From *FBIS-SOV-93-051*, March 18, pp. 44–47.

Kravchuk, L. (1993b) News conference. Radio Ukraine World Service, October 4. From *FBIS-SOV-93-192S*, October 6, pp. 50–52.

Kravchuk, L. (1993c) Speech to the supreme council. Radio Ukraine World Service, October 21. From *FBIS-SOV-93-204*, p. 51.

Kravchuk, L. (1993d) Address to council. Radio Ukraine World Service, October 21. From *FBIS-SOV-93-204*, October 25, p. 51.

Kravchuk, L. (1993e) Statement outlining republic's European aspirations. *Mlada Fronta Dnes*, October 25. From *FBIS-SOV-93-208*, October 29, pp. 61–62.

Krawchenko, B. (1993) "Ukraine: The Politics of Independence." In *Nations and Politics in the Soviet Successor States*, edited by I. Bremmer and R. Taras. Cambridge: Cambridge University Press.

Larson, Deborah W. (1994) "The Role of Belief Systems and Schemas in Foreign Policy Decision Making." *Political Psychology* 15, no. 1:17–33.

Lassassi, A. (1988) *Non-Alignment and Algerian Foreign Policy*. Brookfield, VT: Gower.

Lavoy, P. R. (1993) "Nuclear Myths and the Causes of Nuclear Proliferation." *Security Studies* 2:192–212.

Levy, J. S. (1994) "Learning and Foreign Policy: Sweeping a Conceptual Minefield." *International Organization* 48:287–289.

Linville, P. W. (1985) "Self-Complexity and Affective Extremity: Don't Put All Your Eggs in One Cognitive Basket." *Social Cognition* 3:94–120.

Linville, P. W. (1987) "Self-Complexity as a Cognitive Buffer Against Related Depression and Illness." *Journal of Personality and Social Psychology* 52: 663–676.

Marples, D. R. (1993) "Belarus: The Illusion of Stability." *Post-Soviet Affairs* 9:253–277.

Martin, L. L., and L. F. Clark (1990) "Social Cognition: Exploring the Mental Processes Involved in Human Social Interaction." In *Cognitive Psychology: An International Review*, edited by M. W. Eysenck. New York: Wiley.

Mearsheimer, J. J. (1990) "Back to the Future: Instability in Europe After the Cold War." *International Security* 15:5–56.

Mercer, Jonathan (1995) "Anarchy and Identity." *International Organization* 49:229–252.

Meyer, S. M. (1978) "Probing the Causes of Nuclear Proliferation: An Empirical Analysis: 1940–1973." Ph.D. diss., University of Michigan.

Miller, E. K., and R. Desimone (1994) "Parallel Neuronal Mechanisms for Short-Term Memory." *Science* 263 (January 28):520–522.

Morozov, K. (1993a) Defense minister returns from Riga Conference. Radio Ukraine World Service, May 4. From *FBIS-SOV-93-085*, May 5, p. 47.

Morozov, K. (1993b) Meeting with Les Aspin. Reuters, June 3. From Nexis.

Motyl, Alexander (1993) *Dilemmas of Interdependence: Ukraine After Totalitarianism*. New York: New York Council of Foreign Relations.

Northrup, T. (1989) "The Dynamic of Identity in Personal and Social Conflict." In *Intractable Conflicts and Their Transformation,* edited by L. Kreisberg et al. Syracuse: Syracuse University Press.

Portnikov, V. (1994) "Pobed kravchuka." *Nezvisimaya Gazeta,* July 12, p. 1.

"President Kuchma's speech to the troops" (1994) *Interfax,* August 3. From *FBIS-SOV-94-150,* August 3, p. 31.

Przeworski, A., and H. Teune (1970) *The Logic of Comparative Social Inquiry.* Malabar, FL: Krieger.

Putnam, Robert D. (1988) "Diplomacy and Domestic Politics: The Logic of Two-Level Games." *International Organization* 42:427–460.

Quester, G. H. (1991) "Knowing and Believing About Nuclear Proliferation." *Security Studies* 1:270–282.

Rosenau, J. (1990) *Turbulence in World Politics.* Princeton: Princeton University Press.

Rozanov, A. (1995) Personal interview with Glenn Chafetz, Athens, Georgia, July.

Schwartz, D. N. (1983) *NATO's Nuclear Dilemmas.* Washington, DC: Brookings Institution Press.

"Shushkevich Gives Briefing" (1992) *TASS,* February 24. From *FBIS-SOV-92-039,* February 27, p. 7.

Shushkevich, S. (1993a) Minsk Radio, April 9. From Nexis.

Shushkevich, S. (1993b) NBC Television, August 31. From Nexis.

Skachko, V. (1993) "Slishkom Mnogo Protovorechiya." *Nezavisimaya Gazeta,* April 27, p. 3.

Sokolovskaya, Y. (1994) "Pal Vtoroy Iz Belovezhskikh Zubrov: Kuda Poidyet Ukraina?" *Izvestia,* July 13, pp. 1–2.

Solchanyk, Roman (1994) "The Politics of State-Building: Centre-Periphery Relations in Post-Soviet Ukraine." *Europe-Asia Studies* 46, no. 1:47–68.

Solingen, E. (1993) "Macropolitical Consensus and Lateral Autonomy in Industrial Policy: The Nuclear Sector in Brazil and Argentina." *International Organization* 47:262–298.

Spector, L. S. (1992) "Repentant Nuclear Proliferants." *Foreign Policy* 88:21–37.

Stankevich, S. (1992a) "Derzhavav poiskakh sebya." *Nezavisimaya Gazeta,* March 28, p. 4.

Stankevich, S. (1992b) "Yavlenie derzhavy." *Rossisskaya Gazeta,* June 23, p. 1.

Subtelny, O. (1994) *Ukraine: A History,* 2d ed. Toronto: University of Toronto Press.

Sysyn, F. (1991) "The Reemergence of the Ukrainian Nation and Cossack Mythology." *Social Research* 58:845–864.

Taber, C. S. (1994) "The Interpretation of Foreign Policy Events: A Cognitive Process Theory." Paper presented at the annual meeting of the International Studies Association, Washington, DC.

Tiurina, T. (1994) "Belarus: Neutrality Maybe." *Bulletin of the Atomic Scientists* 50:37–40.

Urban, M., and J. Zaprudniak (1993) "Belarus: A Long Road to Nationhood." In *Nations and Politics in the Soviet Successor States,* edited by I. Bremmer and R. Taras. Cambridge: Cambridge University Press.

Vertzberger, Yaacov (1990) *The World in Their Minds: Information Processing, Cognition, and Perception in Foreign Policy Decisionmaking.* Stanford: Stanford University.

Wagner, R. H. (1993) "What Was Bipolarity?" *International Organization* 47: 77–106.

Walker, Stephen G. (1987) *Role Theory and Foreign Policy Analysis.* Durham, NC: Duke University Press.

Waltz, K. N. (1981) "The Spread of Nuclear Weapons: More May Be Better." Adelphi Paper No. 171. London: International Institute of Strategic Studies.

Weary, G., F. Gleicher, and K. Marsh (1993) *Control Motivation and Social Cognition.* New York: Springer-Verlag.

Wendt, Alexander (1992) "Anarchy Is What States Make of It: The Social Construction of Power Politics." *International Organization* 2:391–425.

Wendt, Alexander (1994) "Collective Identity Formation and the International State." *American Political Science Review* 88:384–398.

Wilson, A. (1995) "The Donbas Between Ukraine and Russia: The Use of History in Political Disputes." *Journal of Contemporary History* 30:265–289.

Wish, Naomi B. (1987) "National Attributes as Sources of National Role Conceptions: A Capability-Motivation Model." In *Role Theory and Foreign Policy Analysis,* edited by S. G. Walker. Durham, NC: Duke University Press.

Yegorova, O., and Ya Yuferova (1992) "My vystradel: Dolyu mirovortsev." *Komsomolskaya Pravda,* August 28, p. 3.

Zaprudniak, Jan (1993) *Belarus: At a Crossraods in History.* Boulder: Westview Press.

Zlenko, A. (1993a) More on Zlenko comments. Ukrayinske Telebachennya Network, March 10. From *FBIS-SOV-93-054,* March 23, pp. 33–34.

Zlenko, A. (1993b) Discussion on Radio Ukraine, July 2. British Broadcasing Company, July 6. From Nexis.

Zlenko, A. (1993c) Policy discussion. *Kievskiye Novosti,* September 17, p. 4. From *FBIS-SOV-93-186,* September 28, pp. 32–35.

Zlenko, A. (1993d) Discussion of European Security, Alliance. Mayak Radio Network, October 12. From *FBIS-SOV-93-196,* October 13, pp. 86–87.

Zlenko, A. (1993e) Ukrainian Television, November 19. From Nexis.

8

"How May the World Be at Peace?": Idealism as Realism in Chinese Strategic Culture

Rosita Dellios

This chapter is an example of the potential explanatory power of "strategic culture." More than just allowing us to project likely Chinese behavior in war, Dellios is able to expand the focus of strategic culture to ask how China will seek to remake the international system. She argues that China will be a stabilizing force in the international system as a result of the logic of its own strategic culture. Power politics would be replaced by wen *politics, which would lead to a less dysfunctional and conflictual international system than the one, based on Western realism, we now have.*

—Editor

There is a famous orientalism that declares: "Let the Chinese dragon sleep, for when she awakes she will astonish the world."[1] In this decade of China's self-strengthening, Western realists seem to be seeing dragons again. Not so their geoeconomic counterparts, who see only markets. Neither the threat nor the opportunity analysts, however, quite see China in the "round"—as a mandala of security in which certain principles have long held sway over matters of survival and, indeed, benefit. An appreciation of China's cultural-philosophical tradition provides a corrective to these blinkered visions. More than that, it suggests a way forward in a world once again questioning the basis for peace in the aftermath of great power contention.

Far from becoming a dragon defying the West, China will be a stabilizing force in the world as it remakes the international system according to the logic of its own strategic culture. Power politics would be replaced by *wen* politics (see below), the politics of Confucian civility. *Wen* politics would lead to a less dysfunctional international system than the one we now have, which is based on Western realism. Thus idealism becomes realism in the truest sense.

STRATEGIC CULTURE AS A CONCEPT

Strategic culture pertains to a people's distinctive style of dealing with and thinking about the problems of national security. This definition does not preclude cross-cultural and enduring approaches to strategy. For example, Chinese strategic culture displays characteristics such as deterrence and psychological warfare that are applicable across time and across cultures. The Chinese do not have a monopoly on these, but they have molded them into a distinctive Chinese approach, just as nineteenth-century European strategic culture—as advanced by Clausewitz and Jomini—is distinguished by the skillful application of physical force. Without disputing the presence of foreign or universal elements in Chinese strategy, it is still possible to argue that there is a uniquely Chinese *approach* to strategy and that it remains even in an age when China has become a powerful nuclear-armed state.

The relationship between strategic culture and culture is a derivative one. Strategic culture derives from culture its mentalities, which it then focuses on issues of peace and war, social order and disorder. The relationship between strategic culture and foreign policy analysis is advisory and, if need be, remonstrative. Its predictive value lies in identifying tendencies, not certainties. Gray (1986:35) expressed the matter well when he observed: "As with sound geopolitical analysis, with strategic-cultural analysis, one is discerning tendencies, not rigid determinants."

Strategic culture's primary strength is awareness and (one would hope) avoidance of ethnocentricity—of American Strategic Man being the measure of all things strategic in the contemporary world order (Booth, 1990:122). Strategic culture attempts to peel away the prejudice of the universality of one's views and values. While not all layers can realistically be removed—just as one's own upbringing cannot be entirely deleted as a source of conditioning—it is nevertheless a worthwhile exercise, for it sufficiently opens those portals of perception that allow for enhanced understanding of others *plus* oneself. Once other ways of conceiving of the world are introduced, it is impossible not to draw renewed conclusions about one's own. Hence, we have arrived at a point at the end of the twentieth century where the hitherto self-referential West is in a position to specialize in interrelationships (Beck, 1994:24), or for the rich to learn from the poor and the West from those it once colonized (Giddens, 1994).

As a specialist term, though not as an idea, strategic culture is relatively new. Historians are accustomed to inquiring into the variety of influences—from the cultural and philosophical to the geographical and historical—that help explain a people's proclivities for dealing with the threats and opportunities of the world around them. An impressive example of this has been the ways-of-warfare literature dealing with China and, to a lesser extent, Vietnam (see Stetler, 1970; Kierman and Fairbank, 1974; Rand, 1979; Boylan, 1982; Lin, 1988; and Ball, 1993). It was only during the Cold War, however, that the need for the conceptualization of strategic culture as an instrument of analysis arose.

Recourse to an alternative schema for comprehending nuclear weapons doctrine was deemed necessary when it became apparent that Soviet strategic thinkers did not share their U.S. counterparts' notions of deterrence. This came from the Soviet insistence on preparing to survive and fight a nuclear war instead of accepting the inevitability of mutual assured destruction (MAD) and, hence, the preferred logic of deterrence. Later, in the early 1960s, the Soviets also rejected a refinement in U.S. nuclear philosophy—the euphemistically termed controlled flexible response. This, of course, was a doctrine of limited nuclear war, and the Soviet leaders argued that it was irresponsible of U.S. decisionmakers to even contemplate such a policy. How could they control the risk of escalation to full-scale nuclear war? In this way the Soviets were becoming a cause of major frustration to Washington in their refusal to cooperate conceptually. After all, what was the point of nuclear deterrence when the other side actively prepared for nuclear survival?

Given the two superpowers' inability to communicate—let alone empathize—over the equivocal nature of their nuclear security, it is not surprising that someone should diagnose the problem and give it a name. In 1977, through a paper from the influential RAND Corporation, Snyder (1977:v) wrote:

> It is useful to look at the Soviet approach to strategic thinking as a unique "strategic culture." Individuals are socialized into a distinctively Soviet mode of strategic thinking. As a result of this socialization process, a set of general beliefs, attitudes and behavioral patterns with regard to nuclear strategy has achieved a state of semipermanence that places them on the level of "culture" rather than mere "policy."

Interestingly, having introduced the term, Snyder dropped it from subsequent publications and admitted (1990) that he never intended it as a serious contender for explanatory power. He saw it as a "blunt instrument," an explanation of last resort.

Others were not so dismissive (see Pipes, 1977; Ermarth, 1978; Gray, 1979; and especially Booth, 1979). They warned against ethnocentrism and urged strategists to widen their repertoire of concerns. "One cannot know one's enemy by stereotyping him," advised Dixon (1976:266). "Man cannot live by the Military Balance alone," Booth cautioned; his advice to strategists was to "be as familiar with value systems as weapons systems" (Booth, 1979:110). By 1986, Gray's persuasive and well-developed application of strategic culture to understanding superpower nuclear strategy bolstered the literature considerably, as did a U.S.-Soviet comparative study edited by Jacobsen (1990).

With the end of the Cold War came the end—at least in that particular milieu—of strategic culture's conceptual incubation. Was it ready to take its place among other approaches to analysis of strategic and security issues? For many, the answer is yes. Booth reminds us that "'realities' in human behavior are in the eye of the beholder. In the strategic domain, as in others, we live in a 'created' world. Strategic realities are therefore in part culturally constructed as well as culturally perpetuated" (Booth, 1990:124). Culture, in other words, shapes everything, including what we call *the real world*. The world *out there* might be a predatory place for a realist, but it is presumptuous to assume everyone is socialized to live and think within these terms of reference. As Booth notes, "It should be stressed that cultural explanations do not exclude other 'useful' explanations and that those other explanations may well themselves contain a cultural dimension. Thus, for example, what happens in the Soviet Union (and elsewhere) is not some game of politics divorced from the history, geography and political culture of that particular state" (Booth, 1990:124).

From Strategic Man to Symbolic Universe:
The Security Mandala

At this point, a further refinement can be made to the concept of strategic culture, using the mandala as a metaphor. Because it is an especially Eastern metaphor, with spiritual rather than instrumental connotations, it is a fitting choice for conceiving of Chinese and other Asian security systems that tend toward holism. The mandala metaphor also helps to release strategic culture from the space-time capsule of Cold War scholarship.

Mandala comes from the Sanskrit word for circle and in its generic meaning pertains to a system of spatial relationships around a center. China as the Middle Kingdom is a mandala concept—a spatial as well as conceptual circle of power with a moral center. The classical Indian strategist Kautilya (fourth century B.C.) modeled international relations in terms of a mandala system.[2] Comprising a center, symmetry, and cardinal points, the mandala serves to create harmony from the polarities, order from chaos. Not surprisingly, its appeal as a metaphor for the idea of security is compelling.

While the basic design concept of the mandala is common to all mandalas, sacred and secular, so too are the basic properties of security common to all peoples (essentially, cultivation of confidence and avoidance of harm). A security mandala, in turn, represents a sense of security (a square) achieved in the universe (a circle) (see Figure 8.1). Mandalas come in many variations, each distinctive and complete in its own right. Similarly, different peoples' orientations vary. For example, it is possible that the quest for security inverts the relationship between square and circle so that the square as the security domain contains the circle in hegemonic fashion (see Figure 8.2). This is the Chinese legalist position, a strategic subculture that made possible the unification of China in 221 B.C. The perpetuation of China as a unified entity after this event, however, required an additional circle around the hegemonic square (see Figure 8.3) to restore the "proper" hierarchical moral order, which should contain, and not be contained by, the security domain. In this way, the previously contained circle becomes the *stabilized world,* the *world at peace,* or the *harmonized world.* Its design is the *yin-yang* symbol (depicted at the heart of Figure 8.3). The traditional mandala of square-in-circle (Figure 8.1) was evident in classical India. Like Confucianized China, India's cultural domain was bigger than its strategic domain, but without the intervening hegemonic complication of the three-layered Chinese model (Figure 8.3). The Concert of Europe, by comparison, could not achieve either of these (Figure 8.1 or 8.3), so it partitioned its security domain into a brittle balance of power (see Figure 8.4). Its stabilized world was more mechanical than the Chinese version because it had not been transformed into a moral center. To do so would have endorsed the hegemonic project (morality as the means to hegemonic power).

The perfect strategic system would define its own mandala (see Figure 8.5). It would need to address an aspect of security at every point of the circle (for example, military, economic, social, ecological). In this ideal security mandala, survival (the square of security) and value (the circle of the universe) become the same in every aspect through permeability. Permeability is the open system of change that maintains a security mandala as a living system. Therefore, it is better to have the permeable *real* security mandala that acknowledges the *ideal* than to grasp for what is beyond reach (Figure 8.5) or to deny its desirability (Figure 8.4). The permeable real is the Daoist ideal (Figure 8.3). This is one window on idealism as realism. To put it another way, it is more "realistic" to become well-adjusted to a living, interacting, changing world where one lives by one's "ideals" through a code of conduct than to be disappointed in not achieving a perfect world, or becoming cynical—and thus acting cynically—about its "imperfections." Cynicism is not realism, for it has no worthwhile creative function beyond self-preservation, often at the implied expense of others. A more logical realism is one that acknowledges the mutuality of not only survival but of improvement on existing conditions. These ideas will be reexamined in later contexts.

Figure 8.1
Traditional Security Mandala

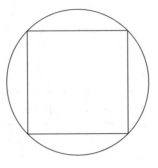

Figure 8.2
Inverted Security Mandala

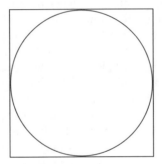

Figure 8.3
Chinese Three-Layered Security Mandala

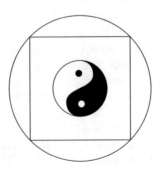

Figure 8.4
Balance of Power Security Mandala

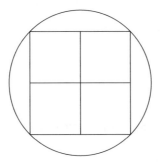

Figure 8.5
Permeable Security Mandala

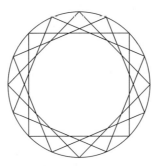

It is now possible to be more specific about the role of a security mandala. It serves strategic culture in much the same way as model building serves science. In turn, in its minimum capacity, strategic culture provides the context for analysis of foreign policy behavior in such a way as to reduce the risk of miscalculation. If it serves this modest peripheral role, it will affect the tone of discussion but not necessarily the power of the other approaches—be they the familiar rational-actor analysis, the more sophisticated hypergame analysis, or the intriguing theory of drama and irrational choice (Bennett and Nicholson, 1994). Because it provides a contextual briefing that could have grave implications for one's findings, strategic culture is ignored to the detriment of foreign policy analysis. It should be the explanation of first resort, the fabric to which other prominent factors are stitched as needed. The limitations of strategic culture are ultimately the limitations of its model building—a security mandala like any other model can be built badly or well. To those who object that there is nothing to show that it exists, the same can be said of all social science models. The test is not so much in predicting events (how many people predicted the collapse of the USSR or the Beijing Massacre or the latest Gulf War?) as in recognizing the milieu in which events unfold. Only then can tendencies be suggested. Again, I do not think that other methodologies, for all their social scientific rigor, can hope to deliver more.

CHINA'S STRATEGIC CULTURE

Foundational Principles

To explore how China in transforming itself might transform the international system according to the logic of its own strategic culture, we must identify systematically the foundational principles of that culture.

Jen *(human-heartedness).*   Expressions of Chinese world order could be therapeutic to the current system untutored in *jen* (human-heartedness, benevolence, or humanity). Instead of swinging between the polarities of the all-consuming state and the all-demanding individual, *jen* provides an ethic for the proper provision of both.

Jen is the key concept of Confucianism, the dominant tradition in Chinese philosophy. A combination of the written characters for "man" and "two," *jen* pertains to human relations. In the *Analects,* Confucius explains *jen* thus: "When Fan Ch'ih asked about *jen,* the Master said: 'Love people.' When Yen Yüan asked about *jen,* the Master said: 'If you can control your selfish desires and subject them to rules of propriety and if you can do this for a single day, it is the beginning of *jen* for the entire world. *Jen* is self-sufficient and comes from your inner self; it requires no outside help.'"[3] "Briefly defined," explains Fung Yu-Lan (1952, vol. 1:68), "[*jen*] is the manifestation of the genuine nature, acting in accordance with propriety (*li*), and based upon sympathy for others."

To the Chinese, self-cultivation is more meaningful than individualism. In this way it is not a question of subsuming one's entire identity for the greater good of the group, but of cultivating oneself in order to be the building block of *jen.* In this way, state, society, family, *and* self are well served. Indeed, thinking more broadly, the world itself is well served, for there is a natural progression to the level beyond state. If the state, through moral leadership, has *jen,* so does its foreign relations, because such relations would be based on the external expression of *jen,* called *li* (or propriety in behavior). The *jen-li* mindset renders power politics (*jen*-deficient relations) the province of the ignorant and therefore barbarous. So the tactical details of dealing with barbarians—through such methods of "using barbarians to contain barbarians"—were subsumed within the grander strategy of tributary relations. Foreign affairs were thus transformed into internal affairs. This arrangement yielded security and economic benefits without the costs of militarism or isolationism. The challenge was how to disarm the barbarians at the gates by encouraging them to partake of the Chinese world through tribute relations. While tribute meant a symbolic submission to civilization (China), it also entailed attractive rewards, both in terms of trade opportunities and the conditions of peace in which they could be pursued. This was an externalization of the internal Confucian social order, which was itself a reflection of self-cultivation. "*Jen* is self-sufficient and comes from your inner self."

Li *(rules of proper conduct).* *Li,* as noted above, is the outer expression of *jen* or human-heartedness. If *jen* is absent, pretentions of *li* are worthless. Worse still, they diminish the person and situation. "The Master said, 'Unless a man has the spirit of the rites, in becoming respectful he will wear himself out, in being careful he will become timid, in having courage he will become unruly, and in being forthright he will become ignorant" (Confucius, 1988:VIII.2).

In the affairs of government, *li* is considered superior to law but does not exclude law from its proper place in society. "To impress restraint before the fact, is *li,*" wrote Sima Qian in his *Historical Records,* "to impose restraint after the fact is law" (quoted in Wu, 1982:407). A seventeenth-century official said: "When the people are at peace, they are governed and live according to the rules of conduct (*li*), but when troubles arise, punishments must be used" (quoted in Pye, 1985:42). Confucius (II.3) put the matter of *li* over law in the following terms: "The master said, 'Guide then by edicts, keep them in line with punishments, and the common people will stay out of trouble but will have no sense of shame. Guide them by virtue, keep them in line with the rites [*li*], and they will, besides having a sense of shame, reform themselves." In explaining the attitude of Confucius, Wu (1982:407–408) points out: "What he aspired after was not merely effective government, but better society. Law at best can be conducive but to the former; only *li* may lead men to the attainment of the latter. Hence, in his mind it is not law before *li,* but *li* before law; and whatever legal institutions there may be, they should all be so constituted as to further the ends of *li.*"

Traditional Chinese international law was, in fact, *li.* It included since ancient times practices familiar to modern diplomacy, such as diplomatic inviolability and repatriation or extradition of persons. In regulating their international relations, the Chinese established a board of rites instead of a ministry of foreign affairs. This highlights the importance attached to correct behavior as distinct from boundary setting.

The "foreign" is transformed to the "known" through rites of propriety based on a recognition of the moral universe. Since "all under Heaven are one," relations should proceed in an orderly fashion in accordance with *li*.

Tien *(heaven, nature, the moral universe, the way of nature and man as one)*. *Tien* in Chinese philosophy has come to mean both the moral universe and the natural universe. There is an assumed interaction of both so that creation is not mechanical but spiritual and purposeful. The concept of *tien* has been used to "denote the power that governed all creation" (de Bary, Chan, and Watson, 1960:5). It is more impersonal than the Christian idea of God, and not as anthropomorphic as a somewhat similar concept to *tien*, that of *shang-ti* (lord-on-high). Expressed more precisely, "Heaven was a more universalized conception. It represented a cosmic moral order. . . . The authority of Heaven might therefore be appealed to in situations where the sanctions of a clan or nation did not extend" (de Bary, Chan, and Watson, 1960:6). *Tien*'s authority leads to the related concept of *tien-ming* or mandate of heaven: that whoever rules must do so virtuously in accordance with *tien-dao* (way of heaven). Otherwise, *tien* will withdraw its mandate and pass it onto another monarch or nation worthy of leadership. Hence the importance of the proper observance of *li* and the cultivation of *jen*. While this describes the dominant Confucian philosophy of traditional China, its aim of harmony is shared by the other influential indigenous Chinese philosophy, Daoism. In their concern with harmony as a social and spiritual value, both incorporate the *yin-yang* school of thought. Indeed, the *I Jing* (Book of Changes), which employs Daoist and *yin-yang* thinking, carries Confucian interpretive commentary.

Yin-yang *(earth-heaven, female-male, waning-waxing, negative-positive, receptive-proactive, hidden-open, defensive-expansive)*. The negative (or defensive) and the positive (or expansive) attributes of Chinese strategic philosophy relate directly to the *yin-yang* concept. The concept may be explained as follows: "Yin and Yang are at the root of all things, and together in alternation they are the moving force of our world and all its manifestations. Yin is seen as passive, yielding, and nurturing, while Yang is active, dominating, and creative. Any circumstance, however intricate, can be described by a string of Yins and Yangs" (Huang, 1987:8). In the words of one ancient philosopher (Chou Tun-yi, quoted in Fung, 1966:269–270), "Movement and Quiescence, in alternation, become each the source of the other."

Yin-yang's alternation is likened to waxing and waning. This marks dynamic change of succession, like the seasons, though in human affairs it is possible to adapt and strive for balance and hence ride the wave of change rather than be beached or drowned by it. In this sense, *yin-yang* is not deterministic, nor is it "struggle," as the Chinese communists found in 1978 when they decided to replace "class struggle" with pragmatism ("seek truth from the facts") in the desire to advance China materially. The philosophy of *yin-yang* is to "flow" in the direction of restoring balance, as distinct from struggling to achieve some superior dialectical resolution, with the latter's implication of a teleological state of affairs. The *qi* (life force) of *yin-yang* is understood to harbor transformative power and may be tapped into by individuals and whole societies. The survival (transformative) capacities of *yin-yang* mean that it is possible to emerge secure even in the most trying of conditions.

For a *yin-yang* perspective on Chinese strategic thought, see Figure 8.6. Its spatial consideration is security mandala (Figure 8.3). This perspective shows that China's strategic philosophy, past and present, may be interpreted to address two essential needs. One is *inviolability* and the other is the attainment of China's *rightful place under heaven*—the closest approximation in Western understanding being "destiny" or "proper place." The first, inviolability, has a defensive orientation and the second, rightful place, an expansive one. They are not opposed but interrelated. Without inviolability, rightful place is difficult to attain. Without the rightful place, inviolability is not assured—as far as one can be assured of the complete security to which inviolability aspires.

Figure 8.6
Chinese Strategic Thought—a *Yin-Yang* Perspective

YIN	*YANG*
Defensive	*Expansive*
Inviolability	Rightful Place Under Heaven

In practice:
Prevent war of aggression
—Great Wall mentality
　("barbarian" invasions
　19th C. Opium Wars
　20th C. Japanese invasion)
—People's War
　("Every Man a Soldier")
—Nuclear people's war
　("Dig Tunnels Deep")
At its extreme:
Idealistic
Thus, do not court disappointment but
sense of purpose
Retain the positive (*yang*)

In practice:
Become powerful
—Middle Kingdom mentality
　(Center of an international
　system based on tribute)
　Toward "a powerful, modern
　socialist state"
—Zhou Enlai, 1975

At its extreme:
Overextends, spills over
into *yin* too fast (destruction)
Thus, do not court superpower status
(due to visibility, enmity, and
transitoriness)
Retain the hidden (*yin*)

The notion of progress to a state of ideal convergence of humanity is idealism beyond reach, just like the perfect security mandala (Figure 8.5) is ideal. The *qi* of *yin-yang* cannot be grasped either but that is its reality; consequently one learns not to struggle or to grasp but to conform. What does one conform to? The answer is idealism as realism—following the *tien-dao* (the way of the moral universe), while being mindful in order to be masterful of transformative relations. These, as noted above, are derived from the *yin-yang* "law" of change (as set out in the *I Jing*).

Wen-wu *(civility-martiality).* Traditionally, China recognizes the superiority of *wen* (civility) over *wu* (martiality). *Wu* was only to be resorted to if *wen* failed and, indeed, *wu* was believed to be most effective or "potent" (see Rand, 1979:116–117) when it was not dominant over *wen.* This meant that (1) "War is not easy to glorify because ideally it should never have occurred" (Fairbank, 1974:7); and (2) when war *is* used, its effectiveness or potency depends on how it relates to moral order (is it a just war?) and whether it is sparingly used as a means for effecting policy. Here the basic framework of *yin-yang* thinking becomes apparent: "The way" or moral order needs to be pursued, and the method of doing so should be subtle and well timed rather than brazen.

"Just war" is thus not a centerpiece in Chinese strategic thought. This is because war in itself is regarded as a phenomenon of failure, be it failure of political virtuosity in the realist sense (Machiavelli's *virtu*) or of moral leadership in the Confucian sense. The discarding of war as a tool of statecraft marks an important intersection in China's strategic cultures. At this juncture, Sun Zi's ideal general who "breaks the enemy's resistance without fighting" (Sun Tzu [Zi], 1988:III.2) finds himself in the company of Mohism's great teacher, Mo Zi, of whom it was said: "Teaching that social well-being derives from universal love, Mo Zi described warfare as mass murder and ridiculed the states of his time for punishing individual thefts and murders while rewarding pillage and massacre" (Zhuge and Liu, 1989:6); and in the company of Mencius, who instructed that peace could come only through unity. When asked who could unify the world, Mencius replied: "One who is not fond of killing can unite it" (Mencius, 1988:53). With the exception of the Legalists, who *did* accept the instrument of force as a legitimate tool for forging unity and thence peace, Chinese strategic culture converged on an attitude of antimilitarism. Complementing this was the suggestion of inclusive *global* security in the *yin-yang* conception of "incorporating the other," and as suggested by the Chinese security mandalas of Figures 8.3 and 8.7. China's own history taught that periods of horrific bloodshed and disorder occurred in contexts of rivalry and disunity; periods of stability came when there was unity in China and Confucian suzerainty in the region.

Figure 8.7
A Classic Security Mandala for China

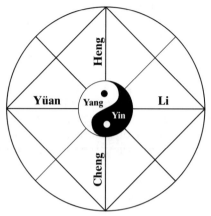

Having made the point about Chinese antimilitarism in principle, there are obvious examples of aggression in practice. The moral-cum-political use of *wu,* not surprisingly, leaves it open to abuse. For example, there is nothing in Confucian philosophy that sanctions the shooting of students; yet the ease with which the army could be used to do so in June 1989, under the justification of restoring political and social order, attests to the double-edged sword of *wu* moral power. In practice it means that China's rulers—past and present, virtuous or not—had to control the power of *wu* if they wished to be assured of their own. Hence, Mao Zedong spoke of power—the party's power—growing out of "the barrel of a gun." Similarly, Deng Xiaoping was also able to retain supreme power through the backing of the army.

Dao *(the way) and* wu-wei *(nonaction, spontaneous action, noninterference, metapower).   Dao* simply means "the way." For Confucianists, *tien* bestows "human nature," and in following our human nature we are in fact following the *dao;* by cultivating the *dao* we educate or civilize ourselves (from *Doctrine of the Mean,* in Chan, 1963:98). The Daoist school of Chinese philosophy has adopted it as its central concern; and its principal proponent, Lao Zi—whose ideas are set forth in the *Dao De Jing* (Book of the Way and Its Power)—speaks of the *dao* as eternal and nameless. To interpreters of the *dao,* it is "the way of man's cooperation with the course or trend of the natural world" (Watts, 1992:xiv).

According to the *Dao De Jing* (Lao Tzu [Zi], 1988:Chap. 37), "Tao [*dao*] invariably does nothing (*wu-wei*) and yet there is nothing that is not done." Moreover, "To make complete without acting (*wu wei*), and to obtain without seeking: this is what is meant by the activities of

Heaven" (Hsun Tzu quoted in Fung, 1952, Vol. 1:285). From these quotations it is possible to appreciate lack of action in a positive light. It is not "inaction," but avoidance of unnatural action (Chan, 1963:791). *Wu-wei* represents an alignment with the *tien-dao,* or the way of heaven.

The key international relations application of Daoism is the endeavor to excel through strength of character rather than force of arms. Right is might, and not the other way round. Fulfilling one's potential comes not from actively seeking it at the expense of the other (person, society, or the environment), like a zero-sum game ("I win, you lose"). It comes from incorporating the other, working with the other, in line with the complementary principles of polarity, *yin* and *yang.* Even if that other is an opponent, one uses the strength of the opponent to achieve one's own safety. This, of course, is a basic principle of the martial arts, where the force of an attacking opponent is not met frontally, but allowed to continue under its own momentum until it reaches its opposite condition of self-defeat. That Buddhist monks used this martial method indicates its ethical acceptability, in addition to its Daoist insight into the "laws of nature," of which *wu-wei* or non-doing is a central concept. Indeed, it was a Chinese strategist, Mingjiao of the eleventh century, who wrote: "A lost country wars with weapons; a dictatorship wars with cunning; a kingdom wars with humanitarian justice; an empire wars with virtue; a utopia wars with nondoing" (quoted in Zhuge and Liu, 1989:8).

Datong *(greater community, grand unity, universal commonwealth, utopia).* This is the global practice of *dao* that Confucius said he never saw; but he speculated that it existed during the Three Dynasties prior to the imperial age. "When the great Tao was in practice, the world was common to all" (quoted in Fung, 1952, Vol. 1:378); he called it the period of *datong* or the Great Unity. Confucius regarded the society for which he strived through the implementation of *li* as only a Small Tranquillity. "Now that the great Tao has fallen into obscurity, the world has become (divided into) families" (quoted in Fung, 1952, Vol. 1:378). The government of Great Unity represented a higher ideal. So *datong* was not imperialism; imperial China was a devolution from *datong.* However, the sentiment of *datong* could be said to have been kept alive through the belief that "all under Heaven are one."

This one-world philosophy of *datong* is an important point for Chinese strategic culture, because it found practical, even if imperfect, expression in the tributary mode of international relations.[4] As noted above, this system of suzerainty was inclusive of others. Essentially, the Chinese international project has been one of seeking order (harmony) through unity. In times of disunity, like the Warring States period (450–221 B.C.), the drive was for unity under one victorious state. It was not a push for independence—the path pursued by the European states and, eventually, the present international system of sovereign states. Applied to today's problems, it is in this light that the desire for political reunification across the Taiwan Strait is better understood.

The psychological indivisibility of Chinese sovereignty was severely shaken at the time when the European treaty system overtook the Chinese tribute system. The Opium War of 1839–1843 not only represents the watershed between the Chinese and Western world orders, but it also established a primary reference point for Chinese national humiliation. This has fueled strategic culture to a remarkable degree. It has meant that while practicing gradualism (such as over the disputed Spratly Islands in the South China Sea or the introduction of market reforms), Chinese sovereignty is never compromised—not just with independence-prone Taiwan, but also with regard to human rights, and particularly democracy-prone Hong Kong with its Opium War connections. "Certain questions left over from history" has been a familiar refrain from the Chinese foreign ministry.

De *(power)*.   This is the word for "power" as it is used in the *Dao De Jing.* It is not coercive or forceful power but the power of virtue and character. *De* can mean both "power" and "virtue." In Daoism it has the sense of latent power, mystical power, potency. It has more in common with power as understood in traditional Asian societies where power is status and has mystical connotations—as distinct from being a utilitarian matter, a means for achieving purposeful ends (see Pye, 1985).

Metapower *(wu-wei, de, indirect power).*   A nation that exhibits a preponderance of Western realist, *wu*-backed power is popularly termed a superpower. This term describes capability and a willingness to flaunt it (status-wise) or mobilize it (for punitive measures) in the interests of system maintenance. In doing so, a superpower exercises hegemonic leadership by (1) setting the standard of international norms and rules of behavior and (2) acting as the guarantor of international stability. Such hegemony may have imperial implication, depending on the prevailing international political fashion. Given all these characteristics of superpower capability, international will, and hegemonic implications, how does it register in terms of *de?* Does the superpower have *tien-ming* (the mandate of heaven) by following *tien-dao* (the way of heaven)? Is its hegemony morally sanctioned? Without a moral center in its security mandala, it cannot be described as a *de*-superpower.[5]

A *de*-superpower is better expressed as metapower. It is more comfortable with the power of *wu-wei* (non-doing) than the power of *wu* diplomacy. This understanding distinguishes the secular Western realist superpower and its implied hegemony, from the Daoist-Confucian metapower with *its* implied hegemony—that is, by the pursuit of international *li* for the purpose of international peace (Small Tranquillity) through the spiritual aspiration for international unity (*datong*). Like *yin* and *yang,* the Western realist's superpower is shadowed by the Daoist-Confucian metapower. The latter (*yin*) force must contain elements of the former (essentially *yang*) force if it is to survive. Hence, in the exercise of *wen* politics, *wu* power is held in reserve. When its use is called upon, it acts decisively. To use once again the analogy of the Chinese martial arts, fighting is avoided; but if it must be engaged in, the blow has to be decisive. The current international system of secular "balanced" power is dysfunctional in that it does not address the question of how the world may be at peace, but only how it may preserve itself. This individualism is characteristic of the Western philosophical tradition but represents its corruption in the absence of moral cultivation. Within the Chinese humanism of *jen,* however, how one can relate harmoniously to others is the appropriate consideration. Contemporary China is now faced with restoring its own *jen* after flirting with extremist groupism and materialism.

In accordance with *jen's* consensual approach, metapower can further be explained as pervasive, indirect influence—which represents the attributes of *li* rather than law. Metapower's historical approximation may be identified as suzerainty. Legally, this refers to the political control of one state over another, but historically, as Watson explains (1992:15), "it means a shadowy overlordship that amounts to very little in practice." More specifically, in Small Tranquillity terms, it amounts to an international system's tacit acceptance of suzerain authority. "Tacit acceptance is the same as acquiescence, and is necessary for any effective hegemony, whether *de jure* or *de facto*" (Watson, 1992:15). Metapower shares with suzerainty the concept of indirect control but adds to it the postsuperpower notion of indirect power.

Foundational Principles Within the Chinese Security Mandala

The neo-Confucianist Yen Yüan's diagram of cosmology may be adapted as a classic security mandala for China. There is a square within a circle and a number of intersecting lines (Figure 8.7). According to Yen Yüan (quoted in Fung, 1952, Vol. 2:636), "The large circle represents the Way of Heaven in its entirety. . . . The operations of the *yin* and *yang* result in the creation of the four powers [*de*]: *yüan* (originating growth), *heng* (prosperous development), *li* (advantageous gain), and *cheng* (correct firmness)." The four *de* (powers) are rendered as dynamic, not static, forces. The principle of permeability is acknowledged: "Thus there is nothing that does not interpenetrate everything else" (p. 637). Potentiality rather than actuality is stressed: "Once one understands that the two forces of the Way of Heaven, the four powers of the four forces, and the production of all things by the four powers, all constitute this original potentiality, ... then one can examine this diagram (with proper under-standing)" (pp. 637–638).

Its interest as a metaphor for a security mandala is the depiction of the four cycles of (1) self-establishment (system transformation, to use the world order language of Kim, 1991), (2) enrichment (system mainte-nance), (3) empowerment (system exploitation), and (4) virtue (or meta-power). China seems to be entering the third cycle, of advantageous gain (system exploitation). Samuel Kim has identified this as a possibility in interpreting China's outlook on the world in the 1980s. A "radical *sys-tem-transforming* approach" under Maoist China before membership in the United Nations, was followed by a "*system-reforming* approach" upon admittance to the UN; this, in turn, was transformed in the 1980s to "*system-maintaining* and *system-exploiting*" approaches "as Beijing be-came more interested in what the UN system could do for China's mod-ernization and less interested in what it could do to reform the [UN] Charter system" (Kim, 1991:21–22).

Cycle 3, of advantageous gain (system exploitation), may, however, be seen as a prelude to indirect global power or metapower (cycle 4), which in turn occasions a new cycle of system transformation (cycle 1). This assumes that a breakdown, through excessive *yin* or *yang* practices at any one stage, is guarded against. An example of excessive *yin* is the police state mentality in internal affairs; excessive *yang* may be exempli-fied by imperial overreach in foreign policy. For China this has meant, on the one hand, avoidance of the burning-of-the-books attitude, which is said to have brought about the early demise of the first dynasty, the Qin; and, on the other hand, avoidance of extravagant displays of state power far from one's center (such as the Ming imperial naval expeditions of the fifteenth century). It was better for the world to come to China and be transformed than for China to go out to the world. Interestingly, in the process, the Chinese world expands to be more inclusive and, therefore, transformative of that which it includes. This may be viewed as system transformation. Simultaneously, China in its diffusion undergoes its own transformation toward cosmopolitanism, as exemplified by the Tang dy-nasty (A.D. 618–906). If history is any guide, China is entering this (neo-Tang) phase of metapower and thence system transformation. The rele-vant cycles of history are well identified by Capon (1989:7):

> Indeed, it is with the historically symbolic Han dynasty that the story of the founding of the Tang begins. Apart from the short-lived Qin dy-nasty (221–06 B.C.) the Han was the only precedent for an enduring and unified Chinese empire. The preface to the founding of the Han Empire was also repeated as the founding of the Tang; for as the Han dynasty was preceded by a brief but immensely determined Qin dy-nasty, so the Sui dynasty (A.D. 581–618), some eight centuries later, es-tablished the foundations of the Tang.

Twentieth-century communist China (including its latter-day "open-door" variant of system exploitation) could be another example of what Capon (1989:9) describes as "a brief but dogmatic reunifying dynasty laying the foundations for another long period of stability."

A SINICIZED GLOBAL SYSTEM?
AN INTERNATIONALIZED CHINESE SYSTEM?

Are we heading for a sinicized global system? Is China approaching a Tang Renaissance? How do *wen* politics overtake Western realism? Because it is a highly strategic culture, China is likely to plan carefully its foreign policy performance—in relation to both domestic and international circumstances. By flowing with the *dao* of the international system, China is thereby cultivating its own, acquiring its individual *de,* its potency. Specific issues that are likely to be played out in the politics of system transformation are global military power, the power of ideas (liberalism in the presence of "Asian values"), and East Asian economic power in internationalizing a new sinitic culture. Hence, the traditional formula of military, political, and economic power considerations in foreign policy analysis is retained as the particularistic entry point into a comprehensive strategic-cultural analysis for Chinese foreign policy behavior.

Military Power

In matters military, Chinese esteem of *wen* warfare in a Western-tutored world of *wu* diplomacy poses a fundamental difficulty for China. It is a difficulty not dissimilar to the one faced by the Celestial Empire in relation to the European colonial powers in the nineteenth century. In other words, today's Western deterrence, both conventional and nuclear, is backed by *wu* capability, which in turn poses the problem of *wu* credibility for China.

It is a problem China had to deal with during the age of nuclear hegemony in world politics, from 1947 to 1989. By nuclear hegemony is meant both the dominance of nuclear politics over other "low politics" and the dominance of the two superpowers (the United States and the Soviet Union) over world affairs because of their ownership and near monopoly of the means of mass destruction.

With nuclear hegemony's end, there emerged an incipient nuclear democracy among the non-Western aspirants of Western power. In other words, those who were not in the exclusive "nuclear club" could not see why they should not try. After all, none of the original members has chosen to leave the club by giving up nuclear weapons. This latest episode of the phenomenon of "anti-Western Westernization" (Ojha, 1969) has been named "nuclear proliferation" by the international establishment. But proliferation is consistent with the protective-cum-empowerment relationship of the old tributary system. To kowtow to the emperor is to kowtow to civilization and thereby be transformed. By being the country most visibly undermining the West's nuclear hegemony (through its own nuclear weapons modernization as well as suspected proliferation), the Chinese are not persuaded by the "grandiose rationalizations" (Ojha, 1969:56) of Western realism.

Obviously, during the nuclear hegemony period, the Chinese nuclear force fell far short of either superpower's forces in size and sophistication. Accounting for only 3 percent of the world's total warheads and holding only a tenth the number of launchers of either superpower, the Chinese had no intention of competing with the U.S. and Soviet mega-arsenals. The aim is not to imitate what is new or foreign, and thereby attempt to become it, but to incorporate-"civilize"-sinicize it into an existing system (security mandala, Figure 8.3).

How has China's nuclear weapons power been sinicized? Its rationale derives from the *yin* desire for inviolability. Never again would China be at the mercy of technologically superior powers, as it had been at the end of its dynastic life. At the same time, China has not developed a mega-arsenal of weapons like that of the Cold War nuclear hegemons. Nuclear weapons power has been rendered more psychologically potent by the absence of declared nuclear policy. We are not told how China would "use" its nuclear power if it had to. But it does pledge never to be the first to use nuclear weapons. What does this mean? It probably means a well thought out deterrence based on sound Daoist principles. There is an interesting parallel here with the Daoist "use of uselessness." In this concept, one has to balance usefulness with uselessness. This is illustrated by adapting a dialogue of the Daoist master, Zhuang Zi (Chuang-Tzu), to explain nuclear *wu* power:[6]

> "If nuclear *wu* power's intention is to be useless, why does it serve on the altar for the defence of this land?"
> "Be still and do not declare a doctrine. It just pretends to be on the altar. By so doing it can protect us from the injury of those who do not know it is useless. If it were not on the altar, we would be still in danger from the arrogance of those with nuclear teeth. Moreover, what this doctrine maintains is different from what ordinary military doctrines do. Therefore, to judge it with conventional morality is far from the point."
> "All know the usefulness of the useful, but not that of the useless."
> (Adapted from Chuang-Tzu, 1989:74–75, 77)

The "usefulness of the useful" has also received strategic consideration in China. Traditionally a land power, China has been expanding and modernizing its naval power since the 1980s. From a strategic-cultural perspective, there can be little doubt that the growth in Chinese naval capability will soon empower China's "will" to reclaim its maritime tribute region in the South China Sea and the near Indian Ocean (bearing in mind that Southeast Asia is a two-ocean region, between the Chinese and Indian oceans). By "will" is meant *rightful place under heaven*—in China's case, this will mean earning its *tien-ming*. Because the mandate of heaven is not achieved by *wu* power, China will have to demonstrate her *wen* credentials. *Wu* seapower then becomes the handmaiden of *wen* strategy by adding a forward deployment capacity to the existing heartland power. This amounts to *wu* credibility in international perceptions.

The Power of Ideas

Turning to the power of ideas, China's presumed desire to create a situation in which the country is unassailable now refers less to physical invasion and more to the invasion of undesirable influences, or "spiritual pollution" (to use the Chinese communist term). Examples of corruption among those holding responsible positions are legion. The authorities have blamed "money worship" for these ills. Modernizing China is taking on the appearance of an economic animal in the form of the three-clawed dragon, as distinct from the more noble five-clawed variety that emerged symbolically at the height of Chinese civilization. Without *li*, according to the perception of history that informs Chinese strategic culture, *luan* (chaos) befalls the nation.

Like most other countries, China regards internal cohesion as a vital element of security. How to maintain internal cohesion is often determined by political culture. From ancient times, China practiced a mixture of idealism and classical realism, represented by Confucianism on the one hand and Legalism on the other.[7] Similarly, China's history has been punctuated by periods of unity and disunity. The commonly held fear that loss of central control will lead to warlordism is to a large extent based on this pattern of experience. Here is where the resurrection of *li* is of more import than the use of punishments or simply succumbing to Western liberalism. The latter would entail China's loss of the (cultural) initiative over the present (political) international system dominated by the West. It would also most certainly mean the loss of Communist Party authority.

Signs that various *li* are being reintroduced include the rehabilitation of Confucius as "a great thinker and statesman" ("Qian Qichen," 1993:11), the publication of inexpensive and well-produced literature for parents teaching their children morality (Fung, 1995), the emphasis on patriotism in schools, and, in the foreign policy sector, China's continuing emphasis on the Five Principles of Peaceful Coexistence[8] and on the need for a "new international political and economic order" (see Kim, 1991). How successful China's center will be in reinforcing *li* and, in the process, its own authority when so much of China is under the spell of "economics first" remains to be seen. It is also difficult to assess how post-Tiananmen China can convince a human rights–conscious world of the country's morality. Moreover, the continuation of nuclear testing had done nothing to endear China to international public opinion.

It is true that the moral view of power does not always guide practice or appear to do so. Nonetheless, failure to transform oneself does not negate the project. Even Confucius is said not to have achieved his ideals of self-cultivation (see Tu, Hejtming, and Wachman, 1992:108). Although China appeared to the West as unscrupulous in selling missiles to the Middle East and in rejecting nuclear arms reduction agreements, immoral in its human rights record, and perhaps provocative in its military buildup in the region—points the Chinese authorities have counterargued[9]—China's time-honored pronouncements still indicate the quest for moral power. One might argue that the two Cold War superpowers, the United States and the Soviet Union, did engage in a moral contention via their competing ideologies of "liberating the world's oppressed classes" versus "making the world safe for democracy." China's view, as illustrated by its condemnatory statements, is more skeptical. China did not approve of the way in which the rest of the world was "manipulated" in the contest between the two strongest nations. The profession of ideals on the one hand and the pursuit of "power politics" on the other could be viewed not only as hypocritical but also irresponsible. Why? Because of the high nuclear force levels and the disregard for "justice," an ideal at the forefront of China's foreign policy rhetoric and posture. China was the only Third World country strong enough to challenge the post-1945 world order of superpower dominance. It has acquired an independent nuclear deterrent and polished its role of international critic, even to the present time. The new post–Cold War order is seen as potentially dangerous not only because of an interfering West (led by the United States), but also because of economic inequalities. This pertains to the Third World that China has been championing for years as part of its antihegemony campaign. In 1991, for example, the call for justice continued (Li, 1991:10):

> As is known to all, poverty of third world countries has many causes, of which the old international economic order and the economic relationship based on exchange of unequal values between the North and the South, which long placed the developing countries in an unequal and unfair position, is the main one. It will get nowhere to impose a particular Western model of development on the developing countries instead of reforming the old economic order. Nor is armed control a fundamental remedy for regional turbulence and conflict.

This type of rhetoric has remained strong in the post–Cold War (and post-Tiananmen) era when China needs to defend its rights to noninterference in its sovereign affairs. Beijing's commitment to antihegemony conforms to the defensive phase of People's War strategy. The "weak" side seeks to erode the capability and will of the stronger invader (the would-be hegemon) until such a time as the final phase of strategic counteroffensive may be launched. Upon accomplishing this task, the victorious defender presumably would not claim the mantle of hegemon for itself. Even if it had built up the capability to do so, it could not act in this way without forfeiting the real prize of its antihegemonic war: the demonstrated victory of its own value system. China, paradoxically, must pursue its antihegemonic interests if it wishes to prevail. Chih-Yu Shih has written a revealing book on Chinese foreign policy called *China's Just World,* in which he contends that "the Chinese not only promote their interests but also embody a worldview that explains why those interests are worth pursuing" (Shih, 1993:13).

China's antihegemonic posture accords with the country's Five Principles of Peaceful Coexistence and its experience—like other East Asian societies—of the hegemonic practices of the West. The "unequal treaties" are an especially painful reminder of the consequences of inequality among nations. Ironically, the Chinese world order, which has so little regard for individualism, is more particular about realizing the theoretical equality of nation-states. In reviewing Chinese national boundary issues in the early days of the People's Republic of China (PRC), Ojha (1969) notes the importance Beijing attached to "not so much a change of boundary lines for their own sake as their renegotiation on a free and equal basis" (p. 65), of being "motivated not by territorial expansionism but by this fanatical obsession with sovereign consent" (p. 65), and of wishing to "neither take advantage of nor yield advantage to any country" (p. 153). Ojha also notes (p. 172) that when China did go to war over boundary issues, it was only after deeper antagonisms or complications presented themselves. Certainly this proved correct even as late as the post-Mao period. The Sino-Vietnamese border war of 1979 had less to do with disputed boundary demarcation than with "punishing" Vietnam for invading Cambodia after signing an alliance treaty with China's enemy, the Soviet Union. The war was meant to teach the Vietnamese a lesson so "they could not run about as much as they desired" (Deng Xiaoing, quoted in Segal, 1985:211). This doctrine of "punitive expeditions" was known in ancient Chinese thought.[10] Its continuance into the future can be expected, especially under conditions of perceived moral assault—such as de jure independence for Taiwan or foreign peacekeeping forces in the areas of disputation in China's claimed southern sea.

There are two forms of punitive expedition that might result. The first belongs to the time of transition between Western realism and *wen* politics. The above examples of moral provocation (perceived interference in Chinese internal affairs) belong to this phase. The transitional nature of the times means that China does not feel confident in having acquired a state of *cheng* (correct firmness, or rightful place under heaven). It is when *heng* (prosperous development) and *li* (advantageous gain) vie for attention with possible plans for punitive action. There are distractions and uncertainties. A victorious outcome is not assured. Nonetheless, if pressed, China would act, even if the victory is more symbolic than real.

Should China reach a position of *cheng,* which makes possible *yüan* (originating growth) and thus the beginning of a new cycle, punitive expeditions are of a different order. They are then administered within the sinicized system rather than against a dominant non-Chinese system. At this point, speculation arises as to how the sinicized world system would function. Again, judging from the dominant strands of Chinese strategic culture, China will have more confidence in the efficacy of *li*. Should this fail, and should "intimidating, cajoling, or subsidizing" others prove fruitless—terms used to describe China's traditional methods (Reischauer and Fairbank, 1970:317)—punishment is likely to be of the decisive variety.

Because the Chinese world order will contain not only China, there is likely to operate a kind of "Confucian family of nations" punitive expedition force—with "claws," to use the dragon metaphor. More specifically, branches of "regional family" forces would prevail, whereby each of the regions enforces its own order. China has never been comfortable psychologically with projecting Chinese force far from its East Asian neighborhood. China could oversee world security, but it could not allow itself to administer it personally. In a sinicized world, such would be the task of the international mandarin classes.

The preceding discussion describes the international system of a sinicized world. What are the transition markers? How does one arrive from "here" to "there"? Reflection on the nature of the present decade is in order. Spurred by an international climate more sensitive to the conduct of *li,* China will be in a better position to occupy her rightful place. Though ironic, the human rights campaign against China affords the country an opportunity to elaborate its own worldview. This, in turn, should widen China's scope to include its more Confucian-literate brethren in Taiwan, Hong Kong, Singapore, and the domains of "Cultural China" that include the Chinese diaspora and the contributions of non-Chinese participants of Chinese affairs—be they intellectual, journalistic or commercial (see Tu, 1991).

Cultural China as a term has become even more significant than *Greater China,* which is largely an economic description. The concept of Cultural China has been developed in the discourse on China by a number of commentators. Among its initiators is a Taiwanese American academic, Charles Wei-hsun Fu, who used the term at a public lecture in Taiwan in 1987 (Fu, 1993) as a means of escaping the deadlock of political China (between Taiwan and the PRC). As Lu (1995) explains: "There is also the connotation that there is something unique and desirable about cultural China, which is lacking in political and economic China." He points out that "cultural China is more fundamental than political or economic China," and that "the former is fundamental to understanding the latter two." Cultural China provides not only a way out from the political impasse that has trapped the contemporary concept of China, but also a way into the world "through a 'discourse community,'" which transcends geographical areas, ethnic groupings, languages and religions" (Lu, 1995). Yu Ying-shih, a (mainland) Chinese American scholar, also wrote on Cultural China (1993), saying that it was ideal for the nonpolitical unification of China. In this way the vibrant and diverse cultures of the Chinese regions (the little traditions) are not overwhelmed by an imposing great tradition.

It is true that in the Chinese periphery the more traditional Chinese mores as well as diverse little traditions have survived. They have acted as the cultural engines of modernization and commercial success. In this sense, like the latest deities on the altar of Chinese culturalism, Lee Kuan Yew, with his "Asian values" message emanating from tiny Singapore, sits alongside Deng Xiaoping with his pragmatism from China proper.

Economic Power

This raises the role of East Asian economic power in "publicizing" a value system that is not European in inspiration. The renewed "unity of all under heaven" has already begun economically in the region. It might again resemble a tribute-trade system in which doing business with China and her Confucian (including Japanese) cultural kin would be a major attraction to foreigners who might otherwise become obsessed with preparing to deal with "the China threat." Tribute would be made materially and symbolically to civilization, a civilization that nourishes the environment in which such economic and cultural transactions can occur. Such a civilization would now be called not China, but East Asia—a geographic and cultural expression spanning Northeast and Southeast Asia. Beijing would be only one of a number of "capitals" (see Harding, 1993:674) acting as the centers of the East Asian tribute-trade system, with APEC (Asia-Pacific Economic Cooperation), or even the proposed EAEC (East Asian Economic Caucus), a forerunner and facilitator. The West's position would be a complementary one, in true *yinyang* fashion. Once the center, it now becomes the periphery, but a periphery that is not exploited in the neo-Marxist sense. Rather, the periphery the West represents is a sustaining one, allowing for the (mutual) pursuit of a middle path between polarities of the group and the individual, duties and responsibilities, the religious-magical universe and the secular-scientific one (or tradition and modernity), economics and politics, ambiguity and distinction.

The United States finds a more sustainable niche in this system, for it is not faced with a confrontational situation, as occurred through needless misunderstanding with the Soviet Union. This was due largely to inadequate strategic-cultural analysis on the part of advisers to both governments. The spiraling of threat perceptions during the frostier years of the Cold War, followed by a "steady state" of animosity that allowed for a working relationship under détente, illustrated how well adjusted the world could become to its nuclear neurosis. That it was a dysfunctional condition became amply evident when the Cold War ended and much of the international community could not fathom, and certainly not condone, Western realism in the form of invasions (Iraq-Kuwait), nuclear testing (especially by France in 1995), and sacrifices of various kinds, from the environment to human rights.

PREDICTABLE ENCOUNTERS

As the current system struggles to find its post–Cold War identity, as Western realism subsides and Cultural China strengthens, a number of predictable encounters can be envisioned. At the military level, there will be a flurry of high-tech arms acquisition programs among China's Asian neighbors, including India. Interestingly, the implied excuse to the West and to each other will be concern to balance the Chinese. Privately, however, these states will be emulating China. Weapons will be almost exclusively employed as national status symbols. The rhetoric of national resilience, comprehensive security, and total defense in conjunction with a calibration of "Asian values" to political management styles will reveal the sinicization of modernity. This is already well under way through the conjunction of traditional Chinese values in the East Asian region (comprising both Northeast and Southeast Asia, marking China's periphery) and indigenous ones (for example, Javanese, Balinese, Malay, Thai, and others).

War is likely to remain last on the list of regional interests. In any case, entrenched consensus politics will slow any developments that could lead to war. Complicated rituals of maneuver within regional forums will also diminish any such possibility. By contrast, "efficiency" (as distinct from pragmatism) in relationships will be deemed callous and instrumental—insults considered worse than war. As Pye once put it: "Sticks and stones can break my bones but words can kill me" (1990:337).

The diplomatic environment would be controlled by a mastery of *li*. The United States, having emerged from the formidable learning process of the Cold War and disinclined to be drawn into a new but equally risk-prone role of global policeman, will be inclined toward supporting this system. The key confrontations will occur, as usual, within the United States itself—between the containment-of-China and engagement-of-China advocates. However, because the United States is unlikely to be assertive in a region that least appreciates (and, from the U.S. perspective, least needs) assertive behavior, Washington will be least troubled by a sinicizing Asia. This will, in all probability, be judged a region of stability. The United States, with its own inherent idealism, is unlikely to interfere with traditional Chinese values—propelled by economic modernity—reaching out into other parts of the world. The reasonable nature of a *jen*-directed society represents more of a help than a hindrance to future U.S. foreign relations. By not being singled out as the solitary superpower, the global puppeteer, or the remaining evil empire, it is possible for the United States to take the Daoist path to longevity: a *wu-wei* policy of metapower. Otherwise, the drawbacks of being a superpower—visibility, enmity, and transitoriness—must be faced.

CONCLUSION

Chinese idealism equates with *li* (proper conduct). From it issues good governance and harmonious relations. True, it is an ideal, but it is not one that others in the Chinese cultural orbit (the East Asians) are unable to pursue. Increasingly, their mutual relations exhibit Chinese idealism (pursued through *wen* politics) rather than Western realism. Proper conduct does not negate self-interest; it redefines it in relation to the greater good. This is why, to take a concrete example, ASEAN (Association of Southeast Asian Nations), regardless of limited economic outcomes, has proved so successful as an exercise in mutually supportive international relations.

Earlier, Mencius was mentioned as the philosopher who advised on how the world may be at peace. By way of conclusion, it is worth reiterating his views, as commentated upon by Fung Yu-lan (1966:180):

> Though the First Emperor was thus the first to achieve actual unity, the desire for such unity had been cherished by all people for a long time previous. In the *Mencius* we are told that King Hui of Liang asked: "How may the world be at peace?" To which Mencius replied: "When there is unity, there will be peace." "But who can unify the world?" asked the King. "He who does not delight in killing men can unify it," answered Mencius (Ia, 6). This statement clearly expresses the aspiration of the time.

It may also be the statement that most clearly expresses the sentiment of our own post–Cold War times. Morality in foreign policy is, paradoxically, and to employ a Deng quote, the truth that can be gleaned from the facts. In this respect, idealism *is* realism. That Chinese strategic culture has not only adopted this idea but prospered from it suggests its continued relevance to China's future and, hence, to a large extent our own. Five thousand years of statecraft capped by one hundred years of humiliation have invested contemporary China with both calculation and reflection in its power relationships. As the Chinese president once said to the U.S. secretary of state: "The fat man didn't get that way with just one bite" (quoted in Kaye, 1994). Similarly, one could add, scholarship in foreign policy analysis cannot expect to acquire "weight" without the study of culture—and strategic culture in particular. Alternative security constructs help break the disservice of ethnocentric thinking in the application of strategic-cultural analysis. If we are to apply strategic-cultural analysis to foreign policy problems, we must begin by experimenting with the conceptual templates of what is called "security."

NOTES

1. This quote is attributed to Napoleon Bonaparte.

2. O. W. Wolters (1968) adopted it for identifying pre-European international relations in Southeast Asia and later used it to mean a single polity or state (see Wolters, 1982; Mackerras, 1995). The concept of mandala in international relations is being developed in contemporary contexts by the Centre for East-West Cultural and Economic Studies at Bond University, Australia (see *The Culture Mandala,* 1994). I am a founding member of this center, which was established in 1993.

3. This is Dun J. Li's translation (1971:74) of the passage. It is more explicit—for example, "selfish desires" instead of "self" as found in D. C. Lau's (1988, XII:1) translation.

4. Traditional China modeled its foreign relations on the Confucian values associated with filial piety. With the Chinese emperor at the head, lesser kingdoms were expected to show submission in return for Chinese protection. Thus, "foreign relations" came under the family metaphor, rendering them familial relations; the Chinese emperor was recognized as the symbolic head of the international household—a rather more literal "family of nations." The tributary system, also known as the tribute-trade system, derives its name from the tribute-rendering activity. Representatives from neighboring countries would bring "tribute" (or gifts) to the emperor in the Chinese capital in exchange for the right to trade with China. Often the envoys returned with more gifts than they brought, but that they kowtowed (from *ketou,* knock the head) to the emperor indicated their recognition of China as the "elder." In this way, China controlled both trade and the unruly potential of its neighbors. Above all, China acted out its sense of civilizational superiority, which is linked to the mandate of heaven concept. The Chinese did not try to convert the "barbarians" through missionaries but to set them an example. It was expected that by coming with tribute to the capital they would be transformed.

5. Notice a coincidental meaningfulness in English of the Chinese-English compound word that emerges. The process of *de*-superpowering any superpower would represent a more Daoist world system.

6. Elsewhere, in more military-oriented writing, I have particularized nuclear *wu* power in the form of guerrilla nuclear warfare (see Dellios, 1989, 1994).

7. Legalism was based on the power of punishment through law and force in international relations, rather than the power of virtue. Legalism was short-lived, but its incorporation of Daoist thinking on the use of deception meant a greater measure of longevity for its "power politics" perspective.

8. These are: (1) mutual respect for sovereignty and territorial integrity; (2) mutual nonaggression; (3) mutual noninterference in internal affairs, equality, and mutual benefit; and (5) peaceful coexistence.

9. There are many examples of Chinese rebuttals, often in the form of long-standing policy statements with regard to China's nonaggressive posture, but sometimes with specific reference to current problems. *Beijing Review* is a dependable source of such statements. See, for example, "Qian on World Situation and China's Foreign Policy," *Beijing Review,* 11–17, October 1993, pp. 8–11.

10. For example, in Li Ch'uan's *Secret Classic of T'ai-po,* the term is used in the context of moral order: "If [the employment] of soldiers does not accord with [the Way of] Heaven, one cannot move [them to victory]; if [the employment] of an army is not modeled on [the Way of] Earth, one cannot carry out punitive expeditions; if [the employment of] attack methods does not match [the Way of] man, one cannot be successful" (quoted in Rand, 1979:115–116). Also, it was a minor theme in Mohist thought (see Mo Tzu, 1973:93, 111–113).

REFERENCES

Ball, Desmond (1993) "Strategic Culture in the Asia-Pacific Region." Working Paper No. 270, Strategic and Defence Studies Centre, Australian National University, Canberra, Australia.

Beck, Ulrich (1994) "The Reinvention of Politics: Towards a Theory of Reflexive Modernization." In *Reflexive Modernization: Politics, Tradition and Aesthetics in the Modern Social Order,* edited by Ulrich Beck, Anthony Giddens, and Scott Lash. Cambridge, UK: Polity Press.

Bennett, Peter, and Michael Nicholson (1994) "Formal Methods of Analysis in IR." In *Contemporary International Relations: A Guide to Theory,* edited by A. J. R. Groom and Margot Light. London: Pinter.

Booth, Ken (1979) *Strategy and Ethnocentrism.* London: Croom Helm.

Booth, Ken (1990) "The Concept of Strategic Culture Affirmed." In *Strategic Power: USA/USSR,* edited by Carl G. Jacobsen. London: Macmillan.

Boylan, Edward S. (1982) "The Chinese Cultural Style of Warfare." *Comparative Strategy* 3, no. 4:341–364.

Capon, Edmund (1989) *Tang China: Vision and Splendour of a Golden Age.* London: Macdonald.

Chan, Wing-tsit, trans. and comp. (1963) *A Source Book in Chinese Philosophy.* Princeton: Princeton University Press.

Chuang-Tzu (1989) *Chuang-Tzu* (translated by Fung Yu-Lan). Beijing: Foreign Languages Press.

Confucius (1988) *The Analects* (translated by D. C. Lau). Harmondsworth, UK: Penguin.

The Culture Mandala (1994) *Bulletin for the Centre of East-West Cultural and Economic Studies* 1, no. 1. Bond University, Centre of East-West Cultural and Economic Studies, Gold Coast, Australia.

de Bary, William Theodore, Wing-tsit Chan, and Burton Watson, comps. (1960) *Sources of Chinese Tradition,* vol. 1. New York: Columbia University Press.

Dellios, Rosita (1989) *Modern Chinese Defence Strategy: Present Developments, Future Directions.* London: Macmillan.

Dellios, Rosita (1994) *Chinese Strategic Culture, Part 1: The Heritage from the Past.* Research Paper No. 1, Centre for East-West Cultural and Economic Studies, Bond University, Gold Coast, Australia.

Dixon, Norman (1976) *On the Psychology of Military Incompetence.* New York: Basic Books.

Ermarth, Fritz (1978) "Contrasts in Soviet and American Strategic Thought." *International Society* 3, no. 2:138–155.

Fairbank, John K. (1974) "Introduction: Varieties of the Chinese Military Experience." In *Chinese Ways in Warfare,* edited by Frank A. Kierman, Jr., and John K. Fairbank. Cambridge: Harvard University Press.

Fu, Charles Wei-hsun (1993) *Xuewen di Shengming yu Shengming di Xuewen* [The life of scholarship and scholarship of life]. Taipei: Zhenzhong.

Fung, Andy (1995) "Traditional Chinese Family Education Study: Family Instructions." Paper presented at the Fourth Biennial Conference of the Chinese Studies Association of Australia, Macquarie University, Sydney, July 5–7,

Fung Yu-Lan (1952) *A History of Chinese Philosophy,* vols. 1, 2, 2d ed. Princeton: Princeton University Press.

Fung Yu-Lan (1966) *A Short History of Chinese Philosophy.* New York: Free Press

Fung Yu-Lan (1973) *A History of Chinese Philosophy* (translated by Derk Dodde), vol. 1, 7th ed. Princeton: Princeton University Press.

Giddens, Anthony (1994) "Risk, Trust, Reflexivity." In *Reflexive Modernization: Politics, Tradition and Aesthetics in the Modern Social Order,* edited by Ulrich Beck, Anthony Giddens, and Scott Lash. Cambridge, UK: Polity Press.

Gray, Colin S. (1979) "Nuclear Strategy: A Case for a Theory of Victory." *International Security* 4, no. 1.

Gray, Colin S. (1986) *Nuclear Strategy and National Style.* New York: Hamilton Press.

Harding, Harry (1993) "The Concept of 'Greater China': Themes, Variations and Reservations." *China Quarterly,* no. 136:660–686.

Huang, Kerson, and Rosemary (1987) *I Ching.* New York: Workman.

Jacobsen, Carl G., ed. (1990) *Strategic Power: USA/USSR.* London: Macmillan.

Kaye, Lincoln (1994) "Don't Tread on Us." *Far Eastern Economic Review,* March 24, pp. 16–17.

Kierman, Frank A., Jr., and John K. Fairbank, eds. (1974) *Chinese Ways in Warfare.* Cambridge: Harvard University Press.

Kim, Samuel S. (1991) *China In and Out of the Changing World.* Princeton: Princeton University Press.

Lao Tzu [Zi] (1988) *Tao Te Ching [Dao De Jing],* translated by D. C. Lau. Harmondsworth, UK: Penguin.

Li, Dun J. (1971) *The Ageless Chinese: A History,* 2d ed. New York: Charles Scribner's Sons.

Li, Luye (1991) "UN Role in Establishing a New World Order." *Beijing Review* 34, no. 39:8–12.

Lin, Chong-Pin (1988) *China's Nuclear Weapons Strategy: Tradition Within Evolution.* Lexington, MA: Lexington Books.

Lu, Martin (1995) "'China Culture' and Its Political Implications." Unpublished paper, Bond University, Gold Coast, Australia.

Mackerras, Colin, ed. (1995) *East and Southeast Asia,* 2d ed. Melbourne: Longman Cheshire; and Boulder: Lynne Rienner.

Mencius (1988) *Mencius* (translated by D. C. Lau). Harmondsworth, UK: Penguin.

Mo Tzu [Zi] (1973) *The Ethical and Political Works of Motse,* translated by Yi-Pao Mei, 2d ed. Westport, CT: Hyperion Press.

Ojha, Ishwer C. (1969) *Chinese Foreign Policy in an Age of Transition: The Diplomacy of Cultural Despair.* Boston: Beacon Press.

Pipes, Richard (1977) "Why the Soviet Union Thinks It Could Fight and Win a Nuclear War." *Commentary* 64, no. 1:21–34.

Pye, Lucian W. (1985) *Asian Power and Politics: The Cultural Dimensions of Authority.* Cambridge: Belknap Press of Harvard University Press.

Pye, Lucian W. (1990) "Tiananmen and Chinese Political Culture: The Escalation of Confrontation from Moralizing to Revenge." *Asian Survey* 30, no. 4.

"Qian Qichen on Major International Issues." (1993) *Beijing Review,* October 11–17, pp. 8–11.

Rand, Christopher C. (1979) "Li Ch'uan and Chinese Military Thought." *Harvard Journal of Asiatic Studies* 39:107–137.

Reischauer, Edwin O., and John K. Fairbank (1970) *East Asia: The Great Tradition,* 8th ed. Boston: Houghton Mifflin.

Segal, Gerald (1985) *Defending China.* New York: Oxford University Press.

Shih Chih-Yu (1993) *China's Just World: The Morality of Chinese Foreign Policy.* Boulder: Lynne Rienner.

Snyder, Jack (1977) *The Soviet Strategic Culture: Implications for Limited Nuclear Operations.* Santa Monica, CA: Rand R-2154-AF.

Snyder, Jack (1990) "The Concept of Strategic Culture: Caveat Emptor." In *Strategic Power: USA/USSR,* edited by Carl G. Jacobsen. London: Macmillan.

Stetler, Russell (1970) "Introduction." In *Selected Writings of General Vo Nguyen Giap,* edited by Russell Stetler. New York: Monthly Review Press.

Sun Tzu [Zi] (1988) *The Art of War* (translated by Lionel Giles). Singapore: Graham Brash.

Tu Wei-ming (1991) "Cultural China: The Periphery as the Centre." *Daedalus* 120, no. 2:1–32.

Tu Wei-ming, Milan Hejtming, and Alan Wachman, eds. (1992) *The Confucian World Observed: A Contemporary Discussion of Confucian Humanism in East Asia.* Honolulu: Institute of Culture and Communication, East-West Centre.

Watson, Adam (1992) *The Evolution of International Society: A Comparative Analysis.* London: Routledge.

Watts, Alan (1992) *Tao: The Watercourse Way.* London: Arkana.

Wolters, O. W. (1968) "Ayudha and the Rearward Part of the World." *Journal of the Royal Asiatic Society,* nos. 3 and 4:166–178.

Wolters, O. W. (1982) *History, Culture and Religion in Southeast Asian Perspectives.* Singapore: Institute of Southeast Asian Studies.

Wu, K. C. (1982) *The Chinese Heritage.* New York: Crown.

Yu Ying-shih (1993) *Wenhua Pinglun yu Zhongguo di Qinghuai* [cultural commentaries and Chinese sentiments]. Taipei: Yun-chen Cultural Publisher.

Zhuge, Liang, and Liu Ji (1989). *Mastering the Art of War* (translated and edited by Thomas Cleary). Boston: Shambhala.

9

Operational Code Evolution: How Central America Came to Be "Our Backyard" in U.S. Culture

Darin H. Van Tassell

Van Tassell captures culture through a different tool of foreign policy analysis: the operational code. He conducts a content analysis of U.S. leaders' statements to uncover the origin of a long-held American cultural belief—that Central America is the "backyard" of the United States, and that therefore U.S. intervention in the region is natural and proper. Tracing from the very earliest days of the Republic, Van Tassell is able to lay out in great detail how the belief started, and how it was expanded and refined over time. Thus, rather than taking culture as a given to be measured and applied to foreign policy, Van Tassell takes culture itself as the explanandum, showing how the belief both led to and was reinforced by actual foreign policy and how, over time, the belief becomes an axiomatic template for action within the culture.

—Editor

DEVELOPING A CULTURAL MODEL
FOR ANALYZING INTERVENTION

Why has U.S. policy in Central America and the Caribbean, in spite of major changes in the international and domestic policymaking environment, so persistently resulted in intervention?[1] During the Cold War years, conventional wisdom held that anticommunist ideology coupled with geographic proximity were driving U.S. policy. But after the Cold War, when one would have expected U.S. behavior in the Central American region[2] to take on a different appearance because of the worldwide decline of communism, the U.S. government militarily intervened in Panama and in Haiti. Scholars are now left with the following research puzzle: Despite a major change in the policymaking environment, the U.S. reaction to matters not to its liking in the region remains the same—it attempts coercive solutions.

Conflicting Explanations: A Review of the Literature

Attempts to explain the occurrence of military intervention (and for that matter, international conflict and foreign policy in general) typically focus on either external or internal factors.

External explanations.   Realists argue that military intervention will be used in cases of power asymmetry to further the national goals of the stronger state. Strong states intervene to install or protect friendly governments.

More specifically in terms of U.S. policy, Latin American specialist Robert Pastor (1986) notes two approaches that fall under the external explanation approach: security and neodependency. The *security perspective* posits that U.S. policy is motivated by a "strategic imperative," because the national security of the United States is defined in terms of the character of the other republics in this hemisphere. Moreover, the security perspective identifies the major sources of insecurity as emanating from outside the hemisphere. Policy output "reflects a rational decision to prevent hostile groups from coming to power" (Pastor, 1986:488). The Reagan administration claimed the problems in the region came from "outside the area," and the crises in the 1980s were seen as "a Soviet-Cuban power play—pure and simple" (Clines, 1984:3).

The *neodependency perspective* asserts that a structural relationship exists between state behavior and the international system (Azar, 1983; Galtung, 1964; Choucri and North, 1989). The existence of such international stratification results in the exploitation of weaker states on behalf of more powerful states. This perspective typically maintains that the capital accumulation process primarily explains state behavior. Moreover, the the crises that have led to U.S. interventions in the Caribbean and Central America are rooted in poverty and injustice, which in turn are primarily a result of the United States fostering a system of economic dependence. Thus, this perspective suggests that the "threats" to the region essentially are economic in nature, not ideological.

Internal explanations.   Other scholars contend that one cannot rely solely on explanations of the external environment to determine the origins of intervention, because internal explanations also play a role.[3] Along these lines, the conventional wisdom has long been that the anticommunist beliefs prevalent in the United States account for conflicts that emerged during the Cold War. Halberstam (1972) and other analysts maintain the importance of focusing on policymakers' beliefs, whose convictions are consequential for understanding U.S. policy output.

ADDRESSING THE CONTROVERSY: THE NEED FOR A CULTURAL MODEL TO EXPLAIN INTERVENTION

Works by Tsebelis (1990) and Putnam (1988) help reconcile the variety of different approaches reviewed here. Tsebelis contends that it is important to realize that policymakers are involved in multiple decisions at any given time. His notion of "nested games" is a reminder that games among actors at the international level—e.g., decisions about going to war—are submerged inside the competitive games among coalition partners at the constituency level. In proposing what he calls a "two-level game" model, Putnam suggests that policymakers often find themselves in two games at once, one internal to the country and one external. Although two-level and nested games provide an intellectual bridge for cutting across the artificially created boundaries of international and domestic explanations of conflictual behavior, a shortcoming is that these theoretical tools alone do not take us far enough, because these approaches tend to subsume the role of *underlying* causes within the nest or treat those causes as a second-level game. However, scholars such as Lebow (1981) help rectify this problem by making a distinction between the immediate and underlying causes of state behavior, a distinction that is crucial for analyzing decisions that produce military intervention.[4]

Traditionally, explanations that stress either external or internal understandings of intervention have tended to emphasize the immediate conditions, which disguise the underlying reasons for coercive policies. As Singer (1961:26) notes, "Goals and motivations are both dependent and independent variables, and if we intend to explain a nation's foreign policy, we cannot settle for the mere postulation of these goals; we are compelled to go back a step and inquire into their genesis and the process by which they become the crucial variables that they seem to be."

Therefore, to gain a better understanding of U.S. intervention in Central America and the Caribbean, one must look to underlying causes in addition to immediate ones. This chapter will suggest that a more compelling approach for explaining the underlying causes for such policies is to treat the immediate causes for U.S. intervention as two-level and/or nested games and filter them through an underlying cause: the lenses of U.S. political culture, which serves as an operational code. This chapter thus offers a glimpse at one of the links between foreign policy and culture.

Seeking a Definition for Culture

Cultural explanations are not now a prominent feature of mainstream political research. In fact, although the concept of culture enjoyed a certain popularity in the 1960s and early 1970s (e.g., Almond and Verba, 1963; Pye and Verba, 1965), and although one occasionally receives an indication of isolated pockets of continuing interest, cultural explanations have largely fallen into disfavor. But cultural factors are among the most enduring and profound sources of foreign policy. The norms, memories, and behavior patterns that constitute a people's culture become largely habitual responses to the requirements of everyday life, so much so that many of the attitudes and relationships that constitute life in the community are unrecognized or taken for granted. Only when challenged do people become sensitive to the all-encompassing nature of their culture, and even under these conditions the culture provides norms for interpreting and rejecting the challenges to it. Thus, despite the growing interdependence of world politics, long-standing cultural factors are highly stable sources of foreign policy. A society's major value orientations serve as foundations for the external goals the society frames and the means it selects to reach them.

This translation of underlying cultural values into foreign policy plans and activities occurs in a variety of ways, ranging from the impact of public opinion on policymaking to the more subtle ways the socialization of foreign policy officials in childhood affects their official behavior. Similarly, every society has mechanisms to preserve memories of past commitments and accomplishments—mechanisms that range from the observance of national holidays to the symbols glorified by political leaders. These concerns for tradition affect the policymaking process through the behavior of generations of foreign policy officials as they function as bearers and perpetuators of their culture (see Chapter 5 of this book). Here I demonstrate that by the turn of the twentieth century, there appeared a set of symbols and concerns that helped shape a "lens" through which U.S. policymakers continue to view events in the Caribbean and Central America.

First, what is meant by *culture?* Isard defines culture as "the body of customary beliefs, social forms, and material traits constituting a *distinct* complex of tradition of a social group" (1992:8). Isard asserts that culture comprises, at least in part, a nation's core interests, geography, perceptions/images, and historical experience. As Brickman (1984:3) reminds us, "Culture, by definition, is information that can be transmitted to future generations without each generation's having to re-experience directly the events from which the information was derived."

Core interests.   Holsti (1967:132–135) argues that core interests are so important that governments and nations commit their very existence to them; therefore, they must be preserved at all times. Others have defined core interests as "those interests which policymakers deem so vital to the continued existence of the state that, if threatened, the decisionmakers perceive the very existence of the state threatened."[5] When threats to these interests occur, intervention is likely.

I contend that core interests over time have become driven not only by security concerns but also by underlying cultural forces. For example, why has the idea of the Central American region as falling within the core interests of the United States not been extended to other similarly situated nations? Why, for example, does not Canada evoke similar concerns? Clearly, core interests are not a function of geography alone.

Perceptions and images.   Core interests by definition are not objectively determined by detached observers (Van Tassell, 1970:11–12). Rather, they are a product of the perceptions and images of policymakers.[6] An implicit assumption within the cultural model approach is that the prospects for intervention become intensified when the core interests of the United States are *perceived* to be threatened in Central America.

Jervis (1976) asserts that it is impossible to explain crucial foreign policy decisions without reference to policymakers' images about the world and the motives of other actors in it. He suggests that the primary source of images is stereotyped interpretations of dramatic historical events, whose strong impact on the thinking of younger people can continue to shape their approach to international problems years later. Policymakers are more responsive to information that supports images they already have than to information that challenges them. Because all but the most unambiguous evidence will be interpreted to confirm the wisdom of established policy and the images of reality on which that policy is based, Jervis suggests that "policymakers will proceed a long way down a blind alley before realizing that something is wrong" (1976:187–191).

A primary argument of my analysis of U.S. intervention in the Central American region is that the dominant image of this region since the beginning of the Republic is that it lies in "our backyard."

The relationship between maps and policymakers' images of the world also proves to be an important and curious link in this regard.[7] Particularly since World War II, special emphasis has been placed on the distortion introduced into political analysis by the reliance on Mercator equator-based projections. Dougherty and Pfaltzgraff (1990:72) note that "such maps failed to present the idea of the earth as a sphere and therefore as having geographical unity and continuity. The Mercator projection provided an erroneous conception of distances—for example, the proximity of the United States to the Soviet Union across the Arctic. Viewing the world as a sphere makes evident that, for example, Buenos

Aires is farther from the United States than every European capital including Moscow." Yet in the minds of most people in the United States, the events of the Western Hemisphere are taking place far closer to home. Policymakers continue to think in geographic terms, many simply inaccurate.

Geography.   Geography is also a critical component of a cultural approach for understanding U.S. intervention in Central America. Indeed, the significance of geographic proximity is readily observable throughout the history of U.S. policy toward the region. In the 1820s, the United States was vulnerable to attack from Latin America, so it made strategic sense for Washington's defensive posture to include a warning that European powers should not attempt to regain their colonies. After almost two centuries, however, despite the changing nature of warfare and technological advances, the actions and statements of U.S. policymakers make it all too apparent that geographic considerations continue to maintain an enormous influence on the perceptions and images that affect the policymaking process.[8]

Historical experience.   Isard (1992:15) specifically highlights how history can provide insights into culture. These historical lessons are important not only for individuals but also for governments, which can institutionalize them. "Once this has occurred," writes Jervis (1976:238), historical lessons "may form the basis of future planning, becoming permanent features of standard operating procedures, creating preferred frameworks for viewing events or preferred options for dealing with contingencies." Such a framework has become the dominant lens through which U.S. policymakers view events in the Central American region. In other words, a cultural context now surrounds the pattern of U.S. intervention in Central America.

THEORIZING ABOUT THE EXISTENCE OF A U.S. "CULTURE OF CONTROL" TOWARD CENTRAL AMERICA AND THE CARIBBEAN

I am persuaded no constitution was never before as well calculated as ours for extensive empire and self-government.

—Thomas Jefferson to James Madison, April 27, 1809[9]

In his discussion concerning the relationship between culture and conflict behavior, Isard notes the existence of *cultural complexes*. A cultural complex may be defined as a group of interrelated cultural traits dominated by one or more essential traits. Isard (1992:11) suggests that societies usually are composed of a number of cultural complexes or "dominant themes," sometimes not fully consistent with one another.

By juxtaposing the "American Experiment" version of U.S. culture with the "City on the Hill" version, Schlesinger (1986) demonstrates that there are contradictory strands in U.S. culture. The American Experiment version, which can be extended to all mankind, is best characterized by the values of participatory government, individual worth, and freedom. The City on the Hill version, however, is characterized by the popularly held and deeply rooted belief that the United States is exceptional, that the United States was endowed with a special moral role and destiny in world affairs and thereby serves as a shining example to the rest of the world.[10]

This essay attempts to demonstrate that the City on the Hill/American Exceptionalism vision has dominated the shaping of policymakers' attitudes toward the Central American/Caribbean region since the early days of the Republic. This sense of superiority has created a paradox— yet another cultural complex: Although it has given the United States an excuse to remain smug and content in an isolationist cocoon, well protected from "corrupt" or "inferior" foreigners, it has impelled the country toward intervention, particularly in Central America and the Caribbean. In addition, this paradox helps account for the historical belief that threats to the United States are external, not internal.

American Exceptionalism

As Schlesinger's work implies, studies of U.S. political culture generally have portrayed the U.S. citizenry as a confident and optimistic people who have a special sense of destiny about the future of their country and its place in the world.[11] The founders of the Massachusetts Bay Colony sharply differentiated America from the Old World, proclaiming, "This is the place where the Lord will create a new Heaven, and a new Earth in new Churches, and a new Commonwealth together" (Baritz, 1964:3). Governor John Winthrop of Massachusetts said in a shipboard sermon in 1630, "We shall find that the God of Israel is among us, when ten of us shall be able to overcome a thousand of our enemies; when we shall make us a praise and a glory. . . . For we must consider that we shall be as a City upon a hill" (Winthrop, 1971:19). The New England Puritans felt that they had embarked on a "mission of cosmic significance" and would provide a "moral example to all the world."

Such sentiments would prove to have unintended, secular implications for national self-confidence during the Revolutionary era of the young Republic. Eighteenth-century historian William Findley (1796) wrote that Americans had "formed a character peculiar to themselves, and in some respects distinct from that of other nations."[12] Tocqueville's *Democracy in America* was particularly important in this regard, for he too informed the world that "the position of America is quite exceptional."

Even U.S. presidents were not immune to the idea of American Exceptionalism. John Adams predicted that the United States "will last forever, govern the globe and introduce the perfection of man" (Davis and Lynn-Jones, 1987:23–24). In a letter to James Madison, Thomas Jefferson wrote that he was persuaded that "no constitution was never before as well calculated as ours for extensive empire and self-government" (Williams, 1980:vii). Moreover, Abraham Lincoln would later suggest that the American Revolution gave the world the final "solution" to the political problems, and that it must "grow and expand into the universal liberty of mankind." His contemporary, William Seward, contended that if America were weakened, mankind's hopes would be "disappointed," and all progress would be "indefinitely postponed," for it was the "ark of safety in which are deposited the hopes of the world" and the "key to progress of freedom and civilization" (Burns, 1957:90).

Williams (1976) also suggests that perhaps a more important although less obvious reason for the U.S. sense of uniqueness may be that despite its large population, vast territory, and historic position as a hemispheric power, the United States views itself as an island nation. This is a major source of the deep-seated and recurring feelings—if ever suppressed—of isolation and insecurity. Such a view of the United States' geopolitical predicament also helps account for the U.S. concern about international instability. As Lyndon Johnson once remarked with reference to U.S. intervention in Vietnam, "Everything that happens in the world affects us, because pretty soon it gets on our doorsteps" (Ahmad, 1980:7).

Along similar lines, what historian Richard Hofstadter (1966) has described as the paranoid strain in U.S. politics is undoubtedly related to feelings of uniqueness and insularity. His insights are particularly useful for understanding why during times of preoccupation with threats to national security, explanations that place the blame on "outside" or "foreign" forces often emerge.

To find the origins of what he refers to as the "paranoid style in American politics," Hofstadter submits it is necessary to go back at least to the first Alien and Sedition Acts of 1798. For example, notice the language from a sermon preached in Massachusetts in 1798: "Secret and systematic means have been adopted and pursued, with zeal and activity, by wicked and artful men, in *foreign* [emphasis added] countries, to undermine the foundations of this Religion [Christianity], and to overthrow its Altars, and thus to deprive the world of its benign influence on society" (Hofstadter, 1966:9). Next, observe the theme inherent in this Texas newspaper article in 1855: "It is a notorious fact that the Monarchs of Europe and the Pope of Rome are at this very moment plotting our destruction and threatening the extinctions of our political, civil, and religious institutions. We have the best reasons for believing that corruption has found its way into our Executive Chamber, and that our Executive head is tainted with the infectious venom of Catholicism" (Hofstadter, 1966:8–9).

Following the first few decades of the twentieth century, however, it would be the communists who would hold this select position on the list, and their position was never more apparent than during the Truman and Eisenhower administrations. Perhaps Joseph McCarthy (1952) himself best captured the prevailing public mood when he said: "How can we account for our present situation unless we believe that men in this government are concerting to deliver us to disaster? This must be the product of a great conspiracy, a conspiracy on a scale so immense as to dwarf any previous such venture in the history of man. A conspiracy of infamy so black that, when it is finally exposed, its principals shall be forever deserving of the maledictions of all honest men" (quoted in Hofstadter, 1966:8–9). Thus, Hofstadter suggests that the United States is prone to search for explanations that point to problems emanating from outside its borders.

These insights are particularly noteworthy for observing U.S. foreign policy toward the Central American region, because as the self-appointed "guardian of the gates," policymakers came to perceive that the United States has a responsibility to control situations that threaten to bring instability. At the turn of the century, the principal threats to the region came in the form of potential European intervention and threats to U.S. business interests. During the Cold War, the threat posed by communism resulted in U.S. intervention in the region. It could be argued that one of the perceived security threats of the 1990s is no longer a communist insurgency but a substance: illegal drugs. It is also worth noting how the drug war is being waged: The main weapons have been to increase border patrols, advocate crop substitution, and assist police forces where the drugs are produced. Again, the threat is portrayed as emanating from the outside.

The following discussion shows how political culture can be operationalized to better interpret U.S. intervention in the region.

DEVELOPING A CULTURAL MODEL
FOR EXPLAINING U.S. INTERVENTION

In offering a preliminary look at the explanatory power political culture has for examining U.S. intervention in the Central American region, the premise is not that political culture explains everything concerning the complexity of U.S. foreign policy behavior. Rather, the premise is that political culture is a powerful yet neglected explanatory variable that has not been used to analyze the pattern of U.S. intervention in this area of the world.

The dominance of the City on the Hill/American Exceptionalism component of U.S. culture makes it necessary to explore how this particular cultural strain has led to the development of an *operational code*— or a powerful set of lenses or screens U.S. policymakers use to view and interpret events in Central America and the Caribbean.

It is perhaps noteworthy at this stage to make the distinction between national role conception (see Chapters 5 and 7 of this book) and operational code. While similar, role conception and operational code tackle different scopes of inquiry. National role conception concerns how the "perceptions of the historical past become linked with" what Holsti (1970) calls "our national self-image or national role conceptions—the way we view our own nation and its place in the world." National leaders may perceive their states as world leaders, as neutral mediators and conciliators, as reliable allies, as aggrieved revolutionaries, as pillars of the international community, as protectors of the weak, and so on.

Whereas national role conception is more about "who we are" and "our place in the world," operational code analysis as used here deals with the lenses through which we see *others*—a subtle, but critical, difference. Recalling the question posed by Hudson in Chapter 1, "Are there different cultures for different foreign policy issues (or in this case, different regions)?" I answer in the affirmative regarding U.S. policy in Central America. Indeed, while the sentiments and tendencies described here may well have existed for other powerful actors and communities at different times, the operational code template presented here is peculiar to events in the Central American/Caribbean region.

While threats to the United States from the region have changed over time, what is missing in most of the scholarship concerning U.S. intervention in the region is the uncanny manner in which threats always seem to exist. That is, the character of the U.S. operational code toward the region is such that policymakers have seldom asked themselves, "Is there a threat?"—rather, they ask, "What is the threat *now?*"

Two aspects of the code help account for the continuity of U.S. intervention over time and the change in the type of events that led to the introduction of military troops.

The first factor is that U.S. policymakers continue to believe that it is necessary to control the character of the region because of its geographical proximity to the United States. As was briefly suggested earlier, history, especially the view that the Central American region is "our backyard," helps account for this underlying factor. As the rest of this chapter demonstrates further, it has long been considered natural for the United States to believe that not only does it have the right to control threatening events in Central America and the Caribbean, but that such actions are necessary as well.

However, the second factor is one involving change; the particular threat the United States has perceived as warranting U.S. involvement has varied over time. For example, anticommunism was merely the primary manifestation of the operational code during the Cold War era. Likewise, the threat of various European governments intervening in Central America and the Caribbean to collect their unpaid debts was the principal manifestation of the code during most of the pre–Cold War years of the twentieth century.

In short, the cultural factors (*underlying* cause) as well as the substance of the threat in each historical period (*immediate* cause) are equally important for understanding the pattern of U.S. intervention in the region (see Figure 9.1).

Figure 9.1
Cultural Model for Interpreting the Unprecedented
Use of U.S. Armed Forces in the Central American Region

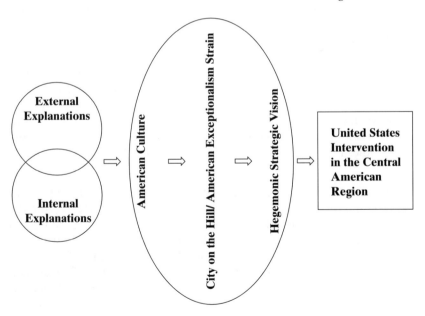

Immediate Causes   Underlying Causes

Research Strategy, Sources of Evidence, and Anticipated Results

To demonstrate the U.S. operational code toward Latin America, and the continuity of U.S. control in the region, I focus on four fundamental policies that shaped U.S. relations with the region prior to the twentieth century: the No-Transfer Policy of 1811, the Monroe Doctrine, the annexation of Mexico in the 1840s during the era of Continental Expansionism, and the Roosevelt Corollary.[13]

To identify the creation of an operational code in these four pre-twentieth-century cases, I apply a modified form of operational code analysis. Originally developed by Leites (1951, 1953) to derive a modus operandi of the Soviet leadership and later modified by George (1969), the operational code approach to understanding foreign policy behavior allows one to identify the most important variables in the decisionmaking process. However, while Leites and George applied an operational code approach to the study of individuals and groups, little has been done to apply it to political culture. Here I seek to determine the extent to which the existence of the cultural components that make up the operational code (core interests, perception, geography, and history) affect the four specific historical policies in question.

The evidence in the four cases falls into two categories. First, some evidence is found in direct quotations from the speeches, public statements, and writings of presidents and top policymakers. Memoirs, important government documents, and some secondary literature sources are cited. Each of the independent cultural variables is examined to determine how it influenced policymakers as they made important decisions regarding the region. Indeed, it is suggested that notions of controlling the Central American region have existed from the beginning of the Republic and that such unquestioned assumptions have been passed on to subsequent generations of policymakers.

One should expect to observe the following kind of rhetoric in the case studies for each of the independent variables:

- *Core interests:* statements that suggest that the United States should be involved because of threats to national security from the region in question, that somehow the very existence of the United States will be threatened or called into question should it not respond; statements that speak of a "sphere of influence"
- *Images:* statements that reflect a sense of American uniqueness and exceptionalism and the people's "God-given right to march to the Pacific"; the belief that the Western Hemisphere is a U.S. hemisphere
- *Geography:* statements that reflect the importance of the region due to its proximity to the United States; statements like "our backyard"

• *Historical experience:* statements that reflect the importance of history in influencing policy

In using policymakers' statements, I am well aware of the need to make clear the difference between rationalization and explanation. I contend, however, that such statements are rationalized only according to what is familiar and acceptable in the culture. The resulting historical pattern should provide empirical teeth to the assertion that an operational code of control toward the Central American region existed in the eyes of U.S. policymakers by the end of the nineteenth century.

The Genesis of a Policy of Control

I know only two things about the Monroe Doctrine: one is that no American I have ever met knows what it is; the other is that no American I have met will consent to its being tampered with.

—Madariaga (1962:74)

From the beginning of the Republic, key U.S. policymakers have coveted Central America and the Caribbean. Kenworthy (1995) contends that when Alexander Hamilton, in *The Federalist* 11, foresaw "one great American system superior to the control of all trans-Atlantic force or influence and able to dictate the terms of the connection between the Old and the New World," his "America" was hemispheric, while his "Americans" were the citizens of the soon to be reorganized United States. As early as 1787, John Adams concluded that the young republic was "destined" to extend its rule over the entire northern part of the hemisphere and anticipated such expansion as a "great point gained in favor of the rights of mankind" (Parenti, 1971:8). Even Thomas Jefferson wrote that it was in the interest of the Unites States to have Spain maintain its hold on Latin America "till our population can be sufficiently advanced to gain it from them piece by piece" (Boyd, 1954:218). Jefferson saw the region as "essential to our tranquility and commerce. . . . Our strength will permit us to give the law of *our own* hemisphere" (Blachman, 1990:121), and he publicly wished, "What a Colossus shall we be when the Southern continent comes up to our mark?" (Kenworthy, 1995:25). John Quincy Adams found such thinking not at all wishful, and he would later write, "I consider the cause of that country [Latin America], as essentially our own" (Bemis, 1943:70). While such statements are insightful by themselves, an examination of four key policies in early U.S. history also finds their roots in such beliefs: the No-Transfer Policy of 1811, the Monroe Doctrine, Continental Expansion ("Manifest Destiny"), and the Roosevelt Corollary.

The No-Transfer Policy of 1811.   To understand better the beginnings of U.S. policy toward Central America and the Caribbean, one must go back to the great territorial questions that arose in North America following the independence of the English colonies. Indeed, it is here that the wishful thinking of John Quincy Adams and others was put into practice, first with regard to the Florida territories held by Spain.

By the early nineteenth century as the Spanish empire began crumbling all over the New World, U.S. policymakers became concerned with the fate of the Spanish Floridas, primarily because the region was surrounded on land by the territory of the United States. President Jefferson instructed the governor of the Louisiana Territory to tell the inhabitants of West Florida (of whom 90 percent were Spanish American émigrés) that "we consider their interests and ours as the same and that the object of both must be to exclude all European influence from this hemisphere" (Lipscomb, 1904:187). Diplomatic historian Samuel Flagg Bemis notes that in this message to rebellious Spanish subjects of American origin in West Florida, Jefferson states the ultimate objective of the Latin American policy of the United States—the exclusion of European influence from the entire Western Hemisphere—but his more immediate purpose was to substitute the sovereignty of the United States for Spanish authority in the adjacent borderlands.[14]

Following Jefferson into office, President James Madison continued to encourage the inhabitants of West Florida to expect help at the appropriate moment. By 1810, Spanish authority had collapsed to the point that the local governor agreed to place it in the hands of the United States, and by 1812, only a few weeks before the outbreak of war with the British, most of the territory was annexed to the new state of Louisiana and the Territory of Mississippi. The British foreign minister in Washington quickly protested the U.S. possession of West Florida, and Madison used the British protest to his advantage in a special message to Congress. Aroused by the possibility of British occupation of the Floridas and remembering the transfer of Louisiana only a decade before, Congress responded to Madison's message by passing the No-Transfer Resolution of 1811:

> Taking into view the peculiar situation of Spain and her American provinces; and considering the influence which the destiny of the territory adjoining the southern border of the United States may have upon their security, tranquillity, and commerce . . . the United States, under the peculiar circumstances of the existing crisis, cannot without serious inquietude see any part of the said territory pass into the hands of any foreign Power; and that a due regard to their own safety compels them to provide under certain contingencies, for the temporary occupation of the said territory; they, at the same time, declare that the said territory shall, in their hands, remain subject to a future negotiation.[15]

In effect, the resolution enabled the president of the United States to take possession of East Florida in case it should be in danger of occupation by a "foreign power," if possible "through arrangement with the "local authorities," but if necessary "by using the army and navy" (Bemis, 1943:29). Indeed, control of the Floridas was deemed vital to U.S. interests. Consequently, Madison soon helped create a situation that would require the United States to gain custody of the region.

A powerful personality among the local authorities was one General George Matthews, who successfully stirred up a revolution among the immigrants from the United States. The Madison administration already had given tacit approval to Matthews's activities but kept itself in a position to repudiate his conduct and sacrifice him if necessary. Bemis notes that "the British Minister protested against this intrigue and the ensuing occupation of Amelia Island. At that very time, his own government had been trying through a secret agent to encourage sedition in the New England states." Madison could not very well affirm an activity in Florida that he vehemently denounced on behalf of the British in New England. So the president repudiated Matthews and dismissed him. But the U.S. army maintained its possession of Amelia Island when the war with the British began in 1812. As the No-Transfer Resolution dictated, the annexation of the Floridas soon followed.[16]

According to Bemis (1943:30), "the No-Transfer Policy of 1811, which crystallized out of the great territorial questions of North America—so vital to the independence, security, and continental future of the U.S.—was the first significant landmark in the evolution of its Latin American policy." In 1811, the policy was carefully restricted to Florida. However, by 1823 and the pronouncement of the Monroe Doctrine, it was applied to all the Western Hemisphere. In short, the No-Transfer Policy is one of the earliest expressions of the U.S. policy of control toward what was the Central American region in the early 1800s.

The Monroe Doctrine of 1823. The desire to control events in Latin America also accounts for why the United States favored the independence movement in the region; "general revolution in Spanish America would be certain to loosen Spain's feeble authority in the borderlands and make it easier to occupy them in case of war with England and Spain" (Bemis, 1943:31). However, such support was not publicly professed at first. Until 1821, when it formally purchased the Floridas from Spain, the United States chose not to jeopardize these delicate negotiations by helping the Spanish-American insurgents. It was not until it was clear that the Latin American independence movements had succeeded that the United States acted to prevent other European nations from acquiring colonies or undue influence in the region. Referring to the newly independent Latin states, President Monroe's secretary of state, John

Quincy Adams, noted the importance of geography on policy when he remarked that U.S. relations with the former Spanish colonies "are more important to the interests of the United States," because the new states "are situated in [this] Hemisphere . . . and one of them borders upon the Territories of this Union."[17] Adams's statements are particularly important when one examines the roots of U.S. policy in Latin America, because Adams was the chief architect of this regime's landmark policy toward the region: the Monroe Doctrine.

On December 2, 1823, President James Monroe gave his annual message to Congress. He declared that the Western Hemisphere was no longer open to European colonization, that the Old and New Worlds were so different that the United States would abstain from European wars, and that the European powers should not intervene forcefully in the Americas. These three points (noncolonization, two spheres, and nonintervention) were designed to warn the monarchies of Europe against crushing the independence of the new Latin American states that had broken from the Spanish empire and to warn Russia against encroachments on the Pacific coast.[18]

Great Britain, which had profited commercially from the breakup of the Spanish mercantile system and therefore did not welcome a restoration of Spanish rule in Latin America, approached U.S. officials with the idea of issuing a joint declaration warning against European intervention. North Americans, who also realized economic benefits from the dismantling of the Spanish empire and who sympathized with the Latin American independence movements, also worried about the European threat. While the United States ultimately rejected Britain's offer, it was a decision that involved much discussion. In fact, Thomas Jefferson counseled Monroe on his decision. Observe how references to the interests, uniqueness, and geographic location of the United States led Jefferson to the conclusion that if the United States wanted to control the Gulf of Mexico region, such a declaration should be made unilaterally:

> Our policy should be never to suffer Europe to intermeddle with cis-Atlantic affairs. America, North and South, has a set of interests distinct from those of Europe, and peculiarly her own. She should therefore have a system of her own, separate and apart from that of Europe. While the last is laboring to become the domicile of despotism, our endeavor should surely be to make our hemisphere that of freedom. One nation, most of all, could disturb us in this pursuit. . . . Great Britain is the nation which can do us the most harm of any one, or all on earth. . . .
>
> I candidly confess, that I have ever looked on Cuba as the most interesting addition which could ever be made to our system of States. The control which, with Florida Point, this island would give us over the Gulf of Mexico, and the countries and isthmus bordering on it, as well as all those whose waters flow into it. . . .

> I could honestly, therefore, join in the declaration proposed, that
> we ... oppose, with all our means, the forcible interposition of any
> other power, as auxiliary, stipendiary, or under any other form or pre-
> text, and most especially, their transfer to any power by conquest ces-
> sion, or acquisition in any other way. (Paterson, 1989:182–183)

In other words, Jefferson—along with John Quincy Adams—persuaded Monroe to reject the British proposal of a joint policy statement
on the grounds of national interests, i.e., the conception that the Western
Hemisphere was a U.S. sphere of influence—not a British one. Moreover, U.S. policymakers feared that a joint declaration would effectively
bar the United States from its cherished aim of acquiring Cuba.[19] However, it would be President Monroe's annual message to Congress on
December 2, 1823, that would constitute the formal U.S. answer to the
European menace. Monroe stated that "the American continents, by the
free and independent condition which they have assumed and maintained, are henceforth not to be considered as subjects for future colonization by any European powers."[20] Additional references to the importance of geography and images of uniqueness are apparent here as
well: "It is only when our rights are invaded or seriously menaced that
we resent injuries or make preparation for our defense. With the movements of this hemisphere we are of necessity more immediately connected, and by causes which must be obvious to all enlightened and im-
partial observers. The political system of the allied powers is essentially
different ... from that of America."[21]

Monroe also added a phrase that suggests how the interests of the
United States had become intimately tied to the rest of the hemisphere:

> We should consider any attempt on their part to extend their system to
> any portion of this hemisphere as dangerous to our peace and safety.
> With the existing colonies or dependencies of any European power we
> have not interfered and shall not interfere. But with the Governments
> who have declared their independence and maintained it, and whose
> independence we have, on great consideration and on just principles,
> acknowledged, or could not view any interposition for the purpose of
> oppressing them, or controlling in any other manner their destiny, by
> any European power in any other light than as the manifestation of an
> unfriendly disposition toward the United States.[22]

What the Monroe Doctrine implied, in effect, was that the United States
would be the sole political and colonizing power in the New World and
that the Western Hemisphere was to be a U.S. sphere of influence (Parenti, 1969:113). Aware of such implications, the "backyard image" is evident in the later comments of Congressman Henry Clay, who predicted
that in half a century Americans, "in relation to [Latin] America," would
"occupy the same position as the people of New England do to the rest

of the United States" (Williams, 1961:217). Although the United States would lack the ability and means required to back up Monroe's words in the coming decades, by the turn of the century the Monroe Doctrine became the unquestioned first principle of policy in the hemisphere.[23]

Continental Expansionism during the 1840s.   After the settlement of the Florida question and the issuance of Monroe, U.S. policy toward Central America continued to be understood best in terms of national security. However, national security issues now began to be defined more in terms of national expansion. The 1840s witnessed an expansionist surge that brought the United States new territories. Texas, Oregon, and the California Territory, after the use or threat of force and much debate, became parts of the expanding U.S. Republic.

Expansionism was certainly not new to the United States. However, when an ideology emerged that not only explained westward expansion as natural and good but indeed godly, it was met with popular enthusiasm. Such a belief became known as Manifest Destiny (see Weinberg, 1935). Although the actual term does not appear until the height of the expansionist movement in the 1840s, notions of manifest destiny were clearly evident in the beliefs of John Quincy Adams, who earlier wrote, "The world [should] be familiarized with the idea of considering our proper dominion to be the continent of North America" (Bemis, 1943:74).

Beginning somewhere around the Louisiana Purchase and ending with the Mexican War[24] (with the exception of the Gadsden Purchase of the southern parts of present-day New Mexico and Arizona in 1853), the story of U.S. continental expansion has been told many times before and is well documented.[25] The 1840s were particularly active. John L. O'Sullivan is credited as the first to give a name to the spirit of expansion sweeping the country in the mid-nineteenth century. "Our manifest destiny," he wrote, "is to overspread the continent allotted by Providence for the free development of our yearly multiplying millions" (Tindall, 1984:512). Note the following excerpts from O'Sullivan's famous essay in 1839. While images of U.S. uniqueness are perhaps nowhere more noticeable, note how the U.S. historical experience and geographic location has led to the "natural" connection between such images and continental expansionism:

> America is destined for better deeds. It is our unparalleled glory that we have no reminiscences of battle fields, but in defence of humanity, of the oppressed of all nations, of the rights of conscience, the rights of personal enfranchisement. . . .
>   . . . The expansive future is our arena, and for our history. We are entering on its untrodden space, with the truths of God in our minds, beneficent objects in our hearts, and with a clear conscience unsullied

by the past. We are the nation of human progress, and who will, what can, set limits to our onward march? Providence is with us, and no earthly power can prevent our procession. . . .

. . . We may confidently assume that our country is destined to be the great nation of futurity . . . for its floor shall be a hemisphere. (Paterson, 1989:255–256)

While one could argue that such words are those of a newspaper editor and not a policymaker, such themes can be found in the words of the U.S. president at the time as well. Indeed, not only were such themes further developed by President James K. Polk during the time he presided over the annexation of much of Mexico, but the ideas expounded by Hamilton, Jefferson, Madison, John Quincy Adams, and Monroe about the creation of an international regime in the New World were now so antithetical to that found in the Old World that by the time of the Mexican-American War, whatever Washington did could not be labeled power politics or imperialism. Indeed, in Polk's first annual address to Congress on March 4, 1845, he argued: "The American system of government is entirely different from that of Europe. Jealousy among the different sovereigns of Europe, lest any of them might become too powerful for the rest, has caused them anxiously to desire the establishment of what they term 'the balance of power.' It can not be permitted to have any application on the North American continent, and especially to the United States" (Kenworthy, 1995:27).

During this very same address, President Polk also saw fit to make the case for the United States to absorb Texas and Oregon. "Foreign powers do not seem to appreciate the true character of our Government," he stated. "To enlarge its limits is to extend the dominion of peace over additional territories and increasing millions" (Paterson, 1989:256). Indeed, one finds his message particularly illuminating, for Polk's image of U.S. uniqueness and his desire to annex the remaining contiguous areas of the continent to make the country safe from external threats appear to have combined to provide justification for such actions. Note also that even though such areas were not part of the United States at the time, Polk clearly perceives them as lying within the core interests of the country:

Foreign powers should therefore look on the annexation of Texas to the United States not as the conquest of a nation seeking to extend her dominions by arms and violence, but as the peaceful acquisition of a territory once her own, by adding another member to our confederation, with the consent of that member, thereby diminishing the chances for war and opening to them new and ever-increasing markets for their products. To Texas the reunion is important, because the strong protecting arm of our Government would be extended over here, and the vast resources of her fertile soil and genial climate would be speedily developed, while the safety of New Orleans and of our whole southwestern frontier against hostile aggression, as well as the interests of the whole Union, would be promoted by it. . . . No one can fail to see the danger to our safety and future peace if Texas remains an independent state or becomes an ally or dependency of some foreign nation more powerful than herself.

. . . Nor will it become in a less degree my duty to assert and maintain by all constitutional means the right of the United States to that portion of our territory which lies beyond the Rocky Mountains. Our title to the country of Oregon is "clear and unquestionable," and already are our people preparing to perfect that title by occupying it with their wives and children . . . upon our soil. . . . The jurisdiction of our laws and the benefits of our republican institutions should be extended over them in the distant regions which they have selected for their homes. The increasing facilities of intercourse will easily bring the States, of which the formation in the part of the territory can not be long delayed, within the sphere of our federative Union. (Paterson, 1989:257–258)

According to one observer of U.S. foreign policy, "Americans of Monroe's day (and Americans ever since) have treated the Doctrine as an exhilarating example of a young republic's magnanimous defense of weaker sister republics against Old World despotism" (Parenti, 1969:113). Indeed, by the turn of the century, such principles had such a tremendous hold on the imagination of U.S. policymakers—and the formula it prescribed for the foreign policy of the United States had become so sacred and unquestioned—that it would be easy for a future president to invoke it in good faith as an instrument of protective imperialism.

The Roosevelt Corollary.   By the end of the nineteenth century, U.S. interests were not limited to areas in the continental United States and Mexico; U.S. officials were willing to go to great lengths to reinforce the country's political dominance in the Caribbean Basin—a region policymakers tended to view as an "American lake."[26] Indeed, the United States ended the nineteenth century by taking Cuba and Puerto Rico, and eventually—in 1917—buying the Virgin Islands from the Danes.[27] The $25 million the United States paid Denmark was a considerable figure if we realize that the United States paid France $15 million for Louisiana and its hinterland, bought Florida from Spain for $10 million, and paid the Russians $7.2 million for Alaska. It was small, however, compared to the $300 million spent to build the Panama Canal. U.S. geopolitical interests in the Caribbean did not begin with the ownership of that canal, but after its completion, the canal became the geopolitical center of gravity in the region.

These were the actual territorial conquests or purchases. However, following the turn of the century, direct annexation of territories was no longer the most expedient way of enjoying "the fruits of empire." Indeed, following the continental expansion of the United States to the Pacific, gaining influence rather than occupying territory became the latest manifestation of the United States' operational code toward the region; sufficient *control* of territory and events was increasingly seen as being more desirable. For example, in response to a boundary dispute between Venezuela and British Guiana in July 1895, Secretary of State Richard Olney cited the Monroe Doctrine and declared that the United States would intervene whenever the actions of a European power in the Western Hemisphere posed a "serious and direct menace to its own integrity and welfare." He further justified the United States' active intrusion into the matter by claiming that the United States "is practically sovereign on this continent, and its fiat is law upon the subjects to which it confines its interposition" (Crabb, 1982:37). Whatever Olney's exercise in circular reasoning meant, it powerfully reinforced the Monroe Doctrine.

Moreover, while many U.S. strategists, such as A. T. Mahan, perceived the Latin nations as neutral, they envisioned the Europeans as either jealous rivals or threatening adversaries. In the Caribbean, the British were the most likely to be seen in such a light. Before the United States had compelled Britain to back down over the Venezuela–British Guiana border dispute in 1896, U.S. officials such as Henry Cabot Lodge regarded the British presence in the Caribbean with deep suspicion. "England," he warned in 1895, "has studded the West Indies with strong places which are a standing menace to our Atlantic seaboard." Clearly the U.S. victory in the Spanish-American War, its acquisition of Puerto Rico and a major base in Cuba, and its control over Panama and its canal project all made the United States overwhelmingly predominant in the region. But by the early twentieth century, U.S. policymakers perceived a new challenger in Germany (Maingot, 1994:29).

Indeed, by 1897, Bismarck was describing the Monroe Doctrine as "an extraordinary piece of insolence," and in 1898 he was predicting that with Spain out of the way in the Caribbean, England and France would drive the U.S. "pygmy navy" out of its waters. "The Monroe Doctrine," he said, "is a spectre that would vanish in plain daylight."[28]

The Germans had eyes on the Danish Virgin Islands, Curaçao, the southern coast of Brazil, and the Galapagos Islands. It should come as no surprise that the Kaiser was an avid reader of A. T. Mahan's geopolitical doctrines and was determined not to abandon the sea lanes and commercial opportunities to the British. German capital and immigrants were deeply involved in both coffee and cocoa plantations and trade throughout the Caribbean region and had made a bid to buy the Panama Canal rights from the De Lesseps Company. In general, German capitalists behaved little differently from U.S. or British capitalists; that is, they expected their national navies both to protect and, when and where necessary, to collect delinquent loans from the Caribbean governments (Bemis, 1943:115).

What perception did U.S. military strategists have of their position in the region as this new competition began? According to the work of one Caribbean expert:

> In 1901, the [U.S.] government assigned the General Defense Board the task of measuring the "actual value of our power of and influence in the Caribbean Sea and upon the coasts of South America." They reported back that if bases were kept in Cuba and new ones built in Puerto Rico, the "principles of strategy and the defects in our geography" indicated that the navy could maintain "mastery" of the Caribbean and "predominance on the Atlantic coast of South America. . . ." Beyond that point control was "doubtful to improbable." In 1902 the U.S. again virtually forced Germany, Britain and Italy to lift their blockade of Venezuela, proving the Board's estimates to be correct. Again, in 1903 the Board considered it "sound strategy" to plan for the West Indies and not the Atlantic coast as a probable theatre of war. By then they had pinpointed the most likely enemy: the "most important war problem to be studied is based on the supposition that Germany is the enemy."[29] (Maingot, 1994:30)

In fact, the historical record suggests that the Defense Board had pretty good intelligence. According to the research of the German archives by Grenville and Young, Germany had considered an attack as early as 1891, and in 1899 the Kaiser personally ordered a war plan against the United States. The Caribbean, and Puerto Rico specifically, would be the first step toward not a conquest of the United States but, in the Kaiser's words, "a firm base in the West Indies and a free hand in South America, which entails a breach of the 'Monroe Doctrine'" (Maingot, 1994:30).

It is in this light that President Theodore Roosevelt's "corollary" to the Monroe Doctrine must be viewed, for it would be Roosevelt who would get credit for converting the long-held premise concerning U.S. control of the character of the region into doctrine.[30] From 1898 to 1932, the United States intervened militarily on numerous occasions in the Central American/Caribbean region. Its occupation forces ran the governments of the Dominican Republic, Cuba, Nicaragua, Haiti, and Panama for long periods; Honduras, Mexico, Guatemala, and Costa Rica experienced shorter occupations.

The United States justified its actions in the region by the so-called Roosevelt Corollary to the Monroe Doctrine, so named because President Roosevelt warned in 1904 that the United States, if necessary, would use force to protect its interests in the hemisphere. He said:

> Chronic wrongdoing or an impotence which results in a general loosening of the ties of civilized society may in Latin America, as elsewhere

ultimately require intervention by some civilized nation, and in the Western Hemisphere, the adherence of the United States to the Monroe Doctrine may force the United States, however reluctantly, in flagrant cases of such wrongdoing or impotence, to the exercise of an international police power.... It is a mere truism to say that every nation, whether in America or anywhere else, which desires to maintain its freedom, its independence, must ultimately realize that the right of such independence cannot be separated from the responsibility of making good use of it. (Ronning, 1970:8)

In light of the previous case studies, the Roosevelt Corollary can be seen as a logical outgrowth of the No-Transfer Policy of 1811, the Monroe Doctrine, and the era of Continental Expansionism. The above statement is a testament to the impact the combination of core interests, images of uniqueness, geographical location, and historical experience had on policymakers: the need to control events in the United States' backyard that were deemed threatening. As U.S. economic interests in the region expanded and the tendency of the nations there to fall into disorder and fail to meet their financial obligations became progressively more evident, the ensuing decades witnessed the United States assuming the self-appointed role of hemispheric policeman, charged with maintaining law and order in the area. Indeed, by the early twentieth century, the United States possessed the power to keep foreign countries out of the hemisphere in general and the Central American region in particular. Success in driving the Spanish out of Cuba in 1898 and the U.S.-backed secession of Panama from Colombia in 1903 firmly established the United States as the dominant military, political, and economic power in the region. In fact, thirty-one U.S. interventions in the region occurred in the first three decades of the twentieth century.

However, U.S. policy toward Central America and the Caribbean came to mean more than simply preventing direct foreign intervention, for it was during this age of Roosevelt's "big stick" that the "idea took root that it was incumbent upon the United States to correct any deficiencies in the internal character of Latin American regimes that might encourage foreign intrusion" (Blachman et al., 1986:330). At the time of the Corollary, the United States perceived political turmoil and economic instability to be particular threats that warranted intervention. While the specific methods for dealing with these threats varied, a minimum policy sought sufficient control to prevent any situation that might make these countries susceptible to foreign entanglement and intervention.

It should become increasingly apparent that the notion of U.S. control in the region as a necessary component of U.S. foreign policy—its operational code toward Latin America—became solidified early on as an unquestioned assumption among U.S. policymakers.

CONCLUSION: NEW WORLD ORDER
OR BUSINESS AS USUAL?

Table 9.1 suggests how cultural values influence the development of the operational code as policymakers perceive events in the Central American region.

Except for the impact of history in the No-Transfer Policy and the Monroe Doctrine, an examination of official documents and remarks by policymakers in each of the four cases produced evidence that points to how cultural variables reflect a need for control in Central America and the Caribbean. By the end of the Continental Expansionism period and the proclamation of Roosevelt's Corollary, however, past U.S. successes and policies clearly had influenced both the rhetoric of policymakers and the output of the policymaking process. The image of the non-U.S. contiguous regions being part of the United States' backyard and the perception that such areas needed to be controlled carried tremendous implications. It must be underscored that Florida, Texas, Oregon, and California were once "foreign" lands that the United States viewed in the same manner that it has viewed Central America in the twentieth century. Indeed, these areas were at the time "Central American" for all intents and purposes. It had been traditional for North Americans to talk in such a proprietary way even before President Monroe unilaterally formulated his doctrine in 1823.

The immediate causes of intervention have changed, but the underlying causes remain the same as in the 1700s. In the case of a pre–Cold War U.S. military occupation of Nicaragua, from 1912 to 1933, the immediate factor prompting intervention was the threat posed by the potential intervention of European bondholders to collect unpaid debts. The conventional wisdom surrounding the motivation for the CIA-backed coup in Guatemala in 1954, the example par excellence of intervention in a Cold War environment, has long been the threat of communism in the region. However, the United States' most glaring use of force in Central America and the Caribbean during the post–Cold War environment—the invasion of Panama in 1989—serves as a reminder that the threat posed by narcotics now warrants intervention. And finally, the second case of U.S. intervention in the post–Cold War environment, the 1994 use of armed forces in Haiti, indicates that yet another threat—this time in the form of massive immigration—constitutes license for intervention.

But in each of these different environments, only the nature of the *immediate* threat has changed. Thus, the twentieth-century interventions can be viewed as extensions of the political culture that has developed since the Puritans first landed in the 1600s. The underlying operational code has remained unchanged.

Table 9.1   Overview of the Case Studies: Does an Operational Code Exist?

Case studies	Cultural Variables Reflecting Issue of Control			
	Geography	Core interests	Images	History
No-Transfer Policy	•	•	•	?
Monroe Doctrine	•	•	•	?
Continental Expansionism	•	•	•	•
Roosevelt Corollary	•	•	•	•

Because U.S. policymakers perceived the need to maintain control over Central America and the Caribbean, related talk of "our backyard" (not "our neighbor's house") reflects this top-down sense of power and position, as do other policymakers' attempts to define whose influence in the region will be deemed "foreign"—that is, non-U.S. (Etheredge, 1985: 193). As one scholar notes:

> Over the past century and a half the United States has built up an impressive collection of weapons and techniques to maintain and promote its interests in its "backyard." These have ranged from direct military intervention, the threat of force, the use of surrogate troops, and clandestine "destabilizing" operations. . . . Although at any particular time one or another of these methods might be the most favored instrument of United States foreign policy, none of them has ever been completely abandoned. There is a high degree of continuity in U.S. foreign policy towards the region, and the United States prefers to keep the widest possible range of options at its disposal. (Pearce, 1982:2)

Although in the post–Cold War world, adjustments may have occurred with respect to the larger international system, such premises remain unchallenged with respect to the Central American/Caribbean region. Will the pattern of intervention continue? Culture, while durable, is anything but immutable. Nonetheless, the self-scrutiny necessary to change this operational code and the "backyard" image of the region in the minds of U.S. policymakers does not appear to be on the horizon. In the absence of such scrutiny, threats will continue to be anticipated and doubtlessly found. Thus, insofar as U.S. intervention is driven by the underlying legacy of exceptionalism and the City on the Hill strain of U.S. culture, the post–Cold War era could result in a steady continuation of the pattern of intervention in the United States' "backyard."

NOTES

I wish to recognize a group of Georgia Southern University students who, while enrolled in my courses on U.S. foreign policy, provided an intellectual climate that stimulated me to think about many of the issues presented here. Robert Bunn, Chris Burke, Dave Coradini, Ashley Corbin, Lee Hyer, Greg Johnson, Raymond Perez, Tom Rhodes, Patti Thacker, Pat Williamson, and Sophia Wood all deserve special thanks.

1. For the purposes of this essay, the concept of intervention is narrowly defined and should be synonymous with the introduction of U.S. armed forces into territory outside the United States. However, *intervention* is often more broadly defined to mean "the calculated use of political, economic, and military instruments by one country to influence the domestic or the foreign policies of another country" (see Schraeder, 1992).

2. Throughout this essay, primarily for the sake of both brevity and clarity, the concept of the "Central American region" or "Central America" can be understood to include both the Caribbean Basin as well as the Central American states themselves. Thus, while not traditionally considered a part of Central America, Colombia and Venezuela are included in the analysis here.

3. See, for example, Lake (1988) and Ikenberry (1988). Although both have concentrated their work in the area of international political economy, their findings concerning the impact domestic politics has on foreign policy making are more than relevant here.

4. While Lebow (1981) is certainly not the first to make the distinction between immediate and underlying causes, his writings are particularly helpful and illuminating. With respect to his classical treatment of World War I, Carr's (1962:ix) attempt to "analyze the underlying and significant, rather than the immediate and personal, causes of the disaster" certainly makes such distinctions as well.

5. This definition of core interests can be found in Van Tassell (1974) and Hughes (1994:79).

6. See Neal (1961). Although Neal focuses on Eastern Europe as existing within the core interests of the USSR, his insights are certainly applicable to Central America and the United States.

7. See, for example, Harrison and Weigert (1947); see also Henrikerson (1975), who writes about the effect of maps on U.S. policymakers. For a suggestion of how maps influenced the "psychological isolationism" of the United States, see Harrison and Strausz-Hupe (1945).

8. An interesting discussion in this regard can be found in Hartlyn, Schoultz, and Varas (1992:4).

9. Quoted in Williams (1980:vii).

10. The writing of Ahmad (1980) is particularly compelling here as well. Some of the better known works in this area date from the generation of scholars who wrote about the circumstances directly following World War II and the Cold War. However, it is interesting to note that such works commonly fail to recognize that American Exceptionalism is as old as the nation itself. See, for example, the work of Boorstin (1972) and Hartz (1955).

11. For an excellent and concise overview of the impact of the U.S. political culture on U.S. foreign policy making, see Kenworthy (1995), Rosati (1993), Hodgson (1976), Dallek (1983), and Baritz (1985).

12. Quoted in Kammen (1993:7).

13. The reasons for the use of force have, of course, changed over time. A table that includes all instances of U.S. military intervention in the twentieth cen-

tury, with accompanying threat-based rationale, is available from the author: Professor Darin Van Tassell, Center for International Studies, Georgia Southern University, Landrum Box 8106, Statesboro, GA 30460–8106.

14. Bemis (1943:28). The "adjacent borderlands" refer to the area from the St. Mary's River, the boundary between Georgia and East Florida, to the Rio Grande del Norte, which was the western boundary of Louisiana as it had been conceived by the French government at the time of the Louisiana Purchase. Other statements by Jefferson provide evidence that early U.S. policymakers also had designs on territory to the north as well. Indeed, Jefferson proclaimed that "if the English do not give us the satisfaction we demand, we will take Canada, which wants to enter the Union; and when, together with Canada, we shall have the Floridas, we shall no longer have any difficulties with our neighbors; and it is the only way of preventing them" (quoted in Williams, 1980:63–64). Such statements underscore the notion that national security threats—in this case from Europe—can be solved by creating "buffer zones" along the U.S. border.

15. United States Congress, *Annals of Congress,* 11th Cong., 3d ed., 1810–1811, cols. 374–376.

16. Substantial portions concerning the events surrounding the No-Transfer Policy of 1811 were borrowed from Bemis (1943:28–31).

17. Unknown author (1902), "Some Original Documents on the Genesis of the Monroe Doctrine: John Quincy Adams and the Monroe Doctrine," *American Historical Review* 7:676–696.

18. Only a few years earlier, the USS *Ontario* was dispatched from Washington and landed at the Columbia River in August 1818—taking possession of what would become the Oregon Territory. Britain had conceded sovereignty here, but Russia and Spain asserted claims to the area.

19. This argument is perhaps best associated with Bemis (1949).

20. From President James Monroe's December 2, 1823, message to Congress, quoted in Paterson (1989:184).

21. Ibid.

22. Ibid., pp. 184–185.

23. For a detailed study of the Monroe Doctrine, see Perkins (1937); for a careful and documented study of the Latin American phase of the Monroe Doctrine, see Whitaker (1940).

24. Incidently, the Mexican War saw 1,721 U.S. citizens killed, 4,102 wounded, and 11,155 dead of disease. The military and naval expenditures were $97.7 million. For this price, and payments made under the Treaty of Guadalupe Hidalgo, the United States acquired more than 500,000 square miles of territory (more than one million if Texas is counted), including the great Pacific harbors of San Diego, Monterey, and San Francisco. These figures can be found in Tindall (1984:534).

25. See, for instance, Van Alstyne (1960).

26. Quoted in Keen and Wasserman (1988:513). It is interesting to note that the U.S. ambassador to Cuba, Earl Smith, used similar language in the 1960s. Smith wrote in his memoirs that no toleration of Castro should be allowed and that action should be taken against Castro out of fear that the Caribbean would grow into a "Communist lake," and that the United States had "a duty and obligation" to intervene if necessary to prevent a communist takeover. See Smith (1962:224, 232).

27. Cuba is somewhat of an exception, for it formally received its independence from Spain following the Spanish-American War in 1898. However, while Cuba may have been independent in name, the Platt Amendment carried provisions that legally gave the United States control of the island.

28. A discussion of German imperial designs in the Caribbean at this time can be found in Perkins (1937:206–207).

29. Maingot (1994:30) draws heavily on the archival research of others who cite the April 14, 1901, and July 29, 1903, minutes of the General Defense Board.

30. The "new" expansionism policy actually was announced formally after the policy had been adopted in the form of Secretary of State John Hay's "Open Door Notes" in 1899. The note announced the primacy of U.S. interests in the neighboring Central American/Caribbean region, as well as in Asia. The "Notes" were "designed to establish principles, or rules of the game," wrote William Appleman Williams, "which Americans considered essential for the immediate and long-range effectiveness of the expansion of their political economy" (quoted in Williams, 1980:129).

REFERENCES

Ahmad, Eqbal (1980) "Political Culture and Foreign Policy: Notes on American Interventions in the Third World." Washington, DC: Institute for Policy Studies.

Almond, Gabriel A., and Sidney Verba (1963) *The Civic Culture: Political Attitudes and Democracy in Five Nations.* Princeton: Princeton University Press.

Azar, Edward (1964) "The Theory of Protracted Social Conflict and the Challenges of Transforming Conflict Situations." In *Conflict Processes and the Breakdown of International Systems,* edited by D. A. Zinnes.

Azar, Edward (1983) "The Theory of Practical Social Conflict and the Challenges of Transforming Conflict Situations." In *Conflict Processes and the Breakdown of International Systems,* edited by D. A. Zinnes. Denver: University of Denver.

Baritz, Loren (1964) *City on a Hill: A History of Ideas and Myths in America.* New York: Wiley.

Baritz, Loren (1985) *Backfire: A History of How American Culture Led Us into Vietnam and Made Us Fight the Way We Did.* New York: Morrow.

Bemis, Samuel Flagg (1943) *The Latin American Policy of the United States: An Historical Interpretation.* New York: Harcourt, Brace.

Bemis, Samuel Flagg (1949) *John Quincy Adams and the Foundations of American Foreign Policy.* New York: Knopf.

Blachman, Morris J., Douglas C. Bennett, William M. LeoGrande, and Kenneth E. Sharpe (1986) "The Failure of the Hegemonic Strategic Vision." In *Confronting Revolution: Security Through Diplomacy in Central America,* edited by Morris Blachman, William M. LeoGrande, and Kenneth Sharpe. New York: Pantheon Books.

Blachman, Morris J. (1990) "U.S. Interests in South America." In *South America into the 1990s,* edited by G. Pope Atkins. Boulder: Westview Press.

Boorstin, Daniel J. (1972) *American Civilization: A Portrait of the Twentieth Century.* New York: McGraw-Hill.

Boyd, Julian P., ed. (1954) *The Papers of Thomas Jefferson,* vol. 9. Princeton: Princeton University Press,.

Brickman, Phillip (1976) "Is It Real?" In *New Directions in Attribution Theory Research,* edited by John H. Harvey, William Ickes, and Robert F. Kidd, vol. 2, Chapter 1.

Burns, Edward McNall (1957) *The American Idea of Mission.* New Brunswick, NJ: Rutgers University Press.

Carr, Edward Hallet (1962) *The Twenty Years' Crisis, 1919–1939*. London: Macmillan.

Choucri, Nazli, and Robert North (1989) "Lateral Pressure in International Relations: Concept and Theory." In *Handbook of War Studies*, edited by Manus Midlarsky. Boston: Unwin Hyman.

Clines, Francis X. (1984) "Reagan Calls Salvador Aid Foes Naive." *New York Times*, March 20, p. A3.

Crabb, Cecil V., Jr. (1982) *The Doctrines of American Foreign Policy: Their Meaning, Role, and Future*. Baton Rouge: Louisiana State University Press.

Dallek, Robert (1983) *The American Style of Foreign Policy: Cultural Politics and Foreign Affairs*. New York: Knopf.

Davis, Tami R., and Sean M. Lynn-Jones (1987) "'City Upon a Hill.'" *Foreign Policy* 66:20–38.

Diehl, Paul F., and Gary Goertz (1988) "Territorial Changes and Militarized Conflict." *Journal of Conflict Resolution* 32:103–122.

Dougherty, James E., and Robert L. Pfaltzgraff, Jr. (1990) *Contending Theories of International Relations*. New York: Harper and Row.

Etheredge, Lloyd (1985) *Can Governments Learn? American Foreign Policy and Central American Revolutions*. New York: Pergamon Press.

Findley, William (1796) *History of the Insurrections in the Four Western Counties of Pennsylvania*. Philadelphia: Samuel Harrison Smith.

Galtung, Johan (1964) "A Structural Theory of Aggression." *Journal of Peace Research* 1:95–119.

George, Alexander L. (1969) "The Operational Code: A Neglected Approach to the Study of Political Decision Making." *International Studies Quarterly* 13:190–222.

Halberstam, David (1972) *The Best and the Brightest*. Greenwich, CT: Fawcett.

Harrison, Richard E., and Hans W. Weigert (1947) "World View and Strategy." In *Compass of the World: A Symposium on Political Geography*, edited by Jans W. Weigert and Vilhjalmut Stefansson. New York: Macmillan.

Harrison, Edes, and Robert Strausz-Hupe (1945) "Maps, Strategy and World Politics." In *Foundations of National Power*, edited by Harold and Margaret Sprout. Princeton: Princeton University Press.

Hartlyn, Jonathan, Lars Schoultz, and Augusto Varas, eds. (1992) *The United States and Latin America in the 1990s: Beyond the Cold War*. Chapel Hill: University of North Carolina Press.

Hartz, Louis (1955) *The Liberal Tradition in America: An Interpretation of American Political Thought Since the Revolution*. New York: Harcourt Brace.

Henrikerson, Alan (1975) "The Map as an 'Idea': The Role of Cartographic Imagery During the Second World War." *The American Cartographer* 2:46–47.

Hodgson, Godfrey (1976) *America in Our Time*. New York: Vintage Books.

Hofstadter, Richard. (1966) *The Paranoid Style in American Politics and Other Essays*. New York: Knopf.

Holsti, Kal J. (1967) *International Politics: A Framework for Analysis*, vol. 14, no. 3. Englewood Cliffs, NJ: Prentice-Hall.

Holsti, Kal J. (1970) "National Role Conception in the Study of Foreign Policy." *International Studies Quarterly* 3.

Hughes, Barry B. (1994) *Continuity and Change in World Politics: The Clash of Perspectives*. Englewood Cliffs, NJ: Prentice-Hall.

Ikenberry, G. John (1988) *Reasons of State*. Ithaca: Cornell University Press.

Isard, Walter (1992) *Understanding Conflict and the Science of Peace*. Cambridge, MA: Blackwell.

Jervis, Robert (1976) *Perception and Misperception in International Politics.* Princeton: Princeton University Press.

Kammen, Michael (1993) "The Problem of American Exceptionalism: A Reconsideration. *American Quarterly* 45:4.

Keen, Benjamin, and Mark Wasserman (1988) *A History of Latin America.* Dallas: Houghton Mifflin.

Kenworthy, Eldon (1995) *America/Américas: Myth in the Making of U.S. Policy Toward Latin America.* University Park: Pennsylvania State University Press.

Lake, David A. (1988) *Power, Protection, and Free Trade.* Ithaca: Cornell University Press.

Lebow, Richard Ned (1981) *Between Peace and War: The Nature of International Crisis.* Baltimore: Johns Hopkins University Press.

Leites, Nathan (1951) *The Operational Code of the Politburo.* New York: McGraw-Hill.

Leites, Nathan (1953) *A Study of Bolshevism.* Glencoe: Free Press.

Lipscomb, Andrew A., ed. (1904) *The Writings of Thomas Jefferson,* vol. 12. Washington, DC: Thomas Jefferson Memorial Association.

de Madariaga, Salvador (1962) *Latin America: Between the Eagle and the Bear.* New York: Praeger.

McCarthy, Joseph (1952) *McCarthyism: The Fight for America.* New York: Devin-Adair.

Maingot, Anthony P. (1994) *The United States in the Caribbean.* Boulder: Westview Press.

Neal, Fred Warner (1961) "U.S. Foreign Policy and the Soviet Union." Santa Barbara, CA: Center for the Study of Democratic Institutions.

O'Sullivan, John Louis (1839) "The Great Nation of Futurity." In *Major Problems in American Foreign Policy, Volume 1: To 1914,* 3d ed., edited by Thomas G. Patterson. Lexington, MA: D. C. Heath.

Parenti, Michael J. (1969) *The Anti-Communist Impulse.* New York: Random House.

Parenti, Michael J., ed. (1971) *Trends and Tragedies in American Foreign Policy.* Boston: Little, Brown.

Pastor, Robert A. (1986) "Explaining U.S. Policy Toward the Caribbean Basin: Fixed and Emerging Images." *World Politics* 38:488.

Paterson, Thomas G., ed. (1989) *Major Problems in American Foreign Policy, Volume I: To 1914.* Lexington, MA: D. C. Heath.

Pearce, Jenny (1982) *Under the Eagle: U.S. Intervention in Central America and the Caribbean.* Boston: South End Press.

Perkins, Dexter (1937) *The Monroe Doctrine, 1867–1907.* Baltimore: Johns Hopkins University Press.

Putnam, Robert D. (1988) "Diplomacy and Domestic Politics: The Logic of Two-Level Games." *International Organization* 42:428–460.

Pye, Lucian, and Sydney Verba, eds. (1965) *Political Culture and Political Development.* Princeton: Princeton University Press.

Ronning, C. Neale, ed. (1970) *Intervention in Latin America.* New York: Knopf.

Rosati, Jerel A. (1993) *The Politics of United States Foreign Policy.* Fort Worth, TX: Harcourt Brace Jovanovich.

Schlesinger, Arthur M., Jr. (1986) *The Cycles of American History.* Boston: Houghton Mifflin.

Schraeder, Peter J. (1992) "Studying U.S. Intervention in the Third World." In *Intervention into the 1990s: U.S. Foreign Policy in the Third World,* edited by Peter J. Schraeder. Boulder: Lynne Rienner.

Singer, J. David (1961) "The Level of Analysis Problem in International Relations." Reprinted in *International Politics and Foreign Policy: A Reader in Research and Theory,* rev. ed., edited by James N. Rosenau. New York: Free Press, 1969.

Smith, Earl T. (1962) *The Fourth Floor.* New York: Random House.

"Some Original Documents on the Genesis of the Monroe Doctrine: John Quincy Adams and the Monroe Doctrine" (1902) *American Historical Review* 7:676–696.

Tindall, George Brown (1984) *America: A Narrative History*, vol. 1. New York: W. W. Norton.

Tocqueville, Alexis de (1945) *Democracy in America.* New York: Vintage Books.

Tsebelis, George (1990) *Nested Games.* Berkeley: University of California Press.

United States Congress. *Annals of Congress,* 11th Cong., 3d ed., 1810–1811, cols. 374–376.

Van Alstyne, Richard W. (1960) *The Rising American Empire.* New York: Oxford University.

Van Tassell, G. Lane (1970) *Toward a Perspective of the Concept of Intervention in International Politics: A Framework for Analysis Applied to American Actions in the Dominican Republic in 1965.* Ph.D. diss., Claremont Graduate School and University Center.

Van Tassell, G. Lane (1974) "Intervention in International Politics: A Conceptual Model." *Georgia Political Science Association Journal* 2:51–71.

Weinberg, Albert (1935) *Manifest Destiny.* Baltimore: Johns Hopkins University Press.

Whitaker, Arthur P. (1940) *The United States and the Independence of Latin America, 1800–1830.* Baltimore: Johns Hopkins University Press.

Williams, William Appleman (1961) *The Contours of American History.* New York: World Publishing.

Williams, William Appleman (1976) *America Confronts a Revolutionary World: 1776–1976.* New York: Morrow.

Williams, William Appleman (1980) *Empire as a Way of Life.* Oxford: Oxford University Press.

Winthrop, Robert C., ed. (1971) *Life and Letters of John Winthrop,* vol. 2. New York: Da Capo Press.

PART 4

AFTERWORD

10

Advancing
Cultural Explanations

Fritz Gaenslen

Taken together, the chapters of this book add to the growing evidence of a major revival of interest in the concept of "culture." Taken individually, each of the chapters attempts, in one way or another, to offer a cultural explanation of foreign policy–related behavior. My purpose in this afterword is to consider these offerings in the context of two broad questions: *When* do we want to make cultural explanations, and *how* do we want to make them?

WHEN

We do not *always* want to make cultural explanations—or so it would seem to anyone who has followed within the social science disciplines the now-you-see-it-now-you-don't history of the culture concept. On many occasions, certainly, we have gotten along comfortably, even gratefully, without it. At other times, however, culture has impressed itself on our consciousness. In thinking about how to make cultural explanations, we may usefully begin by asking just when it is that culture most insistently intrudes.

Historical Perspectives

When did our present-day anthropological notion of culture first come into being? According to Sahlins (1995:10–14), the term originated in the late eighteenth century, the product of German bourgeois intellectuals who, relatively powerless and without the formal unity of a country, sought to express a distinctive national identity (*kultur*) in opposition both to the Francophile pretensions of the Prussian court and to the ambitions of France and England as purveyors of "civilization." The latter term, Sahlins (1995:10) writes, was invented in France in the 1750s, quickly adopted in England, and enthusiastically embraced in both countries "in explication of their superior accomplishments and justification of their imperialist exploits." Culture, Sahlins observes, was a rejection of this universalizing hegemony and of the distinction between "more civilized" and "less civilized" people.

Several features of this account are worth emphasizing. First, the invention of culture appears to have followed upon the construction and contemplation of an "other." Second, this other was not only "external" (France and England), but "internal" as well (the Prussian aristocracy). Third, with respect to both external and internal manifestations of the other, the inventors of culture felt themselves in a position of political disadvantage. Finally, they experienced their disadvantage as both social dislocation and injustice. Culture was not only an assertion of identity and "place," but of equality as well.

Can a similar tale be told about other times and places? A growing literature (Foster, 1991:239–241) suggests that it can. Consider, for example, the importation of the culture concept to Japan. In the view of a number of scholars (Morris-Suzuki, 1995; Najita and Harootunian, 1988), the word *bunka* (culture) first entered popular awareness in Japan in the 1920s as the antithesis to "civilization and enlightenment." Where civilization and enlightenment had been the rallying cry of early Meiji Westernizers—affirming both the achievements of the European scientific and industrial revolutions and a universalist conception of cosmopolitanism—culture was taken as referring to a unique Japanese essence. Why the 1920s? The answer can be seen as having both external and internal components.

Externally, the 1920s saw the inauguration of the so-called Versailles-Washington system, an international order—defined by the Versailles Peace Conference of 1919 and the Washington Conference of 1921–1922—that largely served to protect the interests of Great Britain and the United States and to roll back Japan's position in Asia. Internally, the 1920s saw a growing disaffection in Japan with domestic political and economic arrangements—with "incompetent" politicians and divisive party politics and with the extreme rapaciousness and inequality produced by industrial capitalism. Against these domestic threats, and the perception of Western colonial ambition, culture was an assertion of both national unity and national independence.

Finally, let us consider the introduction of the culture concept—in its incarnation as "political culture"—to U.S. political science. Introduced by Gabriel Almond in 1956, political culture achieved wide currency in the 1960s primarily as a tool for making sense of the problems facing the host of new states that emerged with the demise of colonialism following World War II. As Pye (1991:492) has written, "The emerging nations did not have well-institutionalized governments and therefore there was need for new concepts to describe them." But there is more to the story than this. According to Almond (1980:6–10), the political culture concept had its true beginnings in the confrontation of the U.S. public and U.S. political science with the failure of enlightenment and liberal expectations about the inevitability of democracy. This confrontation was occasioned, most fundamentally, first by the Nazi seizure of power in Germany and then, in the immediate postwar years, by the perceived threat—internal and external—of worldwide communism (also see Pye, 1991:496). To a people revealed in surveys as uniquely proud of their governmental institutions (Almond and Verba, 1963:102), at a time when the "hearts and minds" of the citizens of the new states were seemingly up for grabs, political culture was, at least in part, an assertion of U.S. identity in the face of a threatening other.

What do these vignettes of intellectual history tell us about when to make a cultural explanation? In broad summary, they suggest that the explanatory power of culture will be most impressive when the individuals whose behavior we seek to explain find themselves in circumstances that either make salient their own collective identities or make possible their mobilization of the collective identities of prospective political allies.

To render explicit a so-far implicit feature of these circumstances, let us now consider the origins of the present "culture revival."

Contemporary Perspectives

The present revival of interest in the culture concept can be seen as both a response to recent upheavals in the world's political landscape and the product of several scholarly debates. The recent political upheavals are familiar. They include the "third wave" of global democratization that began with the fall of Portugal's dictatorship in 1974 (Huntington, 1991); the continuing growth since the Iranian revolution of 1979 of Islamist movements in much of the Middle East (Halliday, 1995); the burgeoning phenomenon of "collapsed states" in places like Somalia and Rwanda in Africa (Zartman, 1995); and, perhaps most notably, at the outset of the 1990s, the demise of Marxist regimes in Eastern Europe and the disintegration of the Soviet Union, Yugoslavia, and Czechoslovakia (Bunce, 1996). These upheavals have led many observers to draw the connection, noted above, between culture and "the politics of identity." As one analyst (Street, 1994:96) puts it, they direct our attention "to the way regimes legitimate themselves and the way citizens identify themselves, both processes that suggest a mediating role for culture."

But these political upheavals make vivid another lesson as well. They suggest that cultural explanations will seem most persuasive when the individuals whose behavior we seek to explain are unclear about the structure of rewards and punishments they face—when their situations are characterized by uncertainty. The argument is straightforward and unoriginal (see Geertz, 1964:63–64; Gaenslen, 1986:81–82; Goldstein and Keohane, 1993:16; Crawford and Lijphart, 1995:186): When an existing order has broken down and a new one has yet to be institutionalized, individuals will face continual doubt about their interests and how to maximize them. In these circumstances, cultural beliefs and values can plausibly provide mental antidotes to the problem of a tangible disorder by serving as sources of sociopolitical meaning and as guides to political action.

This point perhaps requires elaboration. I do not mean to suggest here that culture somehow fails to operate in more stable circumstances, or that its influence in such circumstances is unimportant. Rather, my point is methodological. Stable circumstances make it difficult to untangle the influence of culture from other influences; an absence of variance tends to produce overdetermined explanations with little opportunity for discriminating tests. It follows, then, that our cultural explanations are likely to prove more compelling to skeptical readers to the extent that we focus on times of relative turbulence. Does it also follow that, in offering cultural explanations, we ought to avoid the analysis of more stable circumstances altogether? This seems to me to give up too much. My own conclusion is more modest: Analysis of the cultural underpinnings of relatively stable political orders will usefully be supplemented by examining these same orders in times of turbulence and uncertainty.

The political upheavals of recent years have not been the only spur to a revived interest in the culture concept. For some analysts, external worldly events have been less important than internal scholarly debates. The debates include—and I shall use simplifying labels—those between "realists" and "idealists" in the field of international relations, between "rational-choice theorists" and "area specialists" in the field of comparative politics, and between "positivists" and "interpretivists" in the social sciences more generally. The first two of these debates seem to me to repeat the lesson offered above—that cultural explanations will be most compelling when political actors are faced with uncertainty.

Consider, first, the debate in international relations between realists and idealists. Pared to its essentials, the realist position stresses the rationality of decisionmaking units, conceived as nation-states; attributes security-maximizing utility functions to each state; and characterizes the international environment of states as ruthlessly competitive (see Tetlock, 1996). This last point is the most important. In the realist account, the competitive environment does double theoretical duty. First, it serves as the source of policymaker rationality: International competitive pressures are said to create incentives for the clear appraisal of threats, the methodical evaluation of options, and the unemotional assessment of alliances. (Note that it is this assumption that permits realists to treat states as "unitary actors.") Second, the competitive environment serves as the source of foreign policy itself; that is, states are said to pursue the policies they do in response to structural incentives provided by the international system. For present purposes, the idealist objection is as follows: "Given the causal ambiguity inherent in complex historical flows of events, systemic constraint cannot be sufficiently constraining to be a powerful explanatory tool" (Tetlock, 1996). Instead, idealists claim, we must look to the causal beliefs of particular policymakers and to their particular notions of good and bad outcomes. Both the beliefs and the notions, idealists would add, may sometimes be the products of culture.

The second debate that has spurred a revival of interest in the culture concept has been the one between rational-choice theorists and area specialists. This debate can be seen as a more general version of the one between realists and idealists in international relations. Rational-choice theorists seek to understand social and political phenomena as the product of purposive, goal-seeking choices by individuals possessed of stable and ordered preferences; individuals are said to assess their available options and to choose those they expect will best achieve their goals. Area specialists have expressed several reservations about the rational-choice project (see Little, 1991; Gaenslen, 1986). First, they note that although much human behavior can properly be described in rational-choice terms, at least some behavior seems usefully understood as more expressive than instrumental. Second, they observe that the rational-choice description of rationality does not go far enough—that it does not specify the nature of the goals that individuals pursue, the decision rules they use to select among options, and the level of detail needed to describe the environment of choice. Finally, area specialists object to the common practice in rational-choice analyses of merely positing goals, decision rules, and the salient features of the environment rather than investigating them. The result of this practice, they argue, has been the propagation of an ethnocentric and economistic view of both social institutions and human motives that is insensitive not only to such behavioral impulses as love, friendship, loyalty, habit, and anger but, most significantly, to the particularities of cultural difference.

How do the debates between realists and idealists and between rational-choice theorists and area specialists serve to reiterate the lesson that cultural explanations will offer more convincing accounts of behavior in "uncertain" environments than in "predictable" ones? The answer lies in the fact that although the objections raised by idealists and area specialists are telling, they do not completely carry the day. If idealists and area specialists can claim differences between states and between peoples, realists and rational-choice theorists can reasonably claim similarities—core interests of security and well-being that states and peoples share. When environmental constraints can be shown to make salient these core interests, we are likely to find realist and rational-choice explanations persuasive. Conversely, when environmental constraints are demonstrably uncertain, we should expect to find cultural explanations more convincing.

A third debate that has contributed to the revival of interest in the culture concept is that between "positivists" and "interpretivists." However, this debate seems to yield a lesson that contradicts the lessons I have offered so far. At the center of the interpretivist position is a deep skepticism about the possibility of positive social science. Reality, in the interpretivist view, is a word that means little unless enclosed in quotation marks; our apprehensions of reality are never raw, unmediated, or simply objective. Thus, in a critical vein, much interpretivist analysis has sought to show how the practices and products of mainstream social science research encode and conceal value positions that need to be brought to light. More affirmatively, however, interpretivists, relatively unencumbered by positivist methods, have directed considerable energy to cultural analysis more broadly conceived. In particular, they have focused on features of language and discursive practice that would seem, in general, to be necessary elements in our stories about how culture works its effects (see Yee, 1996:94–101). Although positivists would defend themselves with the reminder that performing sociology of knowledge on other people's arguments is not the same as showing these arguments to be logically flawed or factually unsupported, their neglect of language and discursive practice—and of culture—seems less defensible. Yet interpretivists too are easily charged with neglect. As positivists would point out, we still need some way to tell a good interpretation from a bad one.

This Book

My argument to this point has been that we ought to be sensitive to the temporal environment of those whose behavior we seek to explain— that our cultural explanations will be most effective when, in the eyes of policymakers, times are turbulent and/or issues of legitimacy and identity loom large. Does this analysis offer a useful way of looking at some of the contributions to this book?

Consider, first, the chapters by Chafetz and his associates and by Zurovchak. These authors locate their studies at the same historical moment. In the early 1990s, with the breakup of the Soviet empire and the disintegration of the Soviet Union itself, policymakers in Belarus, Ukraine, the Czech Republic, and Slovakia faced for the first time, in effect, the task of making independent foreign policy. The moment, in other words, was "a defining moment." Sensitivity to internal and external others was high, and concerns about legitimacy and collective identity crowded the political agenda. Interestingly, however, the two chapters illustrate different lessons about when to make a cultural explanation. Why did Belarus embrace nuclear nonproliferation and why did Ukraine hesitate? For Chafetz and his associates, the circumstances I have described induced in policymakers a particular concentration of mind: They served to make culture, in the form of different national role conceptions, the object of conscious contemplation. In Zurovchak's account, however, these circumstances did not so much concentrate policymaker attention as diffuse it, with culture influencing behavior below the threshold of policymaker awareness. Why did Slovak foreign ministry officials adopt more centralized and less flexible decisionmaking procedures than their Czech counterparts? According to Zurovchak, both sets of officials behaved "naturally" in the face of novel circumstances; in the absence of pressures to the contrary, they simply acted in accordance with their different cultural assumptions about the proper organization of human relationships.

Like Chafetz and Zurovchak, Breuning and Lotz are each concerned to explain policymaker choices at particular historical junctures. Breuning's focus is on Dutch and Belgian foreign assistance policies circa 1986–1987. Lotz's subject is the U.S. ratification of the North American Free Trade Agreement at the end of 1993. However, neither author is much concerned to explain why culture (in the form of either national role conception or national myth) should be especially salient to policymakers at these specific moments. Instead, both authors can be seen as making a more general argument—an idealist argument—about the uncertainty associated with issues of international political economy. Whatever the international political and economic constraints at the time, these authors suggest, they were not so constraining as to preclude the mobilization of contrasting national role conceptions by Dutch and Belgian policymakers or opposing national myths by Albert Gore and Ross Perot.

Finally, let us consider the chapters by Banerjee, Van Tassell, and Katzenstein. Like Chafetz and Zurovchak, each of these authors focuses on "a defining moment." For Banerjee, the moment is India on the eve of independence, with India's future national identity the object of internal and external contention among Hindus, Muslims, and British. For Van Tassell, the moment is the new American Republic as it struggles for the first time to define its role in Central America and the Caribbean in the face of a wider European presence. For Katzenstein, the moment is the transition between the Ming and Qing dynasties when China first grappled with the issue of how to treat "rebels" on Taiwan. None of these authors, however, provides an illustration of one of my lessons about when to make a cultural explanation. Instead, each of them offers a useful lesson about a related, but different question: How are we to describe a country's culture? Breuning, in her chapter, suggests that important elements for such a description are likely to be associated with significant turning points in a country's history: founding events and major shocks or crises. Banerjee, Van Tassell, and Katzenstein would all seem to agree.

HOW

How are we to make a cultural explanation? My central premise is that demonstrating in convincing fashion the independent influence of culture on political behavior is difficult. To further understand the difficulty, we may usefully turn to the culture concept itself. Following widespread practice, I define culture as the shared assumptions and meanings of a group. However, this definition still leaves plenty of room for both conceptual confusion and problems of operationalization.

Reducing Conceptual Confusion

In its home discipline of anthropology, the culture concept has come under heavy attack in recent years for implying timelessness, homogeneity, and uncontested sharedness. Others have responded, however, that these implications are by no means necessary and have argued instead for a more "historicized" and "politicized" notion of culture (see Ortner, 1995:180). This discussion within anthropology offers a lesson about how to make a cultural explanation: Namely, there is no one best way to do this. How we conceptualize culture—how we treat such issues as timelessness, homogeneity, etc.—should depend on the particular case and our precise theoretical interests.

Still, our conceptualizations of culture should probably be more restrictive than inclusive. Barnes (1994:45–49) cites approvingly a definition of culture by Schein that seems more concrete than most definitions of the term. Here is Schein's (1992:12) most recent wording. The culture of a group can be defined as "a pattern of shared basic assumptions that the group learned as it solved its problems of external adaptation and internal integration, that has worked well enough to be considered valid and, therefore, to be taught to new members as the correct way to perceive, think, and feel in relation to those problems."

Also potentially useful is Barnes's emphasis on the distinction between cultural assumptions and individual beliefs. Culture is not involved in all individual beliefs, he states, but only in those that the individual understands are shared with others. Maintaining the conceptual distinction between cultural assumptions and individual beliefs is necessary, Barnes argues, if we are to understand better the interplay between them.

Finally, on the question of how many people must share beliefs to be labeled a culture, Barnes echoes the point that this should depend on the goals of the analyst. He reminds us, however, following Schein, that culture is a learned product of group experience and is therefore to be found only where there is a definable group with a significant history.

Can we go further in meeting the challenge "to narrow the concept of 'culture' so that it includes less and reveals more" (Keesing, 1974)? One obvious strategy is to disaggregate the concept, as far as possible, into discrete parts (beliefs, values, preferences) and to represent these parts as variables. This strategy will help us minimize vagueness and the unexamined conflation of multiple meanings and, as a result, reduce in our cultural explanations the possibility of circular reasoning (Smelser, 1992:20–25).

Problems of Operationalization

Not all students of culture will find this narrowing of the culture concept congenial. Especially likely to be disgruntled are those who are concerned less with cultural explanation than with cultural description—that is, with representing adequately the sensibilities and outlooks of particular collectivities of people. It is not that this latter task is somehow unworthy. Indeed, against the satisfactions of "thick description" (Geertz, 1973), the straightforward testing of hypotheses can sometimes seem sterile. Certainly, in this book, we get a more vivid sense of China from Dellios's elegant rendering of that country's strategic culture than we get of Belarus or Ukraine from Chafetz's study of nuclear nonproliferation. Nevertheless, the distinction is important. To describe an aspect of a country's culture is one task; to show some impact of that culture on political behavior is another. The first task seems to me to be the primary focus not only of Dellios's chapter, but also those of Banerjee, Katzenstein, Lotz, and Van Tassell. The Breuning, Zurovchak, and Chafetz chapters, on the other hand, appear more concerned with the second task. The cultural descriptions in this latter group may not be as richly textured, but the dependent variables are more clearly specified.

Yet the "worlds" of cultural description and cultural explanation are not so unrelated as many analysts (e.g., Brint 1994:10) would have us believe. First, even those who see themselves as primarily residents of the "world of social science explanation" must, in developing their hypotheses, concepts, and measures, and in making sense of their findings, spend considerable time in the "world of interpretive description" (see Nathan, 1993:936). Thus, virtually all the contributors to this book attempt to operationalize culture through the interpretation of texts and/or utterances. Second, even those who see themselves as primarily residents of the "world of interpretive description" must, if they are to demonstrate the validity of their interpretations, spend considerable time in the "world of social science explanation." Thus, virtually all the contributors to this book wrestle, at least implicitly, with a question I remarked on earlier: How do we tell a good interpretation from a bad one? Let us consider this question more closely.

Although the rules for describing a culture are largely undeveloped, they are probably most developed if we seek to operationalize culture through the mechanism of the sample survey. In this volume, only Zurovchak and Lotz employ surveys to look at culture—albeit in different ways. Even surveys, however, must be interpreted, and we are always free to worry about a host of issues pertaining to the reliability and validity of the results: timing, format, sample size, wording of questions, response stability, representativeness, and the like. Our problems are compounded if we seek to operationalize culture through the interpretation of canonical texts (Dellios) or the public utterances of political elites (Banerjee, Katzenstein, Lotz, Breuning, Chafetz, and Van Tassell). For these approaches, we have even fewer rules to guide us and, therefore, more reasons to worry about reliability and validity. My point, however, is not that we should prefer survey methods to other approaches. In particular, if we wish to show the influence of culture on foreign policy, a focus on what policymakers say seems more than reasonable. My point, rather—and I take it to be Banerjee's as well—is that just as we have developed over the years rules for making sense of survey responses, we need to develop rules for the cultural decoding of public discourse.

How can we do this? Although I hesitate to close off any avenue of inspiration, I do not believe we shall proceed very far in developing rules for deriving culture from discourse if we look to grand theories about discourse in general. Relatedly, I do not believe that a "linguistic turn" will lead us to useful answers about the relationships between language and other forms of knowledge and practice. The controversies surrounding these relationships are so long-standing that they are now described as "classical" (Hill and Mannheim, 1992:382). Instead, just as improvements in survey research have been the product of fine-grained analyses of the results of particular surveys in particular contexts, so I would expect the development of rules for the cultural decoding of discourse to proceed from analyses that were similarly fine grained and similarly context specific. Such analyses would address a variety of questions, including those suggested by Rieder (1994:127–133,146): (1) How far, and to what relevant community, might one generalize the sentiments encoded in a particular speaker's utterances? Is there a difference between the culture of the speaker and the culture of the listeners? (2) Is a particular discourse representative of the discursive field, or are there a variety of discourses? Is there one discourse for genteel settings and another for the back room? Is there one discourse for mobilizing an in-group and another for legitimating the group before outsiders? (3) What are the conditions and occasions that will allow us to presume the sincerity of utterances? What do particular utterances hide as well as reveal? What dividends—tangible or symbolic—do they yield? And what might utterances "do" rather than express? In summary, if we are to develop rules for the cultural decoding of public discourse, we need to pay at least as much attention to contexts as we do to "texts."

Must we wait until rules for the analysis of discourse are better developed to tell a good cultural description from a bad one? Happily, no, but only if, as I have suggested, we are willing to spend considerable time in the world of social science explanation. To evaluate a cultural description, we need to follow the advice of King, Keohane, and Verba (1994:47) and consider the description's observable implications. We need to ask, "If my [cultural description] is correct . . . , what else might I expect to observe in the real world?" In short, the best way to demonstrate that a cultural description merits attention is to use it to advance a compelling cultural explanation.

What are the salient features of such an explanation? Let us consider two recent examples.

Two Examples of Cultural Explanation

Example one. In *The Child and the State in India,* Weiner (1991) offers a cultural explanation for why India, almost alone among the countries of the world, has no effective laws mandating universal education and no effective laws banning child labor. India, he points out, is the largest single producer of the world's illiterates. Weiner attributes this state of affairs to a set of beliefs widely shared by state bureaucrats, social activists, academics, and, more broadly, the Indian middle classes—of whatever political persuasion. These groups, he argues, tend to view social inequality and differential privilege as the natural and proper order of things and to see the role of education as maintaining this order. Educating the poor, these groups believe, will disrupt existing social arrangements by arousing unrealizable ambitions and by creating dissatisfactions that could lead to social unrest. Weiner argues that these beliefs have their origins in religious notions and in the premises that underlie India's hierarchical caste system—notions and premises that resist changes in group status.

Example two. In *Culture of Honor,* Nisbett and Cohen (1996) offer a cultural explanation for differences in homicide rates between Northern and Southern white males in the United States for the period 1976–1983.

Southern white males, they argue, are more likely to be deeply concerned about honor—defined as rights to precedence or status—and to see affronts to honor as requiring a violent response. This set of beliefs, which they term a "culture of honor," tends to have its historical roots, they suggest, in areas where individuals are highly vulnerable to economic loss and where state regulation of conflict is largely absent. More particularly, cultures of honor have been associated historically with herding economies. The U.S. South, Nisbett and Cohen maintain, was originally settled by Scottish-Irish herders, and the higher incidence of homicide among white Southern males today should be seen as a cultural residue of this heritage.

The first thing to notice about these examples of cultural explanation is that they share a common design. Both studies *attempt to explain differences* (in laws; in homicide rates) and both studies *treat culture as an independent variable* (India/not India; North/South). Both studies, in other words, are *explicitly comparative.* If we do not want to say that adopting this design is necessary to offering a cultural explanation by definition, I would suggest that it is at least necessary to offering a cultural explanation that is compelling. In this book, Breuning, Zurovchak, and Chafetz adopt the same design as Weiner and as Nisbett and Cohen.

But adopting the right design is not enough. If we are to offer cultural explanations that are compelling, we need to pursue two additional strategies. The first strategy requires that we focus on the dependent variable and ask: What, besides culture, might account for the observed variation? Can the absence of compulsory schooling in India be attributed to budgetary constraints or to the need by parents and employers for children's income and labor? Weiner shows that India's education budget as a percentage of GNP compares well with those of other developing nations whose records are far superior, and that little relation exists historically between a country's introduction of education and child labor laws and its level of national and per capita wealth. Can the higher homicide rates among Southern white males be attributed to the South's hotter temperatures, the legacy of slavery, greater poverty, or the wider availability of guns? Nisbett and Cohen take considerable pains to show that they cannot. The essence of this strategy is straightforward: If we can eliminate all of the plausible rival explanations for the differences we observe, then the only explanation left standing will be our own—a cultural explanation.

Two further comments about this strategy are in order. First, the strategy is demanding in the sense that thinking up plausible rival explanations can require considerable knowledge. The knowledge requirements may be particularly great for those concerned with the impact of culture on foreign policy. As Hudson observes in her introduction, students in the subfield of foreign policy analysis stand at the interface between the study of international relations and the study of domestic politics. So if we wish to make a compelling cultural explanation from this vantage point, we must eliminate plausible rival explanations in *both* domains. The contributors to this book are generally more concerned with battling the international dragon of realism than the domestic dragon of rational choice.

Second, the strategy of eliminating plausible rival explanations can carry us just so far. With this strategy, we may convince readers of the efficacy of culture in general without convincing them of the precise cultural explanation we wish to advance. We may come to believe that the absence of compulsory education in India has cultural roots without believing that these roots lie in religious beliefs and the premises of the caste system. We may come to believe that different homicide rates in the U.S. North and South are indeed the product of different cultures without giving credence to the idea of a culture of honor. In short, if we want to make our cultural explanations more compelling, we will need to go beyond the elimination of plausible rival alternatives.

A second strategy, then, requires that we focus not on the dependent variable, but on our independent variable. The strategy involves asking a question I posed earlier: If our cultural explanation is correct, what else might we expect to observe in the real world? If a belief in social inequality as the natural order of things is a cultural belief, we should expect to find Marxists, trade unionists, and social workers in India espousing the same education policies as employers and conservatives. This is what Weiner finds. If higher homicide rates in the South are attributable to a culture of honor, we should expect to find (1) that homicides involving arguments, brawls, and lovers' triangles are the principal source of the difference; (2) that Southerners are more likely to approve of violence only for the protection of property, in response to an insult, and as a means of socializing children; and (3) that in laboratory experiments Southerners exposed to an insult express more anger, show more increase in cortisol and testosterone levels, and engage in more dominance behavior. Nisbett and Cohen find all these things. In summary, the strategy of pursuing additional observable implications can help make our cultural explanations more compelling.

CONCLUSION

At the outset of this afterword, I observed that the culture concept is currently enjoying a major revival of interest, a revival that owes its origins to political and economic upheavals worldwide and to theoretical and methodological debates within the political science discipline. Once again we are deciding—rightly—that culture is a concept we cannot do without. But its intractabilities remain. Thus, drawing on the contributions to this book, I have sought to present my thoughts on how to make a cultural explanation compelling. Several chapters make plain, however, that this is but half the task. We want to develop not only cultural explanations of politics, but political explanations of culture. A question for the future, then, is how to do this.

REFERENCES

Almond, G. (1980) "The Intellectual History of the Civic Culture Concept." In *The Civic Culture Revisited,* edited by G. Almond and S. Verba. Boston: Little, Brown.

Almond, G., and S. Verba. (1963) *The Civic Culture.* Princeton: Princeton University Press.

Barnes, S. H. (1994) "Politics and Culture." In *Research on Democracy and Society, Volume 2: Political Culture and Political Structure,* edited by F. Weil and M. Gautier. Greenwich, CT: JAI Press.

Brint, S. (1994) "Sociological Analysis of Political Culture: An Introduction and Assessment." In *Research on Democracy and Society, Volume 2: Political Culture and Political Structure,* edited by F. Weil and M. Gautier. Greenwich, CT: JAI Press.

Bunce, V. (1996) *From State Socialism to State Disintegration: A Comparison of the Soviet Union, Yugoslavia, and Czechoslovakia.* Monograph Series of the Institute for European Studies at Cornell University.

Crawford, B., and A. Lijphart (1995) "Explaining Political and Economic Change in Post-Communist Eastern Europe." *Comparative Political Studies* 28:171–199.

Foster, R. J. (1991) "Making National Cultures in the Global Ecumene." *Annual Review of Anthropology* 20:235–260.

Gaenslen, F. (1986) "Culture and Decision Making in China, Japan, Russia, and the United States." *World Politics* 39:78–103.

Geertz, C. (1964) "Ideology as a Cultural System." In *Ideology and Discontent,* edited by D. Apter. New York: Free Press.

Geertz, C. (1973) *The Interpretation of Cultures.* New York: Basic Books.

Goldstein, J., and R. O. Keohane (1993) "Ideas and Foreign Policy: An Analytical Framework." In *Ideas and Foreign Policy: Beliefs, Institutions, and Political Change,* edited by J. Goldstein and R. O. Keohane. Ithaca: Cornell University Press.

Halliday, F. (1995) "Review Article: The Politics of 'Islam'—A Second Look." *British Journal of Political Science* 25:399–417.

Hill, J. H., and B. Mannheim (1992) "Language and World View." *Annual Review of Anthropology* 21:381–406.

Huntington, S. P. (1991) *The Third Wave: Democratization in the Late Twentieth Century.* Norman: University of Oklahoma Press.

Keesing, L. (1974) "Theories of Culture." *Annual Review of Anthropology* 3:73–97.

King, G., R. O. Keohane, and S. Verba (1994) *Designing Social Inquiry: Scientific Inference in Qualitative Research.* Princeton: Princeton University Press.

Little, D. (1991) "Rational-Choice Models and Asian Studies." *Journal of Asian Studies* 50:35–52.

Morris-Suzuki, T. (1995) "The Invention and Reinvention of 'Japanese Culture.'" *Journal of Asian Studies* 54:759–780.

Najita, T., and H. D. Harootunian (1988) "Japanese Revolt Against the West: Political and Cultural Criticism in the Twentieth Century." In *The Cambridge History of Japan,* vol. 6, edited by P. Duus. Cambridge: Cambridge University Press.

Nathan, A. J. (1993) "Is Chinese Culture Distinctive?—A Review Article." *Journal of Asian Studies* 52:923–936.

Nisbett, R. E., and D. Cohen (1996) *Culture of Honor: The Psychology of Violence in the South.* Boulder: Westview Press.

Ortner, S. B. (1995) "Resistance and the Problem of Ethnographic Refusal." *Comparative Studies in Society and History* 37:173–193.

Pye, L. (1991) "Political Culture Revisited." *Political Psychology* 12:487–508.

Rieder, J. (1994) "Doing Political Culture: Interpretive Practice and the Earnest Heuristic." In *Research on Democracy and Society, Volume 2: Political Culture and Political Structure,* edited by F. Weil and M. Gautier. Greenwich, CT: JAI Press.

Sahlins, M. (1995) *How "Natives" Think: About Captain Cook, for Example.* Chicago: University of Chicago Press.

Schein, E. (1992) *Organizational Culture and Leadership,* 2d ed. San Francisco: Jossey-Bass.

Smelser, N. J. (1992) "Culture: Coherent or Incoherent." In *Theory of Culture,* edited by R. Munch and N. Smelser. Berkeley: University of California Press.

Street, J. (1994) "Review Article: Political Culture—From Civic Culture to Mass Culture." *British Journal of Political Science* 24:93–113.

Tetlock, P. E. (1996) "Social Psychology and World Politics." In *The Handbook of Social Psychology,* 4th ed., edited by D. Gilbert, S. T. Fiske, and G. Lindzey. New York: McGraw-Hill.

Weiner, M. (1991) *The Child and the State in India.* Princeton: Princeton University Press.

Yee, A. S. (1996) "The Causal Effects of Ideas on Policies." *International Organization* 50:69–108.

Zartman, I. W., ed. (1995) *Collapsed States: The Disintegration and Restoration of Legitimate Authority.* Boulder: Lynne Rienner.

About the Authors

Hillel Abramson is research associate at the Center for Health Services Research in the Department of Political Science and doctoral candidate in the Department of Psychology at the University of Memphis.

Sanjoy Banerjee is an associate professor in the International Relations Department at San Francisco State University. He has published articles in *International Studies Quarterly* and the *Journal of Conflict Resolution,* as well as other works.

Marijke Breuning is assistant professor of political science at Truman State University (formerly Northeast Missouri State University). Her recent publications include an article in *International Studies Quarterly.* Together with coauthor John T. Ishiyama, she is currently working on a book manuscript on ethnopolitics integration in the "New Europe."

Glenn Chafetz is associate professor of political science at the University of Memphis and senior research associate of the Center for International Trade and Security at the University of Georgia. He has published a book, *Gorbachev, Reform, and the Brezhnev Doctrine: Soviet Policy Toward Eastern Europe 1985–1990* (Praeger, 1993); and articles in *The Journal of Politics, Political Science Quarterly, Political Psychology,* and other journals.

Rosita Dellios is associate professor of international relations at Bond University on the Gold Coast, Australia. Author of *Modern Chinese Defence Strategy* (Macmillan, 1989; St. Martin's Press, 1990), she specializes in Chinese defense and foreign policy. She is working on a second book on Sino-global relations.

Fritz Gaenslen is associate professor of political science at Gettysburg College. He has published articles in *World Politics, Political Psychology, Sociological Methods and Research, Political Research Quarterly,* and several edited volumes.

Suzette Grillot is a doctoral student and instructor in the Department of Political Science at the University of Georgia, and a graduate research associate for the Center for International Trade and Security. Her research and teaching focus on international relations and the former Soviet Union with particular emphasis on international security and foreign policy issues.

Valerie M. Hudson is an associate professor of political science at Brigham Young University. Long engaged in developing the subfield of foreign policy analysis, she has edited or coedited five volumes, and published in various journals, including *Third World Quarterly, Political Psychology,* and others.

Lawrence C. Katzenstein first became interested in cultural elements of negotiations while serving as director of research of the New York City Human Rights Commission. He has published in *Studies in Third World Societies,* and has a book forthcoming, entitled *Great Disorder Under Heaven.* He teaches at the Institute for International Studies at the University of Minnesota, where he also directs the undergraduate international relations program.

Hellmut Lotz received his M.A. in American Studies from Brigham Young University, and is currently a doctoral student in political science at the University of Maryland at College Park, where his research interests include cultural effects on foreign policy discourse in the United States.

Darin H. Van Tassell is an assistant professor at the Center for International Studies at Georgia Southern University. His primary areas of specialization are the study of U.S. foreign policy, Latin America, and global politics. He has published several articles in academic journals on topics ranging from the practice of U.S. policy, contemporary global economic patterns, and theories of education.

John F. Zurovchak received his doctorate in political science from Ohio State University. He served as associate editor of the *Mershon International Studies Review,* and is currently employed in the executive office of the Midwest Universities Consortium for International Activities, Inc. (MUCIA) at Ohio State University. His research interests include the relationship between national culture and small group dynamics, how images of relative culture influence interactive strategies among competing ethnic groups, and how assessments of relative culture impinge upon economic and political transitions within postcommunist states.

Index

About the Book

During the Cold War years, one could argue that the constraints of the bipolar rivalry dwarfed the domestic idiosyncrasies of nations. Now, however, nations often define national interest in terms of particularistic domestic motivations and imperatives—a change that calls for systematic study of the effect of societal culture on foreign policy.

This collection introduces the reader to the evolution of thinking about culture and foreign policy. The authors also assess the current state of the field, clarify theoretical concepts and frameworks, and investigate appropriate and innovative methodologies for empirical study.